Comprehensive Administration of Special Education

SECOND EDITION

Comprehensive Administration of Special Education

RICHARD S. PODEMSKI
The University of Alabama

GEORGE E. MARSH II
The University of Alabama

TOM E.C. SMITH
University of Arkansas at Little Rock

BARRIE JO PRICE
The University of Alabama

Merrill, an imprint of
Prentice Hall
Englewood Cliffs, New Jersey   Columbus, Ohio

Library of Congress Cataloging-in-Publication Data

Comprehensive administration of special education / Richard S.
Podemski ... [et al].—2nd ed.
      p. cm.
    Includes bibliographical references and index.
    ISBN 0-02-395961-4
    1. Handicapped children—Education—United States—
Administration. 2. Special education—United States—Administra-
tion. I. Podemski, Richard S.
   LC4031.C65 1995
   371.9'042—dc20   94-11499
                                  CIP

Cover photo: front by Barbara Schwartz/Prentice Hall and Merrill; back by Scott Cunning-
    ham/Prentice Hall and Merrill
Editor: Ann Castel Davis
Production Editor: Jonathan Lawrence
Text Designer: STELLARViSIONS
Cover Designer: Gryphon III Design
Production Buyer: Deidra M. Schwartz
Electronic Text Management: Marilyn Wilson Phelps, Matthew Williams, Jane Lopez, Karen L.
    Bretz
Illustrations: STELLARViSIONS

This book was set in ITC Garamond by Prentice Hall and was printed and bound by Book
Press, Inc., a Quebecor America Book Group Company. The cover was printed by Phoenix
Color Corp.

© 1995 by Prentice-Hall, Inc.
A Simon & Schuster Company
Englewood Cliffs, New Jersey 07632

Earlier edition © 1984 by Aspen Systems Corporation.

Printed in the United States of America
10 9 8 7 6 5 4 3 2 1

ISBN: 0-02-395961-4

Prentice-Hall International (UK) Limited, *London*
Prentice-Hall of Australia Pty. Limited, *Sydney*
Prentice-Hall Canada Inc., *Toronto*
Prentice-Hall Hispanoamericana, S. A., *Mexico*
Prentice-Hall of India Private Limited, *New Delhi*
Prentice-Hall of Japan, Inc., *Tokyo*
Simon & Schuster Asia Pte. Ltd., *Singapore*
Editora Prentice-Hall do Brasil, Ltda., *Rio de Janeiro*

PREFACE

In 1968, at the height of the Vietnam War, professor Lloyd Dunn, who had been a successful teacher and diagnostician in special education and would soon retire from the field, published one of his last articles, entitled "Special Education for the Mildly Retarded—Is Much of It Justified?" He set off a debate within the field of education with his remarks:

> I have loyally supported and promoted special classes for the educable mentally retarded for most of the last 20 years, but with growing disaffection. In my view, much of our past and present practices are morally and educationally wrong. We have been living at the mercy of general educators who have referred their problem children to us. And we have been generally ill prepared and ineffective in educating these children. Let us stop being pressured into continuing and expanding a special education program that we know now to be undesirable for many of the children we are dedicated to serve. (*Exceptional Children, 35* (1), 5–22)

Over the last 25 years, the concern expressed by Dr. Dunn has remained at the heart of controversies about special education and programming for children with disabilities. The "mainstreaming" movement begun by enactment of PL 94-142 in 1975 embraced Dr. Dunn's concern by guaranteeing a "free, appropriate public education" for every child. However, we have yet to resolve the issue of how to effectively serve children with disabilities, especially as there is now more intense pressure on schools to adopt an "inclusion" model. For philosophical, legal, social, and economic reasons, many schools are attempting to reduce the amount of time children spend in special classes and to provide substantial support and education for them in regular classrooms. As in the case of the initial impact of PL 94-142, the major responsibility for implementing inclusion and making it work rests with school administrators.

The school administrator has the challenge of forging teamwork among all educators and effectively integrating all program components. Specifically, the attitudes of educators and the issues of "responsibility" and "ownership" of students affects the interpersonal relationships of teachers and other personnel. Although the philosophical assumptions of inclusion for students with disabilities (along with other restructuring and school reform movements that complicate school programming) will be debated by professors, parents, and policymakers, it is the responsibility of regular and special education administrators to create a vision of how inclusion will work and to go about implementing it, just as administrators had to do on the "front lines" 20 years ago with the implementation of PL 94-142.

School administrators must help their faculties reach consensus about what integration means, must understand the legal and ethical bases for inclusion, and must produce an instructional and organizational method to furnish integrated services for students with disabilities using existing resources. This will inevitably entail modification of existing organizational and interpersonal methodologies, strategies, and techniques to successfully overcome obstacles to integration of students with disabilities. With this in mind, we have attempted to provide a comprehensive resource to practicing school administrators that provides sufficient information about both theoretical and practical aspects of the administration of special education. It is our sincerest hope that during the next decade we will continue to strive for practices that are both morally and educationally right for all children.

We would like to express our appreciation to the following persons, all of whom reviewed and commented on the manuscript: George P. Diamond, Northern Illinois University; Kathleen Knops, College of DuPage; Elliott Lessen, Northern Illinois University; Nikki Murdick, University of Arkansas; and Qaisar Sultana, Eastern Kentucky University. We also wish to acknowledge the outstanding work of Ms. Judy Lamon and Ms. Melanie O'Rear, who assisted us with typing the manuscript and other administrative tasks, and Mr. Jimmy Kilgore, who provided invaluable research and bibliographic assistance. Finally, we wish to thank our families for their support and encouragement throughout this project.

Richard S. Podemski
George E. Marsh II
Tom E. C. Smith
Barrie Jo Price

ABOUT THE AUTHORS

Dr. Jim Hale is program leader in educational leadership at the University of North Florida. Dr. Hale has a national reputation in educational finance and has written numerous chapters, research monographs, articles, and papers in the field of educational finance generally, including the financing of special education. Along with Drs. Richard Rossmiller and Lloyd Frohreich, Dr. Hale did the seminal research on costs of special education programs.

Dr. George E. Marsh II is currently a professor in the area of teacher education at The University of Alabama, specializing in interactive educational technology. He began his career as a teacher at the secondary level, then became a teacher of the disabled and learning disabled. He was a director of education for a state school for the retarded, a director of special education for a public school system, a department chairman of special education at the University of Arkansas, and a professor of curriculum and teaching at the University of Miami. He has published several books and numerous articles dealing with special education programming and research and technology in education.

Dr. Anna McFadden has been a special education teacher in public schools and in university settings. She is currently associate professor in education computer technology in the College of Education at The University of Alabama. She has published in the area of special education, including textbooks on instructional methods for mildly handicapped students. Other areas of research and publication have included the use of technology in the instructional process. She has co-authored three textbooks on technology in education; current activities include co-authoring a series of booklets for the National Association of Elementary School Principals, including *The Internet in the Classroom*. Dr. McFadden also serves as a curriculum development consultant to schools throughout the U.S. and American Schools Overseas, with sponsorship by the U.S. Department of State, Office of Overseas Schools.

Dr. Alba A. Ortiz, Ruben E. Hinojosa Regent Professor in the Department of Special Education at The University of Texas in Austin, is one of the nation's foremost scholars in the area of bilingual special education. Dr. Ortiz is the associate dean for academic affairs and research in the College of Education at The University of Texas at Austin. She also directs the Office of Bilingual Education in the College of Education. Dr. Ortiz's research and writing is nationally recognized and her ability to present the important concepts and ideals associated with developing appropriate educational programs for culturally and linguistically distinct exceptional learners is well-known internationally. She is a frequent presenter and invited speaker on topics related to special education, bilingual special education, and bilingual education. She is the immediate past president of the International Council for Exceptional Children.

Dr. Richard S. Podemski is the associate dean for instructional programs and a professor of educational leadership in the College of Education at The University of Alabama. Formerly Dr. Podemski was an associate director of the University Council of Educational Administration in Columbus, Ohio, and a professor of educational administration at the University of Arkansas. Dr. Podemski has published over 50 books, book chapters, and articles focusing on the interrelationship between the field of educational leadership, and the related fields of special education administration, educational technology, and counseling.

Dr. Barrie Jo Price is currently a professor in the Area of Teacher Education at The University of Alabama, specializing in interactive educational technology. She is a former special education teacher, a professor of special education at The University of Arkansas, and a professor of curriculum and teaching at the University of Miami. Dr. Price has authored six textbooks, numerous articles, and presented papers at national and international conferences. She currently conducts research and development in the area of applications of technology to teaching and learning. She serves as a consultant in this area to, among others, the U. S. Department of State, Office of Overseas Schools, and the National Association of Elementary School Principals.

Dr. Tom E.C. Smith is currently professor of special education at the University of Arkansas at Little Rock in the Department of Teacher Education. Formerly, Dr. Smith served as chairperson of the Department of Special Education, University of Alabama at Birmingham, and held an appointment at the Civitan International Research Center, UAB. He was also on the faculty at the University of Arkansas, Fayetteville, for ten years. Dr. Smith has authored or co-authored seven textbooks in special education, and has had more than 30 articles published in professional, refereed journals. Currently, he is the publications chairperson for the Division on Mental Retardation and Developmental Disabilities, Council for Exceptional Children.

Dr. James R. Yates is the John L. and Elizabeth G. Hill Centennial Professor in Education, and chairman of the Department of Educational Administration at The University of Texas at Austin. He is also a professor in the Department of Special Education at The University of Texas at Austin and is associated with the special education administration program. Dr. Yates has more than 80 publications that reflect his scholarship in the areas of technological forecasting methodologies, futures in education, delivery of services to special populations, and issues associated with serving culturally and linguistically diverse populations. He is currently national president of the Council for Exceptional Children, Division for Culturally and Linguistically Diverse Exceptional Learners.

BRIEF CONTENTS

CONTENTS

CHAPTER THREE

Identification, Placement, and Service Delivery   49

CHAPTER FOUR

Tests and Assessment   **75**

CHAPTER SIX
Linguistically and Culturally Diverse Students 129

CHAPTER SEVEN
Impartial Hearings and Litigation 157

CHAPTER EIGHT

Program Evaluation   183

CHAPTER NINE

Personnel   207

CHAPTER TEN
Fiscal Policy   233

CHAPTER ELEVEN
Facilities and Transportation   257

CHAPTER TWELVE
School and Community Relations   281

CHAPTER
ONE

ADMINISTERING
SPECIAL
EDUCATION
IN THE
KNOWLEDGE
AGE

EXCLUSION, MAINSTREAMING, AND INCLUSION

Although references to people with disabilities can be found in ancient historical records of various cultures, legal provisions for people with disabilities were first made in Roman law. However, acceptance of people with disabilities by society has been slow to develop. Shunned, ostracized, feared, and abused in many cultures, people with disabilities have always required protection and special consideration.

Enactment of PL 94-142 (Education for All Handicapped Children Act) in 1975 was the capstone in the history of humane treatment of people with disabilities, the most comprehensive civil rights act yet passed by the U.S. Congress. It guaranteed a free, appropriate public education for every child "regardless of how, or how seriously, he may be handicapped." More recently the Americans with Disabilities Act of 1990 (ADA) extended similar considerations to all children and adults. It is unlawful to discriminate in employment and unlawful to discriminate in state and local government services, public accommodations, transportation, and telecommunications against a qualified individual with a disability.

In the United States, special education has proceeded from a program of *exclusion* to one of *inclusion*. In many nations, without the aid of legislation, the integration or inclusion of people with disabilities is spreading. For example, an article in the *British Journal of Special Education* (Hart, 1992) includes arguments about ways to link special educational needs and the needs of others into a uniform strategy for improving learning for all children.

After the right to an education for children with disabilities was finally won, most school programs for these children were housed in separate buildings or special schools away from the mainstream of education. Gradually, most schools began to include all children (disabled and nondisabled) in the same buildings, but the children with disabilities were often segregated in a separate wing or in special classes. The trend to incorporate children with disabilities more fully into the educational mainstream began with professional objections to segregation. These objections were based on research that demonstrated clearly that the extra expense and a separate curriculum did not result in superior achievement or job preparation for children with disabilities.

In 1990, the U.S. Congress amended the Education of the Handicapped Act and gave it a new name. The amendment, PL 101-476, is known as the Individuals with Disabilities Education Act (IDEA). Although PL 94-142 and PL 101-476 have been successful in protecting the rights of children with disabilities, there has been a tendency to take the act for granted—the regulatory aspects have become routine and financial problems confronting schools have pushed schools toward a more inclusive model.

After nearly two decades, social and economic trends in education are eclipsing the original intention of PL 94-142 and its amendments—the trend toward an inclusive educational model. Promoted by many national associations and groups, but most notably the National Association of State Boards of Education (NASBE), "inclusion" is aimed at (1) creating laws and regulations pertaining to the certification of teachers and programs and (2) funding to place most children with disabilities into general education programs and curricula where services will be delivered to support the general education teacher (rather than "pulling out" children for services or placing them in segregated classrooms). Inclusion is threatening to different interest groups and a possible source of confusion for school administrators.

The Regular Education Initiative (Davis, 1989; Maheady & Algozzine, 1991) is mainly an academic debate that has raged in special education literature about the efficacy of special education programs. It began as a discussion opened by staff members in the Reagan administration who were concerned about both the increase in the number of people with disabilities served by schools since PL 94-142 and the costs (Will, 1986).

In 1968, a similar controversy began over the efficacy of programs for people with mental retardation, a controversy that resulted in "mainstreaming" of children with disabilities into public education. It was shown that students with mental retardation in segregated special classes did not perform better than counterparts in regular classes. Thus, the entire system of segregation was questioned. The controversy was dealt with as a civil rights issue.

Today, a similar problem has developed over the efficacy of special programming for the large group of students who are known as "mildly disabled" or mentally retarded, emotionally/behaviorally disturbed, and learning disabled. In essence, the same arguments about efficacy have resurfaced twenty years later. However, this time the arguments support more than mainstreaming; they call for total integration of most children with disabilities into regular classrooms.

Wang, Reynolds, and Walberg (1986) and Reynolds, Wang, and Walberg (1987) maintain there is a need for the restructuring of special and regular education because special education creates more problems than it solves—for the system and for students—especially for those who are "mildly" disabled. They indicate that more than 80% of nondisabled students could be classified as learning disabled by one or more current definitions. One of their suggestions, that regular classroom teachers be fully prepared to educate such students, would reduce or eliminate many special teachers, many of the problems, and the expense.

Clearly, the biggest problem is the inordinate number of students who may be classified as learning disabled. In 1989, children with learning disabilities represented about 45% of students in special education. As of the 1993–94 school year, children with learning disabilities represent about 50% of children in special education (Ayers, 1994). Anticipating this problem, the federal guidelines attempted to build in methods of holding down the number of students by requiring additional steps and procedures, but the strategy did not work.

The problem is caused by the definition, which is one of exclusion, and by the trend to use learning disabilities as a dumping ground for problem students. Although traditionally the condition was considered to affect approximately 2–3% of the student population, the lack of explicit criteria and the tendency for some professionals to widen the concept to include anyone with any type of learning problem have caused some administrators to experience an "epidemic" of learning disabilities. Over a 10-year period, every category of "disabled" has diminished significantly, except for the categories of emotionally disturbed, which increased slightly, and the category of "learning disabled." In five cities involved in an urban middle-schools project serving principally poor and minority children, the estimates of students with learning disabilities ranged as high as 65% in some schools (Lewis, 1991).

The state of Vermont enacted legislation to implement comprehensive educational services in each district to promote success for *all students through general education programs*. Under this legislation, each school must provide various services for all students in regular classes, but only a relatively small number of pupils may be placed in special classes. Although there have been other experiments of this nature, particularly programs supported by federal funds, the most sweeping changes along these lines are likely to result from the so-called inclusion model.

Similar in concept to the Regular Education Initiative, the inclusion model is a trend to serve students with disabilities in regular classrooms, to reduce the complications and expense caused by assessment and programming needs, and to maintain or improve academics and adjustment of students with disabilities. Unlike the Regular Education Initiative, however, the inclusion concept is promoted by the NASBE. If adopted as legislation and/or regulations, the inclusion model may have a major impact on teacher certification, funding of special education, and placement. In the face of increased numbers of poor students and a shrinking fiscal base, economics are dictating a move in this direction.

Rabe and Peterson (1988) noted that adherence to federal standards in special education was initially vexing to many local school districts because Individualized Education Programs (IEPs) and mainstreaming proved to be controversial. PL 94-142 imposed a significant change of local practices in special education. The use of the IEP disrupted the traditional power of the administration, requiring the involvement of teachers, parents, and students directly in a process unfamiliar to school personnel. In many ways, these trends were precursors to changes that are occurring throughout education today and which remain unsettled. Site-based management, parental involvement, and "empowerment" movements are emerging as part of school restructuring.

The result of 20 years of mainstreaming has been the gradual acceptance of children with disabilities in regular classrooms. In fact, the percentage of children served today in various kinds of educational placements clearly shows this trend: 31.3% in regular classes, 37.3% in resource rooms, 24.4% in separate classes, 5.2% in special schools, and 1.7% in home/hospital/residential settings. The overwhelming majority of students with disabilities, 68.6%, are served in public schools and spend all or much of the day integrated with nondisabled peers. It appears that the successful integration of children with disabilities leads to the next step, inclusion. The underlying theme behind inclusion is that "special education must become part of a unified educational system to better accommodate today's diverse student needs" (Ayres & Meyer, 1992, p. 31).

Thus, the inclusion model is a logical outcome of a progression of changes spanning several decades, and it also addresses needs defined by decreasing funding and fiscal limits. It is becoming evident that there is much overlap in the work of "regular" teachers and "special" teachers. Cannon (1992) and colleagues conducted a study of regular and special teachers and determined that both groups agreed on 82% of essential teaching practices for effective instruction of mainstreamed students. Logically, if what both special and regular teachers do for most children with disabilities is identical, it seems increasingly difficult to support segregated programming, especially if there are no significant differences in achievement and other measures of student performance.

The cost of special education is a major factor to be considered in decision making about inclusion models. For example, in Minnesota, 102 directors of special education listed excess program costs, effects of enrollment on staffing, and billing of resident districts for special services as the most important issues (Ysseldyke, 1991).

To be sure, there is significant opposition to the fusion of regular and special education, as promoted in the inclusion model (Ohanian, 1990). The opposing view is predictable because an entire bureaucracy exists for this population; careers and related programs will fall if inclusion gains acceptance. Some parents object, especially if they are concerned about the combining of categories of disabilities. Although most special educators, especially professors, happily supported the expansion of special education services, a free, appropriate education, and even the mainstreaming of children with disabilities, most are much less sanguine about total inclusion. Some object that general education classroom teachers are not prepared for or even capable of dealing with the needs of children with disabilities. It also threatens the jobs of many teachers and professors by forcing the downsizing of teacher preparation programs. And many teachers in regular classrooms feel unprepared to deal with students with disabilities and would rather that special programs and teachers continue to manage most of the special education programming (Pearman, 1992). Regardless of the view one may have of the inclusion movement in special education, it represents a remarkable historical change because over a time span of a few decades school policy has changed from a policy of exclusion to one of inclusion.

Initial research results have shown that children with disabilities served in regular classrooms do as well or better than similar students in special classes. This reinforces the trend, and it seems likely that many states will follow suit—especially if funding becomes more critical, which seems certain. Therefore, it will become necessary for special and regular education administrators to develop an entirely new relationship to support the inclusion of children with disabilities in regular classrooms. Cooperation will be the key. Special education administrators are likely to play a more prominent role in regular classroom programs, working with and, perhaps, supervising regular classroom teachers. An entirely new set of role relationships will have to be created if all children are to benefit from the changes in educational practice.

PL 101-476 represents the most important school legislation for children with disabilities and is a "living" document that grows and changes with each court interpretation and each amendment. Hundreds of thousands of new teachers will enter the profession by the turn of the century, meaning that a majority of teachers will not have the culture and traditions of the current teaching corps. Today, administrators are confronted with many problems in education because of the reform movement, an aging teacher corps, anticipation of new teachers entering the work force, and a changing student population requiring more services that were once clearly the responsibility of special education teachers.

In an age of significant change and a trend toward inclusion, administrators must be fully knowledgeable of special education law and regulations. Valesky and Hirth (1992) maintain that administrators must possess a knowledge of special education sufficient to implement federal legislation (i.e., PL 101-476, formerly PL 94-142) and to meet proposed objectives of the inclusion movement. They surveyed the state directors of special education and concluded that knowledge of special education law is particularly important for all school administrators. However, a majority of states do not have certification requirements that address this need. Thus, principals are lacking in the training necessary for dealing effectively with special education programs, and university programs seem to be unclear about state endorsement requirements. This is particularly problematic in schools where there are no designated special education administrators.

Hirth and Valesky (1990) conducted a survey of principals' knowledge of special education and found that:

- A majority of principals need to know more about due process, parental notification procedures, services provided to expelled students, and the difference between the concept of mainstreaming and the legal term "least restrictive environment."
- Many principals erroneously believe that all students in special education must receive special education programming and related services.
- Many principals lack knowledge about the extended-year services or special services for students.

PUBLIC EDUCATION IN THE KNOWLEDGE AGE

Over the next decade, public schools will experience a significant increase in the number of students with disabilities who will challenge current teaching models (Haberman, 1991). In addition, the majority of teachers will be new to the profession. And, most students with disabilities will probably receive their education in regular classrooms. Public education will continue to struggle in a climate of change, criticism, and economic limits.

Special education programming has expanded the responsibilities of administrators. Because of changes in the economy and society, programming for students in special education has never been more important. Some authorities worry that the new push for excellence and higher achievement will widen the schism that exists between regular and special educators (Shepard, 1987). It is the mutual responsibility of regular and special education administrators to support unified goals and programs essential to benefit children with disabilities, who comprise a growing segment of the school population. As the inclusion model spreads in education, it is incumbent on administrators to assure that the best possible classroom instruction occurs for all children not only because it is ethical to do so and important for the nation but also because classroom teachers will be the major source of support and instruction for all children, including children with disabilities.

The Knowledge Worker

One of the most important factors affecting schools is the change in the work force and the increased demand for literate workers (Haddock, 1991). This has obvious implications for schools, in general, and for special education, in particular. The world is experiencing wave after wave of political, social, and economic change, the consequences of transition from an industrial to a global economy. The steady erosion of public confidence in schools is a reflection of stresses caused by economic change. As the economy has changed, so have our institutions. Change will be constant in our society, especially because of the rapid development of new technologies that will eliminate jobs and industries while creating new opportunities. Until this decade, most jobs required only minimal literacy skills and very few required knowledge. In the past, it was easier for schools to meet public expectations. Today, all high-paying jobs require high levels of technical knowledge, and even low-paying jobs demand relatively high levels of literacy. This is the crux of school reform in America.

The dropout rate, poor test scores, and other evidence of school failure feed a national fear of permanent economic inferiority. This puts pressure on schools to deal with more advanced subject matter and, at the same time, to deal effectively with students with disabilities, many of whom are not academically talented. Much of the work force will be laid off or forced out of the workplace by new technologies. People will need to learn to be entrepreneurial rather than work "for" someone. Schools will be expected to teach this new concept as well as new skills, such as independence instead of obedience and cooperation rather than competition. Schools will be expected to change dramatically to prepare youth to the highest levels of achievement. But an even greater problem will confront schools in dealing with the preparation of youth with disabilities for an uncertain future. It is an area of particular concern for people with disabilities.

Schwarz and Taymans (1991) reported high unemployment among those with disabilities, including those who had graduated from special training programs. The U.S. Bureau of the Census in 1989 reported that the percentage of men with disabilities working full-time fell 7% during the 1980s, down from 30% at the beginning of the decade; women with disabilities earned 30% less than other women; and, by 1988, workers with disabilities earned 36% less than the nondisabled (Meers, 1992). Many people with disabilities only work part-time. The truly grim fact is that literacy requirements are becoming so high that many youths, if not most, who are functionally illiterate and disabled will have few job alternatives unless they are better educated and the schools work actively with the communities to find employment opportunities.

Expectations of Schools in the Knowledge Age

The impetus for change today is clearly the humbling experience of economic inferiority to Japan and Germany and the serious economic threat from developing nations. There is a demand for higher school standards, higher student achievement, and an emphasis on mathematics and science to meet the international challenge (Kumar, 1991). The greatest problem continues to be how to provide a strong academic curriculum in a democracy that does not also exclude large numbers of apparently less capable students, such as those who are poor, disadvantaged, and disabled. In effect, the current reform movement is still asking our educational system to make all young people literate, both culturally and scientifically, calling for methodologies in schools for combining children with disabilities with nondisabled children in spite of these elevated goals (Johnson & Pugach, 1991).

Some critics argue that a recommendation for a common curriculum is too structured and will serve only college-bound students. This debate picks up the historical threads of the division between those who believe that there is a common culture to be transmitted to youth and those who believe in individualized programs centered around the student's interests and needs. Critics are concerned that the common curriculum will not take into account the unique needs of minority, disadvantaged, and bilingual children, and children with learning and motivational problems (e.g., De Leon & Gonzales, 1991). This is a problem for teachers, teacher training institutions, and administrators.

The vocational education interests in America are strong because the federal and state governments have made significant investments in vocational education over the years. Further, critics argue that many children are not suited for college, and the school has a social and economic obligation to help these students assume their proper role in the work force. The opposite view counters that a strong general education is the best work preparation in an ever-changing, complex world. With thousands of college graduates unable to find jobs in the new "global economy," there is general support for vocational education or technical preparation (tech prep) and apprenticeship programs to assure that noncollege-bound youth will have job opportunities.

Most states have passed legislation to stiffen high school graduation requirements, and there are national efforts to adopt a common curriculum and national standards for achievement with greater emphasis on mathematics, science, English, and foreign language. Higher graduation standards and more rigorous courses may make it increasingly difficult for academically marginal students and students with disabilities to achieve a high school diploma, yet the diploma is a prerequisite for most jobs. It is possible to raise academic standards, but many students will be rejected if tracking is eliminated, unless schools can move toward individualized learning.

Many states have developed minimum performance tests that students must pass either before they are allowed to move to a higher grade or before graduation. The minimum competency testing program, which is popular in many southern states and has spread to other states, is a means of checking skills of students at intermediate points as well as a means of holding schools accountable for the process of instruction. Implications for students with disabilities are obvious.

Some states have developed alternative certification routes that do not require a degree in a teaching field. A variety of models are likely to emerge, especially if efforts of the National Governors' Association gain momentum. The major concern for some educators is that skills in dealing effectively with children with disabilities and young children are not ordinarily acquired in disciplines of the traditional liberal arts program of a university. The implications for instruction of students with disabilities are a major concern, especially because more students with disabilities will be in school in the next decade.

Most state reform packages have been championed by state governors who have attempted to develop business, industry, and general public support for quality educational improvement. Advertising campaigns, blue-ribbon panels, educational commissions, negotiation sessions with education and business groups, and speeches to statewide and local audiences have all been used to increase public support for educational reform. Most of these reform packages have included the passage of increased income taxes, business taxes, and/or sales taxes. State-level measures will most likely be insufficient, and local districts will also have to increase local fiscal support, primarily through increases in property taxes. Many districts unable to meet the new standards because of small student enrollments or inadequate fiscal bases may have to consolidate with neighboring districts.

In an age when governments are broke, the middle class has fewer children, and there is a growing elderly population, there is diminished interest in supporting public education with taxes. Schools will be increasingly impacted by children of poverty when all children will be expected to succeed in a college-prep curriculum.

In the final analysis, it is the action of each teacher with his or her students—teaching and learning—that is important in reform and restoring public confidence. Everything else surrounds this process. Thus, it is important for the administrator to create an environment that maintains excellence in teaching.

RESPONSIBILITIES OF SCHOOLS IN SPECIAL EDUCATION

Cooperation between regular and special education is part of the intent of PL 94-142 and PL 101-476, whether implied or expressed, and is essential if mandates pertaining to education of children are to be successful. From a systems point of view, the only way that cooperation can be assured is by administrative leadership. It is essential that the principal be fully knowledgeable about special education programming. As indicated earlier, this is not often the case. The education and placement of children with disabilities in regular classrooms requires careful planning and leadership. The school administrator, especially the building principal, is in a position to influence such programming. Now, as when the law was implemented, the greatest task for the administrator is to assume a role as an advocate for students with disabilities and to exhibit a supporting attitude for the faculty. Thus, leadership becomes a process of behaving in a proactive manner to assure the best instructional environment for all children, rather than merely complying with the letter of the law.

Responsibilities and Competencies

In line of authority, responsibility for special education devolves in the following order at the district level: (1) the board of education, (2) the superintendent, (3) the assistant superintendent, (4) the principal, and (5) the assistant principal. It is important to note that the special education administrator has been excluded from this list. Many school districts have no supervisor between regular education and special education or director of special education. Further, unless a district specifically employs a line of authority administrator *only* for special education, the special education director, coordinator, or supervisor is considered to be in a staff position. Personnel in such positions perform assigned tasks as deemed necessary for administration, but clearly they are not at the same level of authority, control, and decision-making responsibility as line school administrators.

Some of the confusion and much of the difficulty arising from special education programming result from the fact that school administrators, especially principals, have been willing to default in the area of special education by permitting supervisory personnel or other specialists (e.g., school psychologists) to "call the shots" in special education. This often results in the building-based special education teacher feeling alien to the environment, and programming that reflects the idiosyncratic professional attitudes of one powerful individual. All other teachers can turn to a principal in the building for leadership and support, while the special educator may feel leaderless.

The principal must assure that every teacher assigned to the building is within the principal's scope of authority. All communications should be translated through the principal by supervisory and central office personnel. As with all other regular classroom personnel, all evaluations of the special education teacher's performance should be conducted by the principal. Some principals may not wish to evaluate a special educator's performance because they lack experience and knowledge in special education. Yet, though only a few principals may have certification, training, and experience in all the diverse areas of education available today, most of them are not hesitant to evaluate performances in other areas of the curriculum. Considerable attention has been devoted to improving assessments of teachers, based on objective criteria, which should eliminate this problem if handled correctly.

The Board of Education.   The board of education consists of members of the community either elected by the citizenry or appointed by officials of municipal government to conduct the affairs of the school district. It thus represents the community and provides general leadership in the establishment of school authority. In this context it should, with the assistance of professional school personnel, establish policy, consider relevant state and federal guidelines, and seek appropriate information before making important decisions that affect special education programming. Making the board aware of the importance of special education will pay off in helpful support and policies. In this respect, the board should set the tone for the entire district and establish a philosophy regarding services for students with disabilities; it should ensure that special education is appropriately financed and that special education procedures reflect cooperation between regular education and special education personnel.

The Superintendent.   The seriousness with which lower-level administrative personnel regard the concerns of the special education program will be determined by the attitudes and actions of the superintendent. Thus, the superintendent should:

- Have a clear understanding of the legislation and regulations—federal and state—that pertain to special education.
- Recommend actions to the board to ensure compliance with the law (given the resources of the district).
- Be able to interpret program requirements and communicate district policies to other administrators in the system.
- Be able to organize the staff, or employ sufficient qualified personnel, to implement, conduct, and evaluate the program.

- Make clear the chain of command as it relates to special education programming so that all personnel have a clear understanding of their job descriptions and role.
- Communicate support for the program of special education, especially when changes are required in the system.
- Establish a well-developed philosophy within the district regarding services for the disabled.

The Principal.   Nevin (1979) suggested that the principal's competencies in the area of special education include those required to:

- Ensure due process.
- Interpret federal and state laws.
- Apply appropriate leadership styles.
- Ensure that records comply with the rules of confidentiality and due process.
- Resolve conflicts among program personnel.
- Use evaluation data to make program revisions.
- Determine staff functions and qualifications.

Additionally, we would recommend that the principal should:

- Establish and promote a positive philosophy in the building regarding services for students with disabilities.
- Inform all personnel within the building of the status of special education and define their responsibilities with regard to the program.
- Involve special education personnel in the scheduling of students for class assignments, especially at the secondary level.
- Ensure that an honest effort is made to provide the special educator with sufficient materials.
- Recognize that many students with disabilities also have behavioral problems—problems that should not negatively color the principal's attitude toward students with disabilities or their teachers.
- Assume sufficient interest in the referral and assessment processes of special education to make cost-effective decisions concerning them.
- Seriously consider the evaluation criteria used to make judgments about program effectiveness and communicate such criteria to the special education teacher at the beginning of the program or at the beginning of the teacher's employment.
- Ensure, as educational leader of the school, that the philosophy, goals, and objectives of the special education curriculum are integrated with those of the regular curriculum.
- Assume an active role in supporting the special educator, a teacher who often suffers greater job stress than other teachers.

- Actively seek innovative in-service programs that will benefit the entire staff.
- Assist in communication with parents and special external personnel and agencies.

The Special Education Staff Leaders.   Except in larger districts where assistant superintendents have responsibility for programming, most districts have one or more individuals who serve in staff positions to assist in the management of the special education program. In larger districts, a director or supervisor may be assigned to an assistant superintendent; in smaller districts the director or supervisor may be relatively independent and autonomous. In any event, the special educator fills a position that, for most purposes, is clearly outside the line of authority. Thus, administrative rules and procedures that are not clear may create conflict and confusion. However, although relieved of direct administrative control of teachers, special education personnel are not necessarily in a subordinate position and can work effectively with principals and others to achieve excellence.

Competencies should include the ability to:

- Assist in the development of procedures and policies and in the evaluation of programs.
- Coordinate pupil services.
- Assist in recruitment and coordination of special education personnel.
- Work effectively with all administrators.
- Assist in the development of the budget.
- Establish public relations.
- Manage reporting procedures and monitor necessary paperwork.
- Assist in staffing procedures and in the coordination of support services within the school and from the external community.
- Provide accurate information to internal personnel and external audiences.
- Monitor compliance procedures.
- Assist in diagnoses, placements, and instructional planning.

Legislation and People with Disabilities

PL 94-142, and PL 101-476 as its current amendment, was the most significant federal legislation in a long line of federal attempts to assist the people with disabilities. Although such legislative actions date back to 1822, legislation passed after 1954 is considered to have had the greatest impact on the education of children with disabilities. The administrator should be aware of the following legislative acts and their purposes as they provide an important historical context for understanding special education programming.

PL 85-926. Passed in 1958, this act provided funds for the training of college instructors who would prepare teachers of students with mental retardation.

PL 88-164. Passed in 1963, the Mental Retardation Facilities and Mental Health Construction Centers Act amended PL 85-926 to include training in other major disability areas, not just mental retardation. In addition to expanding teacher training, this act provided funding for the establishment of research and demonstration projects for educating children with disabilities. Also, although not included in the legislation but as a result of its passage, President Kennedy created the Division of Handicapped Children and Youth to administer all programs dealing with children and youth with disabilities.

PL 89-10. This legislation, entitled the Elementary and Secondary Education Act (ESEA), "was the first truly broad-scale aid to education act to be enacted by the U.S. Congress" (B. R. Gearheart, 1980, p. 14). Although the primary focus of this act was on children who were economically disadvantaged, many programs for children with disabilities resulted from its passage. One negative effect was the reorganization of the U.S. Office of Education and the disbandment of the Division of Disabled Children and Youth.

PL 89-313. This legislation was passed in 1965 to provide support for children with disabilities in hospitals, institutions, and other state-administered programs. Although this act did a great deal to improve appropriate services to children with disabilities, PL 94-142, approved 10 years later, created some conflict. Administrators could use PL 89-313 funds for some programs but had to utilize 94-142 monies for others.

PL 89-750. This act, passed in 1966, (1) created the Bureau of Education for the Handicapped, (2) provided for preschool programs for children with disabilities, and (3) established an advisory committee at the national level to advise the Commissioner of Education. The establishment of the Bureau of Education for the Handicapped was important for several reasons. It indicated a commitment at the federal level for the education of children with disabilities, it reflected the growing trend in society that children with disabilities should be provided more services, and its programs demonstrated the potential of shared responsibility, for children with disabilities, among federal, state, and local agencies.

PL 90-480. This legislation, passed in 1968, focused on the elimination of architectural barriers to people with disabilities.

PL 90-538. Called the Handicapped Children's Early Assistance Act of 1968, this legislation focused on children with educational disabilities by establishing experimental demonstration centers.

PL 91-230. This legislation, passed in 1969, (1) consolidated all legislation dealing with children with disabilities, (2) recognized learning disabilities as a new category of disability, (3) included provisions for research, model programs, teacher training, and (4) authorized certain actions dealing with children who are gifted.

PL 92-424. Known as the Economic Opportunity Act Amendments of 1974, this legislation mandated that 10% of those enrolled in Head Start programs be children with disabilities.

PL 93-112. The Vocational Rehabilitation Act Amendments of 1973 included Section 504, which defined and described basic civil rights of the people with disabilities. This section states that people with disabilities should not be discriminated against because of their disability in areas of employment, education, and accessibility to programs and services. Many of the provisions found in Section 504 also are contained in PL 94-142. The major difference is that Section 504 applies to all ages but does not provide funding. PL 94-142 deals only with school-age children and includes provisions for some federal funds.

PL 93-380. Passed in 1973, this legislation mandated that in order for schools to remain eligible for federal funds, they would have to comply with certain requirements related to the education of children with disabilities. The act addressed the following areas of compliance: (1) least restrictive environment, (2) due process procedures, and (3) right to education for all children with disabilities.

PL 94-142. The All Handicapped Children's Act of 1975 is the most significant piece of legislation. It is explained in detail throughout this text and also referred to in its amended form as PL 101-476.

PL 99-457. The Education of the Handicapped Act Amendments of 1986 extend services for children with disabilities from birth to 5 years old. This is an amendment to PL 94-142 and provides incentives for increasing the number of preschool children served by providing federal assistance. The act was implemented fully in 1991.

PL 101-336. The Americans With Disabilities Act (ADA) was signed into law in July of 1990. Simply referred to as ADA, it is a basic civil rights law for people with disabilities. It extends to people with disabilities the same civil rights enjoyed by others through the Civil Rights Act of 1964, which included protection against discrimination on the bases of race, color, sex, national origin, and religion. The act provides for protection in employment, public accommodations, telecommunications, and transportation.

ADA prohibits employers from discriminating against qualified individuals solely on the basis of a disability. Beginning in 1992, employers with more than 25 employees cannot discriminate against qualified persons in selection, testing, and hiring. In 1994, businesses with 15 or more employees must adhere to this regulation.

Also effective in 1992 are provisions that prohibit discrimination against people with disabilities in businesses, such as restaurants, hotels, theaters, stores, and parks. Barriers must be removed in older facilities, and new buildings must be accessible. By July of 1993, interstate and intrastate relay systems must be in place for telephone use. This normally consists of an operator available to facilitate communications for persons, such as those who are deaf, using special telecommunications devices.

ADA also affects public transportation servers. Public transportation officials may not purchase units that are not accessible. Additionally, new bus and train stations must be physically accessible to individuals with disabilities. ADA greatly expands the rights of people with disabilities. Although its impact on public schools will not be significant, it will affect how schools conduct business related to children and adults with disabilities.

PL 101-476. Passed in 1990, the Individuals with Disablties Education Act (IDEA) amended PL 94-142. Although most of the elements of PL 94-142 remain in effect, there were some significant changes in federal law that will be addressed later.

As compared with PL 94-142, IDEA includes the following differences:

- *Terminology.* Referred to as "handicapped children" since 1975, IDEA now refers to children eligible for special education as "children with disabilities."

- *Scope.* The scope of services was expanded to include all instructional settings, not just special education classrooms, and also the work sites and training centers.

- *Special education categories.* In addition to the categories of mentally retarded, hard-of-hearing, visually impaired, speech impaired, seriously emotionally disturbed, orthopedically impaired, other health impaired, and learning disabled, IDEA has added autism and traumatic brain injury and also provides for students with attention deficit disorder.

- *Related services.* In addition to those services provided under the previous legislation, IDEA has extended related services to include social work services and rehabilitation counseling.

- *Age.* Although other amendments have addressed preschool children, IDEA specifically requires that an IEP be provided for all students at the age of 16 for transition to post-secondary programming, and for preschool children when appropriate.

State Legislation

Virtually all states have passed enabling legislation for people with disabilities similar to PL 94-142 and PL 101-476. State legislation is usually compatible with the intent of federal law but at times contains provisions that expand rights afforded by the federal legislation. Certainly each state has promulgated its own regulations for implementing its legislation. This has resulted in the wide variety of practices found among the various states. Administrators must be aware of their own state legislation and regulations and are obligated to comply with those regulations.

THE IMPACT OF PL 94-142 AND PL 101-476

The basic purpose of PL 94-142 was to ensure that all children with disabilities receive a free, appropriate public education in the least restrictive environment. PL 101-476 had two major themes in the 1990 reauthorization: (1) to increase opportunities for minority and economically and educationally disadvantaged individuals to participate fully and benefit from the Act, and (2) to increase the availability of transition services for infants, toddlers, children, and youth with disabilities. In order to provide appropriate services for people with disabilities, educators must become thoroughly aware of its many components: (1) the least restrictive environment, (2) IEPs, (3) the definition of the term *disabled,* (4) nondiscriminatory assessments, (5) parental involvement, (6) due process procedures, and (7) related services.

Least Restrictive Environment

A continuum of services should be made available for children with disabilities, and each child's placement should be carefully considered so that it is as close to the regular class placement as is appropriate for that child's needs and abilities. Self-contained placement or institutionalization is not antithetical to the intent of the law as long as that placement option is the least restrictive for a particular child. In addition to being integrated physically, this concept implies that the placement should be designed so that the child will also be integrated socially.

Supported employment and transition programs, as the names imply, are a type of service that has existed in some form in the past for students, both with and without disabilities. In the future, because of the difficulty of finding gainful employment for youth with disabilities, schools may enter into relationships with community-based organizations and companies to assist less capable youth in finding work and to provide work that is useful and rewarding. This would fall within the guidelines of PL 101-476, especially if similar programs are provided for students who are nondisabled. The extent of obligation could be a debatable issue.

Individualized Education Programs

PL 101-476 requires that an IEP be developed for all children with disabilities. An IEP includes the following concepts: (1) the program is designed for a single child, not a group of similar children; (2) it should only include those elements related to the educational needs of the child, including related services; and (3) the IEP statement is not a plan from which a program is developed, but a specific program to be followed (Weintraub, 1977).

Regulations state that the following individuals shall participate in IEP development:

1. A representative of the public agency, other than the child's teacher, who is qualified to provide, or supervise the provision of, special education.
2. The child's teacher.
3. One or both of the child's parents.
4. The child, where appropriate.
5. Other individuals at the discretion of the parent or agency.
6. Someone familiar with the evaluation of the child, when the child has been evaluated for the first time (Section 121a.344).

Regulations further require that the IEP contain, at a minimum: (1) information on the child's current level of functioning; (2) annual goals, including short range objectives; (3) special and related services; (4) dates the services will be provided; and (5) criteria for evaluation of the program. In addition to these minimum requirements, local or state education agencies may require additional information.

Definition of Disabled

PL 94-142 defined the disabled as those evaluated as being "mentally retarded, hard of hearing, deaf, speech impaired, visually disabled, seriously emotionally disturbed, orthopedically impaired, other health impaired, deaf-blind, multi-disabled, or as having specific learning disabilities, who because of these impairments need special education and related services" (Section 121a.5). IDEA added autism and traumatic brain injury as specific categories, and provided for the student with attention deficit disorder. Gifted and talented children are not included. Some state definitions of special education include the gifted and talented.

Nondiscriminatory Assessment

Professionals have realized that certain assessment procedures are inherently discriminatory for some children. Instruments and procedures must be used that do not discriminate racially or culturally. At a minimum:

1. Tests and other evaluation materials must be administered in the child's native language, or other mode of communication, by trained personnel, and validated for the purpose for which they are used.
2. Tests and evaluation materials should assess areas of academic need, not solely provide a single intelligence quotient (IQ).
3. Tests administered to children with various sensory, manual, or speaking skills should reflect the child's aptitude, not the child's deficits in these skills.
4. No single procedure is to be used as the sole criterion for determining an appropriate program.
5. A multidisciplinary team should be involved in the assessment.
6. The child should be assessed in all areas of suspected disability (Sec. 121a.532).

Parental Involvement

The law requires that parents be involved in all aspects of an educational program for a child with a disability, from the initial referral to the ultimate placement decision. In order to ensure this involvement, schools must inform parents of meetings, arrange them at times and locations convenient to the parents, and allow parents to actively participate in the meetings. All notifications must be far enough in advance to ensure parents the opportunity to attend, and notices must be in the native language of the home. States must develop plans for dealing with parents who choose not to participate. Regardless of these plans, schools must document all efforts in attempting to gain parent participation.

Due Process Procedures

Due process includes the right to examine records, obtain an independent evaluation, receive prior notice before a change in an IEP or other program, and a right to disagree with and appeal a decision made by the school. This provides parents the option of requesting a due process hearing, conducted by an impartial hearing officer, in which both parties to the disagreement present their side of the conflict.

Related Services

Not only are schools responsible for the special education of students with disabilities, but also they are required to provide related services, including transportation and such developmental, corrective, and other supportive services as are required to assist handicapped children to benefit from special education . . . speech pathology and audiology, psychological services, physical and occupational therapy, recreation, early identification and assessment of disabilities in children, counseling services, and medical services for diagnostic or evaluation purposes. The term also includes school health services, social work services in schools, and parent counseling and training. (Sec. 121a.13)

In addition, PL 101-476 extends related services to include rehabilitation counseling and social work services. These services are not exhaustive but merely serve as examples of the types required.

As with any legislation, alternative interpretations and ambiguous provisions and regulations create conflict between parents and schools. These conflicts involve the right of a child to an extended school year, responsibilities for related services, funding responsibilities for residential and private placements, and appropriate versus most appropriate programs. Discussions of court decisions and other legal actions will be discussed in chapter 7. However, a description of these components follows.

The Extended School Year.   The purposes of an extended school year program are: (1) to prevent skill loss or regression that usually occurs over the summer, (2) to provide opportunities to reinforce skills learned during the preceding school year, and (3) to provide training for new skill development. These purposes, although not necessary for some children with disabilities, are required aspects of an appropriate education for others. Basically, what the courts and due process hearings have consistently stated regarding extended school year programming is that, although it is not a right for all children with disabilities, it is an option for all children with disabilities. If a child's disability is such that an extended summer absence from educational programming would cause significant regression, then summer programming for that child should be considered. Whether the additional costs involved should be met by interagency collaboration, local education agencies (LEAs), state departments of education, or a combination of these with federal assistance remains unresolved. Courts have supported extended summer programs for certain students with disabilities at the school's expense.

Specialized Related Services.   Although PL 101-476 regulations specify certain related services that may be provided, the cited services are not to be considered exhaustive or definitive. Court cases and due process hearings have focused on (1) whether or not a child should be provided related services when no special education is provided; (2) whether or not certain services, such as psychotherapy, are medical or diagnostic; and (3) who pays for related services. In most cases, the decision revolves around the definition of related services. For example, a child who requires a catheter in order to attend school in a wheelchair or a child who requires computerized communications devices would have such related services provided at school expense. Because the definition emphasizes that these are services that should be provided to help a child benefit from special education, services that do not assist a child in this manner are not required by law and thus are not the responsibility of the local school district.

Funding for Private and Residential Schooling

Generally, school administrators are not opposed to providing appropriate services to children with disabilities. However, a problem arises from the fact that courts have consistently ruled that cost should not be used as a reason for making a decision about the appropriateness of a special education program for a child. In any event, although states have indicated that the local district is responsible only for providing equal effort for the education of children with disabilities, the local school is ultimately responsible for providing whatever program is necessary to ensure an appropriate program. In cases where a child requires residential placement or other expensive services, schools and state departments of education should attempt to develop interagency agreements to share in the cost. If a child's needs are primarily medical, the school may have a way out of the dilemma, because the law requires only medical services that are diagnostic in nature.

Appropriate Versus Most Appropriate Programs

PL 101-476 requires that each child with a disability be provided a free, appropriate public education; it does not require that the program be the best or most appropriate, but simply appropriate. Thus, the difficulty in providing a program is in the determination of what is appropriate. Given this ambiguity, school administrators should attempt to provide programs based on each child's individual needs. Beyond the provision of such appropriate programming, schools have no legal responsibility.

The State Education Agency

The state education agency (SEA) must submit annual program plans in order to receive federal funds for the education of children with disabilities. These plans must include:

- Procedures for public participation in the development of the plan.
- A policy statement that ensures that all children with disabilities have a right to a free appropriate public education.
- Data indicating the kind and number of facilities, personnel, and services needed.
- Assurance that the state has established priorities in providing services.
- Procedures for the identification, location, and evaluation of all children with disabilities in the state.
- Policies and procedures to ensure confidentiality of all personally identifiable information.
- Information showing the implementation of requirements related to IEPs.
- Procedural safeguards for the parents of children with disabilities.
- Procedures to ensure that children with disabilities are educated in the least restrictive environment.
- Assurances that nondiscriminatory assessment procedures are used.

- Procedures for monitoring local education agencies to ensure compliance of federal and state requirements.

- Details on the use of federal funds, including policies and procedures to ensure that funds are spent in accordance with federal regulations and assurances that all funds received from federal programs for the education of children with disabilities are used in a manner consistent with the goal of PL 101-476.

- Materials required for a comprehensive system of personnel development.

- Policies and procedures for children with disabilities placed in private schools.

- Policies for controlling funds used to educate children with disabilities and for recovering funds used to educate children misclassified as disabled.

- Procedures to ensure that local education agencies have a right to a hearing before final action is taken on a local application.

- Assurances that federal funds are not commingled with state funds.

- Procedures for the evaluation of the effectiveness of programs.

- Assurances that the requirements of a state advisory panel are met.

- Assurances that programs funded with federal funds meet statutory nondiscriminatory employment requirements.

Because the SEA is the monitoring agency for ensuring that the provisions of PL 101-476 are implemented appropriately and because federal funds for the implementation are channeled through the SEA, the role of this agency is critical. Without proper action at the SEA level, the provisions of federal law cannot be carried out adequately. Administrators at the local education agency level must work closely with SEA personnel to maximize efforts to provide appropriate public education for children with disabilities.

In the next decade, the percentage of children classified as disabled is likely to increase, making school administration more complicated than in the past, with respect to special education. Although the school population in the United States includes only about 10% with disabilities, dramatic changes in pupil enrollment over the next decade indicate the proportion of children with disabilities is likely to increase significantly, complicating the job of administration unless efficient means are established to handle the load. No one can deny that serious problems lie ahead because of the large numbers of children with disabilities, especially those labeled as learning disabled, and the number of infants born to drug-addicted mothers, which is currently estimated at 375,000 annually (Lewis, 1991).

The greatest amount of time in special education activities is spent in individual education planning meetings and on filling out special education forms. Other time-consuming duties include reviewing referrals for special education annual reviews, developing IEPs and follow-up system processes, providing special education communications, attending special staff meetings, and preparing and monitoring the special education budget. The trend toward inclusion promises to redefine the roles of special and regular classroom teachers and special and regular administrators. Cooperation between special education administrators and other school administrators is as critical in the era of inclusion as it was to the success of programming for children with disabilities in the past.

CHAPTER
TWO

ORGANIZATIONAL
ARRANGEMENTS

It is important for school administrators to understand the structure of schools as organizations. It is through this organizational structure that the administrator attempts to orchestrate elements unique to that school in order to accomplish educational goals. Organizational structure refers to a broad range of elements such as culture, policy, goals, procedures, staffing patterns, and work responsibilities. These elements are arranged in a particular manner by the administrator, taking into account the unique nature of the school's mission, resources, personnel, and other factors internal and external to the school.

With the passage of PL 94-142, the organizational arrangements for providing special education services to children changed dramatically. To accommodate children with disabilities according to the provisions of this new federal mandate, school administrators attempted to redesign the structures of their schools. Rabe and Peterson (1988) demonstrated that this, and other federal programs, not only forced districts into compliance with rules that caused initial confusion but also disrupted districts that had successful programs before the law. Immediately preceding and for a short time after enactment of the legislation, the professional literature contained many reports about the redesign of special education organizational structures and procedures to provide a free, appropriate education for those with disabilities (Birch, 1974; Reynolds, 1975; Weatherman & Hollingsworth, 1974).

During the 1980s, however, very few articles and monographs dealt with changes in the organizational design of special education. During this decade, state policymakers and local school administrators carefully crafted detailed and often complex rules, policies, definitions, funding patterns, and organizational structures to manage the increasingly large numbers of children who were being labeled as disabled. These activities resulted in the growth of a large special education bureaucracy at the federal, state, and local levels and created a dual system of education, regular education and special education, which many educators believe does not address the real educational needs of children with disabilities.

The challenge for regular and special education administrators in the 1990s and into the next century is to develop new, more responsive organizational structures that will integrate regular and special educational services and empower teachers and other support personnel closest to the instructional setting in ways that truly address the learning needs of children with disabilities.

INCLUSION: A CALL FOR ORGANIZATIONAL REFORM

In 1992, the National Association of State Boards of Education (NASBE) issued a special report on the status of educational services for children with disabilities. This report, *Winners All: A Call for Inclusive Schools* (NASBE, 1992), was highly critical of the current organizational structure of services for children with disabilities and called for the radical reform of all aspects of the way in which special education services are organized and delivered. The report described the growth of special education legislation since PL 94-142 and concluded that since passage of the law a "vast and separate bureaucracy has developed to educate students labeled as disabled" (p. 9). It criticized the system for unnecessary segregation and labeling of children for special services and ineffective mainstreaming practices that fragment both the academic and social aspects of the child's school life. The report states:

> This bureaucracy is characterized by separate and parallel policies for special education students and staff; separate funding mechanisms; separate administrative branches and divisions at the federal, state, intermediate, and local levels; a system of classification for labeling children that is considered by many to be demeaning and nonfunctional for instructional purposes; and a separate cadre of personnel, trained in separate preservice programs, who serve only students with diagnosed disabilities. (p. 9)

The report also criticizes current organizational and instructional practices that in the name of mainstreaming have (1) resulted in lower instructional expectations for children with disabilities; (2) do not provide regular teachers the support services they need in their classes to help children with disabilities; and (3) fragment the mainstreamed child's instructional program through "pull-out" strategies in which they lose instructional time, often miss key elements of the curriculum (such as science), and are "exposed to a dual curriculum that is rarely coordinated across programs" (p. 10).

As a remedy to these problems the NASBE report advocates an inclusive system of education for all children. According to the report, inclusion

> means that students attend their home school with age and grade peers. It requires that the proportion of students labeled for special services is relatively uniform for all the schools within a particular school district, and that this ration reflects the proportion of people with disabilities in society at large. Included students are not isolated into special classes or wings within a school. To the maximum extent possible, included students receive their in-school educational services in the general education classroom with appropriate in-class support. This instruction is complemented with community-based instruction that provides the student with the opportunity to learn a variety of life and employment skills in normal community settings. And principals of inclusive schools are accountable for the outcomes of all of the students in the school. (p. 12)

In a 1993 policy statement on "Inclusive School and Community Settings," the Delegate Assembly of the Council for Exceptional Children stressed the important role of the local school and the regular administrator, especially the building principal, in providing for appropriate services for children with disabilities in an inclusive setting. The policy statement advocates that

> in inclusive schools the building administrator and staff with assistance from the special education administration should be primarily responsible for the education of children, youth, and young adults with disabilities. The administrator and other school personnel must have available to them appropriate support and technical assistance to enable them to fulfill their responsibilities. Leaders in state/provincial and local governments must redefine rules and regulations as necessary, and grant school personnel greater authority to make decisions regarding curriculum, materials, instructional practice, and staffing patterns. In return for greater autonomy, the school administrator and staff should establish high standards for each child and youth and should be held accountable for his or her progress toward outcomes. (CEC, 1993)

Inclusion challenges regular and special education administrators to rethink the organizational structure through which they deliver instructional services to those with disabilities. Inclusive schools require full integration of all aspects of the regular and special education systems and thus greater communication between regular and special administrators, teachers, and other support personnel. To implement an inclusive educational environment, the regular and special education administrators must understand how to manipulate all of the organizational and instructional aspects of the district and the school to provide children with disabilities with appropriate instructional services. Thus, the administrator must understand the elements of organization.

THE ELEMENTS OF ORGANIZATION
Culture

The culture of the school organization refers to the norms, mission, shared values, and philosophy of the school. Cultural aspects of the school, related to special education, are identified in the beliefs and attitudes of teachers, administrators, school board members, and all other members of the school community regarding the rights of children with disabilities to an appropriate education. In addition, these cultural aspects of the school are also identified in beliefs and attitudes regarding the nature of appropriate instructional services for children with disabilities.

Formally these norms, beliefs, and attitudes are identified in school mission statements or school philosophy often found in accreditation reports or as introductory statements in the district policy manual. Understanding the school's culture is important because these various expressions of culture undergird all of the organizational and instructional structures that the school puts into place to serve children with disabilities and affect other instructional elements such as expectations for student performance.

Mission statements are important formal expressions of culture because they describe the school's intent to advocate for children with disabilities and provide appropriate services. A mission statement that advocates inclusion conveys different expectations for all aspects of the service delivery process for children with disabilities than one that views special education from a legal compliance viewpoint. Simpson and Myles (1990) describe four assumptions that illustrate cultural imperatives for general education–special education collaboration:

- The general educator assumes primary responsibility for teaching; the special educator's role is to provide support and resources to enhance student success.
- Social and academic interactions in the general education classroom are beneficial for all students, including those with disabilities.
- Students, parents, and school personnel prefer education in the general classroom to pull-out and other segregated programs.
- Contingent upon appropriate support and resources, most general education teachers and administrators are willing and capable to serve students with mild-to-moderate disabilities in general classrooms (p. 2).

It is the role of the school administrator to assure that the nature of the school's organizational structure and delivery of instructional services are compatible with its culture. Sergiovanni (1991) believes that the cultural and symbolic elements of leadership are important because by articulating and reinforcing values the administrator emphasizes what is important within the school, identifies practices that are consistent with the values, helps new members know what is acceptable behavior, and thus creates a sense of order and belonging among all staff and students in the school.

Policy

Policies are broad guidelines that give direction to an organization and serve to operationalize mission statements or statements of philosophy. In the area of special education, policy dictates the way in which the school will advocate for the rights of and provide services to children with disabilities. A school policy that "aggressively" provides the full range of services needed by children with disabilities in the district conveys a fundamentally different message about what type of behaviors will be required for administrators and teachers than one that states only that the school will provide services "as required by law." At another level, a school policy statement might stipulate the degree of cooperation that the board wishes to foster between regular and special education systems in order to bring about full implementation of services to children with disabilities. In any event, policy statements indicate the extent of the board's commitment to children with disabilities and are used accordingly by employees to guide their decisions. (Illustrative special education policy statements have been developed by the Council for Exceptional Children and can also be found in state department of education manuals.)

Podemski (1981) described the dysfunctional effects of a board policy that advocates the needs of children with disabilities but does not provide for the comprehensive services required to fulfill that policy. Usually in such cases, the board adopted a strong policy because it felt political and legal pressure to do so. However, the board may be unwilling or unable to support the services demanded by such a policy. Such misleading policies can result in internal staff dissension and parental litigation.

Procedures

Procedures describe the customary methods for handling activities (Koontz, O'Donnell, & Weihrich, 1986; Lunenburg & Ornstein, 1991) and serve to specify practices used to implement policies. Procedure statements identify the rules, regulations, time lines, and forms that the board and administration believe are necessary to accomplish the work of the school. In the area of special education, procedure statements would describe the IEP process; the relevant forms; the time lines for referral; the methods of diagnosis, placement, and evaluation; and the persons responsible in each of these areas. Other procedure statements would relate to due process hearings, transportation, program evaluation, and other ongoing special education functions.

Goals

Goals are derived by comparing the intent of policy with the actual operations of the district and are formulated as targets for action that guide the district in its attempts to bring practices and policy into congruence. Goals should be written so as to identify specific expected outcomes and time lines for completion. In the middle 1970s, many school districts established specific goals to bring them into compliance with newly passed federal and state special education legislation. Goals were established to provide for comprehensive child find, to develop comprehensive referral and placement procedures, to provide in-service activities for all regular and special education staff, and for virtually every other aspect of special education services. During the 1990s districts will more likely identify inclusion-oriented goals.

Goal accomplishment must be reviewed regularly. Program evaluation procedures established by the school provide the framework for monitoring and evaluating the attainment of goals. Once a goal is attained, it should be replaced by another goal or set of goals to provide the impetus for further improvement.

Objectives

Objectives are statements of the means that the school and its personnel will use to accomplish goals. In that sense, objectives are subsets of goals. Hampton, Summer, and Webber (1982) note that objectives should be specific, reality-oriented, verifiable, and should specify the time period in which they will be achieved. If a district goal is to train all staff concerning procedures for accommodating children with disabilities in the regular class, the objectives might specify the procedures for achieving that goal. For example, they might specify procedures in assessing the current level of staff knowledge, in developing the content of the relevant in-service training, in making appropriate arrangements for providing such training, in evaluating staff development efforts, and in determining staff needs for further in-service training.

It should be noted that what might be an objective at the district level can be a goal for an individual member of the central office staff. For example, the board may establish policy that all staff will understand the concept of inclusion and the district procedures for implementing this concept. The superintendent would then stipulate staff participation in comprehensive in-service training as a goal to accomplish board policy. One objective in accomplishing this goal might involve the development of a series of staff development training programs. The implementation of that objective might be delegated to a director of staff development or special education administrator or maybe the building principal, who then would view the objective of staff training as a goal to accomplish during the year. The director would then develop objectives to guide achievement toward the goal. Because of the obvious potential for confusion here, it is better to view goals and objectives as two parts of a means-to-ends relationship rather than as fixed organizational elements. However they are viewed, both goals and objectives must be logically developed and used to guide the efforts of personnel throughout the school system.

Organizational Structure

The structure of special education service delivery is the result of decisions that special and regular education administrators make about how to organize personnel and other resources in the district to accomplish special education goals. Organizational structure is important because it defines the patterns of cooperation and communication that employees use to accomplish goals. Although organizational size, district wealth, geography, and other variables will influence the specific character of the special education structure, the administrator exercises a great degree of autonomy in creating the design initially and making subsequent changes in the organizational structure. It is only through basic structural reorganization that schools will be able to set and accomplish desired goals; monitor, adapt, and influence the environment; and deal successfully with changes in educational technology. Changing the structural characteristics and the work environment of schools is within the grasp of every educational administrator.

In order to implement special education goals and policies, the special and regular education administrators must integrate the vertical and horizontal aspects of the organization's structure so that these dimensions work together efficiently. Typically, vertical differentiation is depicted on organizational charts as different levels of the organization, for example (in ascending order of size), classroom, department, building administrator, central office, superintendent, and board of education. The more levels there are, the more complex the vertical structure. More specifically, the vertical design for special education will specify (1) the chain of command, or the authority relationships between subordinates and superordinates; (2) the span of control, or the number of individuals or departments reporting to any one person; (3) the degree of centralization, or the degree to which decisions and work flow are concentrated at the top of the chain of command; and (4) formalization, or the degree to which responsibilities for each position are specified in writing.

Horizontal structure refers to the division of labor by which the school district combines related tasks, responsibilities, or even positions into organizational groups or divisions. The horizontal structure refers to the number and responsibilities of departments within the school and the identification and assignment of tasks to any one position or department. The special and regular education administrators must make sure that the vertical and horizontal elements of organizational structure are well defined and complement each other. In this way, the administrator determines (1) how the various aspects of the special education program should be designed to take advantage of the personnel in the district, (2) the tasks that the special education program must accomplish, and (3) how the special and regular education systems and their staffs will cooperate to accomplish the special education goals of the district.

RELEVANT ORGANIZATIONAL ISSUES

The organizational structure of special education is affected in important ways by the "loosely coupled" nature of schools in the United States and by the "functional authority" of special education. Recently, site-based management has proved to be a meaningful change strategy, and matrix management has emerged as a promising organizational strategy for implementing innovative special education programs.

Education as a Loosely Coupled System

Early educational theorists depicted schools in the United States as tightly organized bureaucracies. However, in many respects, schools can be viewed as loosely coupled systems that are characterized by a lack of integration among the various organizational elements (Weick, 1976, 1982). Although some technical aspects of the school are tightly coupled, much of the structure is less integrated. Weick believes that such loose coupling helps the school deal with its many problems by making it less susceptible to external pressure and radical shifts in the environment. However, loosely coupled organizations are also more difficult to administer, making coordination harder to achieve. The loosely coupled nature of schools in the United States is evident in the education of children with disabilities where much of the responsibility for the service delivery process rests with individual teachers and their willingness to maintain the least restrictive instructional environment for each child. Regular class teachers must refer children, modify their own instructional planning accordingly, and then review the relevant IEPs. Because the special education monitoring process in most schools is not comprehensive, however, many teachers might seek ways to avoid referring children or to incorporate them in their classes and then wait for the system to "catch up" with them. This possibility underscores the importance of a dedicated and committed staff that believes in educating each child according to that child's needs. The staff must be supported by a well-designed organizational structure assuring that dedicated staff are hired and supported in their pursuit of regular and special education goals.

According to Weick (1976; 1982), in order to manage loosely coupled systems, the administrator must make full use of symbols, common meanings, and key values, thereby creating commonly held assumptions to guide the decision making of each individual and to structure their dealings with one another. Through mechanisms such as policy statements, staff development, and group decision making, the administrator attempts to articulate the key values governing the school district and to encourage professionals to use them in their own personal, instructional, and organizational decision making. In a sense, the administrator attempts to "socialize" the staff members to accept common assumptions and then to "resocialize" them as those assumptions change or as certain staff members come to hold different assumptions.

Functional Authority

Koontz, O'Donnell, and Weihrich (1986) defined functional authority as "the right which is delegated to an individual or a department to control specified processes, practices, policies, or other matters relating to activities undertaken by personnel in other departments" (p. 209). In many organizational structures, the special education administrator has line authority over many of the aspects of the special education program or even over an entire area, such as pupil personnel. However, few structures give the special education administrator line authority over services at the building level, although these services may be special education related or involve special education personnel. Thus, the typical organizational design places the special education administrator in a staff relationship with the building principal and the various aspects of the regular education program.

Most special education administrators are given functional authority over all aspects of the service delivery process, even those processes that take place at the building level. That is, the special education administrator is held responsible for ensuring that the entire special education service delivery process is in compliance with applicable laws and regulations and that appropriate instructional and support services are made available to all children with disabilities. The result is that the special education administrator and the building principal share authority for many special education functions, yet the authority relationship between these two remains unclear. Such a situation may not only cause conflict between the two professionals but also create confusion among teachers and other personnel as to whom they are to report to, whose directives they are to follow, and who will evaluate them.

When many staff administrators at the central office hold functional authority over various aspects of operations at the building level, additional confusion and conflict can result. Line administrators, especially building principals, may become subject to the directives of many individuals who have functional authority, as well as to the directives of their own line superiors. The potential disruptive effects of such diffusion of functional authority may cause the principal to become defensive against intrusions by any central office administrator and protective of building level "turf," further inhibiting cooperation between the building principal and the special education administrator and the integration of the two systems they represent. Integration is essential for a sound, comprehensive special education program.

In reality, there are no easy solutions to these problems. The challenge involved in functional authority is to clarify who does what within the system and to make clear the types of cooperation expected among the various administrators and staff. This can be done by redesigning organizational relationships, by revising position descriptions to describe more clearly the responsibilities of each individual, and by bringing people together to define and clarify professional relationships. All of these strategies involve the willingness of the relevant individuals to work together and to "negotiate" their relationships with one another.

Site-Based Management

Site-based management has become an integral part of recent school reform efforts. This concept describes attempts to alter traditional hierarchical, bureaucratic staffing and decision-making relationships and to decentralize authority for decisions to individual schools. Rather than have all decisions made by the superintendent and central office administrators, the individual building administrator and his or her staff are "empowered," that is, given greater autonomy to make decisions. Because they are more likely to be aware of local needs and context, it is assumed that their decisions will be more appropriate in dealing with problems than those made centrally. Because local administrators and staff have been involved in making the decisions, they will more likely be committed to seeing that the decisions are well implemented and work harder to assure success. In exchange for greater involvement in decision making the local staff are expected to be more accountable for expected outcomes.

Site-based management is often coupled with other management concepts, such as deregulation of state and local rules and regulations and alteration in traditional roles and responsibilities of administrators and staff, to provide a more flexible and responsive organizational structure. Reavis and Griffith (1992) have identified common elements in restructured schools:

- The organization is flatter, with fewer levels of management.
- Managers function as coordinators to facilitate work of groups rather than enforce compliance to rules or provide evaluation.
- Decisions are made by groups at the lowest levels of the organization.
- Such decisions cause differential work patterns to emerge to meet the needs of the groups rather than the overarching bureaucracy.
- Collaboration supersedes hierarchical structure.
- The focus on outcomes is the principal basis for making decisions.
- The faculty and staff constantly question all assumptions about the way things have been done so that new arrangements can emerge to meet real needs.

These reform concepts hold real promise in special education because they directly address student outcomes and force administrators to challenge traditional patterns of providing for the needs of those with disabilities. The focus on the local school, decentralized decision making, autonomy for decision making, and local accountability place the principal and staff in a unique position to "do what is necessary" to address the unique needs of the students with disabilities in their building. Within this concept, special education personnel are viewed as an integral part of the local school staff, and the special education administrator facilitates building-level decisions by the principal and staff.

Deregulation of external, prescriptive rules and requirements is essential for this concept to work. Many of the ineffective service delivery arrangements in place since the 1970s have been driven by specific federal and state regulations. These rules have added to the bureaucracy in schools and have not been effective in guaranteeing appropriate services for children with disabilities. Many schools have been more concerned about compliance with rules than with meeting the needs of children. The spirit of deregulation, which accompanies site-based decision making, holds promise by recreating flexibility with which the administrator and staff can respond to local needs.

Matrix Management

One type of management design that appears to hold some promise for special education, especially within the parameters of site-based management, is matrix management (Sage & Burrello, 1986; Yates, 1981). Matrix management differs from traditional management in that it combines educational functions—such as those of regular class teacher, special educator, and psychologists—with organizational tasks—such as instructional planning, budgeting, and IEP development. The matrix design attempts to determine which individuals or which positions must be involved in decision making in order to improve the quality of the decision-making process and to increase the likelihood that the decisions will be implemented. Individuals are involved in the making of a decision or in the accomplishment of a task because of their expertise or position in the organization. Their involvement is restricted to the time necessary to complete the task, and their commitment is to the task accomplishment itself rather than to a particular department or unit.

A special education matrix design, such as that depicted in Figure 2.1, highlights functional responsibilities rather than positional authority. In this design, individuals

Figure 2.1   Illustrative Matrix Role Responsibilities Chart

	Referral	Assessment	Direct Instruction	Related Instruction	Related Services	Other Services			
SPED Administrator									
Building Principal									
Regular Class Teacher									
Resource Room Teacher									
Itinerant Teacher									
Social Worker									
Psychologist									
Educational Examiner									
Assistant Sup't for Instruction									
Other Personnel									

From *Matrix Organizational Structure and its Effects upon Education Organizations* (p. 14) by I. R. Yates, April 1981. Paper presented at the meeting of the Council for Exceptional Children, New York (ERIC Document Reproduction Service No. ED 208 475). Copyright 1981 by the Author. Reprinted by permission.

are involved only to the extent necessary to complete the task. For example, the composition of the IEP committee will vary as the administrator matches staff abilities and knowledge with the type of disability and the instructional needs of the child. After the IEP has been developed, the involved individuals return to their original positions in the organization or become involved in other matrix tasks. In addition to IEP development, matrix designs can be used in instructional planning, program evaluation, and resource utilization.

Yates (1981) cites the following advantages of matrix management in special education:

1. It is able to deal effectively with organizational problems.
2. It senses and solves problems more quickly.
3. It makes better use of each individual's talents.
4. It increases the flexibility, adaptiveness, and responsiveness of the organization.
5. It reduces the span of control for administrators.
6. It reduces organizational complexity.
7. It increases the ability of individuals to influence organizational decisions regardless of their position in the hierarchy.
8. It increases communication between organizational levels and departments.

ORGANIZATIONAL DESIGNS

According to Lunenburg and Ornstein (1991), 61% of students in the United States attend schools with enrollment between 1,000 and 5,000 students. About 28% of all children attend large school districts with 25,000 or more students enrolled, representing only 1.1% of all school districts. In other words, 60% of all children attend small school districts with enrollment below 25,000. Obviously, the size and other factors impact the organizational designs for educational programming.

Lawrence and Lorsch (1967), in their classic study of British industries, reported that there is no "best" organizational design for all types of organizations; rather, each organization must design a structure that fits its mission, environments, and resources. Koontz et al. (1986) stated that each organization's structure "must be designed to work, to permit contributions by members of a group, and to help people gain objectives efficiently in a changing future" (p. 334). Thus, it is important for special and regular education administrators to be able to analyze the characteristics of their organizations and to develop appropriate adaptations. Sage and Burrello (1986) described some of the differences in the organizational structures of special education programs in large school districts, intermediate units, and rural districts. Although these descriptions are useful to some degree, most special education administrators are employed in programs with already established structures. Therefore, their primary need is to be able to analyze the dysfunctional aspects of the organizational structure of the school district in which they are employed (large, medium, rural, or "intermediate unit") and design changes to increase the organization's effectiveness and efficiency.

Large School Districts

Characteristics.   Although the definition of a large school district is relative, most educators regard urban districts or county school systems as large school districts. Large districts have many advantages:

- Sufficient numbers of students in most of the disability categories make it possible to offer comprehensive services for almost all types of children with disabilities. Most large districts even have the necessary number of "low-incidence" children with disabilities to be able to offer complete programs in-house.

- Specialized administrative, instructional, and support staff can provide the full range of services necessary for children with disabilities. This indicates high formalization and high specialization of job positions, as well as a high degree of sophistication in both line and staff positions. With adequate numbers of children, the district can hire specialists to perform specific line and staff tasks. Such specialists usually possess full certification for their positions and perform only those tasks for which they are certified. They thus become expert in their jobs and can help the district adhere to legally and educationally sound practices.

- Most large districts have well-established, comprehensive policies, procedures, goals, and objectives. Formalization extends to staff, parent, and student handbooks, as well as to many procedural handbooks on different aspects of the service delivery process, such as consulting with parents, discipline, and instructional planning.

- Specialized units deal with many of the procedures—assessment, due process, and instructional plan development—involved in comprehensive service delivery (this is an example of formalized departmentalization). Some large schools have one independent unit handling diagnostic assessment and another unit dealing with due process hearings and parental litigation. Frequently, specialized units also plan for and conduct staff development.

- Formalized authority structures attempt to establish clear lines of responsibility and communication. Most large schools have relatively tall organizational charts, indicating reasonable supervisor-subordinate ratios.

- Most large communities have many public and private agencies and services that support the special education program and provide diagnostic, instructional, and remedial assistance to the school in working with individual children or their families.

However, many of the environmental and structural factors that provide advantages to the large school are also the cause of potential problems:

- Increased district size decreases the coupling of administrative units and services between levels of the organization, and even within levels. The task of coordinating services between the building level and "downtown" can become very difficult. Physical distance and the separation of various aspects of the service delivery process can make it more difficult for the special education administrator and the principal to coordinate their activities.

- Horizontal integration between specialized units is more difficult to achieve. As more departments or units become involved in the service delivery process, more communication and coordination are needed to integrate the units in support of each other and of the goals of the special education program.

- The environment of large school districts can complicate the delivery of special education services. Large school districts must deal with the effects of crime, desegregation, low socioeconomic families, racial and cultural minorities, and other social or cultural factors that can affect the incidence and types of services the school needs to provide.

- Large schools must contend with diverse publics that may have different or conflicting expectations for the district and for the special education program. Given tight budgets, parents of nondisabled children may organize to limit services to children with disabilities and thereby clash with advocacy groups organized for the latter.

- The creation of the right blend of centralized and decentralized special education services is probably the most complicated problem for the large school district. Because of the large size of the special education enterprise, many individual services are most efficiently handled in a centralized manner. Yet most of the individual referrals, IEP development, instructional planning, and evaluation take place at the building level. Effective integration of centralized and decentralized functions is often quite difficult to achieve.

Possible Interventions.   The ability to maximize the advantages and minimize the disadvantages of the large district involves cooperation between the special and regular education administrators. Together, they need to design organizational interventions that take into account the unique characteristics of the district, the nature of its organizational structure, district policies and goals, and abilities of individual staff members. Following are some possible interventions:

1. Organizational design interventions should apply to both centralized and decentralized aspects of the organization. The relevant centralized functions include:
   - Planning and policy development
   - Curriculum development
   - General program evaluation
   - Budget development
   - Staff allocation
   - In-service development
   - Program advocacy
   - Public relations
   - Intra-agency liaison

   The relevant decentralized functions include:
   - Selection and placement of personnel
   - Personnel evaluation
   - IEP development and pupil placement

- Instructional supervision
- Building resource management and budget development
- Parent relations

Individual schools should be given autonomy to serve the needs of "their" children with the assistance of centralized support services. The role of the special education administrator and special education services must shift to assist the building principal and staff in dealing with the individual students.

2. Definition of roles and functions may be included in job descriptions and district procedures. Regardless of where they are found, they must be disseminated broadly to all district personnel. Unless staff members know the types of assistance they can expect from each other, the necessary cooperation and communication cannot be maintained.

3. The development of appropriate forms of communication among staff and between different levels of the organization can help overcome many of the dysfunctional aspects of horizontal and vertical complexity. In inclusion settings, new patterns of communication and cooperation that alter traditional ways of doing things may have to be developed.

4. Comprehensive recruitment, selection, and staff development practices are vital to the success of the large school district. Since such districts require large numbers of specialized staff and must deal with constant staff turnover, the personnel office must constantly seek to attract and keep the best qualified staff. It is important that hiring procedures determine whether the staff to be hired understand and support the district's philosophy of service delivery for those who are disabled.

5. Comprehensive in-service training is an important means of improving staff knowledge, skills, and abilities.

6. Comprehensive school-community relations are needed to deal effectively with diverse internal and external publics.

7. Large districts may be able to employ staff members with expertise in organizational development and training and use them to deal with organizational problems as they arise. Such specialists can help bridge the boundaries of regular and special education and bring about better cooperation between departments and organizational levels.

Medium-Sized Districts

Characteristics.   A little over one-third of school-age children in the United States attend schools in districts with between 2,500 and 10,000 students. These medium-sized districts must, like large district schools, be aware of the effects of their organizational structures on their ability to offer comprehensive services to children with disabilities. Following are some of the structural advantages of medium-sized districts:

- Compared with large urban schools, medium-sized schools tend to be located in more stable communities with more homogeneous populations. This can produce the need for multiple school-community relation strategies and minimize the degree to which the special education program must deal with diverse social, economic, cultural, and racial variables.

- The organizational structure is less complex and therefore more easily managed. With fewer levels in the chain of command, the vertical structure becomes more understandable and manageable. Also, because there are fewer separate special education service units, there is less horizontal complexity.

- Responsibility for special education services can be more easily decentralized to the building level. Special education teachers and programs can be functionally assigned to individual buildings, thereby moving them closer to the regular class setting and to the building principal's supervision.

However, there are also disadvantages associated with the medium-sized district:

- The medium-sized district's special education programs may not have large numbers of specialists available to provide the wide range of service delivery processes and specialized instructional placements needed to accommodate all types of disabling conditions. Special educators may serve more as generalists, each offering a wide range of special services. Also, they may not be trained or certified for the full range of services for which they are responsible.

- Medium-sized districts have a smaller student pool to draw upon; thus many of their programs for children with disabilities, especially low-incidence disabilities, carry a higher per-pupil cost than those in larger districts.

- The regular education teachers must assume more responsibility for direct instruction of children with disabilities.

- The school districts must contract with outside agencies for certain programs that they cannot efficiently provide within the district. This increases the problems of coordination and horizontal integration between services at the school and the contracting agency.

Possible Interventions.   Special and regular education administrators in medium-sized districts face a unique challenge in the integration of regular and special education systems. Because there are fewer specialists to handle the full range of services, each regular and special educator must become more willing and able to develop self-sufficient skills in dealing with children with disabilities. The distinctions between regular and special education must be eliminated as much as possible; and principals, teachers, and support personnel must be ready to help all children, whatever their need, and to aid each other in whatever way they can. Technically speaking, the special education administrator and the principal must seek to bring about a functional integration of all the horizontal dimensions of the instructional and service delivery process.

To accomplish this, the regular and special education administrators should employ the general strategies discussed elsewhere in relation to improved communication, comprehensive personnel selection, assignments, staff development, and comprehensive policy and goal statements. The administrators may also wish to use some form of matrix management (described earlier) in establishing responsibilities for various aspects of the special education service delivery process.

Because of their characteristics, medium-sized schools have the greatest potential to successfully implement inclusion by using a site-based management philosophy. These districts have easier control over their administrative and service delivery systems and can more easily focus on the regular class as the prime arena for instruction of children with disabilities. Using methods such as the consulting teacher model (which is discussed later in this chapter), these schools can create new patterns of interactions among regular and special education teachers to accommodate the diverse needs of children with disabilities in the regular class.

Rural Districts

Characteristics.   Although rural school districts have the advantage of being close to the community and of having close personal teacher-student relationships, they are at a disadvantage in their ability to provide the full range of services to children with disabilities, especially those with low-incidence disabilities. Helge (1981) surveyed state department of education personnel in 19 states with large rural populations regarding their problems in complying with PL 94-142. She found a variety of factors that hindered full compliance, such as the following:

1. Cultural factors, such as language barriers, resistance to change, and problems associated with low socioeconomic class.
2. Geographic and climatic factors, such as poor roads, hazardous terrain, and distances between the schools and other services.
3. Socioeconomic factors, such as a low tax base, low levels of financial support, suspicion of governmental interference, problems associated with the migrant status of children and their families, and difficulty in recruiting certified staff and retaining them as they became more experienced.
4. Other factors, such as low levels of parental involvement and organizational limitations that made it difficult to provide a full range of comprehensive services and to develop IEPs.

Due to these limiting factors, the development of a comprehensive special education program in a rural area presents a unique challenge. Rural school districts can accommodate individual differences in children as long as those differences are not too great and there are only a few children who demand highly specialized services. Though such districts typically do not have the financial, personnel, and instructional resources to offer a wide range of specialized programs, contracting with external agencies is often difficult because such agencies may be located at great distances from the school, and the cost of their services may be prohibitive.

Small rural school districts find it difficult to attract and keep qualified staff. Unless they are returning to their hometown or they desire to live in small communities, fully certified special education teachers may not wish to work in small school districts. Theobald (1991) listed the following reasons that rural districts find it difficult to recruit and retain qualified special teachers:

- Social, cultural, and geographic isolation.
- Lack of support services.
- Limited career mobility.
- Failure by university preparation programs to prepare teachers for the realities of teaching and living in rural areas.

Even if the district is able to attract certified teachers, they are usually inexperienced and are likely to leave for better salary and working conditions after a few years of experience. This obviously adversely affects staff continuity and the availability of staff expertise to deal with the education of children with disabilities. Special education administration functions are usually handled directly by one of the district's regular administrators, usually the superintendent, or by a building principal, if the district has one. However, these administrators often have no special training in the education of children with disabilities or in the administration of special education programs.

Possible Interventions.   Although rural districts encounter substantial difficulties in complying fully with special education legislation, they are under the same obligation that larger districts are to provide a free, appropriate education for all children with disabilities. Though some types of accommodation can be made in regular education classes for mild and moderate disabilities in such districts, alternative service delivery systems may need to be used for more severe disabilities.

One solution to the problem of offering comprehensive services in a rural context is the educational cooperative (Kirmer, Lockwood, Mickler, & Sweeney, 1984). In a cooperative, several districts agree to pool their resources so as to be able to offer programs that no one district could provide. PL 94-142 does not specifically make reference to cooperatives, but legislation in most states recognizes this type of organizational arrangement and allows schools to form cooperatives that can then legally receive state special education funds. Such cooperatives have several advantages:

- Because cooperatives allow schools to pool children in each disability group, more disability categories can be served in the local community. This is especially true for low-incidence disabilities.
- More special education specialists can be hired. Schools in the cooperative can share the costs of teachers, assessment specialists, and other personnel and then use these individuals in each school as needed.
- Cooperative arrangements usually provide improved organization and administration of the special education program. Cooperatives can afford to hire a special education administrator who can organize and supervise the entire program in the cooperating districts and thus relieve regular education administrators from this overall responsibility.

- Cooperatives can offer programs that are more cost efficient. Hiring a specialist for just one child is not a very cost-effective use of personnel resources, but such a strategy might be the only one available for a rural district with a student who is blind. Cooperatives allow the cooperating schools to share the cost of personnel and other materials by grouping special education functions, student disabilities, and teaching responsibilities.

Cooperative organizational structures also present some problems:

- Cooperatives require that school administrators and teachers from different districts work together, and such cooperation may not come easily to small school districts where community identity and individualism are valued.
- Because cooperatives often span large geographic distances, travel and communication can be difficult.
- Unclear lines of authority and communication can result in poor coordination of special education services and confusion among special education teachers concerning the officials to whom they report, the nature of their relationship with the instructional staff at each cooperating school, and the range of services for which they are responsible.

Attention to organizational design and proper planning can help to minimize these problems and create a well-functioning cooperative. Following are some planning and design procedures that local administrators should follow in setting up a cooperative:

- Determine the need for a cooperative. The incidence of disabling conditions and child find data should be examined to determine if enough children exist in the geographic area of the proposed cooperative to warrant its establishment. Administrators should be sure that all potentially eligible children have been identified and should determine how many of these have not been referred because suitable programs were not available.
- Consider the cooperative's geographic and political feasibility. The area covered by the proposed cooperative should be such as to facilitate student and staff travel and supervision of the cooperative program. Political considerations, such as the degree to which districts in the area have cooperated in the past and the willingness of the district superintendents to share personnel, should also be considered in determining which districts should be included in the cooperative.
- Establish a lead district to handle the cooperative's finances and to house its central administrative offices and, possibly, some of its instructional facilities. The lead district should have the space and bookkeeping capacity to perform these functions.
- Select a supervisor. The cooperative administrator must be able to deal with several different superintendents and boards of education and to coordinate services in several different schools. The ability to handle these functions well

should be considered, in addition to such traditional criteria as experience and certification.

- Develop a contract. To facilitate communication and accountability in each district and among the districts, the superintendents in the cooperating districts and the special education supervisor should jointly develop a performance contract. This contract should clearly specify the duties and responsibilities of the supervisor and other staff in the cooperative and provide an initial framework for structuring the cooperative. In this way, the superintendents will be aware of the services for which they are responsible and the types of services they can expect from the supervisor and the staff in the cooperative. The following items might be included in such a contract:

1. A statement about the purpose of the cooperative.

2. Specific goals for the year.

3. A contact person in each district.

4. Services that the cooperative will provide to each district and time schedules showing when the various staff of the cooperative will be present in each district.

5. The services and other resources to be provided by each district.

6. Procedures for arbitrating differences between the cooperative and the districts.

7. Procedures for evaluating the supervisor and cooperative staff.

8. Procedures for evaluating the success of the cooperative and for revising the contract.

Intermediate Units

Many states have formalized intermediate units to provide services for children with disabilities among other general education services. Campbell, Cunningham, Nystrand, and Usdan (1985) define an intermediate unit as an "office or agency in an intermediate position between the state department of education and local school districts" (p. 101). Intermediate units originally began as regulating agencies that monitored local schools, and many still fulfill some monitoring functions. However, their major function has shifted dramatically to that of providing educational services.

Approximately 39 states have some form of intermediate unit. Some intermediate units exist as formal regional state agencies and either receive direct support from the state or have independent taxing power. Others are supported by the contributed fees of the member school districts, which purchase from the intermediate unit services that they cannot offer economically, or choose not to offer for other reasons, at the local level. Intermediate units that provide services to children with disabilities are the Board of Cooperative Educational Services (BOCES) in New York, Regional Educational Service Centers in Texas, and the Cooperative Educational Services Agency in Wisconsin.

Most of the advantages and disadvantages that apply to local school district cooperatives also apply to intermediate units that provide special education services. The intermediate unit is, in effect, another means of pooling resources and sharing costs.

Many local districts that cannot afford their own comprehensive special education programs, or do not have enough students to offer certain services, can benefit from an intermediate unit that assumes services and administrative functions. Most intermediate units offer such comprehensive services as media services, computer services, vocational education, and administrative and instructional planning. They usually have their own buses, teachers, buildings, administrative officers, and other support personnel. Thus, intermediate units carry substantial administrative and capital overhead that must be recovered in their charges to local schools.

Although intermediate units provide a useful service for many districts, their utility as a source of comprehensive special education services is dependent upon a number of fiscal, political, and organizational considerations. Burrello and Sage (1979) commented that participation in the BOCES in New York changed during the mid-1970s as alterations in the state funding formula increased the financial advantages of offering special education at the local district level and as state legislation increased the emphasis on a least restrictive setting at the local level. In short, the centralized services offered by an intermediate unit may not be compatible with the least restrictive concern of PL 94-142 or compatible with concepts such as inclusion; this could increase the problems of coordination between the local school and the intermediate unit. Indeed, local administrators may prefer to offer their own programs rather than use those of the intermediate unit if state funding formulas favor local service delivery or if the costs of services at the intermediate unit are not markedly cheaper than those offered by the local school district.

SERVICE DELIVERY MODELS

Although the needs of a child should determine the type of services the child receives, some type of administrative planning is necessary to define the options available to the school. The problem is that once a variety of service plans are organized, the school personnel may be tempted to place the child in an existing service model because it is already administratively intact and is, thus, convenient. Clearly, however, service options should be tailored to meet the needs of the child (appropriate and least restrictive); the child should not be forced to fit into a service model merely for administrative convenience. Indeed, children who are, for example, deaf or blind have performed quite well in regular classrooms with only limited assistance. This is a highly individual matter that cannot be determined solely on the basis of the disability category.

Many textbook authors depict the services that might be offered to children with disabilities in the form of a pyramid or a continuum of services ranging from the most restrictive to the least restrictive environment. Perhaps the most widespread conceptualization of such a pyramid is the "Cascade of Services" model developed by Deno (1970), although others have offered similar models. A continuum or cascade model of services has different levels, each depicting the numbers of students who might be served and the degree of distance from the regular classroom. The corresponding organizational arrangements are partly determined by the "normalization" or mainstreaming philosophy and partly by legal and financial inducements to educate children with disabilities in the least restrictive environment. As the inclusion model seems to be spreading in education, it seems likely that, although many models will be available, the placement for most children will be in regular classrooms. Districts will need to establish mission statements and policies to describe whether they support limited inclusion (i.e., only students with mild disabilities) or total inclusion (i.e., all students regardless of the nature of their disability).

The following models, used in public schools throughout the nation, are based on the levels depicted in most continuum or cascade models. These arrangements will need to be tailored to accommodate the district's philosophy of providing services to children with disabilities, especially in the case of those at the building and district levels, which, if appropriate, will need to be modified to support an inclusion philosophy.

Regular Classroom

It is conceivable that a child with a disability might be placed in a regular classroom with no special services, in which case the child would technically not be considered to have a disability. In fact, many children with disabilities are capable of benefiting from regular classroom placement with some type of support. The support may be rather indirect, as in the case of a child who would benefit from special materials and other considerations, for which the teacher receives supportive services from a special teacher. In districts where there is ample support, consulting special education teachers may deal directly with the regular classroom teacher. This is the preferred model within the inclusion concept.

Expanded Role of the Regular Educator.   Unfortunately, even with the advent of mainstreaming, regular classroom teachers often still feel absolved of any authority, responsibility, and/or involvement in relation to students with disabilities, believing that the special education child is the sole responsibility of special education personnel. This attitude may have resulted from the fact that few regular education preparation programs or state licensure requirements adequately address accommodation strategies for students with disabilities in the regular class. In such circumstances, everyone suffers. The regular classroom teacher feels "put upon" to have the child there; the special education teacher experiences frustration because the child is not learning. More significant, however, is what the child feels and experiences. With the Regular Education Initiative and the inclusion model guiding stated department of education policy and procedures, the classroom teacher will have ultimate responsibility for all children, including those with disabilities.

Implicit in the education of any child is the belief that all parties (e.g., parents, teachers, bus drivers, librarians, etc.) have one primary focus: that the child learn to the best of his or her ability. Either because of tradition or training, regular classroom teachers seem to have a fair grasp of what this means when educating nondisabled learners. However, in dealing with students with disabilities, there are important, but not obvious, responsibilities best handled by the regular classroom teacher. One of the most significant of these involves prereferral activities.

Recent studies have suggested that peer collaboration among pairs of teachers can help regular class teachers identify appropriate accommodation strategies. Pugach and Johnson (1989) reported in their research that regular education teachers profited from consulting with other teachers, even other regular education teachers, about ways of accommodating children with disabilities. This interaction helped the regular class teacher to reflect on how to adapt strategies and techniques that they employed for the majority of children in the class so as to be appropriate for those with disabilities.

Itinerant Model

The itinerant model is commonly used for certain categories of disability that require minimal contact. The itinerant teacher travels from school to school and works directly with certain types of children with disabilities in each school. The most obvious example is the itinerant speech therapist. However, teachers of students who are, for example, blind or deaf also travel from one school to another on a regular basis to deliver direct services to students and to assist the teacher. Obviously, such an approach is less expensive, but only certain children can benefit maximally from it.

Schmidt and Stipe (1991) reported that a majority of itinerant teachers believed themselves to be poorly trained for the job, and 77% questioned their effectiveness. Many states will fund itinerant teachers only if they provide services directly to the child with a disability. This may be only marginally effective because the child will still spend much time in the regular class. Within an inclusion philosophy the itinerant teacher needs to assist the regular class teacher with accommodation strategies and techniques so that the regular teacher can provide appropriate instruction on a continuing basis. The itinerant teacher may also provide direct instruction to the child with a disability within the regular class, assisting the child to meet regular class instructional goals.

Consultant Model

This is a variation of the itinerant model, except that the teacher remains in one or two buildings with large numbers of students to serve. The duties of the teacher may be to enter a classroom and provide direct services to the student and/or to the teacher of a regular class. The effectiveness of this model has been a concern for many years, and it is especially controversial as the trend toward the inclusion model or Regular Education Initiative (REI) gains momentum. It is a model that will remain popular and requires specific kinds of skills that may not be taught in preparation programs (Harris, 1991). Some states will not fund consulting teachers because they do not provide direct services to individual children with disabilities, thus inhibiting the implementation of this useful staffing model.

Chalfant and Pysh (1989) reported that their research indicates that multidisciplinary teacher assistance teams can help regular teachers identify appropriate accommodation strategies. The composition of these teams may include the principal, a consulting teacher, other teachers, and parents. Teachers can successfully use these teams to analyze and better understand problems in the class, describe intervention goals, and develop creative solutions for accommodation. The result is improved student performance and satisfaction with the instructional process. These teams were also shown to be effective in reducing the number of students referred to special education.

Administrative support and school-sponsored training in team building and consultation are necessary for these strategies to be successful. The administrator needs to coordinate teacher schedules so that team members can plan and work together to assure that accommodation strategies are feasible and implemented. With the proper support and assistance it is increasingly clear that regular teachers can identify and implement appropriate and successful intervention and accommodation strategies in their classrooms for children with disabilities.

Resource Room Model

The resource room is the least restrictive of the special education models in which children are removed from the classroom for a portion of the school day for special services. The amount of time a child with a disability might be in the resource room for special services should logically be determined by the actual needs of the student as expressed in the IEP. Often, however, students are assigned to regularly scheduled periods in the resource room in order to fit administrative requirements of the school. The nature and variety of services that a student receives in the resource room must be stipulated in the IEP. But this often raises severe problems in special education programming (Breton, Donaldson, & Gordon, 1991). For example, what is the desired relationship between the regular class and the special class curricula? What are the relationships among the regular and resource teachers? And how can shared teaching responsibilities be assigned and coordinated? Students in these pull-out arrangements often become second-class citizens in the regular class and do not have the continuity provided by ongoing participation in the regular class. Often, too, instructional goals in the resource room are less rigorous than in the regular class or not completely coordinated with the student's personal instructional goals in the regular class. Administrators must create measures to assure that there is articulation and coordination between the regular class and resource room whenever the IEP indicates that a resource placement is appropriate.

Resource Center

The resource center is similar to the resource room except that it is a multicategorical or noncategorical room staffed by special teachers, usually two or more. The students in the center are served in a variety of ways without any particular attention to their labels. The center approach is used for a variety of reasons, including the opportunity for students to get support from different teachers and the opportunity for special teachers to work with one another in a team-teaching atmosphere. The center approach is also economical because materials, equipment, and other supportive aids can be located in one area. However, it also has all the problems that attend team teaching. In some states, the resource center model may not be permitted because of regulatory limitations.

Special Class in Regular School

There are many variations of the special class in the regular school. In fact, in some states it is difficult to distinguish between this model and the resource room approach. The main distinction is that the student in the special class has major instructional contact with the special teacher. In some variations, the student is mainstreamed for some academic subjects in a regular class with nondisabled peers; in others, the student is mainstreamed for nonacademic classes. In still another, more traditional variation, the student with a disability is assigned to a segregated special classroom in the regular building with virtually no contact with other classes or students. This, however, is very difficult to justify on either legal or commonsense grounds.

Special School

The special school is a segregated building that is likely to have several classes for students with disabilities. In a sense, it is similar to a regular public school except that it has no nondisabled students. This was once a very common approach among school districts. The objections to it are based on the same arguments that were raised by the civil rights case in *Brown v. Board of Education of Topeka* (1954). Thus, many districts have abandoned the special school. There are, of course, many private schools that are essentially special schools, although most of these tend to deal with one category of disability, such as "cerebral palsy" or "learning disability."

Residential School

Residential schools are state and private schools that are typically geared to one category, such as "blind," "deaf," "emotionally disturbed," or "autistic." Many states fully fund these special residential schools and pay all expenses for any student who meets criteria for admission. There are a number of residential schools for students who are learning disabled. The clients of such facilities are commonly from wealthy families.

Preschool Models

Since implementation of PL 99-457, services will now be provided for preschool infants, toddlers, and their families. There are many types of services that may be provided focusing on child-rearing practices, skills development, nutrition, and other factors that may be important for an individualized program. After child-find and screening activities, assessment, and placement, the infant or toddler may be included in services that are primarily of two types: home-based programs and center-based programs. Personnel working with families and preschool children will come from many disciplines and backgrounds, but all are supposed to be certified or licensed. In both home- and center-based models, consultation and services can include evaluation, interventions, and periodic assessment of progress. It is likely that most programs will focus on skills development, primarily in the areas of psychomotor, cognitive, and language, but any specific services may also be determined according to the individual's needs. Throughout the remainder of this decade, public school-sponsored preschools will increasingly become more common.

Adult Transition Programs

Schools will now provide transition programs for secondary students with disabilities. In most cases, the program will focus on preparing the student with job skills and connecting the student with agencies and programs or jobs in the community. The primary areas of concern in transition planning are employment, postsecondary education or training, housing, finance, transportation, and related needs in medical care, therapy, interpersonal and social needs, and recreation and leisure activities. For some students, transition plans will involve placement in postsecondary training schools or college.

Models for work-related programs can take the form of work experience, work-study programs, on-the-job training, off-campus workstations, and cooperative programs. Some students, unable to function in competitive work environments, will need to be placed in supported-work programs or sheltered workshops, where they can be gainfully employed. The transition process should carefully match student needs with options in the community. Vocational placement is a serious consideration and requires the involvement of professionals acquainted with job evaluation and job placement. Transition programs are more structured and available in large school districts (White & Bond, 1992) than in rural districts where employment opportunities are more difficult to find (Baumeister & Morris, 1992). Thus, all successful programs require cooperation among personnel in the school, public agencies, private business, and the community in general.

Notifications for referral, evaluation, placement, and transition plans can be adapted from the basic forms used for special education programming. For example, a notice can be sent entitled "Transition Meeting," which essentially explains the purpose of the meeting (to plan a transition from school to community placement) and when, where, and who will attend. Similarly, the Individualized Transition Plan (ITP) would follow the structure of the IEP but would include information of importance to a young adult, such as social security number, referral and assessment of social services, Vocational Rehabilitation Services, and so forth. The goals would be for education, training, and/or employment, followed by the objectives to attain these goals.

Most students with disabilities are eligible for evaluation and work training, which may include costs of training and tools through Vocational Rehabilitation Services. Coordination among Social Services, Vocational Rehabilitation Services, and other agencies will ordinarily be the responsibility of the school until a student is graduated or leaves school. For students who have multiple disabilities, comprehensive planning is necessary and many agencies will be involved in the planning process.

With an expected increase in the number of children with disabilities in schools over the next decade and general economic problems of the nation, support for the inclusion model will undoubtedly grow. This support may occur for no other reason than it will be less expensive than other forms of providing services to students with disabilities.

It seems clear that as special education personnel are expected to provide more direct services to classroom teachers than to students in such a model, there will be less demand for special education personnel as they have been used historically. At the same time, there is a trend for teacher training programs to prepare classroom teachers who are dually trained and certified. The general education teacher, at least at the elementary level, will have both the generic skills of the teaching profession as well as the special skills. And this will alter the special education programming in those districts where such teachers are employed.

IDENTIFICATION, PLACEMENT, AND SERVICE DELIVERY

*This chapter was coauthored by Dr. Anna McFadden, Associate Professor, Area of Teacher Education, The University of Alabama.

THE INDIVIDUALIZED EDUCATION PLAN: PRODUCT VERSUS PROCESS

Procedures of special education assessment, referral, and placement are routine parts of the school bureaucracy eliciting little attention, at least as judged by the lack of interest in professional literature. After passage of the initial legislation (PL 94-142), administrative requirements were the most controversial aspects of special education (aside from concerns about placing students with disabilities in regular classrooms), and many articles appeared in education literature. Fewer articles about the processes of special education have appeared in professional journals since that time. The administrator must, nonetheless, be thoroughly familiar with all aspects of PL 101-476, particularly the IEP process.

The IEP is a unique and central component of special education programming and may become more important in education because of the trend toward greater individualization in education and the placement of children with disabilities in regular classes, as part of inclusion. Schools are held to higher expectations, due to the reform movement; and there are likely to be both national and state outcome assessments. It is also likely that individualized formative assessment of all students may become a critical feature in determining school success.

According to Ludlow and Lombardi (1992):

> In the future all students will be placed in regular classrooms; assignment to special education will be based on needs rather than labels; students will be educated by teams rather than individual teachers; and, programming will be delivered in a variety of settings, selected on the basis of which environment is most conducive to students. (p. 158)

If so, it seems logical to assume that the IEP and other written plans will become more important in determining what is to be done and by whom, as a matter of accountability.

The IEP component requires that a written educational program be developed for each student who has a disability. In fact, IEPs may have become so routine that they are formula driven. As noted previously, adherence to federal standards in special education was initially controversial, and some school districts had filled in forms to comply with regulations with no intention of meeting the needs of students. The use of the IEP also disrupted the traditional power of the administration, requiring the involvement of teachers, parents, and students directly in the process. Although research on this topic is scant and difficult to achieve, observation will show that IEPs are frequently developed with little effort, in a very brief span of time, and are not used to guide educational programming. Reiher (1992) indicated in a study of records that there is often incongruence between diagnostic information and the IEP. This may be testimony to the ability of a system to resist top-down bureaucratic commands; but, in theory, the IEP represented the first attempt to provide individualization in education.

Another observation is the significant time delay from referral to assessment and placement in many schools. Actually, although the law requires specific guidelines, the responsibility is placed on the parents to demand timely delivery of services. Parents of poor and minority children are much less likely to assert their rights (Larue, 1989). If parents are not assertive, a school district may proceed at a pace convenient for its purposes, which technically violates the law and may compromise the educational programs of pupils. Figure 3.1 depicts a special education process typical of most states including elements of the process and timelines.

Figure 3.1   Special Education Process

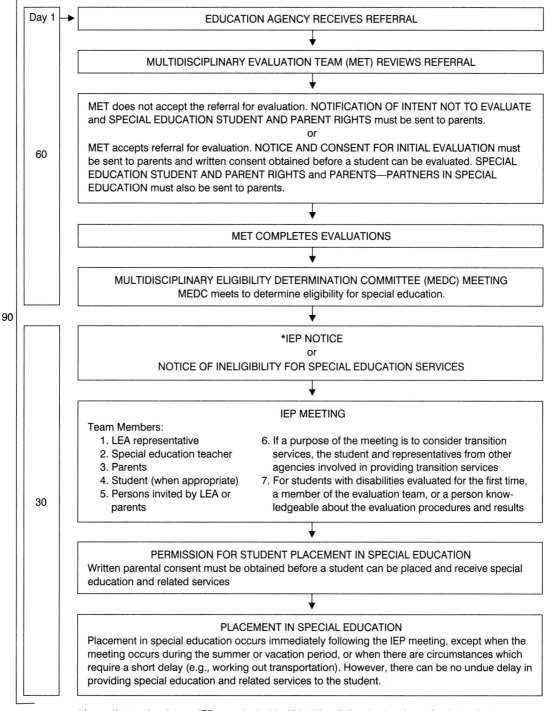

| Day 1 → | EDUCATION AGENCY RECEIVES REFERRAL |

MULTIDISCIPLINARY EVALUATION TEAM (MET) REVIEWS REFERRAL

60

MET does not accept the referral for evaluation. NOTIFICATION OF INTENT NOT TO EVALUATE and SPECIAL EDUCATION STUDENT AND PARENT RIGHTS must be sent to parents.

or

MET accepts referral for evaluation. NOTICE AND CONSENT FOR INITIAL EVALUATION must be sent to parents and written consent obtained before a student can be evaluated. SPECIAL EDUCATION STUDENT AND PARENT RIGHTS and PARENTS—PARTNERS IN SPECIAL EDUCATION must also be sent to parents.

MET COMPLETES EVALUATIONS

MULTIDISCIPLINARY ELIGIBILITY DETERMINATION COMMITTEE (MEDC) MEETING
MEDC meets to determine eligibility for special education.

90

*IEP NOTICE
or
NOTICE OF INELIGIBILITY FOR SPECIAL EDUCATION SERVICES

IEP MEETING

Team Members:
1. LEA representative
2. Special education teacher
3. Parents
4. Student (when appropriate)
5. Persons invited by LEA or parents

6. If a purpose of the meeting is to consider transition services, the student and representatives from other agencies involved in providing transition services
7. For students with disabilities evaluated for the first time, a member of the evaluation team, or a person knowledgeable about the evaluation procedures and results

30

PERMISSION FOR STUDENT PLACEMENT IN SPECIAL EDUCATION
Written parental consent must be obtained before a student can be placed and receive special education and related services

PLACEMENT IN SPECIAL EDUCATION
Placement in special education occurs immediately following the IEP meeting, except when the meeting occurs during the summer or vacation period, or when there are circumstances which require a short delay (e.g., working out transportation). However, there can be no undue delay in providing special education and related services to the student.

*A meeting to develop an IEP must be held within thirty (30) calendar days of a determination that a student needs special education and related services.

Inherent in the IEP process is the understanding that the school district will provide a continuum of programs and services. If the process is, in fact, time consuming, it can be defended on grounds argued that:

1. It creates a structure to assure that assessments will be conducted and appropriate programming will be planned with regard to associated legal considerations of due process and equal protection.
2. It provides teachers an opportunity to help students develop their potentials.
3. It organizes a monitoring process to check student progress.
4. It formally attests to the individuality of each child.
5. It has the potential to forge cooperation between parents and teachers (Turnbull, 1986).

These purposes are likely much more exemplary than actual.

The IEP as a Product

It is true, of course, that at one level the IEP is a form that is completed as part of the service planning and delivery process. But to assume that the form represents the major part of the process can be damaging to the pupil and, at least, violate the spirit of the law. A number of problems can be traced to this restricted, superficial concept of the IEP. The following were identified by Marsh and Price (1980) and remain true today:

- Content area teachers complain about having students with disabilities in the regular classroom.
- Special education teachers complain about the lack of cooperation they receive from regular teachers.
- Teachers resist input from specialists, asserting they offer impractical, inappropriate suggestions for the regular classroom.
- Parents express concern about what is happening to their child while the process unfolds.
- Monitoring personnel question the relationship between daily instructional activities and the comprehensive plan found in the files.
- All parties complain about the amount of time required to complete the IEP process.

The IEP as a Process

There are important differences between viewing the IEP as a product and viewing it as a process. In the first place, the outcome of the product approach is that the proper IEP form is completed and filed; the outcome of the process approach is that free, comprehensive, and appropriate services are provided to students with disabilities. Secondly, in the product approach, the roles of the participants are dictated by the types of information needed for the IEP form and by the static steps needed to complete the form; in the process approach, participant roles encompass actions directed at the acquisition and evaluation of all pertinent information. Finally, in the product approach, the underlying concern is legal compliance with the letter of the law; in contrast, the process approach centers on ethical compliance with the intent of the law.

Acceptance of the concept of the IEP as a broad attempt to analyze and evaluate individual performance data within the context of a particular environment is a commitment to the process approach. The school engaging in the IEP process locates students who may require special education services, assesses their educational needs, and provides appropriate instructional services. The entire process is cyclical in nature, proceeding through program development and annual evaluation, but never really ending. In another sense, the process can be conceived of as involving three stages: (1) the initial stage, concerned with child find and referral, (2) the intermediate stage, devoted to evaluation and placement and completion of the IEP form, and (3) the final stage, involving daily programming and evaluation.

CHILD FIND

Students who are potentially eligible for special education services under state and federal law must first be located by the local district. To fulfill their responsibilities under the law, district personnel must undertake the following child-find activities and administrative actions, which are now routine in America's schools:

1. Screening programs
   - Survey teachers, asking them to identify children with potential problems or about whom they have concerns.
   - Examine achievement test data and other group measures that might identify pupils with possible learning problems.
   - Conduct formal and informal screening of children entering the district in kindergarten.

2. Public awareness
   - Develop community information programs, describing the types of services available and encouraging referral.
   - Provide community awareness programs, emphasizing the rights of students with disabilities and their parents.
   - Contact area physicians and other health related professionals.

3. Interagency cooperation
   - Survey other agencies, such as public health and welfare offices, asking them to refer children who may need special education services.
   - Form an advisory group consisting of parents, community leaders, and representatives of other agencies.

4. Faculty interaction
   - Conduct in-service sessions with regular and special educators on child-find and referral processes.
   - Provide faculty members with referral materials and specific information about problematic behaviors.

There is now a renewed emphasis on this activity, particularly because of the inclusion of preschool children and their families in services. As schools are expected to receive an influx of more children with disabilities over the next few decades, child-find, screening, and referral activities may need to be reexamined to assure they are appropriate and to maintain costs of such programs within reasonable limits.

Administrative Responsibilities

General administrative tasks in child-find activities include:

- Securing copies of all child-find materials and procedures provided by the state department of education.
- Identifying groups in the state or local area that might provide assistance with child-find activities.
- Communicating with local parent groups concerning child-find activities.

Additional actions and responsibilities may be required in particular school situations, districts, or communities. Before finalizing child-find plans, administrative personnel must take into consideration such local variables as:

1. Local attitudes toward individuals with disabilities.
2. The nature and amount of influence wielded by various community groups, such as churches, philanthropic societies, and professional associations.
3. The availability of local media and information on media-use patterns of the population.
4. The existence of particular familial situations in the community that must be considered because of legal, social, or political implications.
5. The informal power structure of the community.

Although the law dictates that child-find activities must be conducted, it is up to administrative personnel to reconcile the legal mandates with local community characteristics. Child-find activities must be conducted professionally in accordance with the law, but common sense may be employed to determine "right" and "wrong" ways to achieve compliance. The right way is to acknowledge that community variables do exist and to work within the context of the local setting. The wrong way is to ignore ethical responsibilities, to give only superficial attention to the activity, and to ignore the relevant local influences, thereby increasing the risk of negative reactions that might adversely affect elements of the program beyond the child-find stage.

THE REFERRAL PROCESS

The purpose of the referral process is (1) to indicate formally that a particular child is not performing commensurate with a peer or a norm group; (2) to request assistance in investigating whether or not a problem exists; and, if so, (3) to elucidate the nature of that problem. The referral process actually begins when concern about the child's performance in the home, classroom, or other setting first surfaces. It continues through the collection of exploratory data to describe more clearly the problem and ultimately culminates in a verification of the problem. Referral may be initiated by parents, teachers, agency representatives from social service groups, or others involved with the child. The two most common sources of referrals are regular classroom teachers and parents; and therefore, they are of the greatest interest and concern to administrators.

Great expense and trouble can be prevented if *prereferral* activities are employed, and excellent information can be gained that can facilitate assessment or prevent referrals. Teachers and administrators should engage in a series of prereferral activities, which can save time, money, and provide valuable information. These activities, though part of the overall referral process, should be completed before any formal referral form is submitted.

Teacher-Initiated Referrals

Typically, teacher-initiated referrals stem from a teacher's concern about a student's daily schoolwork or behavior. The reasons commonly given by teachers for such concern include the child's inability to adequately perform school work, peer relationship problems, below-grade-level performance, and short attention span. Referrals listing such complaints comprise the bulk of the referrals received by most principals or other administrators who are responsible for handling the referral procedures. Although teachers can effectively identify students with potential problems, there are certain problems that can result, especially if there are no prereferral activities. Teachers tend to refer poor readers, more boys, and more African-American pupils; others with an evident need for referral are not considered.

There are indications, also, that teachers tend to refer students who are troublesome but who do not necessarily have a disability according to the definitions. The trend toward inclusion of students with disabilities in general education classrooms would ultimately lead to a different conclusion of this process, assuming that the teacher would expect to keep the child in the classroom rather than wanting the child to be moved to a special class. If the regular teacher is either also trained in special education or receives direct support from special education professionals, the intent is clearly to find ways to assist the child's learning rather than removal. Because federal law requires that students who are referred receive a complete referral conference, teachers should not refer students indiscriminately. Each referral will potentially entail a considerable amount of personnel time and may even cause unnecessary psychological harm to the child, not to mention the expense. The principal or other administrative officer should provide prereferral guidance to regular classroom teachers prior to their initiation of the formal referral process. Such guidance should be given throughout the referral process but especially in the three stages of prereferral: (1) exploration, (2) decision making, and (3) description.

The purpose of the first stage, exploration, is to confirm the existence of a problem. In this stage the teacher alters instructional and environmental variables and monitors student changes in behavior in order to ascertain the relationship between these factors and the perceived student problem.

The purpose of the second stage, decision making, is to determine if the nature of the problem can be examined further through the referral steps. In this stage, the teacher, with assistance from the principal or others, evaluates the information gathered in the first stage and decides whether or not to complete the formal referral request.

The purpose of the final stage, description, is to describe accurately and definitively, on a referral form, the behavior that concerned the teacher.

The following specific teacher actions are performed within each of the three stages of prereferral:

1. Exploration
   - Scrutinize the child's school records.
   - Examine the child's classroom work.
   - Alter major variables in the tasks prompting the concern—materials methodology, instructional schedule.
   - Change seating arrangements.
   - Talk with the child about the concern.
   - Talk with previous teachers about the concern.

2. Decision making
   - Share information gained in Stage 1 with the principal.
   - Formulate one or more questions concerning the data generated in Stage 1 (e.g., Is it possible that medical problems could cause the inattention? Do these same behavioral problems exist in after-school group situations?).
   - Talk with other professionals who might have information relevant to the concern (e.g., speech therapist, special educator, school nurse).
   - Decide if the concern is specific enough to complete the referral form, thereby initiating the referral process.

3. Description
   - Secure the referral form from the appropriate personnel.
   - Complete the referral form, providing required information in objective terms.
   - Collect anecdotal information that accurately reflects the concern; this will be presented at the referral conference.
   - Retain copies of the student's work that are indicative of the problem.
   - Collect copies of peer efforts to illustrate the nature of the problem in the context of peer performance and expectations.

• Formulate one or more hypotheses to explain or describe the concern.

Prereferral actions by the teachers can result in one of several outcomes. All outcomes of the referral process should be given professional attention and may entail administrative actions. However, the central focus is on the preparatory steps resulting from a decision to refer a student for possible special education services (Hoover & Collier, 1991) or to determine that the child does not qualify for special education but that other accommodations need to be made to address the child's learning or other needs. If the outcome of these preparatory steps is a decision by the teacher to complete the referral form, the task must be approached professionally in order to bring the referral process to fruition. In completing the form, the classroom teacher must clearly describe the student behavior or problem in as much detail as possible because the referral form can provide the basis for making assessment decisions and is the formal link between the teacher and other professionals who will deliberate the case.

One of the major by-products of the exploratory activities in prereferral is that the teacher is in a better position to describe concerns about the student's behavior and to document specific examples or evidence of those concerns. Without such exploratory efforts by the initiating party, much of the time in the beginning of referral is spent in trying to precisely define the problem and to understand something of the specific nature of the teacher's concern about the child.

The administrator may assure the integrity of this process by the following actions:

1. General actions
   • See that appropriate referral forms are provided.
   • Provide a teachers' handbook outlining the major activities and components of referral.
   • Communicate the purpose of referral.
   • Support the intent and outcomes of the referral process.

2. Teacher-related actions
   • Confer with teachers concerning prereferral activities.
   • Suggest prereferral activities and offer support for the teacher engaging in those activities.
   • Observe the student in the classroom if deemed appropriate and/or requested by the teacher.
   • Cooperate with the teacher in generating possible alternatives to referral.
   • Assist teachers in completing the referral form.
   • Provide the teacher with information and guidelines in preparing for the referral conference: (a) identify other participating parties, (b) briefly explain the agenda, (c) explain the possible outcomes, and (d) clarify the type of data the teacher should provide.
   • Encourage teacher participation in the referral conference and foster feelings of professional worth.

Parent-Initiated Referrals

Although the usual referring agent is the regular classroom teacher, parents sometimes express a desire to initiate a formal referral procedure. Frequently, the reasons that bring parents to such a point include severe behavioral problems outside of school or extreme concern about the child's lack of academic achievement. In such cases, the first parental contact may be with the building principal. Although most parents will not call the principal directly and request that the referral process be initiated, they may ask for an appointment to discuss problems they are having with the child and to ask for assistance. It will then be the responsibility of the principal to gather as much information as possible in order to provide the proper leadership, possibly resulting in a recommendation that the child be referred. The principal should undertake the following activities:

- Ask the parents the purpose of the meeting; this will give the principal some idea of what to expect.
- Contact the child's regular teacher; the parents may have discussed their concern with the teacher, but this is not always the case.
- Ask the teacher for relevant information, including the teacher's perception of the problem, information concerning the teacher's relationship with the parents, performance data describing the student's daily classroom work, and any previous actions that the teacher and/or parents have tried in connection with the concern prompting the meeting.
- Become familiar with the child's folder.

In this process, the interests of the student, the parents, and the district must be orchestrated in order to guarantee that the parent-initiated referral is properly handled, which may require that administrative personnel cooperatively direct and participate in the referral. In this context, the following specific actions should be taken by the building principal and by the special education supervisor:

- Confer with the parents, discussing steps in the referral process, forms to be used, reporting processes, participating professionals, and possible outcomes.
- Provide assistance in completing the referral form.
- Identify parental expectations relevant to the referral process.
- Schedule the conference at a location and time convenient for the parents.
- Provide information about the conference itself, including the proposed agenda, the type of data to be presented, the questions typically asked during such conferences, and the roles of the participating professionals.

Referral Forms

Although referral forms should be designed to collect responses to a variety of categories, the tendency is for schools to collect limited information. Information that might be included is often available as a routine part of related school activities and is available in school records, especially if they are computerized. Other types of relevant information might be a listing of instructional materials currently being used in the classroom, alternative instructional procedures used and their effects, and brief descriptions of other investigative efforts by the teacher.

As the field of special education has matured, children have grown up. A major concern among parents and many professionals is the need for students to make a transition from school to postsecondary settings. Also, as preschool children will not be included in service, a new category of referral forms will be developed and used for this population. These forms will probably be more concerned with social, psychomotor, and cognitive characteristics of children.

The administrator should review the referral process to determine whether the referral form itself needs revision. In addition to surveying the users of the form, attention should be given to aspects of the process that might suggest the need for changes in the form; for example: (1) the average length of time (number of days) between the initial request for the referral form and its submission for consideration; (2) the frequency of teacher requests for assistance in completing the form or clarifying an item; and (3) the appropriateness of the data produced by the form, as reflected in teachers' responses and the instances in which the form must be returned to the teacher for additional or revised information.

Additional evaluative information can be gleaned from an examination of the referral forms as they are completed by the teachers. The administrator should be alert to possible problems that indicate the need to alter the form.

- Are some items frequently left blank?
- Do some questions consistently prompt teachers to write lengthy answers with limited relevance to the basic issue?
- Are there frequent instances of teachers adding extra pages or writing on the back of the form?
- Are there certain questions to which teachers consistently provide inappropriate answers?

The Referral Conference

The purpose of the referral conference is twofold: (1) to provide a forum for the presentation of data about the student behavior that is of concern to the teacher or other initiating party, and (2) to allow interaction among the professionals that is directed at a collective generation of explanations for the concern and suggestions for possible ensuing actions. Administrative officers must exert leadership to ensure that these purposes are achieved; their leadership role includes planning and conducting the conferences as well as coordinating the efforts of the team members.

Referral Team

Federal guidelines require that the referral team at the conference include the parents and, when appropriate, the child. Obviously, assessment personnel as well as instructional personnel are also expected to attend. State guidelines and local district policies dictate the precise nature of the team membership, but the referring teacher, the building principal or designate, special education personnel, the parents, and, when deemed appropriate, the student consistently function as team members. Others may of course attend in order to provide information about the student, the services, or specific assessment areas. The referral conference must be attended by at least three parties; this helps ensure that it is more than just a meeting between the special educator and the principal. Unless the team membership also includes appropriate professionals, the purposes of the referral process cannot possibly be achieved.

Referral team members must also assume important responsibilities prior to and during the conference. The principal may find it necessary to assist the participants in defining their roles; this requires that the principal understand the actions expected of each participant. Following is an overview of the responsibilities of referral team members:

1. Chairperson (prior to the meeting)
   - Make preparations for the meeting.
   - Send written notices announcing the meeting's beginning and ending times, location, instructions, purpose, and participants.
   - Assist the initiating party in finalizing the referral request.

   (During the conference)
   - Prepare a written record of the meeting, including the minutes, a list of participants, a description of unresolved concerns, and recommended actions.
   - Provide leadership during the meeting to create an atmosphere of mutual interaction.
   - Introduce the participants, providing a brief overview of their professional roles in the referral.
   - Provide a brief overview of all events preceding the referral.
   - Keep the meeting progressing toward the stated purpose.
   - Terminate the conference once the purpose has been achieved and/or closure has been reached.

2. Special educator
   - Provide detailed information about the services included in special education.
   - Supply special information pertaining to assessment approaches and remedial methodologies.

3. Referring teacher
   - Specify precisely the concern about the child that precipitated the referral.
   - Review pertinent test data and achievement information.
   - Present relevant information gleaned from school records and prereferral activities.
   - Suggest one or more explanations for the cause of the concern.
   - Generate suggestions for future courses of action.

4. Parents
   - Present their opinions concerning the student's problem.

- Describe the child's behavior and performance at home.
- Secure information about possible outcomes.

5. Student (if appropriate)

- Provide information concerning personal preferences.
- Present opinions about the problem.

Referral Tasks and Outcomes

The referral team is charged with several important tasks that should culminate in a referral decision, thus completing the referral process. Collectively, the team members must document the existence of a problem to be addressed through the referral process, systematically organize and present all relevant data, and specify the areas of performance that should be examined in further investigations. The members may recommend that additional informal assessment be conducted by the teachers and other professionals. Such action would be followed by an evaluation conference. Beyond that, a comprehensive formal evaluation might be recommended, to be followed by an evaluation conference.

In addition to the above tasks, the building principal or other administrative officer will have to undertake important administrative follow-up activities. These will include filing the completed referral outcome form; arranging for temporary placement, if that is deemed appropriate; completing arrangements and plans for future meetings, if needed; and seeing that formal notification of the referral outcome is sent to the parents and other team members.

Due Process and Parental Involvement

The participation of parents, guardians, or parent surrogates in the decision-making process of referral must be carefully documented and monitored; these participants must be given proper notification and an opportunity to be a part of the deliberations that might affect the rights or educational program of the pupil. Whenever possible, the school should arrange meetings at the convenience of the parents, guardians, or parent surrogates.

Parents must be informed officially of the outcome of the referral conference. If it is determined that the student should receive a formal evaluation, the parents must complete a consent for evaluation and an informed consent for the release of pertinent records.

PRESCHOOL REFERRAL

PL 99-457, Part H, extends services contained within PL 94-142 to preschool children, and these remain in effect under PL 101-476. The laws require that provisions be made for preschool-age children with diabetes between the ages of 3 and 5, an extension of protections in effect for school-age children between the ages of 5 and

21. An important difference is that states were not required to report preschool children by disability category under PL 99-457.

There has been a shift in public opinion about providing services to preschool children, especially with support of conservative politicians who believe that Head Start has been successful. All states have agreed to participate in such services (Odom, Yoder, & Hill, 1988). This has significant implications for local schools, depending upon how services are constructed within individual states. The major concerns are that the state and its agents must meet the following criteria:

- Ensure public awareness, understanding, and support.
- Identify and locate eligible children and families.
- Provide a continuum of appropriate services.
- Specify agency roles, function, policies, and procedures to manage and provide support for comprehensive services.
- Evaluate and improve services provided to children and families.

Many types of services might be included, even prenatal programs to identify at-risk mothers (e.g., mothers who are poor, older, or have medical problems). Thus, attempts may be made to provide proper nutrition and health care; to alert women of the impact of drugs, medications, and inherited conditions; and so forth.

Programs for infants are conceived, generally, as of two kinds: infant and parent-infant. Although programs intend to involve parents as much as possible, most will be conceived to provide direct and indirect services to infants and to prepare parents to deal with skills development. Presently, most programs for infants and toddlers are focused on skills development, primarily psychomotor and language or cognitive development.

There are two types of infant- and toddler-focused programs: *home-based* and *center-based* (Odom, Yoder, & Hill, 1988). Home-based programs involve visitations of professionals (the law requires appropriate certification/licensure) to the home who will assess and recommend activities and services. The center-based program is similar to the home-based, but parents attend a center with a child where services are delivered.

The major problem with preschool services is the logical problem encountered in attempting to diagnose infants and young children, either with labels or generically without them. Such services are based on two assumptions: (1) that children requiring intervention can be accurately and consistently identified, and (2) that the diagnostic process will result in an intervention or a treatment program that will eliminate or reduce the effect of a disabling condition. The entire scope of services in school programs revolves around labeling, but the law and professional opinion oppose labeling of preschoolers for all the reasons that have been given for not using special education labels in the past. Even the process of identifying young children as at-risk and providing them with services actually constitutes a de facto label and might elicit certain negative reactions and erroneous expectations.

Another problem is that there is little research to support long-term treatment plans. MacMillan, Keogh, and Jones (1986) have reviewed research on early intervention programs and determined that the impetus for infant programs stems from the fact that Head Start research showed that children made gains, compared to control subjects, but the gains did not always hold up over time. There was a belief that earlier was better, and the push to intervene, even at the prenatal level, has resulted. Thus, there is no research base that proves any particular strategy or set of strategies will be effective for long-term gains.

Another issue, noted by MacMillan, Keogh, and Jones, is that the motives of interventionists were not questioned in the 1960s when such programs began. But minority-group social scientists, politicians, and community leaders are very concerned about such programs for minority children, especially insofar as these programs deal with issues such as the rights of parents, privacy, promotion of middle-class values, and the lack of verifiable evidence that programs can be effective.

Individualized Family Service Plan

The Individualized Family Service Plan (IFSP) will be required for each infant and preschool child. The plan must include a statement of the child's levels of physical development, cognitive development, language and speech development, psychosocial development, and self-help skills. This requires testing. Tests for young children are notoriously unreliable. Thus, even though a traditional label is not required, the evaluators have to base the need for services on the test scores that presume deviance from norms. This problem will be daunting as states gear up to provide services. The lack of clear and definitive standards, the negative effects of labeling, the lack of professionals, and numerous other sources of complication promise to make this area controversial.

The law stipulates the involvement of the parent in drawing up the plan and a meeting at 6-month intervals until the child no longer receives services or is placed in a school program. The IFSP is regarded by some as merely an IEP, while others consider it to be more encompassing because it involves the family in the treatment plans. Thus, some persons are concerned about family rights to privacy and imposition of middle-class values, as noted previously. And until truly effective intervention programs are developed and identification procedures clarified, significant improvement in the lives of many children may not result despite good intentions.

To illustrate the point, in one of the first statewide preschool screening programs (Thurlow, O'Sullivan, & Ysseldyke, 1986), 45,000 preschool children between the ages of 3½ and 5 were screened in 400 districts. Some districts reported no problems in any of the children, while others reported that all the children presented some disorder. The investigators concluded there was "no relationship between screening referral rates and any of the general social, economic or educational factors" (p. 95).

INDIVIDUALIZED TRANSITION PLAN

As noted previously, PL 101-476 specifically requires that transition plans be developed before students with disabilities reach the age of 16, and such plans must be updated annually until they reach the age of 21. The Individualized Transition Plan

(ITP) is an IEP, but it must include statements of the transition services needed for the students when they leave the school and become adults. As in the case of other IEPs, it must include the students' level of performance, goals, short-term instructional objectives, related services, percentage of time to be spent in regular education, initial and ending dates for services, and annual evaluation.

As White and Bond (1992) make clear, the overall effectiveness of a special education program is the effectiveness of its transition program. The ITP is required for secondary students with disabilities. The plan has all the earmarks of the familiar IEP, except that the strategy is to plan for long-term adult goals based on a transition from school to postsecondary adjustment. Postsecondary planning must be flexible enough to permit someone to change directions, yet specific enough to be meaningful. The typical college student changes his or her mind several times about declaring a major. Plans made in secondary school should permit students with disabilities the same freedom.

The primary areas of concern in transition planning are employment, postsecondary education or training, housing, finance, transportation, and related needs in medical care, therapy, interpersonal and social needs, and recreation and leisure activities. This should become an area of greater concern, especially as jobs continue to become more complex and require higher literacy skills. But, very few schools provide job-related academic skills or occupational services for the majority of special education programs (Okolo & Sitlington, 1988). Fairweather (1989) estimates that less than half of all local education agencies offer transition programs and only one third say they have any staff hired specifically for vocational placement. This creates concern at the secondary level because of the general difficulty of all young adults to get good-paying jobs and the differences in qualifications of those with disabilities who join the pool of job seekers.

Wehman (1992) has revealed numerous reasons why young people leave school, many of whom have disabilities. In the latter instance, even greater long-term problems may exist for youth who are the least prepared for successful occupational adjustment.

In places where job training and follow-up is provided, students can find jobs, but they need continued help with changes and work-related problems. Fortunately, there are some very successful models for students with disabilities that have been tested and improved for decades, primarily for people with mental retardation: work experience, work-study programs, on-the-job training, off-campus workstations, and cooperative programs. Wehman, Wood, Everson, Goodwyn, and Conley (1988) recommend that individualization of the transition process should include eight steps:

1. Identify student.
2. Identify school personnel and adult service personnel to serve as members of the ITP planning team.
3. Identify adult service agencies and organizations for provision of services.
4. Collect relevant information on student prior to ITP planning meeting.
5. Schedule meetings for student.
6. Conduct meetings.

7. Conduct a follow-up of goals and objectives at 6-month intervals.

8. Schedule an exit meeting for student and parents at school completion.

Forms are modified to be used in the transition planning sequence, similar to the process and procedures of IEP conferences. In other words, there is an announcement that a transition meeting is being planned; there are appropriate adult services referral records; and finally, there is the ITP, which has a statement of the employment or postsecondary education goal, the steps to be taken, and the persons responsible.

ADMINISTRATIVE ACTIONS IN DETERMINING LOCAL SERVICE MODELS

Administrative personnel play a central role in developing local service delivery arrangements. Their determinations must be made well in advance of the actual evaluation and placement of students. Their responsibilities include selection of the types of programs to be organized within the district and at the building level, location of the various service options, and supervision and management of the components of the special education program. The following specific administrative questions should be considered in service delivery planning:

- What is the school district philosophy of providing services to students with disabilities? A district that supports inclusion will provide a different array of options for the child and the regular teacher than a mainstreaming program.

- What are the organizational patterns specified in the state special education guidelines?

- What organizational patterns currently exist in the district?

- What placement options exist in each building?

- Does the location of the options seem consistent with the location of the largest geographical location of the population? This becomes significant as population trends change. Thus, the mobility effects on the population of each building should be monitored. This question may pinpoint instances where a special type of class is housed at a particular building simply because "it has always been there."

- What supervisory structure is currently operating to coordinate the various placement options in the district?

- Is there an efficient means of coordinating the special classes (resource or self-contained) with other forms of special services, such as speech therapy?

Examination of the following criteria might also prove helpful to administrators in developing service arrangements for their school or district:

- The state plan and state regulations.

- Demographic data on the student population.

- Data about student service needs.
- The physical characteristics of buildings.
- The locations of other types of services in and outside the district.
- Transportation patterns within the district.

Again, the placement of an individual child cannot be determined merely by the availability of services; the child's needs must dictate the appropriate placement among the available legislative options. Still, administrative leadership in a district can have a profound impact on the effectiveness and efficiency of the service options. To ensure a positive impact, administrators should devote time to plan and organize the numerous components of the placement options. The positive returns will be noticeable in terms of student growth, parent satisfaction, sound fiscal management, and staff and faculty morale.

THE EVALUATION PROCESS

The Federal Register (1977), in clarification of PL 94-142 regulations, described evaluation as the process of determining

> whether a child is handicapped and the nature and extent of the special education and related services the child needs. The term *evaluation* means procedures used selectively with an individual child and does not include basic tests administered to or procedures used with all children in school, grade, or class. (p. 42494)

The administrator must conduct such evaluation prior to any of the following dispositions: denial of special services, placement in special education, transfer, or denial of transfer (from special class to regular class).

The Evaluation Team

The composition of the committee that evaluates and places students in special education is determined by federal, state, and local policies. The members should include the principal or designate; the special education supervisor, director, or coordinator; the referring teacher; the parent(s); the psychologist, psychometrist, or educational examiner; the speech clinician and/or audiologist; the allied health personnel, as necessary; the school guidance counselor; the special education teacher; and the student, when deemed appropriate. The precise composition of the committee and the responsibilities of the various team members will, to a great extent, be determined by the specific aspects of the individual student's case. However, the following general responsibilities are associated with each position on the team:

1. Chairperson
   - Plans and chairs the meeting.
   - Provides leadership to see that all relevant data are presented.

- Coordinates team efforts to analyze and interpret data.
- Ensures that all team members have an opportunity to participate.
- Focuses attention of team members on the total child, not isolated aspects of performance.
- Aids the team in reaching consensus.
- Sees that the meeting culminates in a clearly stated outcome.

2. Special educator
   - Provides professional information concerning service alternatives.
   - Suggests instructional approaches.
   - Reports and review relevant classroom performance data.
   - Provides details about the various areas of assessment as they relate to special services.

3. Referring teacher
   - Provides pertinent achievement data and relevant information concerning classroom functioning.
   - Presents work samples reflecting the child's work in comparison to the peer group.
   - Communicates general information about the ecology of the classroom.
   - Interprets data in terms of expected future classroom performance.

4. Parents
   - Present attitudes and preferences concerning evaluation and possible placement.
   - Ask questions to ensure that they understand the proceedings.
   - Provide information when relevant.

5. Other personnel
   - Present and explain test results and interpretations.
   - Accurately report pertinent student-related nontest data.
   - Identify potential areas of concern or difficulty.

Evaluation Procedures

The administrator responsible for coordinating placement activities must see that all aspects of functioning—academic, socioemotional, sensoriphysical—are examined. The evaluation must be ethically conducted in accordance with the general assessment procedures described in chapter 4. A concerted effort by all professionals is necessary to see that the evaluation process does not become *pro forma,* that it does not deteriorate to a standard battery of tests administered to all students. All information gathered must be relevant to the particular case.

Evaluation is more than merely the administration of formal tests. It includes the presentation of information gleaned from traditional testing situations, assessment information from teachers, information provided by parents, and relevant inputs from professionals in disciplines considered pertinent to the particular case. Thus, a comprehensive evaluation process is one that:

- Reflects a broad approach to assessment in all areas (socioemotional, sensori-physical, academic).
- Includes a wide variety of evaluation strategies.
- Involves professionals with direct experience with the case, with similar cases, or with particular evaluation techniques.
- Incorporates all data into a collective determination regarding the existence of a disability.
- Logically leads to one or more assumptions relevant to planning and placement.

The evaluation process should be outlined in a written policy statement designed to increase the efficiency of the process (1) to reduce the possibility of failure to follow the procedural requirements, (2) to reduce the potential for poor communication and misunderstanding among the participants, and (3) to provide clear definitions of the responsibilities of the team members.

The Evaluation Conference

The following major activities are involved in the evaluation conference:

- Examination of all data collected prior to evaluation, including review of the school folder and referral material.
- Review of the situation that resulted in the referral, including an examination of the ecological details surrounding the referral and data about peer group norms and comparisons.
- Plan and report evaluation data, including the selection of specific evaluation instruments and procedures, the evaluation itself, an objective report of the evaluation results, and the maintenance of complete records of progress.
- Validation of the existence or absence of a disability, which requires the collective interpretation of evaluation data; the generation of hypotheses based on data concerning academic, socioemotional, and sensoriphysical functioning; and the documentation of the presence or absence of a disability.
- Certification (identification) of the primary disability, which involves the collective identification of the nature and major cause of the disability and a statement on the required form as to the primary disability.
- Selection of an appropriate placement, which requires a consideration of the primary disability in the context of other behavioral and performance variables and the identification of the least restrictive placement.

Determination of Outcomes

The major outcome of the evaluation process is the determination of whether or not further actions on behalf of the student are needed. Either special education is required because of the existence of a disability, or the problem does not require special education services. The former outcome, the targeting for special education, is sometimes considered the final outcome. This conclusion mistakenly assumes that the process is primarily administrative, is not intended to produce data relevant to daily classroom instruction, is designed solely to determine placement, or is intended merely to attach a label to the outcome.

A more productive approach is to expect additional by-products from the evaluation process, for example, increased cooperative planning for daily instruction, more productive involvement of special and regular educators, and improved instruction for the student. With this approach, even those cases that do not culminate in an identification for special education placement will benefit because of the additional resources that have been marshalled to aid the regular class instruction of the student.

Related Activities

A report of the evaluation activities and outcome is made on an evaluation conference decision form. Entries on the form should include:

- A written decision or outcome.
- A description of the placement that has been selected.
- A description of all other services needed.
- A statement identifying the primary disability.
- The basis for planning to be completed in the IEP.
- The signatures of all participants in the evaluation process.

During the evaluation process, the parents must be notified in writing prior to the evaluation conference and following the outcome of the conference. Additionally, a parental release form must be signed before special services can be initiated.

Finally, all participants involved in the process should be contacted to ensure that they understand the collective decision and outcome of the conference. The administrative officer in charge of the evaluation process must ensure that all follow-up actions—such as the IEP conference, parental reporting, and the completion of the required forms—are accomplished.

DEVELOPMENT OF THE IEP

If the evaluation process culminates in a decision that a disabling condition exists to such a degree that it interferes with the child's functioning in the regular classroom, a label is assigned and the child is placed in special education. At this point, the IEP must be prepared.

The IEP Form

IEPs were formerly elaborately written documents, revealing considerable thought and labor demonstrated by those who developed such instruments. Today, the IEP may be nothing more than a simple page with goals, objectives, and evaluation dates. The precise format of the IEP is a matter of local determination. To be adequate, the IEP need only include the format shown in Figure 3.2. However, statutory and regulatory requirements dictate certain common elements:

1. A statement of current levels of functioning.
2. The annual goals and short-term instructional objectives.
3. A specific description of the educational services required.
4. The degree of regular class participation by the student.
5. The projected beginning date and duration of services.
6. The evaluation criteria and procedures to be employed.
7. The evaluation schedule.
8. An assurance that the student with a disability is to be served in a least restrictive environment.

Although the task of completing the IEP form once seemed overwhelming, many districts now use coded formats or computerized programs to develop the finished product. However, the task is greatly facilitated by the fact that the IEP is completed only after extensive prereferral, referral, and evaluation activities have been undertaken in a collective effort by numerous professionals. Following is a brief description of the major components of the IEP and the actions associated with each part:

- *Current level of functioning.* The precise nature of the student's present performance must be specified, based on a formal assessment, informal assessment, and observational or behavioral data. Tests and other strategies should be determined by the state plan and/or guidelines as well as by the nature of the problem. The data must be in the form of scores, percentages, grade level equivalents, or levels on standard scales, thereby making possible evaluative comparisons.

- *Long-term goals.* These goals must be based upon the individual student's needs and present performance. They should reflect the priorities of the parents, child, teacher, and professionals, with the best interest of the student as reference. In effect, they provide the skeleton of the IEP and the daily programming plans. The goals may reflect career preparation and independent living skills; health, self-concept, and community adjustment might also be included. They may be based on either a textbook or content approach. A common difficulty is "knowing how much is enough for a year"; this must be addressed cooperatively by all participants. In sum, the more carefully the long-term goals are prepared, the easier it will be to complete the other parts of the planning process.

- *Short-term objectives.* These objectives dictate the steps to be accomplished to achieve daily progress in reaching the long-term goals. The focus of the objectives must be on major needs, because all needs cannot be equally addressed (Turnbull & Schulz, 1979). Teachers must assume a major leadership role in determining these objectives (Torres, 1977). Finally, the objectives must be stated in terms of the learner's behavior, not as a teaching script for the teacher.

Figure 3.2 Sample IEP

Pupil: _____ Sex: _____   *Tests Used:*
Birth Date:_____ Age: _____   Intelligence:_____
Primary Language:_____   Educational: _____
Date of IEP Meeting: _____   Behavioral/Adaptive: _____
Date of Program Entry: _____   Speech/Language: _____
Termination Date: _____   Vision: _____   Hearing: _____
                                     Other: _____

Services Required: Classroom Observation
Resource: _____   Date: _____   Observer: _____
Residential: _____
Self-Contained:_____   *Strengths* (Present level of
Regular Class: _____   functioning):
Related Services: _____   _____
Physical Education: _____   _____
Other: _____   _____
                                     _____
Team Members:
LEA   _____   *Limitations* (Present level of
Parent   _____   functioning):
Teacher   _____   _____
Counselor   _____   _____
Speech Path.   _____   _____
Student   _____   _____
Other   _____   _____

Justification for Placement: *Annual Review:*   Date:_____
_____   (Remarks) _____
_____   _____
_____   _____
_____   _____
_____   _____

- *Educational services.* These services include speech therapy, counseling, transportation, physical therapy, and other types of services. The extent to which the child will participate in these services as well as in the regular class must be specified. The amount of participation must be determined on an individual basis, considering the child's unique needs and situations.

- *Projected duration of services.* The initiation date as well as the date for completion are included on the form.

- *Evaluation.* The IEP must be reviewed at least annually. However, continuous, daily evaluation is not obviated by the annual evaluation requirement. The purpose of the evaluation is to determine whether the child's progress is adequate in terms of the stated goals of the IEP.

The IEP Conference

The IEP conference translates the hypotheses and data collected in the evaluation process into a written program that is used to guide daily instruction for the student for approximately one year. The following describes the tasks for those participants who may comprise the IEP team:

- *School representative(s)* (director of special education, principal, or designate). The school representative arranges conferences, presides at conferences, and can provide leadership.
- *Teacher(s).* Teachers can provide input in the selection of goals and objectives and assist with the placement decision. They also can recommend materials and methodologies, help to identify potential areas of concern, and suggest strategies for avoiding difficulties.
- *Parents.* The parents' support for the student's goals is most important. Parents are able to demonstrate understanding of the plan and its purpose. They can identify potential areas of concern and suggest strategies for avoiding difficulties.
- *Others* (e.g., psychologist, medical personnel, social worker, physical therapist). Other support personnel report suggestions from various other disciplines that might assist those directly responsible for instruction. They also describe related services that might be incorporated.
- *Child* (when appropriate). The child, if possible, should provide input about his or her circumstances and also react to the suggestions of the team.

Specifically, the IEP conference must produce (1) a completed IEP form signed by all team members, (2) guidelines for implementation of the IEP, (3) identification of the responsibilities of those involved in implementation, and (4) review and evaluation plans. All of these components must be in compliance with state and federal regulations.

Parental Involvement

Parental involvement is a procedural safeguard that protects the rights of children with disabilities and their parents or guardians as part of due process. Due process has two primary components: the right to advance notice and the opportunity to be heard. The notice requirements of PL 94–142 and its accompanying regulations apply both to children who have not yet been in special education programs but are being considered by the schools for initial identification and to children in special education programs who are being considered for reevaluation or a change of program.

Parental involvement involves prior written notice to the parents before any change of status, written parental consent prior to placement and beginning of services, and the opportunity to review the child's records. If the school refuses a parental request, such refusal must be in writing. However, refusal of parents' requests to review their child's records can result in the initiation of due process proceedings.

Preventive Administrative Actions

Administrative leadership can also prevent many of the problems that may impair the school system's ability to comply with the requirements of the IEP process. For example, administrators should:

- Beware of the tendency to make long-term goals reflect only academic goals; this would be particularly inappropriate in cases of students labeled emotionally disturbed.

- Help anxious teachers understand that the instructional progress of a student is not their sole responsibility. Such teachers' fears about measuring student progress can lead to an oversimplification of goals and objectives.

- Remind teachers that the daily lesson plan should be directly related to written IEP goals and objectives. Help the teachers to examine their own plans, using the written IEP as a reference.

- Reduce unnecessary concerns and facilitate the monitoring process by accurately presenting the role of monitors of the state department of education.

- Clarify the relationship between student growth and teacher effectiveness evaluations; point out that the purpose of the IEP is to structure student learning, not to provide a method of teacher evaluation.

The evaluation team (similar in composition to the placement/IEP team) must collectively review the IEP at least once a year. The review should be more frequent if changes are warranted by student behavior or parental request. These reviews can produce changes in the objectives used to guide the student's educational program, in the type of service model used, in instructional approaches and materials, or in the kind of special education services employed.

During the evaluation of the written IEP, decisions are made as to whether or not to continue special services. If student performance dictates that services should be continued, the decisions must address the types of services to be provided. Specifically, the evaluation should answer the following questions:

1. Is the child progressing?
2. Is the child progressing at an adequate rate? If not, why not?
3. Are the specifications in the IEP being implemented?
4. Are the services being provided consistent with the type of services identified in the IEP?
5. Have professionals associated with the case performed in accordance with their responsibilities as identified in the IEP?

THE ADMINISTRATOR'S ROLE: MAKING THE PROCESS WORK

Administrators must understand that the entire referral–placement–service delivery process should be conceived as a comprehensive and integrated whole, not as discrete and unrelated functions. To do so requires that the school have both a broad range of placement options that can be tailored to individual student needs and cooperation among all student personnel. By now it should be obvious that there is a need to abandon traditional dichotomous notions of regular and special education in favor of a more enlightened view of a wide spectrum of services for students with disabilities, beginning with the regular class. Implementing such a view requires leadership from the principal and support from the special education administrator. Further, it requires involvement and cooperation among a wide spectrum of professionals, including the classroom teachers and specialists, who can function smoothly as a decision-making team and can cooperate to provide appropriate services for children with disabilities.

Several factors will determine the success of the placement process. The key will be administrative leadership, but also important will be the skill, attitudes, and willingness of the regular and special education personnel to alter traditional instructional arrangements to better address student needs. The administrator helps set instructional goals for the building and facilitates organizational and instructional arrangements, and as such helps the faculty implement the district's philosophy of special education. Within an inclusion model, for example, the administrator may need to assure that class size and the distribution of children with disabilities in any one class facilitate instructional goals for the class and that the regular teacher receives needed assistance from special education or other personnel. Nonetheless, all personnel may need in-service training in emerging instructional models for children with disabilities, team-based instructional planning and service delivery, group decision making and planning, and alternative student assessment and evaluation processes.

Further, emerging service delivery models potentially will require new relationships between the building principal and the special education administrator. These relationships should model the district's philosophy of providing services for children with disabilities and should center around the primary role of the regular class placement within the regular school. Ultimately, the success of the district in providing appropriate services for students with disabilities will be related to administrative leadership.

TESTS AND
ASSESSMENT

The gateway to special education programming is through testing. Testing in American education is a multimillion-dollar industry and millions of standardized tests are administered to children each year (Neill & Medina, 1989). As the school reform movement has concentrated more on student achievement scores, testing in American education promises to increase. However, testing is rarely used for daily instruction but rather for placement or summative assessment. Students who receive the most testing are, undoubtedly, those admitted to special education programs. In addition to the ordinary tests that a district may require of all students, there are those deemed necessary to make judgments about eligibility and retention in special education programs. It is likely that much of the testing in public schools is unnecessary and useless and may often be harmful to students and to education in general. From the administrator's perspective, testing is an area of vulnerability for litigation, a great expense, and a time-consuming activity.

A basic issue in special education has been the need to provide children, especially minority children, with nondiscriminatory testing and assessment procedures. These are explicit in federal law. In an effort to protect children from discriminatory testing, many more tests are often given. However, the chances that a student will deviate in some way on some measure increase with the number of tests administered, especially if unreliable tests are used, which also increases the probability that a problem will be identified. This is a dilemma for the school administrator.

Nondiscriminatory testing procedures date back to litigation in the field of special education. Most notable was the case of *Diana* v. *State Board of Education of California* (1972). This lawsuit was originally filed on behalf of a child in a school district where intelligence tests in the English language were administered to children who lacked facility with the language and appropriate cultural experiences. The school district was ordered by the court to reevaluate all Mexican-American children who had been placed in special education.

Another notable case was *Larry P.* v. *Riles* (1979), in which plaintiffs made an effort to prevent the California public schools from evaluating minority students with intelligence tests. In this case, approximately 30% of the students enrolled were African-American, but nearly two thirds of the students in classes for students with mental retardation were African-American. If for no other reason, the plaintiffs viewed the practice as discriminatory because of the disproportionate number of African-American children represented in special education, and the court concurred.

There have been many other cases involving the assessment of minority children for special education. It all points to the need to provide administrators with the fundamental rationale behind the regulations governing assessment and the need to exercise adequate practices to protect the interests of the pupils and the school. Ultimately, accountability for the school assessment program belongs to administrators, even though they may have had little prior training in this highly technical and complex area.

There are at least two concerns regarding testing programs: the validity and reliability of particular instruments used and the judgments made by personnel about test scores (which reflects the training and attitudes of the evaluators). Administrators must have an adequate level of knowledge about assessment procedures because of the potential for problems in this area of special education and also because so many of the current criticisms in education concern standardized achievement tests, competency examinations, and the evaluation of student progress. Further, administrators must provide leadership to other members of the assessment and placement team. These members look to the administrator for guidance and suggestions about the appropriateness of tests and testing procedures. Moreover, because testing programs are quite expensive, consuming large parts of dwindling school budgets, the well-informed administrator is in a better position to make cost-effective decisions.

THE PURPOSES OF ASSESSMENT

Assessment in special education is undertaken for the purposes of screening, placement, program evaluation, and evaluation of pupil progress. Typically, assessment is regarded as a comprehensive process, of which testing is but one component. For most school personnel, special education testing is the process by which children are "diagnosed" or labeled to determine eligibility for special education placement. In its most optimistic description, assessment in special education might be said to be a process by which the needs of the school, the pupil, and the parents are satisfied, thereby enabling the teachers to embark upon the most desirable approach to instruction and treatment of problems. In its most pragmatic description, it is the process by which a student is legally labeled for special education placement. The extent to which both of these descriptions may converge depends upon the skill of examiners and the validity of the assessment instruments.

Generally, public education has not conducted itself well in the area of standardized testing. The record is replete with abuses of instruments, the misdiagnoses of students, wholesale labeling of minority children, and stigmas attached to children who perform poorly on tests. Testing and its consequences can be harmful.

Screening

In general, screening is a process used to identify a wide range of problems among children of school age; specifically, in the present context, it is a step in the process of determining the eligibility of students for special education. Many schools actively attempt to identify children with hearing, vision, and speech problems, especially in the early elementary school years. Specific instruments and devices may be used routinely in order to detect children who need specialized attention. In such screenings, the students' health, vision, hearing, behavior, speech and language development, motor development, and academic performance are scrutinized. Some of these screenings can be integrated in child-find activities.

A strong reliance on teachers' referrals and inexpensive screening instruments can be justified on the grounds of economy. Unless otherwise required by the state to use specific kinds of commercial screening tests, the school may develop its own inexpensive screening program, using teachers' evaluations and locally developed screening devices and procedures. In addition to measures of classroom performance, schools may use teacher-made tests, checklists, rating devices, interviews, inventories, record review, sociometric ratings, and observations.

In screening, the administrator should be concerned with the following:

- Is the screening program consistent with federal and state requirements in terms of scope, frequency, and appropriateness?
- Are all sources of information (teacher observations, classroom performance, and information from parents) fully used?
- If the procedures comply with regulations, are appropriate referrals and dissemination of findings being made, such as those to medical personnel and parents?
- Are there appropriate follow-up activities to determine the actions to be taken by school personnel and external professionals as a result of the screening? For example, should parents or others follow up on the suspicion that a hearing problem might exist?
- How expensive is the screening process? Can steps be taken to get the same information without costly instruments and personnel or time-consuming activities?
- Can fewer personnel be used more efficiently to gather screening information within a shorter time?

Screening should not be viewed as a process of labeling. A child who is identified by screening may or may not have a problem. The purpose of screening is to economically "sift" the population to find students who may have problems. If screening and assessment practices are sound, the number of pupils identified by screening should be relatively small, and a majority of students identified through screening will probably not have problems sufficient for special education placement. If most students who are screened also end up with a label, either the screening process is very good (in which case assessment seems to be redundant) or, more likely, something is wrong with the screening process.

Placement

The flow of activities in the special education assessment process leads from referral to assessment in specifically defined steps. The relevant activities are, by now, clearly described in federal, state, and district regulations, for example, the referral conference and the evaluation conference as parts of due process procedures. However, the specific timing and nature of the process will vary across states and districts, depending upon a number of variables.

A great variety of formal and informal tests are used to determine the eligibility of children for special education, in accordance with state and federal regulations and definitions of disabling conditions. Some states have adopted specific definitions and criteria in making determinations of disabilities, and others use vague terminology and provide little guidance for the school.

In this context, placement deserves particular attention. It is at this point that a decision may be made to label a student, change the student's educational status, and begin the process of special education. It is also here that the needs of the child are supposed to be determined. The initial structure of the Individualized Education Program (IEP), the nature of the needed special education services, the extent to which the student may be integrated into a regular class, and the nature of the related services are all determined on the basis of decisions of the placement committee. If parents resist the decision of assessment personnel in the placement conference, a variety of actions, such as due process hearings and litigation, may ensue. If the assumptions of the assessment personnel are faulty or the tests that have been used are inappropriate, the assessment decision may unfairly characterize the student. Particularly in the event of a due process hearing or litigation, the school administrator must have confidence that the assessment procedures were conducted efficiently and effectively.

Program Evaluation and Pupil Progress

Test data are used to chart the effectiveness of programs by examining the gain scores of children on various measures over the course of an academic year. The special education teacher may use such data in an attempt to evaluate the IEP. The administrator and others may examine such scores to make judgments about the overall effectiveness of the program, based on the collective average gains of the special education students in the program. With these procedures, caution should be taken to avoid errors in determining the types and numbers of children involved and the specific activities of the special education teacher (which may or may not correlate with the assessed factors). The statistical results of tests may, at face value, indicate great gains or losses, but they may not be accurate because of error in the use of the test instrument.

PROCEDURAL SAFEGUARDS

In assessment, specific due process safeguards must be considered by the school. These safeguards stem from the litigation and professional standards concerning the assessment of minority children and the labeling of a child as disabled. For example, to deny a child with a disability access to public education has been held by the courts to be unreasonable. It has also been determined that it is unreasonable to label a child as disabled without justification.

In the American culture, the labels of "emotionally disturbed" or "mentally retarded" are not socially desirable. However, there is much less cultural resistance to the label of "learning disabled." Similarly, conditions of blindness, deafness, or muscular dystrophy are not necessarily socially stigmatizing; indeed, there is a certain empathy or sympathy expressed by most people with regard to such disorders. In sharp contrast, schools can expect to encounter resistance and conflict in attempts to label children as mentally retarded, emotionally disturbed, or behaviorally disordered. Thus, special procedural safeguards are afforded to students who are assessed to determine if they need special education. These safeguards stemmed from cases in which minority children were classified as mentally retarded and involved the constitutional guarantees of the Fourteenth Amendment.

Procedural due process in assessment concerns the notification and consent of parents and/or the student with regard to special education and the selection of appropriate and valid tests. Decisions made on the basis of this process are to be interpreted legally as a change of status in the student's school program. PL 94-142 and PL 101-476 stipulate the following procedural safeguards in assessment:

- Tests and other evaluation materials are to be provided and administered in the child's native language or other mode of communication unless it is clearly not feasible to do so.

- Tests are to be validated for the specific purpose for which they are used.

- Tests are to be administered by trained personnel according to the instructions contained in the manual.

- Evaluation material must include tests that examine specific areas of educational need, not just a single intelligence quotient.

- Tests are to be selected and administered in order to reflect the child's aptitude or achievement level (or whatever the test purports to measure) without reflecting impaired sensory, manual, or speaking skills, except in cases where the purpose of the test is to measure sensory, manual, or speaking skills.

- The evaluation is to be made by a committee (a multidisciplinary team or group of individuals) including at least one individual (a teacher or specialist) who has knowledge in the area of the suspected disability.

- No single procedure is to be used as the sole criterion for placement (i.e., in determining the child's label and educational program).

- The child is to be assessed in all areas of the suspected disability, including, where appropriate, health, vision, hearing, social and emotional status, general intelligence, academic performance, communicative status, and motor abilities.

In addition, PL 101-476 provides for (1) nondiscriminatory and multidisciplinary assessment of educational needs, (2) parental involvement in developing the educational program, (3) placement in the least restrictive environment (LRE), and (4) the IEP. PL 101-476 incorporated the following provisions related to nondiscriminatory assessment in the processes of labeling and placing students in special education: (1) testing in the native or primary language of the child; (2) the use of evaluation procedures to prevent cultural or racial discrimination; (3) the use of valid assessment tools; and (4) the use of a multidisciplinary team to develop placement decisions.

These regulations are difficult to interpret without some understanding of the definitions of disabilities and some guidance in interpreting the adequacy of test instruments and test data. Hence, administrators, relying on consultant personnel, must collect sufficient information on these subjects in order to make their own judgments.

SPECIFIC ASSESSMENT PROCEDURES

Since its inception the prevailing assessment model in special education assessment has been the clinical method. Loosely interpreted, this model requires that one or more qualified examiners attempt to discover a child's problems, but they use a variety of tests and interpretations of test behavior that are not strictly objective in interpretation. Thus, much of the assessment process is based on statistical regression analysis, which has two distinct problems: (1) students are not likely to have even performance in all traits measured (this does not mean that low trait scores are necessarily deficient though they may be interpreted as such), and (2) regression analysis tends to underestimate at the low end and overestimate at the high end. For example, Evans (1992) argued that the regression model does not accurately assess a severe discrepancy between IQ and achievement scores because there is a bias in the detection of severe discrepancy at lower IQ levels, an artifact of the statistical method employed. Similarly, comparisons of IQ and reading scores for gifted children invariably classify such children as deficient in reading although they may be reading 3 or 4 years above their age mates or grade equivalents.

The clinical method (including the use of tests) is an unscientific approach for two reasons: (1) except in more clear-cut medically related conditions, it is not systematically applied because the conditions that examiners attempt to assess do not have clear-cut, objectively determined symptoms; and (2) valid tests for clusters of symptoms that may be identified as syndromes are, as in the case of most medical conditions, not available. Mental retardation, specific learning disabilities, and emotional disturbance are convenient descriptions of behavior developed for communication among professionals. These descriptions have, through constant use, assumed an esoteric status because they appear in professional literature and legal documents. However, they are not true conditions in the same sense as, for example, diabetes. Diabetes is a condition with known symptoms, disease processes, and parameters that may be reliably identified with valid tests. The condition really exists, rather than as a contrivance or an intellectual abstraction.

There is, as yet, no true condition of learning disability in the same sense that there are conditions in medicine, although research may lead to characteristics inherent in pupils that clearly distinguish learning disabilities from poor achievers. Yet many teachers, parents, and administrators seem to believe that an assessment that results in the label "learning disabled" confirms that the child has a real disorder, as indicated in such remarks as, "He has learning disabilities." In fact, the pupil is characterized this way according to professional criteria of educators and psychologists merely for the purposes of planning and programming, although many professionals sincerely believe in the existence of some underlying neurological problem responsible for school failure. As yet "learning disabilities" is not a condition that may be clearly discerned using medical, physiological, or biological criteria. Recently the criteria used by professionals have come under intense scrutiny and criticism, especially because the number of children served in this category has increased by 100% in only a decade.

There are, of course, certain medical conditions served in special education, and this may suggest that all disabilities or disabling conditions have the same scientific status. For example, by using precise measures, medical tests, and accepted criteria, it is possible to determine fairly accurately the extent to which children cannot hear or see. Whenever nonmedical conditions are grouped in the same category as actual medical diagnoses, there is a tendency to regard them all collectively as the same type of discrete condition. This is a mistake in learning disabilities, emotional disturbance, and mental retardation.

Emotional disturbance and mental retardation are especially confusing because children who are placed in either category at the low or severe end of functioning may have a complex of medical problems. The typical child with mental retardation in special education is one who performs poorly in school but who will be able to attain vocational success in the community. At the low end of the continuum are children with severe and profound retardation with a variety of medical problems in addition to extremely low IQ scores. Many such students have congenital or genetic disorders that cause damage to many processes of the body, including the central nervous system. In the emotionally disturbed category are children who have learned to be disruptive but who may, through effective treatment, learn to be sufficiently well behaved to function within the bounds of accepted behavioral standards. In the same category are those with genetic conditions, such as schizophrenia, that may be susceptible to appropriate medical treatment.

When considering specific assessment procedures, administrators should remember that state guidelines pertain to each assessed condition. These guidelines may vary considerably across states, as in the case of descriptive terminology. In any event, at the local level, it is customary for examiners to proceed with conventional approaches for each condition; each disability has its own general procedures.

Learning Disabilities

A student with a specific learning disability is one who has a significant discrepancy between achievement (usually in reading) and ability, compared with a student of the same age, intelligence, and experience. The discrepancy, found to exist on the basis of test scores, may be said to be caused either by a subtle cerebral deficit or by impaired psychological processes, such as impaired visual perception or perceptual-motor abilities or other disorders that apparently interfere with learning to read or to perform other school tasks. Additionally, such students are sometimes said to be hyperactive, have poor attention spans, or have short-term memory disorders.

These disorders may be considered as causative or incidental, depending upon the circumstances and the theories of the examiners. In any case, there is very little scientific foundation for such processes as visual-perceptual or perceptual-motor disabilities. In fact, if they exist, the extent to which they cause conditions of underachievement is not known. The evidence to date indicates that treatment of such "process or modality disorders" by means of therapy does not result in either improved academic performance or in improved functioning of the modality.

Recently, new terminology (new conditions) have been employed to describe students with learning disabilities, added to the hundreds of terms that have existed in the past. One is Attention Deficit Disorder (ADD), and people with this disorder are said to be a subgroup of the population. ADD supposedly describes pupils with an inability to attend normally to incoming stimuli. Perhaps recognizing its complications for federal legislation and the economic burden it may entail, IDEA included it as a category to study, with recommendations to be made to Congress about the possibility of including it as a specific category. One recent article (Goodman & Poillion, 1992) referred to ADD as an acronym for "Any Dysfunction or Difficulty." Although "attention" has always been used to describe pupils in the LD category, it has become a specialized area of study.

Also, certain clinics claim to diagnose and remediate a condition called scotopic sensitivity, a complex disorder based on several descriptions of visual disorders that do not otherwise interfere with apparently normal vision. Treatment is accomplished with specifically prescribed colored lenses, the tints and hues of which are unique to each individual and can only be determined by the expert who is knowledgeable in this procedure.

Another visual condition, which as yet has no name, was reported in the *New England Journal of Medicine* (Geiger & Lettvin, 1987), which immediately gave it professional credence in the minds of many. In essence, this study examined persons with dyslexia (learning disabilities) who were compared to nondisabled readers. It was not clear how many subjects were in the study, nor was it clear how the subjects with learning disabilities were defined, except that neurologists said they were dyslexic. The study concluded that persons with dyslexia tended to learn to read outside the foveal field, and nondisabled readers do not. From this article may come new methods of diagnosis, new treatment regimens, and an attempt to treat students with learning disabilities by having them read through a "peep hole" in a piece of paper to suppress interference from the peripheral field of vision. The scientific bases for these claims, like many others in this area, remain in doubt.

The definition of learning disabilities has changed over the years. Early professional opinion described it as a form of mild brain damage that interfered with reading (owing to its historical connection with the notion of aphasia or dyslexia in adults). Today it is described as a complex of conditions with treatments spanning many activities that have included such therapies as creeping and crawling on the floor, walking on a balance beam, drawing geometric shapes, visual training exercises, taking Ritalin, drinking coffee, diet changes, allergy medication, biofeedback, yoga, spinning in chairs, and wearing colored glasses. Until there is an authoritative definition, there will be many points of view about what constitutes learning disabilities.

With so many opportunities to find problems in a child because of a lack of clear-cut criteria, the opportunities for diagnoses of learning disabilities increase geometrically. Presently, many schools have extremely high numbers of students with learning disabilities and as much as half of the population with disabilities so categorized.

Mental Retardation

The diagnosis of mental retardation requires a determination that a child have significantly subaverage intelligence. This is usually an IQ score that is more than two standard deviations below the mean. Thus, depending upon the test, an IQ score below

70 or 69 is considered to be significant. Performance in all areas of functioning is also expected to be low, and achievement and general development should coincide with the low functioning. A measure of adaptive behavior is also required in order to protect culturally "different" children from misdiagnosis (although tests of adaptive behavior have correlated highly with IQ tests, meaning they measure the same traits and are probably interchangeable). In reporting an IQ, examiners should not disregard the standard error of measurement. A pupil with a score of 70 could very well have a "true score" above or below 70. If a mistake is made, the pupil must suffer the consequences by having an inappropriate label attached and opportunities diminished because of lower expectations.

Behavior Disorders/Emotional Disturbance

Behavior disorders are suspected when a child pathologically deviates from age or social peers in areas of conduct or displays withdrawal, inadequacy, or immaturity to a significant degree. Although tests of intelligence and achievement may be used here, the clear intention is to assess social functioning and interpersonal relationships. Due to psychiatric connotations, the condition is often labeled as a behavior disorder rather than as an emotional disturbance. Placement and programming are predicated on the behavioral adjustment of the pupil, with less attention to academic training. It is common to find programming for students with behavior disorders to be similar to that for students with learning disabilities, or even to that for students in the regular school curriculum; the distinction is in the label, not necessarily in the treatment.

The most important consideration from the school's point of view is that students with mental retardation, learning disabilities, behavior disorders, and emotional disturbances have more similarities than differences (Smith, Price, & Marsh, 1986). They are essentially tested with the same instruments, placed in programs that differ only marginally, and receive nearly identical instruction and treatment. Thus, in recent years these youngsters have been grouped together under the label of "mildly disabled" for educational programming. Some 21 states now have such programming.

Medical, Health, Sensory, and Speech Disorders

Diagnoses of medical, health, and sensory disorders involve a determination that a child has a particular medical condition to which the school must respond so that the child can profit from instruction. In contrast, speech problems of children are relatively easy to discern by specialists employed in most schools. Most medical, health, and sensory disorders (such as blindness or hearing impairments) will ordinarily have been examined by specialists prior to the age of school entry; those arising after school entry are treated by medical specialists and others in allied health fields. Thus, the criteria for placement are usually rather explicit, based on accepted medical criteria. In these cases, there is much less chance of a dispute arising over labeling; however, the extent to which the student will be integrated in regular classes and will receive other services may still be problematic, depending upon the school, the nature of the child's needs, and the disparity between parents' and educators' perceptions of service. In general, although the school must make determinations and adhere to procedural due process, the assessment burden for most conditions in these categories falls on the shoulders of external personnel (though the school may pay for some of the assessments).

Autism and Traumatic Brain Injury

Autism and traumatic brain injury are included as specific categories in PL 101-476. Both categories have adequate medical criteria, in most cases, to make a diagnosis without much guess work.

TYPES OF ASSESSMENTS

The use of specific assessment procedures will depend upon the nature of the pupil's suspected condition, certain professional conventions, and a variety of state regulations. In general, assessment tests may be categorized as ecological, perceptual, spoken-language, written-language, and mathematical.

Ecological Assessment

Due to special requirements or federal legislation, children with behavior disorders or learning disabilities are ordinarily observed in their natural environments. This may or may not be the case with other disabling conditions, depending upon state requirements and the personal preferences of the examiners. Regardless of the suspected condition, observations of all students in their classroom are extremely useful, for a variety of reasons. Through such observations, valuable information can be obtained—information that cannot be elicited by paper and pencil tests or obfuscated by a teacher. There are now techniques available to make the observation process both efficient and inexpensive. Approaches include (1) simple observations without any guidelines, (2) observations in which behaviors are counted, (3) checklists and rating forms completed by teachers, (4) sociometric techniques, and (5) valid and reliable observational approaches (in which observers are trained to be in agreement about what they are observing and recording).

Perceptual Assessment

Primarily in the area of learning disabilities (although other areas may be involved), examiners employ tests of visual perception, perceptual-motor functioning, auditory perception, memory for aurally or visually presented information, and motor functioning. Although priorities may be allotted to one or more of these areas of assessment (some instructional programs base training on one specific area), the basic claim is that poor functioning in any of these areas may explain why children fail in school. Thus, it is argued, training may not only improve functioning in each area but may also improve a student's overall ability for academic achievement. To date, there is no impressive evidence to substantiate these assumptions (Kavale & Forness, 1987; Larsen & Hammill, 1975), to confirm that the constructs being measured are real, or that the tests used to measure the relevant abilities are valid or reliable (Salvia & Ysseldyke, 1978).

Spoken-Language Assessment

Testing in the area of spoken language might be directed at pupils suspected of having learning disabilities, mental retardation, speech disorders, and hearing disorders. Tests of overall language development might be given; there are few high-quality tests that require a child to offer more than just descriptions of vocabulary words. More frequently, there is the tendency, especially with learning disabilities, to look in the area of language for presumed correlates of learning failure. Thus, tests of syntax, morphology, and semantics are used, as well as specialized assessments of other correlates of language, such as linguistic functioning. Many of these terms may sound highly technical. However, such tests involve only simple activities, such as demonstrating an ability to use grammatical structures, to understand spoken language, to use verbs properly, to use tenses, and to be expressive.

Written-Language Assessment

Written-language assessments are used mainly with students with learning disabilities. In other areas, written-language tests are applied only after placement has been made. Unfortunately, there are few good standardized tests to examine the written work of pupils for diagnostic purposes or tests that will provide information more significant than that provided by actually examining the written work of students. Some existing tests in this area are concerned with spelling and formation of letters.

Mathematics Assessment

In the area of mathematics assessment, diagnostic and achievement tests are used routinely for students with learning disabilities and mental retardation. However, because reading is considered to be much more significant in our society, few children suspected of having learning disabilities are placed on the basis of assessed disorders of mathematics.

COMPONENTS OF ASSESSMENT

After referral activities are completed and the decision is made to conduct an evaluation, examiners must turn to the following components of the assessment process:

- *Educational functioning.* The examiners attempt to determine educational functioning by assessing achievement in subject and skill areas and also, perhaps, by examining so-called learning styles, preferences, strengths, and weaknesses of the student.

- *Social/emotional functioning.* A determination is made as to the referred pupil's emotional status, social skills, relationships with others, and general ability to function independently.

- *Physical sensory.* Vision, hearing, speech, motor, and medical examinations may or may not be given, depending upon the circumstances. If the referred pupil has no apparent need for a medical examination and has passed all screening tests for visual impairment, hearing impairment, and speech disorders, assessment in these areas need not be conducted.

- *Cognitive functioning.* An intelligence test and a test of adaptive behavior are administered.

- *Language functioning.* The language and speech abilities of the child may be examined. If the child has passed all screening tests, however, this may not be required.

- *Ecological assessment.* The child's functioning in the classroom, home, and neighborhood may be examined by a variety of means. Included here would be social work or case study reports.

PERSONNEL INVOLVED IN ASSESSMENT

Depending upon its size and resources, the school may have full-time examiners, may assign part-time assessment duties to personnel with other major duties, may contract with personnel from outside the district, and/or may use reports and evaluations of professionals in the community who are incidentally involved with the assessment process. The following personnel might be involved:

- *Psychologist, school psychologist, psychometrist, or psychological examiner.* Certification or licensure of these individuals is governed by state regulations. Also, certain national professional organizations may have standards that influence the practice of these professionals. In general, persons who conduct assessments using intelligence tests and personality instruments fall into this general category because the administration of individual intelligence tests typically requires someone with credentials and training.

- *Speech pathologist or audiologist.* Most districts employ a speech therapist or pathologist who works with children with speech and language disorders. Some districts also employ audiologists to deal with hearing assessments. These personnel will participate in evaluations by conducting hearing and speech screening, by administering in-depth hearing, speech, and language evaluations, and by playing a role in the evaluation committee's deliberations.

- *Allied health personnel.* Districts may employ school nurses and occupational, recreational, or physical therapists or may contract with physicians for specific types of assessment. It is not uncommon for children to be evaluated by an optometrist, ophthalmologist, neurologist, and pediatrician, as well as by the family/general practitioner.

- *Guidance personnel.* In some schools, the school counselor may play an important role in assessment; some counselors may conduct the psychological examinations, rather than the school psychologist.

- *Social worker.* Larger districts may employ a social worker to collect information from the family, to provide social and educational histories, and to do case studies.

- *Teaching personnel.* Regular classroom teachers and special educators should be involved in all assessment activities; they are best equipped to provide information about the students. Compared with other personnel, they are likely to have more frequent contact with students, to see them in instructional environments, to provide information about school performances, and to assist in making short-term and long-term educational plans.

- *Rehabilitation counselor.* In transition planning and evaluation of older students, specialists in the assessment of work potential and training needs of students may be used for making assessments. In most states, rehabilitation counseling is provided under state and federal statutes.

TYPES OF TESTS

Many types of educational tests exist that can be classified into one or more of several categories. These categories of tests include individual, group, objective, subjective, power (no time limit), speed, verbal, nonverbal, nonlanguage, criterion referenced, and norm-referenced.

Depending on the size and wealth of the district, tests may be administered by school personnel or professionals outside the school. Small, rural districts may contract for services for most types of testing; in such districts, very few tests will be administered by school personnel. Large, wealthy districts may find it more economical to use not only psychologists and other specialists but also persons in allied health professions and disciplines. In such districts, only medical examinations and highly specialized evaluations may be conducted outside the district's purview. In any event, except in instances where parents assume responsibility for the examination, the district's administrators will have responsibility for the testing program.

The most logical way to classify assessment tests is by the domain or area in which the assessment is made. The following are domains of interest in special education (Salvia & Ysseldyke, 1978):

- Intelligence
- General achievement
- Reading
- Arithmetic/mathematics
- Spelling

- Written expression
- Language
- Perceptual ability
- Sensory ability
- Behavior/personality

Except for medical and other highly specialized tests (such as the electroencephalograph, which would not be administered by the school), most tests can be classified under 1 of these 10 headings. Another way of classifying tests is by the way in which they are constructed and the purposes they serve.

Norm-Referenced Tests

Traditionally, the most common type of test, regardless of the domain, has been norm-referenced. Norm-referenced tests have an objective scoring format, standardized procedures for presentation, and norms for comparison of a person's score with others representing the same age and other characteristics. The test is designed so that a representative sample of subjects across certain ages and grades will be included. Performance on the test is determined by how the subject compares with the normative sample of those who took the original test. Performance on such tests (depending upon the content) may be expressed in terms of IQ, reading level, grade level, percentile, or some other score that reflects relative standing on the norms. Although such scoring permits global interpretation of performance, it provides little other useful information.

A norm-referenced test will not tell what a student can or cannot do or what a student has or has not learned; rather it tells the relative standing of the student compared with those who established the norms. The student's relative standing on the test can be influenced by others who took the test and by the nature of the test items. If the norms are scores of subjects who are greatly different from the person who takes the test or if the items on the test reflect knowledge or skills the student has not been exposed to, it is unfair to characterize the performance of the student in terms of the test scores. Even if the student is similar to the normative population and had comparable experiences and instruction, the norm-referenced test only provides a global picture of performance. These are troublesome aspects of the assessment process when using norm-referenced tests.

Criterion-Referenced Tests

A criterion-referenced test is based on the sequence of skills in a particular area of the curriculum. It is commonly used to determine performance of a subject without regard to who else took the test, as is the case in norm-referenced testing. However, criterion-referenced tests are useful only to the extent they accurately reflect skills in a sequence. Still, for purposes of planning and assessment of progress, criterion-referenced tests are useful; from them it is possible to determine what a student actually knows or what a student can do (in contrast with a norm-referenced test, in which one can only compare relationships of performance).

Unfortunately, by regulation and tradition, the placement process in special education relies heavily on norm-referenced tests. Thus, little useful information is made available to parents and teachers, except that a student is characterized in terms of numerical points on a scale. Criterion-referenced tests would add significantly to the assessment process, particularly in marking progress and determining instructional plans.

Curriculum-Based Assessment

A trend in education, generally, is outcomes-based education. In outcomes education, progress toward standards and goals is measured. These standards and goals may be mandated, as in the National Educational Goals, or recommended, as in the National Council of Teachers of Mathematics recommendations; and they may be adopted at state levels, as in Utah and Maine. Outcomes are interactions between individuals and educational activities that include skills, knowledge, and attitudes and are affected by the processes used (Ysseldyke, Thurlow, & Shriner, 1992). As outcomes-oriented models become more widespread or mandated, criterion-referenced assessments may increase in popularity.

Related to criterion-referenced tests are those designed for curriculum-based assessment. Items are usually much more numerous, reflecting content of the local curriculum; they are usually related to specific targets of educational intervention. The use of independent, objective scoring procedures permits information about how the student performs in the curriculum at important junctures, rather than how the student stacks up against others.

The approach can be used as a method of making eligibility decisions about students being referred for special educational evaluation (Shinn & Habedank, 1992). Specific curriculum steps can be identified for the student, instructional approaches can be tailored, and extraordinary progress is possible because teacher and student are constantly on task. It seems reasonable to expect that this type of instruction will spread to regular classrooms and nondisabled students.

As computers become more prominent and powerful in education, it is theoretically possible to measure a student's learning curve within curriculum domains, permitting instruction, remediation, and assessment as a by-product of daily instruction. The computer will do the work. Fuchs (1992) reported on a computerized use of curriculum-based measurement to examine the performance of students in math in 10 sixth-grade classrooms; he found that teachers were able to incorporate students with disabilities into class instruction by knowing how to plan large group instructional interactions.

Another form of assessment that is related to the concept of the curriculum (but radically different) is the alternative assessment known as portfolio assessment. Portfolio assessment is a form of educational measurement that requires teachers to collect products (such as videos, writing samples, papers, and paintings) as indicators of student performance, rather than test scores. Rather than using evidence to compare a child with another child or with norms, objective criteria are established for the child to meet, and assessed by means of actual observed performance or products that demonstrate competence. The underlying concept is that the child should produce evidence of accomplishment of curriculum goals that can be maintained in a portfolio for later use.

Informal Tests

Informal tests are designed primarily for the purpose of determining how a student performs in a specific area. The goal of these tests is not to find out what the student can achieve at a particular level but how the student behaves when attacking problems. An informal test does not have norms, nor does it necessarily consider a broad spectrum of an underlying curriculum. Most commonly, its purpose is to examine academic and problem-solving behaviors.

Examples of informal tests include the independent reading inventory, the error pattern analysis, and the examination of the processes of arithmetic. The process of informal testing is similar to that used in developing expert systems to find out how a person reasons and makes decisions.

Group and Individual Tests

Tests may also be classified as group or individual. A group test is used with an entire class or other large group; an individual test is designed for use with one student at a time. For the most part, because of the precise information that can be obtained and the depth of the examination, only individual tests are used in assessment for the purpose of deciding on the placement of students with disabilities. In group tests, the students must be motivated and usually must be able to read and follow directions without assistance. Some professional organizations, like the Council for Exceptional Children and the American Psychological Association, have taken the position that group tests should not be used for any reason other than screening.

Power and Speed Tests

Tests may also be classified in terms of power or speed. A power test is not timed; a speed test is timed. In some tests, parts may be timed and extra points may be awarded, not just for the accuracy of a response but for the speed with which the response is delivered.

STATISTICAL PROPERTIES OF TESTS

The most important properties of standardized tests are the statistical characteristics reported in the test manuals. The sections that follow include the most common statistical properties of test instruments.

Mean

The simple arithmetic average of scores in a test is referred to as the mean. This is the simplest estimate of the common performance of subjects on a test.

Median

The median is similar to the mean in that it expresses information about the central tendency of scores. Rather than a simple average, however, it is the middle score above which and below which half the scores fall. In establishing norms, the median is often used to separate the performance of subjects at each grade level.

Standard Deviation

The standard deviation is a unit measurement that relates the standing of a score in terms of the exact percentage of cases from the average or mean. The standard deviation tells the examiner the percentage of scores falling between points on the distribution of scores of a test.

Standard Error

It is important to know how much error there is in a score because any score on a test is only an estimate of the true score (e.g., for an IQ or reading grade level). The standard error shows the band of confidence within which a subject's score may be expected to fall. The greater the standard error, the greater the variation in the estimated score and the less confidence there is in the score, especially if it is to be used to aid in deciding whether or not a student should be considered to have mental retardation.

Neill and Medina (1989) make a good point when they note that the error of measurement is ignored in practice. For example, a student might have an IQ score of 117 and be barred from a program for the gifted (an IQ of 130 is usually required), when the estimated true score could actually be 130. Even in classroom testing, where teachers ordinarily assess students for grades with teacher-made tests that have no reliability or validity, distinctions may be made between an "A" or a "B" grade solely on the basis of a tenth of a point difference on the raw score. The differences between "A" and "B" students, or "B" and "C" students, are probably determined more by chance than actual differences among students in mastery of the content.

Reliability

The reliability of a test is generally defined as the extent to which it will yield the same results on repeated administrations or the ratio of true variance to obtained variance. If a student has a certain score one day and a much different score on the same test a few days later, the test is not very useful because it is probably unreliable. Reliability in test manuals is usually expressed as a correlation coefficient. Reliability coefficients of .60 are usually regarded as appropriate only for screening purposes. Tests are usually considered highly reliable if they reach about .90. Of course, there are other types of reliability, such as equivalence, stability, and internal consistency, which should be examined.

Validity

The validity of a test is the degree to which it actually measures what its developers say it measures. According to some critics (Salvia & Ysseldyke, 1978), many types of tests, such as perceptual and personality tests, do not measure what they are said to measure. In assessment, a test would not be valid if it were used to measure curriculum objectives that are not taught. For example, some special education students are taught to read in phonetic programs that eliminate words that do not have a sound and written symbol correspondence. Such students are often required to take tests that cover words and reading skills they have never been taught.

Just because a test maker says a test is valid does not mean it is. Validity is difficult to determine in education and psychology because we are not always sure that a trait really exists or the instrument we use is actually measuring the presumed trait. This is characteristic of personality traits and also for many of the processes presumed to underlie learning disabilities. Some of the traits may be nothing more than creative invention or curious correlates that seem to have validity.

Types of validity are content, construct, and criterion-related (concurrent and predictive). Content validity concerns objectives in the domain (e.g., reading objectives). Construct validity is the method used to determine that a test measures more subjective or theoretical conditions (constructs) such as personality traits (e.g., moodiness or processes in learning disabilities). Concurrent validity refers to a correlation between a given test and another test administered at the same time. Some examiners and test developers often correlate two tests and presume they measure the same thing. Predictive validity refers to the ability of a test score to predict performance in the future. Predictive validity is difficult to achieve, but this does not mean that tests with this presumption will not be used. For example, SAT scores have been shown to add virtually nothing in predicting college performance based on GPA, but they are still used (regardless of the expense).

Norms

The norms of a test are the scores reported for the people who were originally tested to standardize the test. If a person who takes a test has a background and experiences that are much different from those of persons in the normative sample, the test may be unfair. The issue of norms is a basic concern in the testing of minority students because they are compared with norms that reflect different experiences, opportunities, and privileges.

TYPES OF SCORES
Percentile

The percentile is one of the most common and easily interpreted scores. The percentile enables the examiner to determine the rank of an individual score in a distribution of scores for 100 subjects. A score at the 50th percentile means that the performance of the subject is equal to or greater than 50 out of 100 people; a score at the 85th percentile means that the performance is equal to or greater than that for 85 out of 100.

Developmental Scores

Common types of developmental scores are chronological age, mental age, and grade equivalents. Of these, the grade equivalent is the most common. If a student receives a score reported as a grade equivalent, such as 3.6, the score is interpreted as equivalent to the level of third grade, sixth month. Unfortunately, such scores are not very useful because they do not relate to equal intervals. They also vary greatly from test to test, depending on the learning experiences of the sample used to norm the test. Thus, it is not uncommon to find highly disparate scores for the same subject in a series of similar tests. As a result, a new approach, the Lexile method, is used in reading assessment (Stenner, Horabin, Smith, & Smith, 1988). The Lexile method rates reading content by the difficulty of the vocabulary.

Standard Scores

Deviation IQ scores on individual intelligence tests, Z-scores, T-scores, and stanine scores are examples of standard scores. Such scores are related to percentiles and can be interpreted in the same way that standard deviations are interpreted.

REPRESENTATIVE TESTS IN SPECIAL EDUCATION

Administrators, members of the referral team, and test examiners are all accountable for the tests they select, for the validity of their assessment approaches and interpretations, and for decisions they make on the basis of test data. Yet, important decisions that affect the lives of children continue to be based on professional interpretations of data from poorly developed, invalid, or unreliable tests and the whims of examiners.

Ysseldyke, Algozzine, Richey, and Graden (1982) demonstrated that although many tests are given in the process of learning disabilities assessment, teachers do not refer to or use data before or during intervention, the data do not differentiate successful from unsuccessful students, and there is overlap between scores of underachievers and scores of those labeled "learning disabled." In other words, the test scores do not predict or classify which students have learning disabilities and which students do not; it is apparently some subjective process inherent to the examiners.

Administrators must be aware of the limitations of test instruments and the limitations of their staff. They must realize that the school is vulnerable to litigation because of their assessment decisions. And they must therefore be able to make informed judgments about which tests to use, how the tests are employed, and how interpretations of the test data are made (Marsh & Podemski, 1982).

With implementation of PL 99-457 and discrepancies within PL 101-476, a new era of abuse may be imminent. Tests will be used to assess preschool children for preventative and ameliorative services. However, labels should not be applied to such children, especially because of the inability to predict which children will have school adjustment problems. Labeling a 2-year-old as emotionally disturbed, behaviorally disordered, or learning disabled is fraught with danger (Mallory & Kerns, 1988). Eligibility may present problems with assessment and services because a label is not required. However, inappropriate labeling of children may cause harm, even if the labels are not recognized ones but informal ones invented out of the assessment process to categorize children. Reporting that a child may develop learning disabilities, for example, may wrongfully change expectations and status for the child.

To illustrate the point, reference is made to one of the first statewide preschool screening programs (Thurlow, O'Sullivan, & Ysseldyke, 1986). A total of 45,000 preschool children between the ages of 3½ and 5 were screened in 400 districts. Some districts reported no problems in any of the children, but others reported that all the children presented some disorder! The investigators concluded there was "no relationship between screening referral rates and any of the general social, economic or educational factors." Without specific procedures, highly reliable instruments, and highly trained personnel, such results are likely to be repeated with implementation of PL 99-457. What damage will be done to normal toddlers and babies? How much litigation will be defended with public money?

Similarly, gifted and talented programs (technically within the area of special education) rely heavily on testing. Many approaches have been considered, but the common practice, which is probably discriminatory, is to classify children as gifted if they have good grades, high standardized achievement test scores, and exceed an IQ score of 130 on a test of intelligence. As a consequence, most children who are identified are white students from upper-middle-class homes. "Talent search" projects in some schools have been able to find poor minority children with low scores and poor grades who, with appropriate programming and motivation, were able to ultimately demonstrate high achievement.

There are literally thousands of tests that may be used to evaluate students in special education. Aside from special testing for visual impairment, hearing impairment, and health disorders, a few instruments are commonly used in most settings and form the foundation for basic decisions made about students referred or placed in special education programs. (These are discussed in the following sections.) However, there are many other reading tests, mathematics tests, and other instruments that might be employed, and these should be similarly evaluated by administrators and staff.

Stanford-Binet Intelligence Scale

The Stanford-Binet Intelligence Scale was the first scale to gain widespread popularity in school assessment, and it is the forerunner of most modern intelligence tests.

It yields a mental age with a deviation IQ of 100 and a standard deviation of 16 points. The test yields measures in four areas of cognitive functioning: verbal reasoning, abstract/visual reasoning, quantitative reasoning, and short-term memory. Although recent changes in the test are an improvement over the 1972 edition (it is now in its fourth edition), the Binet is not as widely used today because of the popularity of the Wechsler Scales.

Wechsler Scales

The Wechsler Scales are composed of four different scales for school-age children and youths/adults: the Wechsler Intelligence Scale for Children–Revised (WISC–R), the Wechsler Adult Intelligence Scale–Revised (WAIS–R), the Wechsler Preschool and Primary Scale of Intelligence (WPPSI), and the Wechsler Intelligence Scale for Children–III (WISC–III). The WAIS–R is used for subjects over the age of 16. Each of the tests uses three scales: verbal, performance, and full scale. There are a total of 12 subtests in each test; each subtest has a mean of 10 and a standard deviation of 3. The mean for each scale is 100 with a standard deviation of 15. The Wechsler Scales are technically adequate, with good reliability and validity. Minority students were included in the standardization.

The Wechsler Scales have unfortunately been used in certain unscientific ways, for example, in attempts to determine perceptual problems in children and to validate the existence of learning disabilities on the basis of differences in scores between and among the scales. In this connection, administrators should remember that a battery of psychoeducational tests is not comparable to a medical test. The use of a pattern as a preconceived category for labeling is impossible to justify. Ryckman (1981) indicates that the overlap between nondisabled and learning disabled populations on test performance is so great that a search for profiles to distinguish learning disabled subgroups is a fruitless effort. Still, thousands of children are classified this way each year, even though thousands of other children with the same profile do not have any difficulty in school.

Wide Range Achievement Test–Revised

The Wide Range Achievement Test–Revised (WRAT–R) is widely used as a quick method to obtain a gross measure of achievement. The original WRAT was developed in 1936 and has been widely criticized because the authors did not report test-retest reliability and the norms were old (although the reliability coefficients for the test are high). The WRAT–R also reports high reliability coefficients, but little information is known about the representativeness of the normative sample, such as racial, socioeconomic, or geographic variables or children with disabilities. As with the former test, such criticisms will probably not affect the spectacular sales of this instrument.

The WRAT–R, like the WRAT, has a limited and questionable normative population, limited behavior sampling, and questionable validity. It will continue to be used in profile analysis for comparisons with the WISC–R. This cannot be defended. The popularity of the test is undoubtedly due to the short time it takes to administer it, with most testing sessions lasting only 10 to 20 minutes; but, what is gained in speed is lost in depth. It is too brief to indicate diagnostic information and may not reflect the actual skills taught in the school. Its use in the school testing program should be limited to screening.

Peabody Individual Achievement Test–Revised

The Peabody Individual Achievement Test–Revised (PIAT–R) yields age equivalents, grade equivalents, percentile ranks, and standard scores for behaviors in reading, mathematics, written expression, spelling, and encyclopedic knowledge. It is used as a screening device for students between the ages of 5 and 18. It may not reflect the curriculum of a school and would be of limited use as a test for progress and retention in special education.

Peabody Picture Vocabulary Test–Revised

The Peabody Picture Vocabulary Test–Revised (PPVT–R) assesses standard English receptive vocabulary in individuals between the ages of 2 and 40. It is used as an alternative for children with poor expressive skills because the child need only point to an answer for most questions. It is popular because examiner skills are minimal and the test can be administered quickly.

Woodcock-Johnson Psycho-Educational Battery–Revised

The Woodcock has become quite popular in some programs because it has a wide variety of subtests. It also has a unique feature in that it not only incorporates grade level scores and normal curve equivalents but it can also be used for criterion measures and can compare performance with a particular age group. It covers subjects in reading, mathematics, written language, and cognitive abilities for those between the ages of 2 and 95.

Bender Visual-Motor Gestalt Test

A test that deserves special consideration is the Bender test, a simple test that only requires a subject to copy nine geometric designs on a piece of paper. Even though its reliability is low, its norms are inadequate, and its validity is questionable (Salvia & Ysseldyke, 1978), the instrument has been used to diagnose brain damage in children and adults, to test visual perception, and to diagnose emotional disorders. It has not been demonstrated that the Bender can measure visual-motor perception, perceptual disabilities, brain injury, or emotional disorders. It certainly cannot be used to diagnose learning disabilities or minimal brain damage as a single criterion (though such a diagnosis can frequently be found in student records) or to measure intelligence.

There are a number of other perceptual tests that require the student to copy designs or identify them in some kind of configuration. Special education, especially the areas of mental retardation and learning disabilities, as well as the so-called area of minimal cerebral dysfunction, is based heavily on perceptual theories of development and functioning. The notion is that children experience difficulty with academic subjects because of a deficiency in a perceptual process. But, the validity of such instruments has been questioned and some researchers, such as Harper (1979), clearly state that perceptual and perceptual-motor measures are not useful in diagnosis and classification.

PRESCHOOL ASSESSMENT

With the inclusion of preschool programs, similar procedures for identification and assessment of infants and toddlers will be followed as used in public schools. Although labels are not required, the law does require that assessments be made. Thus the same dangers exist here as with older students, except that testing infants and toddlers is even more difficult and unreliable.

Numerous scales exist for screening young children, usually based on developmental milestones. But there are wide ranges in "normal" development. Although precocious children are easy to identify, early walking or talking does not necessarily mean that a child will be gifted or that the child will not ultimately have school problems. Late walkers and talkers, similarly, may make slow, normal, or accelerated progress when they enter school. The predictive validity of preschool instruments is not adequate to make long-term projections with confidence.

For infants, there are three common instruments used for assessment: the Bayley Scales of Infant Development, the Cattell Infant Intelligence Scale, and the Gessell Development Test. These tests generally measure motor developmental milestones, language, and social behaviors. The Bayley is a mental and motor scale, the Cattell provides a mental age and IQ score, and the Gessell provides a developmental age for motor, language, and person-social behavior.

Other tests that are used with preschool children, appropriate for age, have been described previously, such as the Stanford-Binet Intelligence Scale and the Wechsler Preschool and Primary Scale of Intelligence. Special tests for cognitive assessment exist for students with visual and hearing impairments and for students with motor and speech difficulties.

GIFTED AND TALENTED

Because giftedness is recognized as an exceptionality by special educators but is not included in federal legislation that focuses on disabling conditions, many of the comprehensive standards pertaining to students with disabilities do not apply. Schools tend to follow similar procedures for identification of gifted and talented students as prescribed for pupils with disabilities, even attempting to meet time deadlines. Actually, the referral process is very similar, emanating from parents and teachers.

As previously noted in this text, it is unfortunate that giftedness suffers from some of the same definition problems that predominate in learning disabilities or mental retardation. In practice, a single IQ score on the Wechsler or Binet scales is essential, in addition to other evidence that might be required. Another view is that the child may seem to have ordinary intelligence but be highly talented in artistic endeavors. But unless a child is clearly a prodigy in some field of the fine arts, he or she will not likely be provided special programming. Although there may be considerable debate about using IQ scores, and although the definition of gifted and talented may go beyond test scores, it is common for schools to identify these children on the basis of an IQ score of 130.

POTENTIAL AREAS OF CONCERN

Aside from potential harmful effects of testing, the most important consideration in special education assessment is the extent and expense of the assessment program. In terms of the return on investment, testing is a very expensive activity and one with questionable benefits. Yet psychoeducational testing has become a multimillion-dollar industry. New tests, many of which are neither well designed nor particularly useful, are released to the market each year. In general, standardized tests should be questioned if they provide little information that can be used directly by referral or placement teams or by teachers in the classroom. It should be a major concern that many diagnoses are based on faulty definitions and vague criteria for disability. This is especially true in the areas of mental retardation, learning disabilities, emotional disturbance, and assessment of minority children.

The label of "learning disabled" has become a dumping ground for problem children because the label is less objectionable and because the state funding formulae support programming in this area. With the anticipated increase of more poor and disadvantaged children, the learning disabled population may swell beyond any boundary of reasonableness. The Regular Education Initiative and the inclusion model are partly a response to the unfortunate trend of labeling children without necessarily providing them with a better program than they would receive in a regular classroom.

Any incorrect use of tests, faulty interpretation of test results, misdiagnosis, or misclassification may result in conflicts with parents or in litigation. The most important concern is that all criteria used for eligibility are interpreted with extreme care and that tests, examiners, and conditions of assessment are carefully monitored.

Another concern involves the trust placed in the evaluation committee. Even the best-trained, most experienced examiners are dealing with areas of suspicious validity when they make determinations about such disabilities as mental retardation, learning disabilities, and emotional disturbance. For example, a customary practice in the area of learning disabilities is to conduct a profile or scatter analysis on the WISC–R, a practice proposed by those who invented the disorder of minimal cerebral dysfunction. No significant body of research has yet been established to validate the utility of scatter indexes for diagnosis. Yet, this is precisely the way diagnosis is approached by a majority of examiners. Any use of a test that deviates from the way in which the test was designed for use must be defended by the school.

The administrator's best defense against testing problems is to consider the assessment practices of the school in a logical sequence and then examine each aspect. First, the requirements of the state should be analyzed. Frequently, persons in the state education agency, who may often lack relevant expertise or be influenced by policies, are given the responsibility to develop regulations about assessment in special education. The school administrator should, therefore, examine each state requirement to see if it violates accepted principles of assessment or legal interpretations of the courts. The local district plan should also be similarly examined. And second, the competence of the examiners should be evaluated. Although examiners may hold all the necessary degrees, licenses, and certificates, the administrator should remember that many of the laws and much of the litigation regarding assessments has resulted from the errors of apparently qualified examiners.

Procedural safeguards in assessment provide a level of security for both the local district and the affected parents. The administrator can ensure that parents and teachers are given full access to test reports and evaluations, that records are policed, that irrelevant information is removed from the records, and that the records are protected under terms of the privacy acts. Above all, the administrator should ensure that students are viewed as individuals whose test scores have limited meaning beyond the school arena. No test score should be used to characterize a personality, a mind, or a life.

In sum, the administrator should be aware that the more complex or theoretical the assessment problem confronting the committee, the more unreliable the decision is likely to be. The greatest problems can be anticipated in the areas of learning disability, mental retardation, emotional disturbance, and preschool assessments.

The administrator should remember that the definitions of the more complex conditions in the largest areas of special education are weak, that the investment of time and money in special education assessment is unrelated to outcomes, and that the process may affect children adversely. The administrator should realize that regardless of how good or bad the tests are, school personnel make the decisions. Time, effort, and money in selecting and training teachers, administrators, and other staff may pay off in fewer problems and less expensive assessment. The cautions of Neill and Medina (1989) should be heeded: "Standardized tests are consistently sold as scientifically developed instruments that objectively, simply, and reliably measure students' achievement, abilities, or skills. In reality, however, the basic psychological assumptions undergirding the construction and use of standardized tests are open to question and often are clearly erroneous" (p. 689).

CHAPTER
FIVE

STUDENT-RELATED
ISSUES

Student-related issues have always been important in special education programming because of the nature of the students who require special considerations. The amount of time and effort devoted to this part of administration seems to vary, depending upon variables such as geographical location, the size and nature of the district, the cultural context of the school population, and the expectations of the school's community. To a greater or lesser degree, national trends and events impact student-related management at the building or district level, such as federal legislation, court rulings, and education trends.

Parental and community involvement with education often focus on the academic aspects of school, namely the curricular offerings and test scores. This has become more prominent in recent years, as school reform has forged a public consensus that standardized test scores define quality. Other components of board policy, such as dress code, grading policies, and rules for attendance, often receive less attention from parents and others until a specific incident or general fad among students diverts attention to these and similar student-related issues.

All aspects of student management in special education must be clearly described in board policy. By now, districts have undoubtedly developed policies for serving students with disabilities; however, these policies may not always be communicated adequately to school personnel. Even with efforts to include quality-circle-type strategies for involving teachers and community members in systemwide planning and site-based management, there may be only superficial awareness of the existence of schoolwide, formal policy for administering special education programs, and few parents may be aware of policy statements on student-related issues. Thus, many teachers and parents may be unaware of the specific nature of the school philosophy and policy as they relate to student management of both general and special education students on a daily basis, especially if the district is large with a massive central office bureaucracy. The lack of such information indicates a serious administrative gap that could result in misapplication of policy, a possibility fraught with legal and ethical implications. Clearly, schoolwide policy pertaining to student-related issues must be communicated to all parties, possibly beginning with students themselves.

ENROLLMENT PROJECTIONS

Building adequate and appropriate policy for handling student-related issues for all programs, including special education programs, begins with an accurate count of currently enrolled students and estimates for the future. Determining projected numbers of children with disabilities is often difficult because there are not clear, accepted definitions of disabling conditions among states and districts, especially in learning disabilities. Visual impairment, hearing impairment, and other conditions are not disputed, but the categories of emotional disturbance and learning disabilities are confusing.

In the area of learning disabilities, educators have persistently focused on new ways to define the condition, new aspects said to be related to learning disabilities, and debates about just what the term *learning disabilities* means. A comparison of professional journals of the early 1970s with professional journals of today shows that many topics about students with learning disabilities remain the same. (In literature regarding areas such as mental retardation or deaf education, professional concern is related to better treatment methodologies, not to whether or not the conditions exist.) Yet, accurate enrollment projections are vital for the administrator, because many aspects of the special education program are based on student ratios in traditional special programming or using inclusive models. Enrollment projections can affect:

- *Staffing.* Marked increases or decreases in all disability categories or in any one category of disability will affect the need to reduce, reassign, or increase the number of faculty and support personnel.
- *Cost.* Do the data demonstrate a need to alter the budget? A decrease in students may not mean that a decrease in required funding is possible. In contrast, even a small increase in a specific category, such as for the health impaired, may be extremely expensive. If such changes become visible in the projections, the school may need to consider contingency plans.
- *Scheduling.* Changes in the anticipated numbers of any one disability will impact upon the building master schedule and, hence, upon the class schedules for individual children and teachers.
- *Equipment and supplies.* Along with possible changes in the overall instructional program, dramatic changes in enrollment will affect the need for instructional equipment and supplies. These items must be purchased in advance and in appropriate quantities in order to secure discounts and to ensure that they arrive on time for use in the instructional program.

Problems with Definitions of Disabilities

The incidence of various categories of children with disabilities will vary greatly, depending on how the conditions are defined, the practices of examiners, and the characteristics of the community. Disorders of hearing, vision, speech, and health are generally defined more uniformly in terms of acceptable medical criteria, and the incidence may be more accurately anticipated. But the conditions of mental retardation, learning disabilities, and emotional disturbance/behavioral disorders may have vague definitions, variable criteria, and significant subjectivity in determination. This is even more complicated when different variables are thrown into the mix, such as bilingualism (Ortiz & Wilkinson, 1991).

The learning disabilities category is of particular concern to the administrator. Federal regulations have historically attempted to develop ways to hold down the number of students who might be classified as learning disabled. In fact, the Regular Education Initiative (REI) and the inclusion model were stimulated partly because of the problems with the prevalence figures for the learning disabilities category. At federal and state levels, there has been concern that so many students might be identified as learning disabled that most of the available appropriations from federal and state sources could become encumbered for one category.

Children should not be denied services, but overreferral should also be avoided. Because the problem has become more complex within each state, state departments of education are attempting to avoid the need to interfere with definitions and diagnostics by focusing on service delivery, namely placement in regular classrooms rather than special classrooms or mainstreaming. This stems from both economic and logical influences: (1) it is too costly to provide such a number of students with learning disabilities with special classes (in some districts one fourth to one half of the population can qualify); and (2) it is more practical to maintain such students in regular classrooms, provided their teachers are trained and supported to deal effectively with the students. Moreover, as indicated previously, the methodologies used for students with learning disabilities, mental retardation, and behavioral disorders are nearly identical (Smith, Price, & Marsh, 1986); and general education and special teachers have high agreement about the essential instructional goals that should be used with these students. There is also significant overlap between educational outcomes for students with disabilities and students without disabilities.

A vague definition will result in increased or decreased numbers of students, depending upon professional attitudes of examiners and social impetus. A psychological examiner who liberally interprets test data, especially with profile analyses based on test scatter, will yield many more students with learning disabilities than one who requires statistical evidence of a significant difference between scores on a profile.

A review of the prevalence figures since 1976 shows great differences over time. In 1976, the number of children with disabilities nationally was estimated to be 12% of the school population; by 1979, this had dropped to an estimated prevalence of 8%. More recent estimates put the figure at 10.02%. Comparison of prevalence figures from 1979 and 1989 estimates showed marginal increases or decreases for all categories except in learning disabilities. In 1993, the category of learning disabilities accounts for almost half of all students classified in special education (Ayers, 1994).

When the category of learning disabilities was conceived in the 1960s, it was presumed that, as a rule of thumb, it would represent about 1–2% of the school population; now it represents nearly 5% of the school population. This category accounts for nearly half of all children with disabilities served nationally and represents greater percentages in some local school districts (Ayers, 1994). The reasons for this phenomenon are legal, social, and professional.

The law requires children with disabilities to be served, and in order to be served, these children must be classified. All categories of special education have fairly clearcut identification procedures, except learning disabilities and emotional disturbance. However, there is an aversion to classification as emotionally disturbed and mentally retarded. Yet, they seem to be acceptable classifications for many minority children who have problems in achievement or perceived differences in behavior. With the increase in the number of minority children, there is an overall increase in the percentage of children who are so classified.

In practice, an administrator should be highly suspicious of prevalence data that depart markedly from the national prevalence in mental retardation, learning disabilities, and emotional disturbance. If a district has a higher proportion of minority children and children of low socioeconomic status who tend to score lower on standardized tests, the first hypothesis might be that some external factor may be influencing the data. For example, there may be a tendency for examiners to classify more students in these categories, especially learning disabilities. In such instances, care should be taken to ensure that assessment procedures are fair and not biased because of cultural or racial differences.

Unless there are unusual circumstances affecting the population of students in a community, the administrator should not expect prevalence figures for children who have health, speech, and visual impairments to vary greatly from one district to another. It should be noted, however, that although prevalence refers simply to the number of children at any one time and place, in special education this will depend upon the operational criteria and assessment practices, as well as the characteristics of the community. Thus, the greatest problem for administrators in the next decade may well be dealing with the explosion of learning disabilities because of vague criteria and subjective interpretations of examiners. As more minority children from families of lower socioeconomic status enter the schools, creating a majority of minorities in many districts, there is greater potential for larger numbers of students to be classified as learning disabled. And in some schools, the majority of students in the school may conceivably be classified as learning disabled. This will undoubtedly become a major problem because of its implications for student services, staffing, and finance.

The professional debate about the REI, which is now being supplanted by regulatory reality in the form of the inclusion model, would bolster the regular classroom teacher and retain students with mild disabilities in regular classrooms. This is becoming a viable alternative to special class placement, especially if it can be demonstrated that special education programs are no more or no less effective than regular programs but more expensive and confusing for school administration and disruptive of student learning activities.

The existence of special services will increase the number of children in certain categories. For example, if a school district implements programs for young children with hearing or visual impairments, families will move to such communities to take advantage of the programs. This will complicate the process of enrollment projections considerably.

The extent to which inclusion is used will greatly affect staffing patterns. Ludlow and Lombardi (1992) anticipate the following trends by the turn of the next century:

1. All students with disabilities will be placed in regular classrooms for the major portion of the school day.
2. Assignment to special education services will be based on needs rather than labels.
3. Students will be educated by teams of teachers.

Enrollment Data Sources

One approach an administrator may use to validate local prevalence figures is to secure data from other districts with similar characteristics (community factors, size, wealth, enrollment, etc.) and simply compare data. If there are wide variations, a study should be undertaken to determine why. The same approach can be used to compare schools in the same district and to compare changes over time. A notice-able variation might occur in low-incidence disability figures and in their health-related conditions because as programs begin to build and services improve in a district, families will move into it. Thus, programs for the hearing impaired, for example, may grow dramatically over a period of years because of the tendency of parents to look for communities where they can place their children with that disability. This mobility factor alone may cause an apparent disproportion of incidence for certain classes of disabilities.

To make projections and comparisons for planning purposes, the administrator can use data from the following sources:

- *State agencies.* Most states attempt to assist in estimating prevalence by examining statewide data and offering definitions and criteria for placement. The most important consideration is for the school to follow all pertinent guidelines and regulations established by the state education agency (SEA).

- *School census.* The administration should collect data on existing programming (calculate the total percentage and the percentage by diagnostic category) and apply them to the estimated number of students expected to attend the school in following years. The prevalence figures may vary considerably at the secondary level because of a tendency for students to be discharged from special education and to drop out of school. Also, while conducting the regularly scheduled school census, census enumerators might ask specifically for information about preschool children who are suspected of having a disability.

- *Child find.* The school must use well-trained faculty members and volunteers to identify children with disabilities. If screening activities are reasonable, tailored to reduce overreferrals, and properly executed, the school will be able to generate stable estimates of anticipated children with disabilities over a period of time. The only factor that might affect such estimates would be changes in definitions or assessment criteria. Child find is no longer as difficult as it was in the last two decades because of the increased knowledge of medical personnel and others involved in social services and the fact that child-find programs have become routine.

  In some regions of the country, child-find activities may be made somewhat more difficult by religious and cultural attitudes. These attitudes may result in families hiding the fact that they have a child with a disability (as is the case with newly arrived Haitian families). For certain other immigrant groups from countries with repressive governments, there may be suspicion of school representatives asking questions about family members. Administrators in such areas will have to work very closely with all social service and religious organizations in order to make child find truly effective.

- *Referral.* Referral sources (teachers, parents, physicians, etc.) should be reviewed to determine the number of referrals from each. If certain patterns are evident among particular schools or with particular teachers, the administrator may consider checking the reliability of the referral process.

Computing Enrollment Projections

Enrollment projections are usually calculated regularly for the entire school population by attendance or central office personnel with responsibility for research and planning. Although several methods can be used, most school districts calculate only aggregate data about total enrollment with breakdowns for each grade level. Although these data are important for districtwide planning, the special education administrator must have more precise estimates of expected students with various disabilities, and this information needs to be shared with the building principals as it affects building-level planning.

The first step in making projections is to determine the length of time for which the projections are made. Long-term forecasts that project total school population for 10 to 15 years may help the district plan building programs, but because they involve only aggregate data, they are not useful for short-range program planning. And they may not be useful for the long term if there are sudden economic changes in the community. Projections of 3 to 5 years are most useful for instructional and program planning because they can more accurately depict trends for various subgroups in a total, stable population sample. These projections should be updated annually in order to spot changes quickly and to make the necessary adjustments.

To compute projected enrollments, administrators must make certain assumptions:

- They must assume that future enrollments are a function of general community and environmental conditions, such as housing patterns, new construction, community economics, net migration of residents, birth rates, and shifts in industry.

- They must also assume that future enrollments are related to programmatic variables, such as pupil dropout patterns, procedures to determine the promotion or failure of students, and the availability of local special education programming and nearby private programming options.

Administrators must be able to detect general trends for these variables in order to adjust general projections. Simple estimated projections can be made using a linear model; more complex approaches involving additional variables may require the assistance of a statistician with access to demographic data and a computer.

Linear Model. With the linear model, the school uses past demographic projections made by the district, a state agency, or a university to project total district student enrollment for a period of 1 to 5 years. The district then calculates for each category the average percentage of children with disabilities who have been enrolled for the last 3 to 5 years. In the absence of past trend data, the district can use general prevalence rates and simply compute, for each future year, estimates for those disability categories for which data are available.

Cohort Survival Method. A better approach, especially for 5-year projections, is to employ a more complex model that takes into account more variables. One such approach is the cohort survival method. This method requires that the administrator do the following:

1. Obtain actual student enrollments for each grade for the last 5 years.
2. Divide the kindergarten enrollment of each previous year by the kindergarten enrollment of the subsequent year to determine the change ratio for each year.
3. Calculate the average of the 5 change ratios, and use this average to estimate projected kindergarten enrollment for the next 5 years.
4. Calculate the survival rate for each grade during each of the past 5 years, based on the district's past enrollment figures. For example, the percentage of students in the second grade who remained in the school and were enrolled in the third grade would be examined.
5. Average the percentages calculated for each grade to determine an average survival ratio for that grade.
6. Compute future enrollments by multiplying the current enrollment for each grade by the average survival ratio for that grade and then repeating that process for each of 5 subsequent years.

The resulting figures may be adjusted for any dramatic changes in internal or external conditions. For example, some communities might anticipate that an industry will move into the district.

One district was impacted by the relocation of a high technology company. As a result, school enrollments in the primary grades were expected to increase by several hundred students over a period of 3 years. The school district had not anticipated this growth and had to make immediate adjustments in its enrollment projections. Other districts, such as those in Florida, California, and Texas, must pay attention to international developments within the Caribbean and Latin America when trying to predict student enrollment data. Changes in immigration policy and/or political upheaval may produce unexpected enrollment patterns, as, for example, in the rapidly growing numbers of Haitian students enrolling in Florida's Dade County Schools.

For most districts, the more complex models are necessary to provide accurate projections. Fortunately, microcomputer enrollment packages are becoming more available, thus making such models easier to apply. Of course, additional help in determining enrollments is always available from university personnel or outside consultants. Advances in the power of personal computers and increasing sophistication of software have made it possible for administrators to handle predictive responsibilities right at their own desks.

STUDENT RECORDS

Because of the importance of student files and records for both administrative and legal purposes, the special education administrator and the principal must establish and monitor procedures regarding the use, access, care, and storage of student records.

Use and Access

All school districts must maintain student records and other files for state and federal reports. The method of collection, storage, and retrieval will determine the ease with which relevant data can be made available for decision making. For some time, larger districts have used computerized systems for the retrieval and manipulation of coded data, handled by the data processing department within central administration.

The administrative officer responsible for guaranteeing confidentiality must identify precisely which student data and records are covered under various regulations. An educational record is defined by the Department of Health, Education, and Welfare as being directly related to a student and maintained by an educational agency or institution or a party acting for the agency or institution. Turnbull, Strickland, and Brantley's (1982) definition of accessible records, which still stands, is "any records in the possession of the school system related to a student even if they are created by independent sources or contractors for service" (p. 73). Examples of accessible records are test results and any materials shared with a multidisciplinary team for the purpose of planning and decision making. Materials prepared and kept solely by an individual for private use rather than collective decision making are not regarded as accessible records. Information in accessible records that identify an individual student includes the following items (Federal Register, 1977):

1. The names of the child and the child's parent or other family member.
2. The address of the child.
3. A personal identifier, such as the social security number of the child.
4. A list of personal characteristics or other information that make it possible to identify the child with reasonable certainty.

In recent years, access to student records has become a somewhat sensitive issue among parents as well as administrators. School administrators have reported instances of teachers misplacing records and sharing confidential data in inappropriate situations. As a result of litigation regarding the use of such records, some administrators have become extremely protective. There are even reported instances in which teachers are not allowed to view the student folders but must rely instead upon summaries prepared by administrators, school counselors, or others. And some school policies stipulate that teachers can examine records only in the administrator's office.

Administrative concerns related to access involve the questions:

- Will records be maintained properly?
- Will they remain intact?
- Is it possible that confidentiality will be compromised?
- What guarantee is there that teachers will not be careless with the folders and unintentionally allow inappropriate access?
- Do the teachers behave professionally enough to handle records?

And teacher concerns related to access involve the questions:

- How can program planning proceed without access to student folders?
- Does the administration consider teachers too unprofessional to handle student folders appropriately?
- Is the teaching function considered secondary to planning and other administrative activities?
- Will teachers be held legally responsible for mishandling records even when their actions are in compliance with school policies?
- Are psychometrists considered more professional than teachers and therefore allowed freer access to records?

Clearly, administrators, as the agents responsible for ensuring that all policies and regulations are implemented accurately, must protect the interests of both the students and the district. At the same time, teachers must have access to student information and must be trusted to behave professionally. The basic issue here is one of professional behavior and the need for trust and confidence among all parties.

In the final analysis, the use of student records must be predicated upon their availability by the best and easiest means possible to the professionals involved. If student records are not accessible to those professionals whose decision making depends upon such access, there would appear to be no reason to keep the records. Although this may be stating the obvious, it is an important point to keep in mind when dealing with not only access but also the confidentiality, storage, and transfer of student records.

Confidentiality

Federal regulations require the following safeguards to ensure the confidentiality of student records (Federal Register, 1977):

1. One administrative officer should be appointed to monitor the use of student records and to assume overall responsibility for protecting their confidentiality.
2. All persons collecting or using personally identifiable data must receive training regarding the confidentiality and use of student folders.
3. A record of the names and positions of all district professionals who have access to the personal data must be maintained.
4. The records must be made available for public inspection as required.

Section 513 of PL 93-380 ensures that parents have access to the educational record of their child. This legislation, commonly called the Buckley Amendment, also allows parents to ask for a hearing to challenge data in the folder that they consider inappropriate, either because it is inaccurate or because it might be considered misleading.

Teacher access to student records must conform to the confidentiality safeguards cited previously. In addition, the details of teacher access should be specified in the district's storage and retrieval policy. Access to the records by third parties must also conform to district requirements; such access requires the written consent of the parents.

Storage

Storage of student files is also being impacted by existing and emerging technologies. Storage was traditionally conceptualized as a folder—in the case of special education students, often a very thick folder. Collective storage was a file cabinet. Obviously, the spread of computerized data storage, the growing sophistication of CD-ROM storage systems, and databases in general have all combined to change this image of student files.

In reality, in many schools already, no one in the central office ever really handles an actual folder; it is a computer file instead, reviewed on the computer screen. Even so, the following steps should be taken by the administrator in developing local policies and procedures for the storage of student files:

1. Examine state guidelines for specific record storage procedures in special education programming.

2. Study the patterns of use of student folders in the district, including periods of use, personnel who require access most frequently, and relevant organizational procedures.

3. Secure faculty input in evaluating existing procedures and designing new policies for record storage, even if you are using computer technology. This is especially important if a local area network is being implemented and/or planned. Faculty use of files should be facilitated by the technology, not impeded by it.

4. If traditional, paper-based folders are used, establish storage policies that ensure the locking of storage facilities and efficient and effective means of signing folders in and out. In a computerized environment, recording access to the folders, appropriate opportunities for examination of the records by teachers and other professionals, and means for guaranteeing confidentiality are more manageable and may simply require a slight shift in issues. For example, some orientation may be required for new users and an appropriate security system must be developed, typically based on timed access, passwords, limited purpose access, and other such strategies (developed and refined in industrial settings yet appropriate for educational management).

When assuming a position in a district with existing storage policies, an administrator should review and evaluate those policies. Thereafter, the policies should be examined regularly because litigation, new legislation, and/or newer technologies may require modifications to ensure compliance.

Transfer

In the event student records are transferred to courts under judicial order, the parents must be informed of their rights concerning access and confidentiality. This is the responsibility of the administrator designated to coordinate district record-keeping procedures and confidentiality requirements.

Federal regulations specify the requirements relating to school records that are no longer needed because of graduation or transfer to another school. First, the school must inform the parents when personally identifiable information is no longer needed to provide educational services to the child. And second, such information must be destroyed at the request of the parents. However, a record of the student's name, address, phone number, grades, attendance record, classes attended, grade level completed, and year completed may be maintained without time limitation (Federal Register, 1977).

School records of a child with a disability may be retained indefinitely, unless the parents specifically request that they be destroyed. Parent requests for destruction of records may occur because of parental concern that, even with confidentiality safeguards, inappropriate use of the information may occur in the future. The use of information technology may even heighten this concern for some parents. However, district representatives might suggest to parents the possibility that the child or family might need the records at some point in the future and urge caution in making the decision to request their destruction. An alternative is to divide the file, especially if electronically maintained, into an active file of current information and an archive of previous information and actions, stored separately.

GRADING PRACTICES

A decade of criticism and examination of the schools in both the professional and popular press, a slipping public image, the educational reform movement, and the general demand for higher standards have all focused attention on grading practices. Unfortunately, when traditional grading practices are used and evaluations based on the normal curve are rigidly enforced, students with disabilities in the mainstream are likely to be graded severely without standards of equity, in spite of their limitations or needs. In fact, the entire system of education in the United States tends to reward students who are memorizers.

Selby and Murphy (1992) conducted a study of mainstreamed student in the sixth and eighth grades and examined tests and letter-grade procedures used by their teachers. They discovered that students tended to feel helpless in attempts to earn high grades but blamed themselves for the low grades they received. This sets the stage for considerable controversy and conflict, especially at the secondary level where percentages or letter grades have been used traditionally to compare the achievement of a student with others in the same class or grade level. In fact, grading practices may come under closer scrutiny, in general, as there is a decided trend toward more individualization, cooperative learning, and constructivist learning.

Putnam (1992) examined 360 teacher-made tests used in English, math, science, and social studies in junior high and found that the most frequent kind of question was multiple choice and that the majority of questions were asked at the knowledge level. Much of the lack of motivation and other problems in education may be directly related to the nature of classroom evaluation.

Grading special education students on a different scale or a "Kelley Curve" does not work well in an environment struggling with issues of quality as measured by grades and scores. At the same time, however, quality may be unsuitably defined. That is, it may not be defined by the percentage of students *passing,* but by the percentage *failing* (i.e., "We have a really good mathematics program; only about 10% of the top students are able to get through it!"). True quality for a school should be measured by how many students learn and succeed (pass), not by how many fail to do either.

Other points of contention include questions such as:

- Should GPAs for gifted and advanced students be calculated on "quality" points, meaning a "B" in an Advanced Placement (AP) class is worth more toward the GPA than an "A" in a regular class?

- Should students with learning disabilities, given consultation and mentoring through some type of enrichment and/or academic support program, be allowed to obtain the grade of "A" or "B," just like those who do not receive special assistance?

As yet there have been no substantive litigation or SEA decisions concerning grading procedures. State guidelines also contain little information on this subject. Though some states are currently reviewing their positions on grading, graduation requirements, and diplomas for students with disabilities, most states give local schools the authority to decide such issues. In any case, the administrator should examine all state regulations pertaining to grading and should consider policymaking an important priority. If, as seems now certain, the trend toward outcomes-based education continues (Ysseldyke, Thurlow, & Shriner, 1992), the relationship of traditional letter grades to assessment will be questioned. A letter grade reflects the teacher's opinion, if not measurement, of how a student performed. Outcomes will also assess the teachers by holding them accountable for learning.

Grades and the grading process can be expected to grow in importance and in the amount of attention received from parents. As students with learning disabilities and other disability groups progress through the system and pursue postsecondary education and training, grades will take on new importance. Also, for other, less academic goals, such as entering the job market, grades will also become important, especially as they represent a more significant gatekeeping function, that is, admission to or denial of work.

The basic issue regarding grading policies for students with disabilities is whether such students should be compared with nondisabled students on the basis of classroom tests and other teacher evaluations, despite the fact that such tests also reflect deficits related to specific disabilities. In most settings, grades are assumed to communicate something distinctive about the students, based upon the competition among them. However, this assumption is ill-founded. A student who earns an "A" in biology in one class cannot logically be compared with another who earns an "A" in biology in another class, in another school in the district, in another district in the state, or in another state. This is because there are no universally accepted criteria for each course of study. What one teacher believes to be important content objectives may differ drastically from another teacher's criteria for the same course. Thus, a grade reflects only the ability of a student to pass teacher-made tests and to satisfy other requirements unique to a teacher's class.

In short, teacher-made tests and the decisions made with them have unknown reliability and validity. Although great pains are taken to assure that valid, reliable tests are used in classification, this is not true in teacher-made assessments, often of equal or greater significance in a child's future. In fact, grades are often used to punish students. Although a student may earn points through some system of grading, entire letter grades can be removed for such things as misbehavior or missing class.

Teacher-made tests and grading practices typically lack reliability and validity. The common practice of point spreads (e.g., A = 90 to 100) cannot be defended, nor can the use of surprise quizzes and extra-point assignments. Even the most traditional and prestigious MBA at Harvard is proposing to drop the grading curve for evaluation of students in favor of more relevant criteria for assessment. If grades are largely affected by social impacts, students with disabilities will be discriminated against.

Certain questions arise when letter grades are used for students both with and without disabilities:

- Does an "A" mean the same thing for a student with a disability and a student without a disability when the former has received the grade for progressing up to a certain level of ability but still falls far short of what the majority of students in the regular class are able to achieve?

- Will the highest-achieving student without a disability who earns an "A" be lowered in status as a result?

- Will this lead to a debasement of standards?

- In this situation, has the student with a disability received the curricular and instructional modifications necessary to compete with students in the regular class?

In fact, as we have noted, many students with disabilities can compete successfully in the regular class, especially if the Individualized Education Program (IEP) committee has identified appropriate class modifications for the students with disabilities. In such cases, the students with disabilities can and should be graded on regular class standards. However, the regular teacher should be sure that the grading methods and procedures employed do not reflect the child's disability and that the child has every opportunity to demonstrate competence.

For students who participate in special education class placement in accordance with their IEPs, different grading considerations apply. The basis for the identification of students with disabilities rests primarily on the fact that they deviate from their age peers in one or more dimensions. Most of them deviate in grade level achievement. We would question the fairness of determining grades on the basis of such classroom measures, especially if the tests used with those with disabilities are not supposed to reflect their deficit. This is not an unimportant distinction; unless it is addressed by the school, challenges will be made by parents before local boards of education and ultimately in the courts.

If grades are based upon the interaction between measures of the ability of a student and criterion measures, with the IEP as the foundation for establishing the latter, a fair assessment can be made, and the school is not as vulnerable to litigation. Indeed, if schools would accept mastery learning as a basic teaching-learning concept, grading difficulties would be diminished greatly. Each student's performance would be determined on the basis of the interaction of the student with the curriculum, not on the basis of how other students perform. Student achievement would become a matter of criterion-referenced assessment.

Reynolds and Birch (1977) made a statement that still applies to grading practices for those with disabilities: "What students and their parents require is honest and useful information. In day by day, week by week operations, the grading information of greatest value is on progress in meeting objectives set for that student's unique program" (p. 63). A criterion-referenced or mastery learning system that uses the IEP as a base satisfies this requirement as long as the IEP is appropriate for the child. As more schools are using curriculum-based assessment procedures, which may even spread to students without disabilities, there may be a better match between student performance and grades on an individualized, rather than group competitive, basis. In any event, the special education administrator and especially building administrators must exert leadership in establishing appropriate grading policies for students with disabilities and in helping regular educators, parents, and the community at large to understand the purposes and operation of such policies.

DIPLOMAS AND GRADUATION PRACTICES

Economic trends in this country have "raised the ante" for many special education students. Employers as a group complain about declining literacy of workers and the overall dearth of good candidates for jobs, even in fast-food establishments. As a result, employers, now more than ever, are expecting applications to arrive with at least a high school diploma, preferably a college degree. (At the time of this writing, the U.S. Army no longer accepts recruits without a high school diploma or equivalent.) All of this combines to put greater pressure on special education personnel and administrators to ensure that the students in their charge have every opportunity to succeed and receive a diploma—the key to those jobs and to economic independence.

The issues of graduation requirements and diplomas for students with disabilities are interrelated; grading practices that are used will determine the degree to which the student has earned credit for courses required for graduation. There are several approaches to establishing and meeting graduation requirements:

- *Pass/fail.* In this approach, only one general diploma is offered, usually accompanied by a transcript.

- *Certificate of attendance.* This document indicates that the student has met minimum attendance standards but has not completed requirements for a diploma.
- *Regular diploma.* This is the normal diploma signifying that the student has met all graduation requirements.
- *Special education diploma.* This diploma indicates that the student has met the requirements of the IEP but has not completed the standard courses or other requirements for graduation.
- *Differentiated diploma.* This document indicates that the student has met requirements for a specialized curriculum, such as vocational, college preparatory, or severely disabled.
- *Competency certificate.* This certificate is awarded to all students who pass a minimum competency test.
- *IEP approach.* Graduation here is contingent upon successful completion of the student's IEP, indicating the curricular and instructional modifications that the student has required.

One may ask if the graduation diploma is really important. Generally, the courts say that it is. Although there have been no specific special education legal cases, in *Mohavongsanen* v. *Hall* (1976) the court held in favor of a student who sued a university for failure to award a diploma. In this case, though the student had completed all course work, he had failed to pass a special examination that was implemented as a requirement approximately 6 weeks prior to completion of the student's course of study. The court held that the university had breached a contract implicit in the requirements for graduation specified in the catalog. Most significantly, the court ruled that the diploma was a property right that could not be denied without due process. Although the case was ultimately reversed on appeal, the higher court did not contradict the contention that a diploma is a property right. It thus can be reasoned on behalf of students with disabilities that a high school diploma is a property right. Therefore, failure to receive one (either because of the inability to pass a competency test or because of not having access to the curriculum upon which the competency test was based) denies the student equal protection under the law.

Most states award three types of certificates to signify completion of high school: a regular diploma, a special diploma, and a certificate of attendance. Usually the state leaves the decision regarding which graduation options to use to the local district. Thus, one district may award a certificate of attendance and a neighboring district may not. This depends upon local politics and other factors. Such policies should be developed with considerable care.

Many, if not most, students with disabilities at the secondary level are capable of meeting the regular requirements for graduation. The practice of awarding a special education diploma simply because a student who has earned credits for graduation has received special education services can be challenged because it is clearly discriminatory. Presumably, such a diploma is supposed to indicate that the student was not capable of the highest achievement or of competing in specific academic classes; and, somehow, it is supposed to protect the prestige of the regular diploma awarded to students without disabilities. The logic here is weak. In addition, the school is vulnerable to litigation on the basis that the student who gets the special education diploma has been discriminated against because of a disability.

The diploma does not represent standard accomplishments across schools, districts, and states. Moreover, insofar as it has served a gatekeeping function in our society, it has generally excluded those with disabilities. Even if a diploma were able to show precisely the competencies a student has achieved in the school curriculum, it would be of little real value beyond serving to keep students from entering certain kinds of jobs or programs. Moreover, it does not determine what a student may be able to accomplish in the future. There are many students with poor high school achievements or poor achievement in the first year or two of college who have excelled in subsequent professions. To eliminate such students from consideration in college training programs merely on the basis of a diploma that lists their competencies—and, by implication, their inadequacies—might be a disservice.

Minimum Competency Testing

Competency tests, like diplomas, raise issues of concern to those with disabilities as well as to minority groups.

- Is the curriculum upon which the competency test is based available to the students?
- Are the tests for students with disabilities valid and reliable?
- Do the tests that reflect the standard curriculum apply to students who have been in special education?
- If a student is exempt from a competency test, is the student denied a diploma?
- Should students with disabilities be excluded from tests in order to prevent a negative skew in the distribution of class or district scores?
- What are the consequences of this for the student?

State and local district competency tests or graduation requirements that deny students with disabilities a diploma or graduation must be designed and implemented in such a way as to ensure that the standards are equitable and nondiscriminatory to the class of students affected. If the policies or regulations require de jure exclusion or create de facto exclusion of students with disabilities in terms of their access to the curriculum, to specific classes, to promotion, or to graduation and a diploma, the affected students will be able to find relief in case law precedents.

Tracking

An approach that has been used in many districts, especially at the secondary level, is to develop a watered-down curriculum and then restrict students with disabilities and low-achieving students to courses in the lower track. In *Mills* v. *Board of Educa-*

tion of the District of Columbia (1972) and *Hobson v. Hansen* (1967), the courts held that tracking is discriminatory, that it is a form of segregation. If the students who tend to be assigned to a program are overrepresented in terms of race, cultural group, or disability, the effect is de facto segregation. Tracking is especially offensive when it places limitations on students. For example, some high school programs require students who take any basic (low track) class to take all basic classes. This is truly discriminatory in every sense because no allowances are made for diversity of abilities and interests. In many classes, students with disabilities are capable of competing successfully if they are given the same considerations and accommodations as students with visual impairments. One of the most senseless approaches is to create self-help curricula for the majority of students with disabilities. All students with learning disabilities with average or above-average intelligence are capable of dressing, eating, grooming, and social amenities; such programming for them is both insulting and a waste of time. However, many students with mental retardation seem to be immune to such inane programming.

In tracking, the curriculum is designed to enable students to earn credits that are required for graduation but may not be important or relevant for the individual student in a particular class or sequence of classes. Moreover, morale may be low among teachers assigned to instruct in the low track. In contrast, some secondary schools have demonstrated that students with disabilities are able to perform to high standards in regular classes and honors classes. The key to such success lies in the personal and curricular support provided to regular classroom teachers, the assistance of special teachers, and the leadership of the administration.

Any type of course substitution can be considered discriminatory if care is not taken to consider the effects. Obviously, students may be excused from certain types of classes if they cannot possibly compete, and another course may be used in place of the one waived. But, if the substitute course is to meet the requirements for graduation, the school should take care in how it interprets the student's record in moving toward that goal.

Accommodation

Accommodation is the practice of altering or modifying the materials, methods of instruction, or curriculum to enable students with disabilities to meet the requirements of a class or course of study. For example, a student who cannot read efficiently may be given readers, taped lessons, and other aids. Students with disabilities thus master the same content that is mastered by nondisabled students, although with different methods of acquiring the relevant information. The method of accommodation appropriate for each student should be discussed by the IEP placement committee and stated in the IEP, thus providing guidance to the teacher who incorporates these methods into the instructional planning for the student. Several methods of accommodation are in use, including:

- *Course substitution.* This approach is used when the disability prevents the student from taking a course or would make such a course inappropriate. Examples are substituting adaptive physical education for regular physical education and, in the case of a student with a hearing impairment, substituting music history for music appreciation.

- *Time alterations.* This method allows students to take longer to complete individual courses or courses of study. Fewer courses could be carried during each semester, and students might remain in school until the age of 21 to satisfy requirements. The IEP may be used to design and specify time requirements, course load, and other aspects.

- *Modifications in the curriculum, instructional methods, or materials.* There are many instructional aids available for those with disabilities (e.g., taped lectures or books and braille books) that can help the student achieve class objectives. Alterations in the reading levels of tests can also be used to help the student achieve certain objectives.

- *Development of a special education curriculum corresponding to the regular education curriculum.* In this approach the curriculum objectives for regular and special education are the same, but the instructional methods are different in that they are suited to the student's needs.

- *Alternative approaches.* Other methods a school may use to help students achieve graduation are work-study programs, work experience, vocational or job entry/early graduation, college entry/early graduation, independent study, and night classes or high school equivalency tests.

EXTRACURRICULAR ACTIVITIES

Extracurricular activities become increasingly important as the school becomes the setting for the social activities and interests of adolescents. If school policies deny students with disabilities access to such activities, serious complications could ensue. For example, if the school requires a particular GPA in order to be eligible for involvement in certain clubs, organizations, or athletics, some students with disabilities will have open access, and others may be restricted.

In some instances, the practices and policies of a school in determining eligibility and participation in extracurricular activities may be challenged on the basis of discriminatory practices, especially when a student's disability is not considered in accommodation or grading practices. However, if fairness doctrines are adhered to, policymaking in this area can be developed in such a way as to minimize conflict.

DISCIPLINE

Teachers and administrators often may assert that the ability to manage a classroom is one of the most important of teaching skills. In the present context, "to manage" is interpreted to mean the ability to establish and maintain an appropriate learning environment. To create such an environment, the teacher must accomplish several important tasks (Marsh, Price, & Smith, 1983):

1. Develop programs to treat and prevent problem behavior in the classroom.
2. Design personal growth programs to assist in the development of self-concept.
3. Provide support in those instances in which interventions are being implemented by other professionals.
4. Create a positive milieu for group learning.

Obviously, the teacher-preparation program must assume responsibility for providing basic competencies. Although most professionals agree that the teacher is the school person with significant responsibility for influencing socioemotional development of students, the specific range of methodologies to be employed by the teacher is a matter of differing opinion among professional educators and psychologists. Therefore, because consensus cannot be reached among professional educators as to which intervention must be used in the classroom to facilitate socioemotional growth of the students, this decision must be made at the classroom level, based upon student and teacher personalities and other such variables (especially in the case of special education students). These daily classroom management decisions can be greatly affected by administrative actions that support a conventional belief that the administrative policies and procedures within which the teacher must function can also influence the quality of the instructional environment.

Administrators can develop rapport with teachers, provide "informal clout," and thereby affect classroom operations through personal relationships and professional respect (not unlike Peters and Austin's [1985] "management by walking around"). This is particularly relevant in the area of student management and discipline.

Lessons found in the business environment and transplanted to education include building a "can do" attitude among teachers (Pino, 1988). Delegating responsibility to teachers can facilitate improved classroom management. Each person along the line has responsibility and the ability to intervene. Administrators, like other managers, can acknowledge and reward teachers who successfully deal with certain types of classroom behavior. That does not mean rewarding them by giving them all of the "problem children," as is often claimed! It means acknowledging their initiative and supporting their decision.

If a teacher's decision was not on target, the administrator should confer informally with that teacher, brainstorming with him or her about ways to handle particular students. The obvious impact of this is to convey to teachers that everyone is in this together. The feeling of having a support team to help review and analyze decisions without the threat of punishment or ridicule contributes greatly to the evolution of initiative and creative problem solving.

Administrators will need to encourage teachers to attempt various interventions before referral and involvement with other types of services. By actions and words, even more than by policy, hands-on administrators are able to develop feelings of commitment and personal responsibility in teachers. This can be accomplished through being interested, spending time on the problems and solutions, and listening to teachers' ideas.

When something is not working, the tendency is to spend valuable time trying to assign blame, whether in one's professional activities or one's personal life. Teachers may even be found to blame the student's problems on the student. Although all logical adults recognize the futility of such searches for blame, it will require administrative leadership to prevent this from becoming the overriding activity when dealing with classroom behavior. As instructional leaders, strong administrators can focus discussions on the alterable aspects of the situation, emphasizing the desired behavior, and concentrate discussion on observable behavior.

Effective teachers must have a big bag of tools and tricks of the trade. Even more importantly, administrators must allow a broad range of instructional approaches to be used. Administrators can encourage teacher control over the selection of teaching materials and increase teacher participation in curriculum decisions.

Specific Strategies

There are a few specific strategies for dealing with so-called discipline problems that seem to be somewhat common to a wide range of schools. Examination of one of the most controversial drug therapies makes it obvious that the use of some of these strategies involves a clinical designation of a behavioral condition made by medical professionals outside the school environment. However, even these medically and psychologically based treatments sometimes fall to the school to implement and/or to monitor.

Drug Therapy.   Drug therapy was an extremely popular strategy for the last two decades. The purpose of medication has often been the need to decrease the frequency of undesirable behavior or to change behavior that significantly interferes with the acquisition of academic skills. Underlying the strategy is the assumption that, if the interfering behaviors could be eliminated, achievement would be facilitated, and the student would be more desirable in the classroom setting. Although there does not seem to be as much concern expressed about drug therapy, administrators and classroom teachers have been left with unresolved concerns about drug therapy as a means of dealing with behavior and discipline problems. This may become a broader concern as, because of inclusion policies, general education teachers begin to become responsible for supervision of medication for children with disabilities.

Questions center around the shortage of evidence that drug therapy alone produces an increase in learning. Other issues include the tendency on the part of teachers to assume that the therapy itself is sufficient as treatment for poor achievement, without instructional intervention. It is apparent that appropriate instructional activities must accompany drug therapy in order for any benefit to result. There is a lack of definitive proof that children treated with central nervous system stimulants demonstrate anything other than temporary, short-term improvement. Despite the fact that this may seem like a concern of the family and the attending physician, if drug therapy is to be used, educators should be alerted to the possible side effects and be well informed as to the types and categories of drugs involved.

Before initiating communication with parents about the use of drug therapy, administrative personnel should be aware of the roles and responsibilities commonly involved in such therapy. Most importantly, because drug therapy is a medical intervention (not an educational one), a physician (not a teacher or school administrator) should recommend the use of drug therapy. The following limited responsibilities should be assumed by school personnel:

- Development of policy and procedures to govern administration, including preparation of an administration form, a monthly review of the forms on file, and procedures for the maintenance of drugs and accompanying forms.
- Dispensing of medication, including maintenance of records of medication of child (room number, date/time the medicine was given, type of medicine, and person designated as responsible for the medication) and a policy that requires that a designated person be present to witness the student taking the medication.
- Storing of medication, including the development of a written policy that provides limited access and secure storage and requirements for the labeling of drugs (name, physician, designated school agent, and instructions).
- Notification to school personnel as to possible side effects, both expected and unexpected.

In addition, teachers should be aware of the legal implications of drug therapy for students. Administrative personnel should check the insurance policies governing drug administration in the particular situation. In this connection, the National Education Association's Educator's Employment Liability Policy includes some coverage; however, prescribed drugs administered by a teacher in a nonemergency situation are apparently excluded. Also, it should be noted that members of the American Federation of Teachers have for some time been advised by an attorney not to assume responsibility for giving medication in a nonemergency situation (Axelrod & Bailey, 1979). In particular, as noted previously, school personnel involved with special education students who receive drug therapy should be aware of the major types of drugs used and their possible side effects.

In sum, the administrator responsible for special education students should be certain that all personnel, regular or special, who are involved with the student undergoing drug therapy are informed about professional responsibilities, the types of medication, the legal issues, and any other matters that may aid them in performing the necessary support functions. Failure to provide such information can jeopardize the welfare of the child, foster misunderstandings between the child and school personnel, and place undue pressure on all parties involved.

All use of drug therapy must be documented. The following items should be included in such a form:

- Student's name.
- Date.
- Teacher's name and room number.
- Copy of prescription and written statement concerning recommended dosage.

- Statement from physician indicating possible side effects, positive and negative, as well as expected behavioral changes.
- Signature of physician.
- Parental statement including permission for school personnel to administer medication as prescribed.
- Signature of parent.

The IEP Approach. The IEP approach requires important administrative actions that allow and support the integration of two dimensions of discipline: the policies of the school as they pertain to classroom management and the management methods used by the teacher. Disruptive class behavior may indicate the child with a disability is misplaced and acting out frustration. The committee should be convened and possible changes in the IEP should be discussed. Such a discussion assumes that the teacher has available a variety of instructional and student-management techniques. Teachers who are able, in various ways, to alter curriculum approaches and classroom situations are less concerned about discipline problems (Joyce & Weil, 1986). Thus, administrators in districts in which teachers seem to be consistently occupied with disciplinary problems might consider addressing the discipline issue indirectly; that is, to devote staff development time to practical strategies for individualization, daily schedule patterns in the classroom, and the use of materials in learning centers or learning packets. Such approaches can produce significant changes in the class situation and thus in the behavior of students.

However, the classroom teacher must assume primary responsibility for discipline and must be able to use various disciplinary approaches with students with disabilities. Two possible strategies are the use of token economies and the use of learning contracts. Another widely used technique is time-out. Time-out means removing the child from the immediate classroom situation on the assumption that the classroom environment is reinforcing negative behavior. Time-out is extremely effective, but it can become controversial when improperly used. Care should be taken to see that teachers are aware of the following caveats:

- The time-out area should always be within sight of the teacher or another person in order to ensure that the child is safe.
- The period of removal should not exceed 5 minutes.
- The time-out area should be safe for the child. In addition, especially with students with disabilities, time-out should not be accompanied by scolding and lecturing; all that is needed is a brief explanation of the violation before being sent to time-out.
- After the time-out, the child should be required to return to the task that was under way at the initiation of the time-out to avoid use of the technique by the child as a means of escape.

Corporal Punishment. Corporal punishment is defined as "any process which intentionally inflicts a physical hurt upon any part of a human body for the purpose of punishment or correction of the person or with the hope of deterring the same person, or others, from committing acts which necessitate his being punished or corrected" (James, 1963, p. 304). In most school settings, the term means the paddling or spanking of students. Many authorities have cited the negative effects of corporal punishment (Erickson, 1978; Marsh et al., 1983; Martin & Pear, 1978; Smith, Polloway, & West, 1979), and some have described its differential use with ethnically and socially diverse groups of students (McFadden, Marsh, Price, & Hwang, 1992). Parental groups often become militant when corporal punishment is employed. Yet it continues to be an accepted strategy in many public schools. Punishment has been criticized for causing psychological harm to children (e.g., Hart, 1987), and some parents have questioned the school's authority to strike children. In districts where community sentiment or school administrators are opposed to the practice, corporal punishment has been banned. But schools have the right to impose such punishment despite objections of parents.

In *Ingraham* v. *Wright* (1977), the U.S. Supreme Court established the right of schools to use corporal punishment, ruling that due process does not require a notice or a hearing prior to imposition of corporal punishment. But in *Garcia* v. *Miera* (1987), a lower court stipulated the right of parents to sue for "grossly excessive" corporal punishment. The acts of expulsion and suspension, if used as punishment, are more difficult to deal with because courts have held that suspension and expulsion interfere with the right of children to an education (e.g., *Stuart* v. *Nappi* [1978]). Thus, in states and districts where it is permitted, a school may impose corporal punishment without complications of due process procedures but may not apply less severe measures without notification procedures.

Corporal punishment has been most controversial because of alleged race and gender bias (Shaw & Braden, 1990), because it has been associated with arbitrary decisions of school personnel, or because it has been administered for insignificant misbehavior (Children's Defense Fund, 1975). Wayson (1985) reported that most instances of school misconduct are really only minor infractions of school rules, which do not constitute serious maladaptive behavior.

Little is known about disciplinary practices with students with disabilities, which is important because many students with disabilities may unwittingly come into conflict with school codes and informal mores because of intellectual and behavioral problems inherent in their disability. McFadden et al. (1992) reported on race bias, gender bias, and bias in punishment of students with disabilities, with the range of punishments that might be administered by the school, and found the following:

1. The most common disciplinary problems of pupils with disabilities were defiance of school authority, bothering others, and fighting.
2. Students with emotional and learning disabilities accounted for most referrals among those with disabilities.
3. The most common disciplinary action for students with disabilities was corporal punishment.
4. For fighting, 56% of those with disabilities received corporal punishment compared to only 36% of those without disabilities.

Although much controversy in public education has surrounded corporal punishment of African-American children, banning this method of punishment would leave minority students and students with disabilities vulnerable to unfair treatment with other methods of punishment. As the proportional enrollment of those with disabilities and minority children is expected to increase significantly over the next 2 decades, schools must develop alternative instructional and disciplinary practices in order for available school time to be used productively in the pursuit of teaching and learning.

The potential for misuse of corporal punishment is magnified in the case of students with disabilities. They may exhibit irritating, abrasive, or socially disruptive behavior and therefore often become the targets for punishment. At the same time, because of their various disabilities, they may become more critically affected by such methods. This raises the issue of the personal liability of the educator who administers corporal punishment. The courts have held educators personally liable for monetary damages if they fail to take into account the student's personal characteristics in determining the appropriateness of corporal punishment. In the case of students with disabilities, administrators must first determine whether the student's misbehavior is a function of the student's disability.

In any event, because parents of students with disabilities are typically sensitive to the treatment received by their children in school, corporal punishment with these students would appear to be a high-risk action. However, if administrative personnel prefer to consider it as a disciplinary option, a detailed policy must be in effect to protect the due process rights of the child. Such a policy should include the following points:

- Corporal punishment should be used only after other alternatives have been tried and proved unsuccessful.
- The teacher should determine that the misbehavior of the student is not a function of a disability. If the behavior and the disability are related, modifications in the IEP or classroom instructional techniques should be explored.
- Before administering corporal punishment, students should be advised of the rule and the infraction for which they are being punished, and they should be allowed to state their own positions.
- The corporal punishment should be administered in the presence of at least one other certified staff member, and not in a spirit of malice or anger.
- The punishment should be reasonable and take into account factors such as the child's age, physical condition, and emotional state.
- A formal record of the punishment—including the infraction, alternatives employed prior to corporal punishment, the nature of the punishment, and the signatures of the administrator, referring teacher, and witness—should be completed and filed in the principal's office.

The frequency with which teachers employ corporal punishment with each student should be charted. In cases of excessive referrals by a teacher, the administrator should intervene and assist the teacher in developing alternative, classroom-based, student-management strategies. If one student is frequently referred, the administrator should explore the possibility of misplacement and reconvene the IEP committee to consider alternatives.

SUSPENSION AND EXPULSION

Suspension is the removal of a student from the school for a period of up to 10 days. Expulsion is a more permanent removal of the student for the remainder of the semester or year. Because most state constitutions guarantee education as a property right, removal of a student from education can be accomplished only after formal due process. Suspension or expulsion is a problematic issue with any student, but it is especially controversial when the student has a disability. Specifically, it is considered an extreme form of discipline that should not be used casually or extensively. In addition, the impact upon the child should be considered, and there should be explicit policies as to its use, especially with students with disabilities.

Some administrators have mistakenly interpreted certain court cases to mean that students with disabilities cannot be suspended or expelled. The ruling in *Doe* v. *Koger* (1979), that P.L. 94-142 did not protect the child from the school's authority to discipline unruly behavior, may have contributed to this interpretation. However, in that case the court also determined that the school could not use expulsion if the cause of the disruptive behavior was the child's disability (Lemley, 1982); this position was upheld by the court in *S-1* v. *Turlington* (1981). In the latter case, the court further held that a trained and knowledgeable group of professionals, not a school official, must make the decision as to whether the child's disability was the cause of the disruptive behavior. Thus, it is clear that a student with a disability can be suspended or expelled only after a hearing and only if the cause of the disruptive behavior is something other than the child's disability. In *Doe* v. *Maher* (1986), the Supreme Court ruled that schools cannot expel students with disabilities while there is an ongoing administrative appeal. This has been referred to as the "stay put" rule (Turnbull, 1993) and is a reversal of previous opinion that indicated that a child with a disability can be suspended if his or her presence poses a danger to himself or herself, to other students, or to the school staff (Cartwright, Cartwright, & Ward, 1989). Pending a hearing, school staff must develop alternative intervention strategies that implement the student's IEP without excluding the student from school.

In-house suspension means that the student is not allowed to participate in all or part of the educational programming scheduled for the day. If the in-house suspension interferes with the delivery of the instruction detailed in the IEP, then, under the governing rules for service to the student, it must be considered a change in educational placement and treated as such. If in-house suspensions last 10 consecutive days, due process procedures must be followed. McFadden et al. (1992) found that in-house suspension was preferred to formal suspension for students without disabilities. The study also found that formal suspension and corporal punishment were used more often for minorities and students with disabilities who exhibited inappropriate behavior.

There would appear to be alternatives to expulsion, including time-out, a behavior modification program, a half-way program, or an after-hours or in-house suspension program. The administrator should note that some of these alternatives require programming changes and, therefore, should involve the IEP committee.

When it is determined that a student should be suspended, formal due process must be followed. At a minimum, due process should include an oral or written notice of the charges, an informal hearing with an explanation of the evidence, and an opportunity for the student to deny the charges and present his or her own version of the case.

Because expulsion involves removing the student from the school for a substantial period of time, more detailed due process procedures must be followed to protect the student's right to an education. In such cases, the following are required:

- A written notice to the parents or guardians.

- A formal hearing before the board of education, at which time the superintendent presents the evidence of the student's wrongdoing and the student (or the student's lawyer or lay counsel) can present evidence of his or her innocence.

- An opportunity for the student to see and challenge all of the evidence presented against him or her.

- An opportunity for members of the board to question all parties.

- A formal, written decision by the board to expel the student, to reinstate the student, or to administer less severe punishment.

CHAPTER SIX

LINGUISTICALLY AND CULTURALLY DIVERSE STUDENTS

* This chapter was written by Dr. James R. Yates, Professor, Department of Educational Administration, and Dr. Alba A. Ortiz, Professor, Department of Special Education, The University of Texas at Austin.

A changing demography is reshaping American education. Projections indicate that by the year 2000, the nation will have 260 million people, and one in every three will be African-American, Hispanic-American, or Asian-American (Allen & Turner, 1990). Population statistics suggest that dramatic changes are also occurring in America's public schools. Thus, educators must be prepared to teach students who are from racially or ethnically diverse groups, who speak a language other than English, and who are less secure financially and physically (Yates & Ortiz, 1991). This chapter begins with an overview of forces that affect both general and special education and then presents information and describes practices to help administrators design special education services appropriate to an increasingly heterogeneous student population. The focus is specifically on services for linguistically different students, who comprise the fastest growing minority population in this country.

ETHNICITY

The number of African-American, Hispanic-American, and Asian-American citizens in the United States is dramatically increasing. Since 1980 the Hispanic-American population has increased by more than 50%. By 1995, more than one third of the youth in this country will be minorities. Birth rates suggest that these demographic trends will continue—the average age of Anglo-American women is 32, of African-American women is 25, and of Hispanic-American women is 22. By the year 2000, the number of minority students whose first language is not English is also projected to increase by approximately one third. Already, almost one in five children between the ages of 5 and 17 lives in a home where English is not the first language. By far, Spanish speakers comprise the largest segment of the language minority population. And of concern is that schools have not been successful in educating these students, as evidenced by high drop-out rates, low academic achievement, and high rates of referral to special education (Ortiz et al., 1985).

That membership in a racial or ethnic minority is often correlated with lack of school achievement (National Assessment of Educational Progress, 1985) should be of interest to educators and policymakers because schools will continue to feel the effects of the changing demography well into the next century (Staff, 1991a). In Texas, for example, the majority of public school students are already minorities, and the majority of kindergarten students are Hispanic-American. For a number of years, all big-city schools have served a "majority minority" student population.

ECONOMIC STATUS

Today, parents, families, and educators advocate more strongly that schools work cooperatively with families and that they involve parents in educational decisions affecting their children (Kagan, 1989). Special education has historically required parent involvement. Unfortunately, the demography of the current and emerging school population is such that children are less likely to live in homes that would facilitate increased cooperation, interaction, and contact on the part of parents. Increased numbers of children today live in single-parent homes headed by a female parent (Archer, 1987). Almost one in five children is born out of wedlock. In some states, such as Texas and New Mexico, approximately one half of pregnant women receive no prenatal health care (*USA Today,* 1991).

Projections indicate that an increasing percentage of children—be they Hispanic-American, African-American, or Anglo-American—will be living below the poverty level (Policy Analysis for California Education, 1989). At least one fourth of America's children live below the federal poverty line. The Center for the Study of Social Policy (cited in Staff, 1991b) indicates that 43.8% of African-American children and 38.2% of Hispanic-American children live in poverty.

Suffice it to say, the concept of the "stay-at-home mother" raising children is a thing of the past. Two thirds of today's 5-year-olds have working mothers (Hodgkinson, 1988). In general, atypical family configurations are negatively associated with school attainment exemplified by standardized tests, grades in schools, promotion to next grade, and graduation rates (Yates, 1987).

OTHER ENVIRONMENTAL FACTORS

The negative behavioral and learning effects on children born to parents who are chemical abusers are becoming increasingly evident (Brooks-Gunn & McCarton, 1991; Kronstadt, 1991; Zuckerman, 1991). The use of crack reached epidemic proportions in the mid-1980s, and children born to pregnant users of crack are now entering schools. In addition, schools will be called upon to serve more students who have experienced the consequences of sexually transmitted diseases, such as HIV infection. Increasingly, children are emerging from environments of physical and sexual abuse, neglect, malnutrition, and homelessness (Vincent, Salisbury, Strain, McCormick, & Tessier, 1990). Although the cumulative effects of these circumstances are not clearly understood within the school environment, there is little reason to believe that children can be prepared to learn if they are hungry, tired, ill, and abused.

IMPLICATIONS FOR SPECIAL EDUCATION

The preceding data suggest that schools (and special education as a subset of the general education system) must accommodate a student body with changing characteristics (Yates, 1988). The current and emerging students are more likely to be minorities, to be poor, and to speak a language other than English. These characteristics have significant implications for special education, given the evidence that teachers reflect an unconscious bias toward students along social class, racial, and gender lines (Brophy & Good, 1974; Gartner, 1986; Shepard, Smith, & Vojir, 1983; Shepard & Smith, 1983; Algozzine, Christenson, & Ysseldyke, 1982; Ysseldyke, Algozzine, Richey, & Graden, 1982). Children who do not have a readily identifiable disability are being considered for special education placement in increasing numbers. In fact, research shows that teacher referrals are often based on such extraneous factors as race, sex, physical appearance, and socioeconomic status as opposed to the need for special services (Bennett & Ragosta, 1984). In the case of limited English proficient (LEP) students placed in programs for students with learning disabilities (Cummins, 1984; Ortiz et al., 1985) and students with speech and language disorders (Ortiz, Garcia, Wheeler, & Maldonado-Colon, 1986), the data gathered as part of the referral and evaluation process and the decisions made using these data suggest that professionals do not adequately understand limited English proficiency, second language acquisition, and cultural and other differences that mediate students' learning.

In addition to evidence that the background characteristics of students influence referral, there is a growing body of literature indicating that many students served in special education experience difficulties that are "pedagogically induced" (Cummins, 1984). According to Hargis (cited in Gickling & Thompson, 1985):

> These children, who are in fact the curriculum casualties or curriculum disabled, would not have acquired their various labels had the curriculum been adjusted to fit their individual needs, rather than having tried to force the children to achieve in the artificial but clerically simpler sequence of grades, calendar and materials that comprise the curricula. (p. 209)

Although there is often a requirement that the individual who initiates the special education referral must substantiate interventions undertaken to improve a student's academic performance prior to referral, this is frequently not done (Gartner, 1986). Gartner concludes that we have the worst of alternatives in place: (1) a process that makes it easy to refer a student, with no procedure to check if the referral is a matter of prejudice against the child or a failure of the school to meet the needs of the child; and (2) a system that provides little incentive for prevention. According to Gartner, this situation is lamentable because most special education students could be better served in a general education system if that system were to provide greater attention to individual needs, adapt learning environments to accommodate diversity, provide training and support to increase the ability of school staff to respond to student diversity, and fund efforts aimed at prevention, rather than allocate resources to costly remedial programs.

Frymier and Gansnedner (1989) report findings from a *Phi Delta Kappan* survey that indicate that troublesome solutions are being proposed in response to the widespread failure of minority students. Teachers and principals oftentimes feel that the most effective approach with at-risk students is to refer them to special education. Almost three fourths of the principals surveyed indicate that they regularly retain students, but barely one fourth consider retention to be effective. Of the teachers in the study, 91% indicate that individualization of instruction is effective, yet only slightly more than three fourths report that they regularly use such techniques. Is the rather dramatic and steady increase in the number of students served in special education (19.2% in the last 10 years [U.S. Department of Education, 1988]) a reflection of these more systemic problems reflected in the attempts by the educational system to adapt and serve appropriately a growing, heterogeneous population? The fact that the majority of students are served in programs for students with learning disabilities (43.6%) or students with speech impairments (25.8%) provides further reason to question whether these students truly have disabilities or whether the system is choosing special education as an alternative to multicultural education.

These issues raise many questions for special educators:

- Why are members of multicultural groups disproportionately represented in special education programs?
- What characteristics of school organization contribute to overrepresentation and underrepresentation of multicultural populations in special education?
- Which perceptions, prejudices, expectations, and biases of school personnel contribute to disproportionate representation?
- What options prior to formal referral to special education are available to culturally and linguistically diverse students who are experiencing difficulty?
- What components of teacher preparation and professional development are needed to ensure appropriate instruction for culturally and linguistically diverse populations?
- What role must school leadership personnel play to ensure appropriate services to culturally and linguistically diverse students?
- What characteristics and/or actions of parents contribute to special education representation?
- How can system efforts be modified to appropriately identify culturally and linguistically diverse students?
- What assessment instruments and procedures are needed to assess and place culturally and linguistically diverse students in special education programs?
- What analysis framework or model should be utilized to interpret a culturally and linguistically diverse student's performance relative to special education eligibility criteria?
- What cultural, social, linguistic, economic, and demographic variables are examined in the assessment process? What weight is given such demographic variables when determining disabling conditions?
- Who is responsible for diagnostic, placement, and instructional procedures? To what extent are bilingual and/or English as a Second Language (ESL) personnel interacting with special education diagnostic and instructional personnel?
- How is language dominance and proficiency determined and how is this information used in the special education placement process?

These questions and others must be addressed to increase both the level and appropriateness of service for culturally and linguistically diverse students with disabilities. The changing demography underscores the critical need to focus attention on special education service delivery for this population of students.

VARIABLES RELATED TO LINGUISTICALLY AND CULTURALLY DIVERSE STUDENTS

The development of appropriate special education services for linguistically and culturally diverse children with disabilities is complicated by various factors:

- *Inadequate assessment procedures.* Assessment instruments and procedures are inadequate for the purpose of identifying disabilities among linguistically and culturally diverse children. This inadequacy is not given sufficient consideration when decisions are being made about special education eligibility and instructional programming.

- *Lack of trained assessment personnel.* There is a lack of skilled personnel who can test children in their native language and who are qualified to interpret performance in light of the linguistic and cultural characteristics. As a result, modifications in assessment procedures (e.g., using an interpreter) can have significant negative effects on the outcome of the assessment and can compromise decisions made on the basis of data obtained under such circumstances.

- *Lack of trained special educators.* Many linguistically and culturally diverse students are not provided an appropriate education because of the lack of trained special education personnel. Of particular concern is the lack of personnel who can provide instruction in the student's native language (Ortiz & Yates, 1981).

- *Gap between knowledge and practice.* Although there is a growing body of research to guide the education of linguistically and culturally diverse children with disabilities, there is a gap between existing knowledge and practices common in today's schools. Fortunately, both federal and state bilingual and special education rules include safeguards against discriminatory practices in the provision of services for language minorities. These provisions, appropriately implemented, can improve the education of children with disabilities from linguistically and culturally diverse backgrounds.

Figure 6.1 suggests a service delivery process for multicultural populations. Recommendations for ensuring nondiscriminatory identification, assessment, placement, and instructional planning are discussed in the following sections.

PREVENTION OF INAPPROPRIATE REFERRALS

Because of the diversity of student backgrounds and the range of abilities typically found in regular classrooms, it is expected that some students will experience academic difficulty. Very few students' problems, however, can be attributed to a disability. National incidence figures indicate that only 10–12% of the student population has disabilities (Kaskowitz, 1977; Ortiz & Yates, 1983). Linguistic, cultural, socioeconomic, and other background differences are not considered disabilities; the special education assessment process must clearly document that a student's learning difficulties are not the result of factors such as limited knowledge of English or lack of opportunities to learn. Consequently, prereferral interventions aimed at identifying the sources of the problem and improving the student's performance in the mainstream should be attempted before referral to special education is considered.

Prereferral strategies acknowledge that students experience academic failure for a variety of reasons other than the presence of a disability. In practice, prereferral intervention generally refers to a teacher's modification of instruction or classroom man-

Figure 6.1   A Special Education Service Delivery System for Linguistically and Culturally Diverse Students

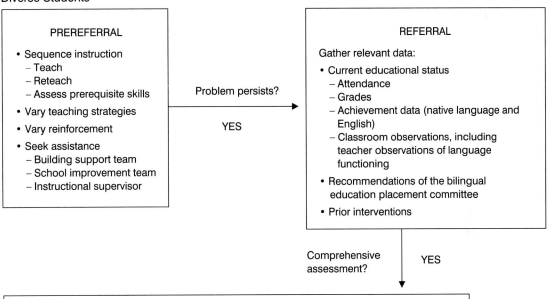

PREREFERRAL

- Sequence instruction
  - Teach
  - Reteach
  - Assess prerequisite skills
- Vary teaching strategies
- Vary reinforcement
- Seek assistance
  - Building support team
  - School improvement team
  - Instructional supervisor

Problem persists?

YES

REFERRAL

Gather relevant data:

- Current educational status
  - Attendance
  - Grades
  - Achievement data (native language and English)
  - Classroom observations, including teacher observations of language functioning
- Recommendations of the bilingual education placement committee
- Prior interventions

Comprehensive assessment?   YES

COMPREHENSIVE ASSESSMENT

Assessment personnel, whether they be bilingual or monolingual, must be trained to assess LEP students.

Eligibility Assessment

- Determine dominant language
- Determine language of assessment
  - If native language dominant, assess in the native language, but consider English language functioning level
  - If English dominant, assess in English but consider native language functioning
  - If no clear dominance can be established, assess in both
- Select assessment battery
  - For both native language and English language assessment
  - Both formal and informal procedures

IEP Assessment

- Determine academic, developmental, or behavioral deficits
- Provide information about strengths and weaknesses
- Identify modification of instructional context, setting, methods, or materials for regular education (including bilingual education and ESL programs) and special education

Assessment adaptations required?

YES

Figure 6.1, *continued*

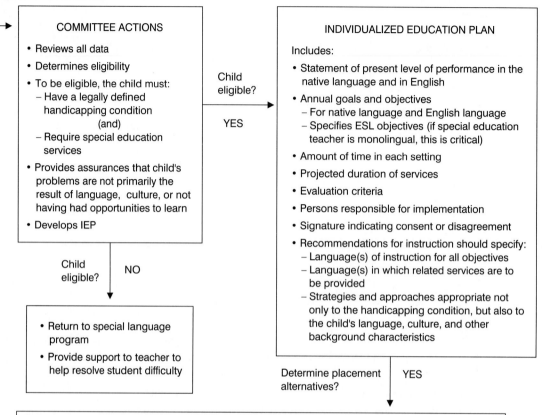

COMMITTEE ACTIONS

- Reviews all data
- Determines eligibility
- To be eligible, the child must:
  - Have a legally defined handicapping condition
                (and)
  - Require special education services
- Provides assurances that child's problems are not primarily the result of language, culture, or not having had opportunities to learn
- Develops IEP

Child eligible?

YES

Child eligible?

NO

- Return to special language program
- Provide support to teacher to help resolve student difficulty

INDIVIDUALIZED EDUCATION PLAN

Includes:

- Statement of present level of performance in the native language and in English
- Annual goals and objectives
  - For native language and English language
  - Specifies ESL objectives (if special education teacher is monolingual, this is critical)
- Amount of time in each setting
- Projected duration of services
- Evaluation criteria
- Persons responsible for implementation
- Signature indicating consent or disagreement
- Recommendations for instruction should specify:
  - Language(s) of instruction for all objectives
  - Language(s) in which related services are to be provided
  - Strategies and approaches appropriate not only to the handicapping condition, but also to the child's language, culture, and other background characteristics

Determine placement alternatives?   YES

ADAPTATIONS

- If no bilingual examiner is available
  - Contract services of bilingual professional
  - Train bilingual education professionals in the district to assist monolingual appraisal staff
  - Train other bilingual professionals in the district to assist with evaluations
  - Train nonprofessionals in the district to serve as interpreters
  - Train community professionals to serve as interpreters
  - Train community nonprofessionals to serve as interpreters
  - In all instances, train monolingual appraisal staff (e.g., training in relation to linguistic, cultural, and other variables that influence student performance)
- Document efforts to obtain trained bilingual evaluators
- Examples of acceptable adaptations for diagnostic* purposes include:
  - Use of local norms
  - Testing of limits to obtain information about student potential (i.e., varying the mode of response, removing time limits, teaching task and then retesting)
  - Use of test normed outside the United States

* *Not to be used for eligibility decisions*

CONDUCT THE ASSESSMENT

DOCUMENTING PROCEDURES AND REPORTING RESULTS

- Record all adaptations
- Describe nature of bilingual evaluations—it is recommended that the child be tested in one language first and then the other
- Do not report scores if norms are not appropriate to the student being tested
- Do not report scores if testing did not follow standardized procedures (e.g., if test is translated from English to other language or if a testing of limits procedure is used)

ADMISSION, REVIEW, AND DISMISSAL COMMITTEE

Must include:

- A representative of
  - Administration
  - Appraisal
  - Instruction
- The child's parent
- The student, if appropriate
- A representative of the bilingual education placement Committee:
  - Should be someone with expertise to help the ARD committee determine the influence of language and other sociocultural variables on performance
  - Cannot be the parent designate unless he or she is the referred student's parent or an employee of the district

SELECT LEAST RESTRICTIVE ENVIRONMENT

- Hospital or treatment center
- Homebound
- Residential
- Special day school
- Full-time special class
- Part-time special class and part-time special language program (i.e., bilingual education or ESL)
- Special language program with resource room services
- Special language program with special education consultation
- Most problems handled in the special language program

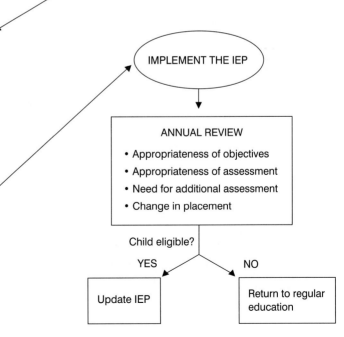

IMPLEMENT THE IEP

ANNUAL REVIEW

- Appropriateness of objectives
- Appropriateness of assessment
- Need for additional assessment
- Change in placement

Child eligible?

YES

NO

Update IEP

Return to regular education

agement, before referral, to better accommodate students who are difficult to teach and who do not have disabilities (Fuchs, Fuchs, Bahr, Fernstrom, & Stecker, 1990). With increasing frequency, prereferral processes are also designed to minimize inappropriate referrals by strengthening the teacher's capacity to intervene with a greater diversity of student background characteristics, for example, differences in language and culture and differences in academic skills, abilities, and interests.

Language and Culture

Each social group holds certain important cultural values and beliefs that children consciously or unconsciously learn (Carter & Segura, 1979). The result of such socialization is the transmission of language and cultural traits that are manifested in particular behavior and distinctive ways of perceiving and organizing the environment (Ramirez & Castaneda, 1974). Often, behavior appropriate to an individual's reference group is interpreted as deviant because it does not conform to the desired or expected behavior of members of the Anglo-American society. This discrepancy may result in the inappropriate referral of bilingual children to special education.

Behaviors directly or indirectly related to language proficiency constitute the most frequent reason for referral of language minority students (Carpenter, 1983; Garcia, 1984; Ortiz & Maldonado-Colon, 1986; Ortiz & Yates, 1983; Shepard & Smith, 1983). This may be because teachers are unaware that many of the behaviors that would be considered indicators of disabilities for Anglo-American students are normal characteristics of students who are in the process of ESL acquisition (Ortiz & Maldonado-Colon, 1986). For instance, behaviors such as limited comprehension and production of English (Dulay, Burt, & Krashen, 1982), errors in pronunciation, syntax, and grammar, and limited receptive and expressive vocabulary characterize second language learners. Yet these same behaviors are listed as problem behaviors on checklists typically used to refer students to special education. Although these checklists are intended to aid in detecting problem behaviors that warrant special education intervention, in actuality, if educators have not been trained to distinguish linguistic and cultural differences from disabilities, they contribute to inappropriate referrals.

Teachers must be trained to incorporate the students' culture and language into the teaching-learning process, to communicate value and respect for the students' own diverse backgrounds, to reinforce the students' cultural identity, and at the same time to teach critical language, academic, and social skills. Educators must go beyond incorporating traditional aspects of the students' culture (e.g., food, music, festivals, and clothing) into the curriculum, acknowledging the contemporary social, political, and economic experiences of multicultural populations. They should also respond to and use cultural referents during instruction, respecting the values and norms of the home culture even as the norms of the majority culture are being taught (Tikunoff, 1985). To accomplish this, curricula and instructional materials should be reviewed to determine whether they present both minority and majority perspectives and contributions and to determine whether they are relevant to the students' language and culture. If student failure can be attributed to the use of inappropriate curricula or to ineffective instructional materials, then referrals to special education are unwarranted. And efforts should focus on modifying or creating more effective instructional programs.

Security and well-being are threatened when children are immersed in an environment in which the language of instruction is one they do not comprehend or speak. Children feel threatened because of an inability to communicate needs, to manipulate new environments, or to understand the expectations held by peers and significant others in the setting. Indeed, before the advent of special language programs such as bilingual education or ESL instruction, LEP students were almost always destined to fail. They were required to meet two expectations simultaneously: (1) to learn English without benefit of an organized, sequenced ESL program; and (2) from the first day of school, to perform tasks in English successfully, although they did not speak the language. In part, this may be why drop-out rates among language minority students are so high. Fortunately, legislation and litigation (PL 90-247, Bilingual Education Act of 1968; *Lau* v. *Nichols,* 1974) have mandated that schools offer programs for LEP students so that they are not excluded from participation in school activities and can learn English effectively.

Instruction should be consistent with what is known about language acquisition and about the interrelationship between first and second language development (Garcia & Ortiz, 1988). The native language provides the foundation for acquiring ESL skills (Cummins, 1984; Krashen, 1982). Educational programs that empower students have strong special language programs (e.g., bilingual education and ESL programs), which promote native language conceptual skills as a basis for English communicative competence and literacy development (Cummins, 1984). In bilingual education, children are provided an opportunity to acquire academic skills in their native language while receiving ESL instruction. Effective implementation of these special language programs is an excellent prereferral strategy. When taught in a language they understand, students experience academic success, thus minimizing the need for referral to special education. Conversely, programs that prematurely shift students into English-only instruction interrupt the natural language development sequence and interfere with intellectual and cognitive development. It is this interference that can lead to academic failure and eventual referral to special education (Cummins, 1984; Ortiz et al., 1985).

Achievement Difficulties

Learning problems occur when students are in classroom environments that do not accommodate their individual differences or learning styles. For example, LEP students who need native language or ESL instruction, but who are taught solely in English without any adaptation of the curricula, can be expected to experience academic difficulties. Other children have achievement difficulties but must be served in the regular classroom because their problems cannot be attributed to disabilities. A student who has not learned to read due to excessive absences, for instance, can overcome this deficit when instruction is individualized or when remediation programs are provided. Children with disabilities, however, have major disorders that interfere with the teaching-learning process. These students require special education instruction to prepare them to be successfully mainstreamed into regular classrooms, as appropriate, and to help them achieve their maximum potential. Failure to distinguish between these types of learning problems can result in the inappropriate referral of language minority students to special education and contributes to the disproportionate representation of these students in special education, particularly in classes for students with learning disabilities (Cummins, 1984; Garcia & Ortiz, 1988; Ortiz & Yates, 1983; Tucker, 1981).

Adelman (1970) suggests that instruction be carefully sequenced as follows:

1. Teach basic skills, subjects, or concepts.
2. Reteach skills or content using significantly different strategies or approaches for the benefit of students who fail to meet expected performance levels after initial instruction.
3. Refocus instruction on the teaching of prerequisite skills for students who continue to experience difficulty even after approaches and materials have been modified.

Documentation of this teaching sequence is very helpful if the child fails to make adequate progress and is subsequently referred to special education; information about strategies that have worked and strategies that have not worked with the student is required background information.

Support Systems for Teachers

When teachers are unable to resolve student difficulties on their own, support systems to assist them in examining the problem and developing other solutions should be available, as should alternatives other than special education referral. Regardless of the specific prereferral approach selected, it is critical that teachers be provided a vehicle for resolving problems at the campus level so that they do not have to experience long delays until external support can be provided (Chalfant, Pysh, & Moultrie, 1979). Chalfant and Pysh (1981) recommend the use of Teacher Assistance Teams (TATs)—committees comprised of regular classroom teachers elected by their peers—to facilitate prereferral problem solving. Members of the support team meet with the referring teacher to discuss presenting problems, to brainstorm possible solutions, and to develop an action plan, which is then implemented by the referring teacher with the support of team members. The team conducts follow-up meetings to evaluate the effectiveness of the proposed interventions and to develop other instructional recommendations if necessary. The end products of the support team are specific recommendations for individualizing instruction for the student, recommendations for informal assessment to be conducted by the child's teacher or by team members, and/or referral for special help, including referral to special education, if appropriate. In most instances, 70–80% of problems considered by these teams can be resolved without special education referral (Chalfant & Pysh, 1989; Ortiz, 1990).

TATs are only one example of how a prereferral process can be implemented on school campuses. Some schools use child-study teams while others have "campus improvement" teams, which are excellent vehicles for helping teachers solve students' learning and behavior problems. The key purpose of prereferral intervention, regardless of how it is put into operation, is to eliminate factors other than possible disabilities as the cause of school problems. This implies that prereferral intervention cycles through an exploration of system, school, program, and teacher variables before attention turns to identifying conditions inherent in the child to explain learning problems.

REFERRAL TO SPECIAL EDUCATION

If mainstream alternatives prove to be of no avail within a reasonable period of time, a referral to special education may be appropriate. As a result of the prereferral process, evidence critical to determining eligibility will already be available, that is, verification that:

1. The school's curriculum is appropriate for linguistically and culturally diverse students.
2. Problems are documented across settings and personnel not only in school but also at home.
3. Difficulties are present both in the native language and in English.
4. The child has been taught but has not made satisfactory progress.
5. The teacher has the qualifications and experience to effectively teach the student.
6. Instruction has been continuous, has been appropriately sequenced, and has included teaching of skills prerequisite to success.

A child who does not learn after this type of systematic, quality intervention is a likely candidate for special education.

Referral information should help educators distinguish linguistic, cultural, and other student differences from disabilities. To this end, data collected must include information about linguistic and sociocultural variables that may affect student progress. For example, referral information should describe the child's language dominance and his or her proficiency in both English and the native language. Such data are critical in determining the language of testing if a comprehensive evaluation is recommended. In addition to information typically provided as part of the referral (e.g., hearing and vision screening and medical history), the following information should be provided for linguistically and culturally diverse students:

1. The student's current educational status, including attendance, grades, achievement data, use of the native and the English language, and the teacher's classroom observations.
2. Results of a home-language survey documenting the extent of use of languages other than English in the home and community context.
3. Documentation of previous educational efforts and strategies provided for the student and the results of these efforts, including participation in or considera-

tion for other special programs (e.g., bilingual education, ESL, or compensatory education) operated by the district.

4. Information reported or provided by parents, including documentation that they have noted similar problems and/or their verification that the presenting problem is atypical of the student's cultural group.

5. The recommendation of the school's bilingual education placement committee for LEP students.

The screening of LEP student referrals should involve personnel who are bilingual and/or have training associated with the education of LEP students or multicultural populations. Ideally, a representative from the bilingual education placement committee would assist in screening—someone who could help interpret student behavior in light of linguistic, cultural, and other background characteristics. Bilingual personnel would also be of great assistance in obtaining information about the child from parents. A bilingual educator can help parents understand the special education process and its implications for their child's education.

Parental Participation

The due process rights of parents must be safeguarded throughout the special education process. Typically shared at the time of referral, the parents' rights document should be available in writing and on cassette tapes in English and/or in the language typically spoken by the parent. If this is not possible for low-incidence languages, school district personnel should ensure that someone proficient in the parents' language can explain the document and the decisions that are being considered that will affect their child's education.

Parental consent forms should include all information relevant to the process, including a description of all evaluation procedures, tests, records, or other reports that the school will utilize as a basis for decision making. Parents must be informed that their consent is voluntary and that it can be withdrawn at any time. In addition, they must be advised that they have the right to bring to meetings and deliberations someone who can serve as their advocate. Districts should routinely ensure that parents have access to such advocates. These advocates should be familiar with special education so that they can assist parents in understanding and interpreting the information presented. Schools should make every effort to include someone on the special education decision-making committee who is fluent in the parents' native language.

School personnel complain that minority parents do not care about, or fail to take an interest in, their children; they also complain that parents do not support schools and teachers. This attitude may actually stem from a conflict between the values and perceptions of school personnel and those of parents. For example, parents from lower socioeconomic status environments may have priorities that supersede their children's education (e.g., meeting immediate needs associated with feeding, clothing, and sheltering their family). Under these circumstances, school conferences may be a luxury that parents can ill afford. In many minority cultures, teachers, like clergy, are professionals to be revered. When this is the case, parents may feel that they will better serve their children by "staying out of the way" so that professionals can do what is best for their children. In such instances, concluding that their behavior signals a lack of interest is an injustice.

In order to empower their students, educators should attempt to actively involve parents and other community members in the schooling process. Collaborative approaches between school and home allow parents to develop a sense of their own effectiveness in relation to their children's education, which, in turn, results in students' increased interest in school learning as well as improvement in behavior.

Comprehensive Individual Assessment

State and federal laws include procedural safeguards to assure that the assessment process is nondiscriminatory for linguistically and culturally diverse populations. These include requirements that assessments be:

- Administered in the child's demonstrated dominant language or other mode of communication unless it is clearly not feasible to do so.
- Validated for the specific purpose for which they are used.
- Administered by appropriately trained, licensed, and certified personnel.

Moreover, legislation mandates that assessments be multifaceted and prohibits making eligibility decisions on the basis of a single measure or criterion.

Beyond the requirements of law, there are a number of significant assessment and program-planning concerns that must be addressed (Ortiz & Yates, 1988). Assessment data used for educational-planning purposes should verify that the child's problems are not directly attributable to a different language, culture, lifestyle, or experiential background. These assessments should include analysis of sociological variables, including factors within the child's family and community environment that may be influencing learning and behavior patterns. These data must be obtained through communication and cooperation with parents. Students are not eligible for special education if the only deficiencies identified are directly attributable to a different language or culture or to not having had opportunities to learn.

When assessing linguistically different students, appraisal personnel should first determine the student's dominant language using formal or informal assessment procedures and information submitted with the referral (e.g., teacher observations of language use in the classroom or results of a home-language survey).

Assessment should be conducted in the student's dominant language; if no clear dominance can be established, it is recommended that instruments be administered in both languages or in the native language of the child's parents. Assessments should also yield data to describe the child's relative language proficiency, that is, a comparison of the level of skill in the native language to the child's English proficiency. Moreover, assessments should focus not only on describing students' conversational skills but also should measure mastery of the more complex, abstract dimensions of language uses that are related to literacy development, including, for example, the child's ability to use language for the purposes of problem solving, evaluating, and inferring (Cummins, 1984). In many instances, students have adequate conversational skills in English but not enough proficiency to understand academic language such as that used by teachers or found in textbooks. It is this lack of academic language proficiency that may lead to academic failure. The assessment should provide information about strengths and weaknesses as well as necessary modifications of instruction relative to the disability and to the student's linguistic and cultural characteristics. Methods and materials for instruction in regular education (i.e., bilingual education or ESL programs) and in special education should also be identified.

Assessment Personnel

Because of the critical shortage of bilingual psychologists and educational diagnosticians, assessment of LEP children continues to be a major problem in today's schools. Districts have the responsibility to document all efforts made to obtain the services of a bilingual professional to conduct native language assessments when such evaluations are required. When no bilingual examiner is available, an interpreter may be used. Figure 6.1 suggested alternatives that can be used in the absence of bilingual evaluators.

Because of the shortage of bilingual appraisal personnel, it is important for special education personnel to collaborate with bilingual educators in order to provide native language assessments and to increase the likelihood of accurate diagnoses. The special education–bilingual education linkage can take a variety of forms. Bilingual educators can provide current language data describing native language and English language skills. They can conduct informal as well as formal assessments to describe students' native language functioning. For example, if they are taught how to conduct curriculum-based assessments, bilingual educators can provide native language achievement data that can then be compared against measures of English language functioning. Bilingual educators, with training related to special education, can also be effective interpreters and assistants in the assessment process.

Adapting Testing Procedures

Because of the lack of standardized instruments normed for minority populations, school psychologists and educational evaluators frequently adapt instruments and procedures when testing linguistically and culturally different students. It is important to alert consumers of assessment data that although these adaptations provide helpful diagnostic data, test scores are invalid because standardized procedures have been violated. This point has to be emphasized because of the importance given to outcomes of standardized testing in making special education eligibility decisions. Given this, all adaptations of testing procedures should be documented in assessment reports, including the nature of bilingual evaluations (e.g., whether the assessment was conducted by a bilingual evaluator versus achieved with the use of an interpreter or whether the assessment involved instruments normed for languages other than English versus items translated on the spot). In addition, test scores should not be reported if standardized procedures are violated or if norms are not appropriate to the student being tested. Instead, patterns of performance should be described.

Special Education Placement Committee

The special education placement committee reviews all data from the comprehensive assessment and establishes eligibility for special education services. The committee ensures that national origin minority group students (or linguistically different students) are not assigned to special education on the basis of criteria that were developed solely based on command of the English language. The committee also ensures that students are not placed in special education if the only deficiencies identified are directly attributable to a different cultural lifestyle or to not having had educational opportunities.

The special education placement committee typically includes at least three members to represent the areas of administration, instruction, and assessment. The committee must involve the student's parent or a designated parental representative and the student where appropriate. In the case of LEP students, a professional representing the bilingual education placement committee or a professional with the expertise to interpret linguistic and sociocultural influences on learning should serve on this committee. These individuals can help analyze performance in the native language and suggest interventions appropriate to the child's background characteristics.

The administrative representative must have the power to provide and/or supervise special education, special language programs, or other related program services. This administrator must have the authority to ensure that the recommendations of the special education placement committee are implemented and that resources and personnel are assigned across programs so that there is a satisfactory commitment to the child's education. An important responsibility of the administrator is to achieve cooperation among instructional personnel in order to integrate resources and services.

THE INDIVIDUALIZED EDUCATION PROGRAM

The IEP delineates priority goals and objectives and provides recommendations for instruction. In addition to the traditional components of an IEP (e.g., annual goals/objectives and specialized instructional methods and materials), several additional components must be addressed for language minority students.

Language of Instruction

The dominant language should be the language of instruction. As a rule of thumb, children whose dominant language is other than English should receive instruction in that other language; children whose dominant language is English should be instructed in English. If no clear dominance can be established, other variables may be taken into consideration, including the child's age, language preference, level of motivation, and previous language experiences, as well as the parents' attitudes. The primary language of instruction, however, should be the language through which the child learns best.

A common misconception is that LEP children with disabilities should receive English-only instruction because they are likely to experience difficulty in mastering language skills. This decision is often rationalized by the belief that it ensures that the child can communicate in the language of this country. The literature in language acquisition and bilingual education, however, does not support such a rationale. Unless children first master their native or primary language, they will have difficulty developing second language skills and will, in all likelihood, experience difficulty in cognitive skill development. Contrary to popular belief, increased exposure to English does not improve or hasten second language acquisition (Krashen, 1982). Consequently, submersion or "sink or swim" programs in which children are placed in the special education classroom with native English speakers, without native language or ESL support, will not be successful.

Language Use Plan

Because students with disabilities are likely to receive services from several instructional or related services personnel, it is important to include a language use plan as part of the IEP. The language use plan essentially describes who will be using which language, for what purpose, and in which skill or subject. For each objective specified in the IEP, a person is designated as responsible for instruction leading to attainment of that objective. For bilingual students, the IEP should specify the language in which instruction or other services will be provided not only by special education and regular classroom teachers but also by speech pathologists, counselors, occupational and physical therapists, and others. Specifying the language of instruction will assure that instruction is consistent with the student's language status.

One of the dilemmas of recommending native language instruction is that there is a lack of bilingual special educators to provide such teaching. Given the shortage of such personnel, it is critical that monolingual special educators recognize that LEP students will not profit from specially designed instruction until they develop adequate English language proficiency. It is, therefore, important that the student's ESL instructional needs be a part of the IEP and that special educators become familiar with the most current practices and research on second language teaching.

Instructional Recommendations

The IEP should include recommendations for teaching strategies, techniques, and materials that are linguistically and culturally relevant and are appropriate to both the child's language status and to the disability. Cummins (1984) cautions against an overreliance on strategies that emphasize direct instruction in English. Strategies that emphasize repetition, drill and practice, and independent seatwork present difficulties for LEP students because activities are frequently stripped of context and therefore lose meaning and purpose. Of particular concern is that language lessons, which emphasize sentence patterns or drills and which focus on linguistic structures, may actually interfere with the second language acquisition process.

Reciprocal interaction teaching models are more effective than transmission models for minority language students with disabilities. Reciprocal interaction teaching is characterized by genuine dialogue between student and teacher, in both oral and written communication, and focuses on development of higher levels of cognitive skills, rather than on basic skills. For example, reading is taught using top-down approaches, which emphasize comprehension, rather than bottom-up approaches, which emphasize word recognition. Literacy skills are taught using approaches such as language experience stories, dialogue journals, shared book experiences, and creative writing tasks, with an emphasis on developing high levels of competence in the native language. Moreover, teachers do not teach language as a subject, but instead, consciously integrate language use and development into all curricular content.

A simple, yet very helpful, suggestion is that districts develop IEP forms for bilingual students. In this way, goals and objectives related to the development of native language skills and the acquisition of English can be incorporated into instructional programs, culturally appropriate materials can be recommended, and procedures for coordinating services can be addressed.

Least Restrictive Environment

Language minority students should have access to the same types of placement options as are provided for monolingual English speakers in special education. This right is frequently misunderstood when placement decisions are made for LEP children. A second misconception is that because the child has a disability and may have difficulty mastering English skills, he or she will be confused by bilingual instruction and should be removed from bilingual education (Ortiz, 1984). Such reasoning ignores the fact that native language proficiency will determine the level of success in acquiring English language skills (Krashen, 1982). Placement in special language programs should be continuous, if appropriate, and teachers should be provided with help in adapting classroom programs to meet the child's special education needs. Figure 6.1 showed the range of possible placement alternatives that should be available to LEP students with disabilities. It is critical that these students be placed in programs or a combination of programs that provide the highest likelihood of success.

A major problem in providing appropriate placements for LEP students with disabilities is the shortage of special education personnel who are bilingual and who have specialized training for serving language minority students. Unless special education programs and instruction are adapted to be consistent with the student's language status, educational prescriptions will fail to yield results; the child will not understand the language of instruction and that instruction may not be relevant to the student's culture or other background characteristics (Wilkinson & Ortiz, 1986). Also, the failure to meet the student's language needs in special education will prevent the LEP child from having the free, appropriate education required by law.

Service Delivery Models

Recently, school districts have begun to explore alternative service delivery models for bilingual students. Such programs are designed to allow the integration of children with disabilities through mainstreaming or placement in either a bilingual education or an ESL program where these students can interact with nondisabled peers (Ambert & Dew, 1982).

The ideal service provider is a bilingual special education teacher or therapist who has training specific to the education of LEP students with disabilities (Ortiz & Yates, 1982). The bilingual special educator can provide dual language (native language and English language) instruction to meet needs associated with the child's language status as well as the disability. A second alternative is the employment of teachers who have dual certification in bilingual education and special education. The disadvantage of this model, though, is that the required knowledge may not be integrated (i.e., the teacher may know how to work with bilingual students and with special education students, but not with bilingual students with disabilities).

LEP students with disabilities can be served by a team consisting of a bilingual educator and a monolingual English-speaking special education teacher who has been trained in ESL instructional strategies. The bilingual education teacher actually takes the lead in instruction because he or she can teach in the child's native language and thus is responsible for services designated in the IEP that are to be provided in the native language. The special educator provides consultation as to how this instruction should be modified to address needs associated with the disability. The special educator provides ESL instruction and is responsible for implementing the IEP objectives to be accomplished in English. The benefit of this model is that children with disabilities have access to personnel trained in the complementary disciplines of bilingual education and special education. These teachers meet to review student progress and revise instructional programs accordingly. Another advantage is that parents have access to someone who speaks their language, and they are, therefore, more likely to be involved in the child's educational program. Even in districts that do not have special language programs, training monolingual special education teachers in ESL instructional strategies is a viable alternative for serving LEP students.

Bilingual paraprofessionals can be teamed with monolingual English-speaking special educators to assist with the implementation of objectives specified in the IEP. The special education teacher provides ESL instruction and instruction in content areas in English. (Caution must be exercised to ensure that the linguistic requirements of academic tasks are consistent with the child's English language development.) The teacher aide provides native language instruction under the supervision of the teacher. This model has the obvious advantage that the child has access to someone who speaks his or her language. If teacher aides are provided with training specific to the responsibilities and tasks they are asked to perform, they are invaluable resources for the monolingual teacher. Without such training, children may essentially be denied appropriate educational opportunities.

In order to provide linguistically and culturally relevant special education services, there must be an interface between bilingual education and special education personnel. Special educators can provide training and assist in adapting aspects of bilingual education or ESL curricula so that LEP children with disabilities can be integrated into these programs. Likewise, bilingual educators and ESL teachers can assist special educators in adapting curricula, instruction, and materials in terms of the child's language, culture, and other background characteristics.

Continued eligibility for special education is determined every 3 years after a comprehensive reevaluation. If the student is eligible, the IEP is revised. An adequate IEP for LEP children cannot be developed without the effective input of the complementary disciplines of special education, bilingual education, and ESL programs.

SCHOOL REFORM INITIATIVES

Today, school reform is the top priority of the general public, the business community, policymakers, and school practitioners. Much of the effort to reform schools has ignored or been ignorant of the implications of these reforms relative to culturally and linguistically diverse students. Even reform efforts within the complementary discipline of special education have often reflected this same lack of sensitivity to the needs of culturally and linguistically diverse students with disabilities.

Inclusion

A progression of conceptual and procedural steps designed to provide a normalized context for the schooling of students with disabilities has developed in recent years. In the late 1960s, integration was the focus of debate, followed in the 1970s by a focus on recommendations for mainstreaming, and in the 1980s by a focus on the Regular Education Initiative. The 1990s reflect a further progression of advocacy for individuals with disabilities to receive services in regular contexts under the nomenclature of full inclusion. Definitions of full inclusion vary (Hollis & Gallegos, 1993), but they generally include the requirement that there is placement only in general education classes for all students with disabilities.

Advocates and opponents of inclusion primarily use philosophical and logical presentations, although there are some studies examining integration (Fuchs, Fuchs, & Fernstrom, 1993). The discussions of full inclusion have resulted in a variety of position statements by various professional and parent organizations (The Association for Persons with Severe Handicaps, 1992; CASE, 1993; Division for Learning Disabilities, 1993; Learning Disabilities Association of America, 1993; National Association of State Boards of Education, 1992). Neither these position statements nor the literature surveyed for this chapter includes any formal or overt mention of the issue of culture or language as a variable associated with the concept of inclusion. This oversight reveals that the educational establishment has not yet become consistently conscious of a dramatically changing demography of school students and the critical nature of language and culture to the educational success of this diverse population.

In order to stimulate thought concerning these matters, the following questions and comments are posed:

1. For purposes of full inclusion, is a bilingual education classroom considered a regular classroom? Bilingual educators would answer in the affirmative. If this is the case, discussions must immediately be expanded in a number of areas. For example, it will be necessary to develop appropriate training of bilingual educators so they can effectively meet the needs of individuals with disabilities. Additionally, the content of training programs for special educators will need to be expanded to include knowl-

edge of second language acquisition and native and second language instruction, including necessary adaptations of this instruction for LEP students with disabilities. If LEP students with disabilities are instructed through ESL programs (i.e., they are not taught by bilingual teachers), then the regular classroom teachers who will be teaching these students will need to develop both ESL and special education competencies.

2.   In inclusive schools and programs, who has administrative responsibility for serving individuals with disabilities who are also culturally and linguistically diverse? The *who* and *how* questions surrounding coordination of services across bilingual education, ESL, and special education—traditionally distinct, parallel administrative units—have yet to be addressed in the inclusion debate. Territorial concerns between special education and regular education increase as bilingual education, ESL, Chapter I, and other support programs are included in the debate.

3.   With inclusion, how are entitlement program funds allocated? What are the necessary procedures for mixing special education, bilingual education, regular education, and other program funds as full inclusion is implemented? Can these cross program allocations occur without changes in law and policy? If mixing occurs, what are the procedures for program cost accountability?

4.   As inclusion is implemented, how are due process and civil rights safeguards provided and assured? There are various federal and state programs designed to address the specific needs of individuals with disabilities, those who are LEP, and others. Each has certain unique features in addition to accompanying governmental rules, regulations, and safeguards. Are the complexities of integrating these separate program rights and responsibilities under conditions of an increasingly diverse clientele going to result in increased litigation that seeks clarification of rights, roles, and responsibilities through the courts?

5.   When special services (special education, ESL, bilingual education, Chapter I, etc.) for several categories of individuals are delivered in the regular classroom, what measures of achievement and accountability will be used? Will common standards of output satisfy all such program accountability requirements?

6.   Under conditions of full inclusion, who is responsible for the instructional adaptations, decisions, development, and implementation required for students with disabilities who are also culturally and linguistically distinct? For example, one of the instructional supports frequently mentioned to accommodate students with disabilities in regular classrooms is to provide additional personnel such as teacher assistants. When an LEP student with disabilities is present in such a classroom, would this assistant need to be bilingual?

7.   Are the public measures of accountability, such as standardized achievement test scores, adjusted for classrooms of full inclusion? If so, for which individual students will these measures be adjusted or adapted, and what levels of adaptations will be deemed acceptable? Will varying weights of adjustments be assigned, and if so, to what types of classroom circumstances? For example, is the standard of accountability adjusted only on the basis of the severity of the disability or also for limited English proficiency? For how long are adjustments available? Are they available until the child achieves academic English language proficiency comparable to Anglo-American

peers? Are such adjustments "attached" to individual students, classrooms, schools, or school districts? The public report card, used nationally and in some state and local communities, would take on a different interpretation under the complex full inclusion of disability, language, and culture. The rather simplistic accountability standard of aggregated achievement test scores would certainly become a more complex task under conditions of inclusion.

8.   Under assumptions of full inclusion, what additional expertise is necessary during placement decision meetings and IEP development for language minority students with disabilities? This issue is seldom considered when determinations are made regarding who should be represented at such meetings. Most typically, the interest is grounded on whether the groups specified by law or policy are represented, such as representatives of administration, instruction, assessment, and parents. Given the complexity of determining appropriate instructional adaptation for language minority students who may also have a disability, the question of importance is the depth of knowledge or expertise the person has, rather than the educational role category the person represents.

9.   For successful inclusion, who is responsible for the professional development activities necessary to serve all students in the regular class setting? The current shortage of specialized personnel would be amplified by the need for expertise and knowledge across the lines of disability, severity, language group, and culture when all students are served in the regular classroom setting.

10.   For full inclusion to succeed, what attitudes and values are necessary? How are values measured to determine readiness of staff for full inclusion? Is there an expanded range of necessary professional values when including culturally and linguistically distinct students who also have disabilities?

11.   Under conditions of full inclusion, what changes in relationships, responsibilities, and procedures are necessary concerning related services or support areas such as speech pathology, counseling, occupational and physical therapy, or school psychology? Although these relationships have always been complex, to expand them to include issues of language and culture surely increases the complexity. For example, because only a small number of trained bilingual speech pathologists or school psychologists are available, most regular educators will not have the benefit of consultation from personnel trained specifically to work with linguistically and culturally diverse learners with disabilities.

12.   With inclusion, what are the preservice and certification changes necessary? Obviously, additional competencies beyond those typically provided in regular and special education preservice and/or certification programs will be required if teachers are to be prepared to effectively serve linguistically and culturally different students with disabilities. How to incorporate even more specialized content is a complicated issue given existing training requirements (e.g., the requirement that students earn a regular education certification as a prerequisite to special education endorsement) and the time it takes to complete a special education training sequence. Inclusion adds yet another dimension to the specialized skills needed by educators who serve multicultural populations who also have special education needs.

Site-Based Decision Making

An emerging school organizational structure associated with decentralized decision making is commonly called site-based decision making. Site-based decision making has its roots in the decentralized management concepts of Japanese manufacturing and can be found in the sociological literature on the advantages of participative management. Increasingly, public schools are considering ways to adapt school organizational structures to fit these decentralized concepts.

The specifics of site-based decision making are varied and almost idiosyncratic to the specific site (Wagstaff & Reyes, 1993). However, some of the common characteristics of this organizational structure have specific implications for services delivered to students with disabilities who are culturally and linguistically different. For example, it is typically advocated that local decision-making groups have the freedom to determine the specific use of financial resources at the local school site. Unfortunately, special population groups often have to fight hard to get entitled program funding because such groups are frequently overlooked or funds are diverted from their needs. One could anticipate that local decision-making groups may be no more, and perhaps less, sensitive than traditional policymakers to the needs of special populations and therefore could make allocation decisions disadvantageous to the typically greater costs associated with serving these students (Tsang & Levin, 1983). Additionally, some states, by policy, have exempted bilingual education and special education from accountability for local site management and de-emphasized the categorical restrictions on the use of special population funding (Carmichael, Dyer, & Blakely, 1992).

Another concern of special population funding is the suggestion that local efforts be rewarded or punished based on changes in student achievement as measured typically by standardized testing. If there is a loss of funds or other sanctions based on insufficient achievement, special population students may be blamed. In fact, such students, depending on how standardized test scores are aggregated and used, may reduce the aggregated average achievement. The concern is that local decision-making councils, under these conditions, may seek ways to exclude special population students from either services or resources.

Lack of representation on decision-making councils has historically been one of the concerns of special education and was a large incentive for much of the litigation and legislation supportive of the need to include special population parents and students in educational decisions. Special education and bilingual education administrators are all too familiar with the intense efforts often needed to bring the special needs of students to the conscious recognition of local leadership.

It has been general practice to bring in the special education or bilingual education expert when the local campus has a special population problem. If such expertise associated with special populations is not included on local decision-making teams, there may be at best an oversight of the needs of special population students. For example, out of a lack of knowledge, local decision makers may restrict the amount and level of expertise that is brought to the campus and thereby restrain the quality of decisions concerning special population students. As a result, without outside expertise, the complex curricular and instructional needs of special population students may not be recognized by the local site-based teams. There is already evidence that this is the case. A national study of site-based decision making by Wagstaff and Reyes (1993) found that special population professionals or parents were rarely represented on the local decision-making teams.

National Educational Goals

A cornerstone of the educational reform movement has been the emphasis on determining, and insisting on, a set of national standards of educational performance. Although there is little resistance to an articulation of appropriate national educational achievement goals, a clear danger exists that such goals may be insensitive to the needs of special population students. For example, an examination of the work of the National Education Goals Panel (1992) and the literature that the work of this panel has spawned (Young, 1993; Riley, 1993) does not suggest any specific recognition or concern for special population students. Each of these national goals has implications for special population students:

1. *All American children will start school ready to learn.* If this goal includes the recognition that many special population students will have needs that require schooling earlier than the traditional 5 to 6 years of age and that readiness to learn is a varying developmental phenomenon, perhaps this goal is without bias toward special population students. There is, however, increasing concern that early intervention may actually hamper the normal linguistic, intellectual, and cognitive development of LEP students, and especially LEP students with disabilities. For example, there is a critical shortage of bilingual educators and bilingual special educators; this shortage is greatest in the early childhood arena. Of specific concern is the question of what happens to very young children for whom the native language acquisition process is interrupted because they are instructed by teachers who neither speak the student's language nor have ESL expertise. It is also difficult to ascertain how parents who do not speak English can be trained to be effectively involved in their children's development if early childhood professionals responsible for working with such parents speak only English. Without personnel who can serve linguistically diverse children in early childhood programs, it will be very difficult for these children to reach school ready to learn.

2. *At least 90% of our students will graduate from high school.* If this goal is not equating the traditional high school diploma as the standard of graduation, this could be a powerful goal for special population students. In reality, there is controversy over special diplomas and boards of education making a variety of decisions related to graduation requirements and processes. Unfortunately, some of these decisions exclude students with disabilities and primary languages other than English.

3. *Our students will demonstrate competency in challenging subject matter and will learn to use their minds well, so they may be prepared for responsible citizenship, further learning, and productive employment.* If this goal reflects the need to expose all students to enriched learning opportunities that transcend basic skills and drill and practice, special population students could benefit substantially from

this national goal. Often students with disabilities and/or LEP are thought to be best served by a curriculum of basic skills to the exclusion of enriched curriculum and learning opportunities.

4.   *American students will be first in the world in science and mathematics achievement.* This goal for some implies a special allocation of resources to gifted and talented students. Other special population students have a clear need to develop competence in math and science if they are to function independently in the emerging high-tech society. Such students are sadly at risk of being forgotten in the program development activities associated with this national goal. Additionally, any discussion of math and science curriculum needs to include the curriculum and instructional needs of special population students in these content areas. For example, there was one innovative effort to place on CD ROM a specially designed earth science curriculum for seventh-grade level science students. But when asked how students with disabilities or LEP would access the program, the developers indicated that such students had not been a part of the thinking or planning when the program was developed.

5.   *Every adult will be literate and have the knowledge and skills necessary to compete in a world economy and exercise the rights and responsibilities of citizenship.* Participants in the national debate concerning this goal need to recognize that worthy individuals exist who may not be literate and that the value of competition may not be appropriate to all cultural groups. For example, some cultures place greater value on cooperative production than on competition.

6.   *Every school will be safe and drug-free and offer a disciplined environment conducive to learning.* If this goal is to be met, substantial effort must be given to appropriate programming for students with behavioral disorders and drug-induced behaviors. Unfortunately, much of the discussion concerning this goal is related to "zero tolerance" programs, alternative school placements, increased police presence, and so forth. To date there has been little discussion of developing programs that may prove successful in treating such antisocial behavior.

Suffice it to say, educational and societal reforms must be considered carefully for their impact upon special population students and communities. The historical tendency for such reform to ignore or be insensitive to the educational needs of such individuals reinforces the fact that special populations must be active, alert participants in these reform debates to assure appropriate futures for special population students.

Given the dramatic increase in students that are different across a range of demographic variables, it is no longer either appropriate or acceptable for schools to continue to search for the blame or cause of lack of student achievement within the characteristics of the students. It is appropriate and essential for schools today to begin to ask, "How can we serve students that arrive with characteristics that have historically been consistently correlated with poor academic performance?" Regular and special education administrators must examine their schools' policies and procedures for those areas that are discrepant with the realities, including the family-life circumstances, of the student population. Educational administrators, teachers, and special service personnel must begin to examine whether their knowledge and procedures of practice are appropriate for the types of students and the needs that such students bring to the educational context. Teacher preparation programs and other professional training must begin to examine whether preparation procedures supply educational professionals with the knowledge and skills required to be effective with the existent and clearly emerging heterogeneous student population. Researchers must begin to probe deeply into those areas that hold promise for allowing the educational professional and educational organizations to serve a heterogeneous student population appropriately and effectively.

IMPARTIAL
HEARINGS AND
LITIGATION

The Individuals with Disabilities Education Act (IDEA), Section 504 of the Rehabilitation Act of 1973, the Americans with Disabilities Act (ADA), and other legislation have significantly improved educational services for children with disabilities. Before this legislation was passed, a great deal of litigation was required to help alter the dearth of services provided for this group by public schools (T. E. C. Smith, 1990; Smith, Finn, & Dowdy, 1993). Often, prior to the implementation of PL 94-142 in 1978, schools refused educational programs for children with disabilities, and parents were without recourse. Laws and litigation helped change these practices; however, the passage of federal and state laws has not guaranteed appropriate services. Often schools and parents do not agree on what an appropriate educational intervention includes (Smith, Price, & Marsh 1986; Turnbull, 1993), and there are still situations where schools simply do not provide appropriate programs for all their students.

Disagreements between parents and the school about the needs of a child with a disability can result in due process hearings or litigation. For example, the parents of a child with visual disabilities may want a local school to provide an educational program, but the school may want the child enrolled in the state's residential school for children who are blind. In another example, parents and school officials may disagree over which of the three primary curricular tracks (academic, vocational, or general) to use with their child (Polloway, Patton, Epstein, & Smith, 1989). The parents may want the school to use a study-skills approach and the school may want to use a more traditional method (Smith & Dowdy, 1989). When such disagreements occur, both the school and the parents have the right, provided by IDEA, to request a due process hearing and, failing satisfaction, to seek judicial relief in state and federal courts (Goldberg & Kuriloff, 1991). Although not required by law, many states require a mediation effort before parents can request a due process hearing, the advantage being that mediation generally finds both parties to be less adversarial and more willing to arrive at a compromise (Dobbs, Primm, & Primm, 1991).

DUE PROCESS HEARINGS

When Congress passed PL 94-142, it required states to provide opportunities for parents and schools to seek administrative relief from special education disputes (Goldberg & Kuriloff, 1991). The purpose of due process hearings is to provide school officials and parents the opportunity to present their views concerning the education of a child and to have an impartial hearing officer make a decision based on the evidence and testimony presented (Smith et al., 1986; Turnbull, 1993). Regulations implementing IDEA state that a parent or school may request a hearing when there is a disagreement concerning the identification, evaluation, or educational placement of a child or the provision of a free appropriate public education (Sec. 121a.506). According to Boscardin (1987, p. 391), "the due process provisions within the original Public Law 94-142 are designed to protect the right of handicapped children and their parents."

Fewer than 1% of eligible students and parents have requested due process hearings (Florian & West, 1989). In the only national study about hearings, Smith (1981) reported that a total of 3,691 hearings had been reported in 38 states. Hearings were requested most often for children with mental retardation, followed by children with learning disabilities and children with emotional disturbance. The majority of hearings were requested by parents, a finding consistent with later findings (Special education, the attorney fees provision of PL 99-372, 1989; Wood & Carros, 1988). Decisions were issued in favor of the parents in fewer than 40% of the cases. Table 7-1 presents a summary of the data on these issues.

These data, and other evidence, suggest that schools have the advantage in due process hearings (Dobbs et al., 1991; Goldberg, & Kuriloff, 1991; Special education, the attorney, 1989).

Table 7-2 summarizes data about the different perceptions of hearing fairness. It appears that parents also feel that hearings favor schools—88% of school officials viewed hearings as fair compared with only 41% of parents. Factors that might create an advantage for schools include "availability of legal services; experiences in due process proceedings; availability of experts such as special education teachers, examiners, and supervisors; and better financial resources" (Smith 1981, p. 235). Regardless of this apparent advantage, IDEA has provided parents with the right to present grievances and to have an impartial hearing officer determine a solution to the impasse, a right that was not always available to parents before passage of the act.

Legal Requirements

Impartiality of Hearing Officers.   To assure the objectivity of hearings, due process hearings must be conducted by an impartial hearing officer. Rather than specify the qualifications of hearing officers, the regulations exclude individuals who would have conflicting interests in the hearings. Section 121a.507 states that hearings may not be conducted (1) by a person who is an employee of a public agency that is involved in the education or care of the child or (2) by any person having a personal or professional interest that would conflict with that person's objectivity in the hearing (Turn-

Table 7-1   Issues and Decisions in Due Process Hearings Concerning Children with Disabilities

Issue	Hearings	Decision in Favor of Parent	Decision in Favor of School
Requested by parents:			
Referral	5	3	2
Evaluation	57	24	33
Placement	1760	649	1111
Other	109	43	66
Requested by school:			
Referral	1	0	1
Evaluation	15	1.5	13.5
Placement	37	15	22
Other	21	5	16

From "Status of Due Process Hearings" by T. E. C. Smith, 1981, *Exceptional Children, 48,* p. 235. Copyright 1981 by The Council for Exceptional Children. Reprinted by permission.

Table 7-2 Distribution and Relative Disparity of Parents' and School Officials' Perceptions of the Special Education Hearing

Interview Questionnaire Variable	n	Perception (% Response)			Significance and Trends of Disparate Perception[a]
		Positive	Neutral	Negative	
Opportunity to present their position					
Parents	36	58.3	16.7	25.0	n.s.
School officials	43	83.7	16.3	0.0	
Legal rights accorded to them					
Parents	37	51.4	24.3	24.3	Officials more positive***
School officials	43	95.4	4.6	0.0	
Fairness accorded to them					
Parents	37	40.5	24.3	35.2	Officials more positive***
School officials	40	87.5	7.5	5.0	Parents more negative*
Adequacy of hearing officer's explanations					
Parents	37	59.5	21.6	18.9	n.s.
School officials	42	81.0	11.9	7.1	
Accuracy of hearing officer's decision					
Parents	36	36.1	19.4	44.5	Officials more positive***
School officials	41	80.4	9.8	9.8	Parents more negative**
Satisfaction with hearing officer's decision					
Parents	36	33.3	8.3	58.4	Officials more positive**
School officials	43	72.1	16.3	11.6	Parents more negative***
Overall satisfaction with hearing					
Parents	37	35.1	10.8	54.1	Officials more positive*
School officials	43	69.8	20.9	9.3	Parents more negative***
Current response to hearing experience					
Parents	36	11.1	22.2	66.7	Officials more positive**
School officials	40	47.5	20.0	35.5	Parents more negative*

Note: The sum of percentages across each row for parent and school officials perceptions, respectively, is 100%.

[a] Tests for significant disparity between parent and school official perceptions are based on the standard error of proportional differences (Ferguson & Takane, 1988) corrected for simultaneous statistical contrasts across 8 questionnaire variables by the Bonferroni method (Miller, 1966).

* $p<.05$. ** $p<.01$. *** $p<.001$.

From "Evaluating the Fairness of Special Education Hearings" by S. S. Goldberg and P. J. Kuriloff, 1991, *Exceptional Children, 57,* p. 551. Reprinted by permission.

bull, 1993). In some states, hearing officers are appointed by state education agencies; in others, local education agencies make the appointments (Turnbull, Strickland, & Turnbull, 1981). In one court case, *Mayson* v. *Teague* (1984), the Eleventh U.S. Circuit Court of Appeals ruled that public education personnel could not be appointed as hearing officers (Wood & Carros, 1988). Probably the least biased method of assignment of hearing officers would be to select hearing officers on a random basis, with the opportunity for disqualification in case of a conflict of interest.

Meeting the two exclusionary requirements detailed in the regulations provides only minimum safeguards concerning the impartiality of hearing officers. In addition, Turnbull et al. (1981) suggest (1) that more than one hearing officer be appointed for each case to avoid scheduling conflicts; (2) that race and sex be considered in selecting the hearing officer pool; (3) that there be no previous employment record between the school and hearing officer; and (4) that parents not be hearing officers. Although these suggestions concern hearing officers appointed by local education agencies, in states where state education agencies make the appointments, similar requirements should be considered (Smith et al., 1986).

Qualifications of Hearing Officers.   Although the regulations make provisions for excluding persons as hearing officers, there is no mention of specific requirements or qualifications *for* hearing officers. The regulations only exclude persons who might be biased in favor of either party (Turnbull, 1993). As a result, hearing officers come from varied backgrounds and receive different types of training in the various states. Not surprisingly, the majority of hearing officers are attorneys. Individuals from this profession at least have knowledge about law and proceedings in an administrative appeals process. The most common form of training for hearing officers is seminars, with periodic in-service sessions, conducted most often by the State Education Agency. In the past, training was provided by the National Association of State Directors of Special Education, regional resource centers, local education agencies, and universities.

Rights of Parents and Schools.   Both parents and schools have certain legal rights in due process hearings:

- To be accompanied and advised by counsel and by individuals with special knowledge or training with respect to the problems of children with disabilities.
- To present evidence and confront, cross-examine, and compel the attendance of witnesses.
- To prohibit the introduction of any evidence at the hearing that has not been disclosed at least 5 days before the hearing.
- To obtain a written or electronic verbatim record of the hearing.
- To obtain written findings of fact and decisions (Goldberg & Kuriloff, 1991; PL 94-142, Sec. 121a.508).

In addition, parents have the right to declare the hearing open or closed and the right to have the child present at the hearing. It is the hearing officer's responsibility to ensure that all rights are respected. The hearing officer may delay the hearing if it is determined that any rights have been denied and that such denial would affect the outcome of the hearing.

The Hearing Process

Request for Hearings.   The due process hearing is a relatively simple process that is initiated when either party, the parents of a child with a disability or the local school district, requests a hearing. Specific policies for requesting a hearing vary from state to state, but they usually require nothing more than a simple written request submitted to the local education agency, the county superintendent's office, or the state education agency. Once a hearing has been requested, the hearing must take place unless the requesting party withdraws the request. There is no procedure for denying a hearing to parents or school personnel. In states that require a mediation effort, a meeting is scheduled at this time.

Format of Hearings.   Federal guidelines do not dictate the format for hearings. Therefore, administrators must determine the general format for hearings in their particular states. Most states require the following stages:

1. Call to order.
2. Opening statement by the hearing officer.
3. Opening statement by both parties.
4. Presentation of evidence and testimony by both parties.
5. Summary statement by both parties.
6. Closing statement by the hearing officer.

Witnesses are asked questions by one party and then cross-examined by the opposing party.

Role of the Hearing Officer.   The duties of the hearing officer begin before the due process hearing is held and end only after a decision has been rendered. The hearing officer's role encompasses three phases: preparation for the hearing, conducting the hearing, and rendering the decision.

Prior to the hearing, the hearing officer confers with all parties to ensure that the hearing has been scheduled at a time and place convenient for the parties and that both parties are aware of their rights during the hearing process. The hearing officer determines if witnesses for both parties have been notified and are expected to attend the proceedings. A verbatim record of the hearing is required, and the hearing officer must confirm that provisions have been made for such a recording. However, the hearing officer may expect the school district to handle the actual arrangements for obtaining the transcript. State guidelines should indicate whether an electronic (taped) recording or a transcript by a court reporter is preferred. Finally, the hearing officer brings a complete set of documents to the hearing necessary for use during the hearing, including a copy of the request for the hearing and an outline of its format.

During the hearing, the main function of the hearing officer is to guarantee that all necessary testimony and evidence are entered into the record. Because the decision can be based only on the information entered into the record, this function is extremely important. The hearing officer ensures that both parties to the hearing have a fair opportunity to present testimony and evidence and to cross-examine witnesses for the opposing side. The fairness and orderliness of the hearing is strictly within the control of the hearing officer. If one party, for example, has an attorney who attempts to dominate the proceedings, it is the hearing officer's responsibility to intervene. Hearing officers may also question witnesses. If, for example, certain information is not clear, the hearing officer should ask questions to clarify the issues. Although the format closely resembles that for court proceedings, hearings are not trials and, therefore, are more informal and open. As long as they are well organized and properly conducted, they should provide the maximum opportunity for necessary information to be presented by both parties.

Following the hearing, hearing officers must review all testimony and evidence and make a judgment to resolve the dispute between the parents and the school. Hearing officers must try to consider all pertinent information as it was entered into the record and then make a decision based on federal and state guidelines, accepted special education methods, and valid assessment techniques. Ultimately the hearing officer must prepare a written decision that includes the following elements: (1) personal identifiable information, (2) the issue and purpose of the hearing, (3) a finding of fact (summary of relevant evidence), (4) the decision and its rationale, and (5) the steps required for appeal.

The decision should be clear and concise and written in a way that is understandable by both parties. Although school officials or parents may not agree with the decision, they should realize that the hearing officer has tried to render an unbiased, reasonable, and appropriate judgment about what is appropriate for the child (Smith et al., 1986). And, both parties must adhere to the decision or appeal the decision to state or federal court.

How to Avoid Hearings

Due process hearings can be "difficult, emotionally draining experiences that can lead to early 'burn out' for school personnel" (Edmister & Ekstrand, 1987, p. 7). Regardless of who wins the decision, the aftermath can be very trying for everyone involved. Unfortunately, hearings often result in an adversarial relationship between school personnel and parents (Dobbs et al., 1991). However, win or lose, parents and schools must work together following the proceedings to try to provide appropriate educational programs for children. Therefore, the best approach, in most situations, is to avoid hearings to begin with.

Although there is no guarantee that schools will be successful in avoiding hearings, there are several steps that can be taken to help defuse potential hearing situations. Table 7-3 summarizes these steps.

Mediation.   Although not required by IDEA, mediation is recommended as a step to reduce conflicts between parents and schools over special education issues. Mediation can be defined as a structured informal process coordinated by a third party that attempts to resolve differences (Dobbs et al., 1991). It is less formal than a due process hearing but more formal than a routine school conference. In order for mediation to have a chance for success, the mediator must have certain competencies. The mediator must (Ekstrand & Edmister, 1984):

- Know the facts.
- Know the issues.
- Know the positions of the parties.
- Have alternatives for resolution.

Table 7-3   Summary of Steps to Avoid Hearings

Step	Description
Focus on the Child	• Attempt to provide appropriate services to all children with disabilities. • Focus on what is best for the child.
Involve Parents	• Go beyond minimal legal mandates to involve parents. • Have a positive attitude toward parental involvement. • Solicit as much parental input as possible.
Utilize Nondiscrimination Assessment	• Ensure that all legal steps aimed at nondiscriminatory assessment are utilized. • Utilize subject judgments when working with a child from a minority culture.
Document Everything	• Document all encounters and interactions with family members. • Send all correspondence by registered or certified mail. • Keep a written record of phone conversations and face-to-face encounters.
Request Mediation	• Even in states where a mediation step is not mandated, attempt to mediate. • Bring in a third party to mediate.

From "Special Education Hearings: How to Do Them Correctly" by T. E. C. Smith and R. S. Podemski, 1981, *Executive Educator, 3,* p. 22.

- Assure that the parties know the ground rules.
- Eliminate adversarial conduct.

Issues Related to Hearings

Preparing for a Hearing. The person responsible for preparing and presenting the school's case varies from district to district. However, regardless of whether this individual is the principal, the director of special education, the school counselor, or some other school employee, he or she should take the following steps (Edmister & Ekstrand, 1987):

- Select appropriate documents.
- Choose and prepare witnesses.
- Become knowledgeable about the facts of the case.
- Conduct the prehearing briefing.

Table 7-4 presents a checklist that can help school districts prepare for a due process hearing. Although there is no way to guarantee a successful outcome for a hearing, following these steps can aid in preparing the basis for one.

During the Hearing. During the hearing, the attorney or designated school representative, who is trained in the hearing process or who has had experience in hearings, should present the school's case. Although hearings are frequently adversarial, they do not have to be. It is possible that both parties will enter into a process that results in good decisions for the child and resolves issues without the hearing officer having to render a decision. By avoiding an adversarial relationship, both parties can benefit.

Smith and Podemski (1981) suggest that during the hearing, close attention be paid to testimony presented by witnesses. This close scrutiny is important for effective cross-examination and as a guide to determine if it will be necessary to recall witnesses or to rebut previous testimony. Recall of witnesses should be done only if major points need to be strengthened or refuted. A recall of witnesses only to emphasize minor points is not likely to affect the decision of the hearing officer.

Witnesses should be instructed prior to the hearing regarding the following (Edmister & Ekstrand, 1987):

1. Maintain professionalism at all times. Hearings are serious business; a level of formality should be kept.
2. Avoid talking except when testifying. Information may be conveyed to the case presenter by note.
3. Avoid giving information either orally or by note to a witness while that person is testifying.
4. Take notes that may aid the case presenter or attorney with direct examination or cross-examination.
5. Avoid conversing with the hearing officer and discussing hearing issues with the opposing party during breaks.

Table 7-4   Checklist to Prepare for a Due Process Hearing

- Has an attorney been retained?
- Does the attorney have knowledge concerning special education legislation and litigation?
- Has the attorney been involved in due process hearings?
- Has the attorney been briefed on the current case?
- Have the key issues in the case been determined?
- Is there an adequate defense for the school's position?
- Have potential witnesses been identified?
- Has the attorney been involved in prehearing discussions concerning the case?
- Has the attorney been provided with all documentation concerning the case?
- Have all due process safeguards been afforded the child and parents?
- Does the school have documentation on all parental involvement?
- Has the attorney had the opportunity to meet with all of the school's witnesses?
- Has the attorney rehearsed questions with witnesses?
- Has the parents' case been anticipated?
- Are rebuttal points available to the parents' case?
- Is the hearing scheduled for a time and place convenient to the parents?
- Have arrangements been made (either by the school or state department of education) for a transcript of the hearing?
- Have copies of the written evidence to be presented been made available to the parents at least five days prior to the hearing?
- Have all reasonable attempts been made to resolve the issues prior to the hearing?
- Has the case been adequately staffed to ensure optimum preparation of the case?

6. Maintain composure if witnesses are sworn (placed under oath); remember that a hearing is a legal process.
7. Stop testifying and wait until the question is resolved if there is an objection by either side. (p. 9)

Follow-up to the Hearing.   When the hearing is completed, the school should consider the following actions (Smith & Podemski, 1981):

1. Review the hearing and determine if the school's case could have been presented in a better manner.
2. If the decision is in favor of the parents, carefully review the transcript and the decision of the hearing officer to determine if an appeal is appropriate; the appeal of a decision without adequate grounds is a fruitless, time-consuming process for all parties.

3. Immediately implement the decision of the hearing officer. This will show good faith on the part of the school and may help to mend relations with the parents. Attempts to reduce residual conflict will help in future dealings with the parents.

Roles of School Personnel

Teachers.   Because due process hearings attempt to resolve issues between the school and the parents of children with disabilities, the teachers who have direct contact with the child in question are likely to be called upon to provide testimony and/or written evidence either for the school or for the parents. Thus, these teachers (both special education and regular classroom) should assist the school administrators as the school prepares for the hearing, be available to provide testimony, and above all, present testimony accurately. In preparation for the hearing, the teachers involved should meet with key school personnel, including the attorney or other individual who will represent the school, to discuss possible testimony (Edmister & Ekstrand, 1987). In order to be well prepared for the hearing, potential witnesses should rehearse all possible questions and answers, including those that may be posed by the parents' representative. Teachers called upon to testify in a due process hearing should be prepared to respond by (Edmister & Ekstrand, 1987):

1. Giving honest, succinct, and sufficient answers to questions without volunteering tangential or irrelevant information.
2. Deferring to another witness if appropriate (e.g., an administrator deferring to a direct service provider).
3. Taking time to reflect before answering.
4. Not being defensive.
5. Saying "I don't know" if that is the case.
6. Asking clarifying questions. (p. 10)

Special Education Administrators.   With their knowledge of special education programs, practices, budgets, and local policies, special education administrators are likely candidates to organize the school's case. In this task, they should work closely with the school's attorney or representative to prepare the best case possible. In particular, they should:

- Present their opinion concerning the disagreement.
- Determine whether to enter into a due process hearing or to acquiesce to the desires of the parents.
- Provide a rationale for supporting the school's case.
- Identify the school personnel who should provide testimony.
- Present necessary written evidence.
- Interpret state and federal regulations and guidelines that support the school's case.
- Determine the logistical procedures to be followed in setting up and conducting the hearing.

Following the planning stage, special education administrators should ensure that all necessary records are available to the parents as well as other school representatives. Evidence that is to be presented must be exchanged with the parents at least 5 days prior to the hearing, and administrators should make sure that this requirement is met. They should also make sure that all relevant school personnel attend the hearing. This may include planning for substitutes if the hearing is held during school hours.

During the hearing, special education administrators should monitor the progress of the hearing and remind the school's representative to bring up points that may not have been anticipated. To counter unexpected evidence, the school's case may need to be altered. Because of their knowledge of special education programming, administrators of special education are in a good position to advise the school representative.

Following the hearing, special education administrators must ensure that the decision of the hearing officer is implemented. If an appeal is planned, the administrators should provide input as to whether it is warranted, and if it is, the grounds on which is should be made. Regardless of the hearing outcome, whether in favor of the school or the parents, special education administrators are in a good position to work with the parents to resolve any remaining conflicts and to reestablish rapport between the school and the parents.

Principals and Superintendents.   The principal and the superintendent are responsible for assuming leadership roles in the preparation for, conduct of, and follow-up to a hearing. In these tasks, they must be available for planning, be present at the hearing in case their testimony is required, present accurate testimony if called upon, ensure that required school personnel are in attendance at the hearing, and be responsible for securing information necessary for the presentation of the case. Although many of these responsibilities may be delegated to other individuals, such as the special education administrator, the ultimate responsibility for these aspects of the hearing rests with the principal and superintendent.

A further major role of the principal and superintendent in a due process hearing is to carry out the decision of the hearing officer. This should be done in a manner that facilitates the working relationships between the school, the parents of the child involved in the hearing, and the parents of other children with disabilities. The attitudes of school administrators before, during, and after a due process hearing may be an important factor influencing the need and desire of other parents to follow the hearing route.

State-Level Appeal

If the due process hearing is conducted by an agency other than the state education agency, many states allow either party to appeal the decision to the state education agency for an administrative review before initiating civil litigation. In states that have the original hearing at the state level, administrative review is not available to the aggrieved party following the initial due process hearing. In those states where state-level reviews are available, PL 94-142 requires that the reviewing official (1) examine the hearing record; (2) confirm that appropriate procedures were followed at the hearing; (3) seek additional evidence as necessary; (4) afford both parties the opportunity to present additional evidence and/or testimony, if the reviewing officer deems such actions necessary; (5) make a decision independent of the hearing officer's decision; and (6) give copies of the decision to both parties (Sec. 121a.510).

Federal regulations do not specify who is to conduct the state education agency review. Some states specify that the reviewing official must be the state superintendent of public instruction or designee. Other states require that the reviewing officer be an impartial hearing officer. Regardless of the reviewing official, state-level reviews provide an opportunity for both parties of the hearing to appeal the decision without entering into formal litigation.

School administrators in states that provide for state-level reviews should be prepared to take advantage of the process in the case of an adverse local hearing decision. Because the review process requires little time and expense on the part of the school, it should be pursued if there appears to be a chance that the hearing decision will be reversed. However, administrators should not request such a review in an attempt to delay the implementation of the hearing officer's decision; such an attempt would be futile because the decision of the hearing officer must be implemented even during an appeal process. Requests for review should not be made unless the school determines that there is a strong chance of reversing the original decision. To appeal on any other grounds is simply to burden the administrative review process.

Examples of Due Process Hearings

The following two case studies are examples of actual due process hearings. In each case, the facts related were taken from the hearing transcripts.

Case 1—Issue: Placement.   In this case, the Alpha School District sought to change the educational placement of John Jones. The proposed placement was to be a self-contained classroom at the Alpha Junior High School. The parents of John wanted to continue the child's placement in a day service center, where he had been for the past year. John, age 14, was evaluated as having moderate mental retardation. The school district argued that the least restrictive setting for the child would be the self-contained classroom for children with mental retardation, which was located in the junior high school.

The hearing officer ruled in favor of the school. The rationale for the decision was (1) that the school district could provide an appropriate educational program; (2) that the school program allowed for some contact with children without disabilities, whereas the day service center did not; and (3) that the individualized education plan used by the day service center was very similar to the one developed by the school, and neither plan indicated that the child required placement outside the public school program.

Case 2—Issue: Extended Year Programming.   The parents of Jim Smith requested that the Beta School District provide a 12-month education program for their son. The school contended that the child needed only a regular 9-month program. Jim was 16 years old, nonverbal, and had an IQ in the range of 20. He had been classified as having severe mental retardation. The hearing officer, agreeing that the child did not require an extended year program, ruled in favor of the school. In justifying this decision, the hearing officer made the following points:

1. Litigation had set the precedent that although extended-year programming was not required for all children with disabilities, it should not be ruled out as a consideration.
2. The key factor in determining if an extended school year is required is that the child would regress significantly without such programming.
3. In this case, the evidence did not show that Jim would regress to such a degree.
4. Although it was obvious that a 12-month program would have been beneficial, it was not shown to be crucial. The courts have ruled numerous times that local schools are only required to provide an appropriate education program, not the best possible program.

LITIGATION

Litigation dealing with the education of children with disabilities, as with litigation on all other education issues, has increased dramatically during the past decade (Smith 1990; T. E. C. Smith et al., 1993). As early as 1974, Laski noted that individuals with disabilities were beginning to access equal services through the court system. Since that time, litigation in the area of educational rights for students with disabilities has continued to increase.

Prior to the early right-to-education cases of *Pennsylvania Association for Retarded Citizens (PARC)* v. *Pennsylvania* (1972) and *Mills* v. *Board of Education of the District of Columbia* (1972), litigation was rare in the field of special education (McAfee, 1987). Since these early cases (Prasse, 1986), "the legal influences on special education programs and subsequently on services to handicapped children [are] without equal when viewed in the context of public school education in general" (p. 311). The result of much of this litigation has been a significantly improved educational system for students with disabilities (Prasse, 1988).

Litigation in special education began growing rapidly following the passage of PL 94-142 in 1975. Since then, "special education has been under a legal spotlight" (McAfee, 1987, p. 47). McAfee lists nine emerging issues in special education litigation. They include:

1. Malpractice (failure to learn)
2. Misdiagnosis
3. Immunity from liability
4. Impact of a handicap on standard of care
5. Confidentiality
6. Access to emergency services

7. Use of aversive consequences

8. Child abuse and corporal punishment

9. School violence

In view of potential litigation in these areas, McAfee suggests extensive teacher training to better prepare professionals for legal actions.

Despite efforts to avoid litigation through mediation, due process hearings, state-level reviews, and informal meetings, some disputes cannot be resolved. In these instances, schools may decide that litigation is the only alternative. This decision should be made by a team that includes the superintendent, other central administrative personnel, principals, and the teachers who deal with the child in question. Also, assessment personnel, counselors, and other ancillary personnel may be involved in the decision. Before deciding to enter into litigation, the team should specifically determine (1) whether all administrative and informal remedies have been attempted, (2) whether litigation would in fact result in an appropriate education for the child and (3) whether the school has a legitimate case. Ultimately, the decision to enter litigation belongs to the school board. The superintendent should present the recommendations of the team to the board and allow them to make the final decision.

The Court System

Litigation dealing with special education can be filed in state or federal courts. Because IDEA has precedence over state legislation, the majority of cases are filed in federal courts. There are three levels in the federal court system: district court, appeals court, and the United States Supreme Court (Turnbull, 1993). Cases are initially filed in district court; there are nearly 100 such courts. If one party appeals the decision of a district court, the appeal is filed in 1 of 13 circuit courts of appeal (McCarthy & Cambron-McCabe, 1987).

Decisions rendered by district courts apply only to that district. Similarly, decisions issued in courts of appeals apply only to cases in that particular district. Appeals to an appellate court decision may go only to the United States Supreme Court. This court deals with nearly 5,000 cases each year but issues a decision in fewer than 5% of them. The decisions of the appellate court stand in the remainder of the cases or the cases are remanded back to the appellate court (McCarthy & Cambron-McCabe, 1987).

The Litigation Process

Whether litigation is initiated by the school or by the parents, school administrators should ensure that the school's case is adequately prepared. Although attorneys will handle the legal preparation, school administrators are responsible for the administrative preparation. Table 7-5 summarizes the major activities of the litigation process.

Table 7-5   Major Activities in a Litigation Process

Staffing the Case	Organize the case to present the best case possible. Include teachers, related services personnel, assessment personnel, and all individuals with knowledge of the child. Use experts as necessary. Consider the legal and educational issues in the case.
Selecting Witnesses	Consider all individuals who could provide important testimony for the district. Include experts as necessary.
Rehearsing the Case	Rehearse questions and answers with witnesses. Rehearse questions likely to be raised by the opposing side.
Consulting During the Case	Ensure that someone will be available to assist the school's attorney during the case. This should be someone with knowledge of the case and expertise in special education.
Implementing the Decision	Regardless of the decision, ensure that the school implements the decision to the maximum degree possible. If the decision is in favor of the parents, staff the case to determine the feasibility of an appeal.

Staffing the Case.   Under the direction of attorneys, school officials should organize their case to present the best defense possible. All individuals involved in the special education program of the school, including the teachers of the child and ancillary personnel, should be involved in the staffing process. The time required in this preparatory phase will depend on the complexity of the issue, the nature of the child's disability, and the issues involved. During this phase, the superintendent should chair the proceedings or delegate this responsibility to another administrative official. The director or supervisor of special education for the district might be a good choice for this role.

Issues to be considered in the staffing process should include (1) the legal basis for the school's stance, (2) the educational programming rationale for the school's position, (3) the appropriateness of the school's suggested course of action for the child, and (4) the reasons the parent's desires are considered inappropriate. The school's attorney should be involved in the discussion during the entire preparation phase.

Selecting Witnesses.   Depending on the nature of the defense, witnesses who can provide evidence and testimony that best support the contentions of the school should be selected. Further, the selection should be based on the individual's (1) role in the education of the child, (2) role in the overall special education program of the district, (3) knowledge of special education programming, and (4) expertise on the issue in question.

Rehearsing the Case.   The school's case rehearsal should include questioning of potential witnesses, rehearsal of questions that will be used in the case, and role playing the provision of answers to the questions likely to be asked by the attorney for the parents. The school should be prepared to rebut testimony presented for the parents. By anticipating such testimony, the school's case can be made with a better chance for success. Without such rehearsal, the school may find itself presenting evidence that is not required or rebutting evidence that was not presented. For example, if the attorney for the school does not know how a friendly witness will answer particular questions, the school officials may be embarrassed when the witness turns out to be a witness for the parents. Rehearsal also lessens the anxiety of witnesses. By knowing what questions to anticipate, the witnesses should be more at ease while testifying. Although it may not always be possible to anticipate questions by the attorney for the parents, a thorough review of the parents' previous concerns expressed in due process hearings, in official complaint forms, or in informal conversations is likely to reveal the line of questioning that will be used.

Consulting During Testimony. During the court proceedings, someone who is knowledgeable about special education should be available to consult with the attorney. Though knowledgeable in legal proceedings, case law, and statutory regulations, the attorney may not have sufficient knowledge about special education issues to ask specific follow-up questions. Also, as the case progresses, the attorney for the parents may present evidence or testimony that requires the school to rethink its case. In such cases, someone with knowledge and experience in special education must be available to provide assistance to the attorney.

Implementation of the Decision. Following the hearing, the school must proceed to implement the decision as completely as possible, regardless of whether an appeal is being made. By implementing the decision, the school shows good faith and a positive attitude concerning the child with the disability. If the decision is in favor of the parents and an appeal is considered, the team of administrative personnel, ancillary personnel, and teachers who have contact with the child or with the special education program must meet to discuss the merits of such an appeal. If the consensus is that an appeal is warranted and there is a chance of overturning the verdict, a recommendation for appeal should be made to the school board. As with a decision to file suit, the ultimate decision concerning an appeal rests with the school board.

Role of Administrators. The superintendent, special education administrator, other central administration staff, and building-level administrators should play key roles during special education litigation. As always, the superintendent has the responsibility for organizing the case for presentation and recommending actions to the board. The superintendent should probably assign an administrator to assume the leadership role in the decision-making process and in the preparation process. This individual should report to the superintendent. Beyond that, the special education administrator should be called upon for assistance.

Administrators must generally keep abreast of current and previous court cases and rulings involving the rights of children with disabilities to receive a free and appropriate public education. They must be particularly cognizant of the legal implications of district-level decisions. This kind of careful monitoring can save districts a great deal of time and money.

MAJOR LITIGATION CASES IN SPECIAL EDUCATION

Although there have been hundreds of court cases filed in the area of special education, there are still only a few that are considered landmark cases. These cases continue to set precedence for special education issues and will be discussed in relation to particular special education issues.

Right to Education

Students with disabilities were actually denied their right to public educational programs prior to PL 94-142 and to various court cases. Two specific cases filed in the early 1970s resulted in the right-to-education principle for all students with disabilities.

Pennsylvania Association for Retarded Citizens (PARC) v. Pennsylvania.   An early litigation case that produced a landmark decision concerning the right of children with disabilities to receive an appropriate public education was *PARC* v. *Pennsylvania* (1972). The suit was filed in 1971 by the Pennsylvania Association for Retarded Citizens and 13 children with mental retardation on behalf of all children with mental retardation being denied a public school education. The action challenged the Pennsylvania laws that denied educational programs to children with mental retardation who were considered uneducable, unable to profit from educational programs, under the mental age of 5, or outside the compulsory school age. According to Laski (1974), "expert testimony so overwhelmingly demolished the factual underpinnings of the statutes that a consent decree was negotiated in which Pennsylvania acknowledged its responsibility to provide free public education and training to all children" (p. 16).

The three-judge panel approved a decree preventing Pennsylvania from denying free educational programs to children with mental retardation. The judges concluded that the majority of persons with mental retardation could benefit from education and training and that those few who could not were capable of some self-care (Laski, 1974). Finally, the court required Pennsylvania schools to seek out and provide services to children with mental retardation in their districts and to update programs for students with severe disabilities (Turnbull, 1993).

Mills v. Board of Education of the District of Columbia.   Another landmark right-to-education case was *Mills* v. *Board of Education of the District of Columbia* (1972). In this case the plaintiffs filed suit on behalf of children with disabilities who were denied educational programs in the District of Columbia. The plaintiffs represented children who were classified as having physical, emotional, social, and mental disabilities. The court's decision thus expanded the Pennsylvania agreement to children with various disabilities. The decision also prevented schools from using limited finances as a reason for not providing services (McCarthy & Cambron-McCabe, 1987). The fact that the court declared financial limitations as moot has, in effect, kept school districts from declaring that services would be provided if funds were available. Thus, the precedent was established that decisions about services must be made on the basis of the child's need, not the district's fiscal capability to provide services (Turnbull, 1993).

Implications of PARC and Mills.   The case of PARC and Mills resulted in the irreversible decision that students with disabilities had a legal right to a free appropriate education. Furthermore, this education was to be provided in integrated settings with nondisabled students when at all possible. Also, schools could no longer use limited funding or lack of students with disabilities as excuses for not providing programs. These cases in effect told schools to go out and find students with disabilities, and also, to find the money necessary to provide programs for these students.

Nondiscriminatory Assessment

Prior to the 1970s, school psychologists and other assessment personnel assumed that standardized, norm-referenced tests represented the best methods for identifying children as having various intellectual levels. Children were routinely identified as having mental retardation on the basis of a single examination with an IQ test. Although later found to be inappropriate, professionals at the time thought that certain validated IQ tests could accurately be used with all children.

Unfortunately, it took the courts to recognize that many tests used to identify children as having a disability, especially IQ tests, were generally discriminatory for some children. In particular, students from minority racial groups were found to be at a major disadvantage when taking certain IQ tests, which apparently had been developed for children from the majority culture. Although several court cases dealt with the issue of discriminatory assessment, probably the two most often referred to are the Diana and Larry P. cases.

Diana v. State Board of Education of California.   In *Diana* v. *State Board of Education of California* (1970), the plaintiffs contended that the test used to evaluate and place Mexican-American and Chinese-American children were biased against those two groups. The case was resolved when the court approved a

> stipulation in which the parties agreed to develop a test that would not be biased against Mexican-Americans, to provide statistical data on the numbers and percentages of various ethnic and racial groups, and to retest and evaluate all Mexican-American and Chinese children presently placed in such classes. (Gearheart, 1980b, p. 20)

Many facts pointed out in this case found their way to PL 94-142 (MacMillan, Hendrick, & Watkins, 1988).

Larry P. v. Riles.   *Larry P.* v. *Riles* has been referred to as the "premier case involving bias in intelligence tests and placing children in programs for the mildly retarded" (Prasse & Reschly, 1986, p. 333). This case, probably more than any other case, brought to the attention of the public the reality of disproportionate placement of minority racial groups in special education programs for children with mild mental retardation.

The case was filed on behalf of all African-American children in California who had been placed in special education classes for children with educable mental retardation (EMR) based on standardized intelligence (or IQ) tests. Although the litigation in Larry P. focused specifically on the tests used to make placement decisions, several related practices were also challenged by the plaintiffs. These practices included disproportionate enrollments in special education classes, placement procedures used for EMR classes, the central role of individual IQ tests in the placement decisions, and state requirements mandating the use of IQ tests in the placement of children with EMR. The decision was in favor of the plaintiffs, parents of African-American children classified as mildly mentally retarded, on both statutory and constitutional grounds. The decision determined that the schools' method of assessing and placing children were wrong in two ways. First, standardized tests were determined to be discriminatory toward African-American children. Second, the history of placement of African-American students in EMR classes indicated unlawful, segregated intent (Prasse & Reschly, 1986). To correct these past practices, the court required extensive actions, including the following (Prasse & Reschly, 1986):

1. Prevention of using standardized tests on African-American children for identification as EMR and placement in EMR classes.
2. Approval of tests as nondiscriminatory and valid.
3. Provision of data to support the use of certain tests.
4. Elimination of many African-American children from EMR classes.
5. Reevaluation, without using standardized tests, of every African-American child previously identified as EMR.
6. Development and implementation of an individualized educational plan for every child found to have been misdiagnosed.

Implications.   The cases of Diana and Larry P. did not totally end discriminatory assessment practices. Unfortunately, many children are still misidentified through inappropriate assessment practices. The two cases did, however, alert professionals in special education that certain tests, which prior to that time had been considered near-perfect, were limited in the valid information they could give for some children. Special education professionals began considering additional information, along with IQ test results, when making eligibility and programming decisions about students.

Extended Year Programming

After the implementation of PL 94-142, students with disabilities generally gained the right to appropriate educational programs, but there were still some issues that had to be resolved through the courts. One issue that was not dealt with specifically in PL 94-142 was extended year programming. Did the schools have a responsibility for providing special education during the summer months, or did their responsibility end during June, July, and August?

Armstrong v. Kline.   In this case, the parents of three children with severe disabilities filed suit challenging the legality of Pennsylvania's policy of refusing to consider or fund education programs for children with disabilities beyond the normal 180-day program provided for children without disabilities (Turnbull, 1993). The suit was cross-categorical, representing children with all disabilities in Pennsylvania. The plaintiffs contended that the 180-day rule violated PL 94-142. They wanted the policy declared illegal and provisions made for the state and local education agencies to develop programs for children with disabilities without the 180-day limitation (Alper, Parker, Schloss, & Wisniewski, 1993; McCarthy & Cambron-McCabe, 1987; Stotland & Mancuso, 1981).

The court ruled in favor of the plaintiffs, stating that

> certain handicapped students require a continuous program of special education and related services in excess of the normal 180 days school year and that any handicapped student who requires such a program is entitled to receive it from the Department of Education and their local school district without cost or other financial liability.

It was acknowledged in the decision that PL 94-142 requires that children with disabilities receive appropriate programming unique to their needs. The 180-day limitation on programming was found to deny certain children their right to an appropriate education (Lehr & Haubrich, 1986).

Implications.   The Armstrong case has had a major impact on all school districts. The decision in this case resulted in state departments of education and local school districts establishing policies and procedures for determining which students need extended school programming. Many students with disabilities in need of summer programming are currently receiving such programs as a result of this case.

Disciplinary Issues

Probably no area of PL 94-142 has received as much attention from school administrators as discipline. Can schools use the same disciplinary methods with students with disabilities as those they use with nondisabled students? Several court cases have focused on this issue, especially in the area of school expulsion.

S-1 v. Turlington.   This case developed when a group of students with mental retardation were expelled from school for various forms of misconduct, including sexual acts against fellow students, willful defiance of authority, insubordination, vandalism, and the use of profane language. The students were expelled for part of the 1977–78 and all of the 1978–79 school years (McCarthy & Cambron-McCabe, 1987). The original decision in *S-1* v. *Turlington* (1981) from the District Court for the Southern District of Florida ruled that local and state education agencies had to provide procedural due process rights and educational services to students with disabilities who were expelled for misconduct. The school district contended that the misconduct was unrelated to the disabilities of the students and therefore should result in expulsion following due process procedures followed for students without disabilities (White, 1981).

The Fifth Circuit Court of Appeals upheld the lower court's decision, affirming that the school did not determine whether the misconduct was related to the disability. The ruling stated that (1) expulsion constitutes a change of placement for children with disabilities and (2) expulsion is an appropriate disciplinary measure for children with disabilities, but a cessation of educational services is not. In addition, the court stated that the responsibility to provide due process rights to students with disabilities in expulsion cases rests with the school, regardless of whether or not parents request such rights (Lemley, 1982).

Honig v. Doe.   This was the first case that dealt with discipline and students with disabilities to reach the U.S. Supreme Court. In this particular case, John Doe, a 17-year-old boy who had been placed in a developmental center for students with disabilities, lost control and choked another student and deliberately broke a window. He was suspended for 5 days, and the principal recommended that he be expelled. A second student in the case, Jack Smith, had been diagnosed as having emotional disturbance since the second grade. By the sixth grade, his educational program had been reduced to half days. After making lewd comments to female students, he was suspended and recommended for expulsion (Bartlett, 1989).

These two students were joined in *Doe* v. *Maher* (1986). The Ninth Circuit Court found in favor of the students, and the school district appealed to the U.S. Supreme Court. The Supreme Court ruled on two of the issues in the case and upheld the Ninth Circuit in both instances. On the first issue, the Court concurred that the state is responsible for providing an appropriate education to a child with a disability when the local school district does not do so. On the second issue, the court agreed by a vote of 6 to 2 that schools cannot expel students with disabilities pending the outcome of an administrative review process (Bartlett, 1989). In other words, schools cannot expel students with disabilities while there is an ongoing administrative appeal. This has been referred to as the "stay put" rule (Turnbull, 1993). Thus, during the interim, school officials must develop alternative intervention strategies that implement the child's IEP without excluding the student from the school. The ruling seems to alter previous assumptions that students who posed a threat to themselves or others could be excluded from the school environment.

Implications.   The implication of these two court cases is that schools cannot discipline students with disabilities in the same way they discipline nondisabled students. The key is to determine if the inappropriate behaviors exhibited by the students with disabilities are in any way related to the disability. This is the first determination that must be made by school personnel.

Another major result of these cases is that in order to expel a student with a disability, due process procedures must be followed. Expulsion is considered a change of placement comparable to moving a student from a self-contained classroom to a resource room.

Minimally Versus Maximally Appropriate

PL 94-142 resulted in students with disabilities gaining access to appropriate educational programs. However, schools did not initially know how to interpret the requirements of the law in regard to how much intervention was enough. Were schools required to do whatever it took to maximize the abilities of students or were they simply supposed to provide access to an appropriate program? The first case to reach the U.S. Supreme Court regarding PL 94-142 answered this important question.

Board of Education v. Rowley.   The Rowley case was the first that dealt with PL 94-142 to reach the U.S. Supreme Court. In this case, the parents of an elementary-age child with a hearing impairment requested that the school district provide a sign language interpreter to the classroom. The hearing officer, the federal district court, and the federal court of appeals ruled in favor of the parents, concurring that without the interpreter, Amy Rowley was not able to obtain the maximum amount of information from the classrooms and was therefore not receiving an appropriate educational program.

In the summer of 1982, the U.S. Supreme Court surprised many professionals and advocates by reversing previous decisions in the Rowley case. In its analysis, the Court concluded that Congress had not intended that the schools try to maximize the educational performance of students in special education. Instead, the EHA's purpose was basically to open the schools' doors to them, granting them access to educational opportunities (Turnbull, 1986; Brady, McDougall, & Dennis, 1989).

As expected, the decision shocked many people interested in special education programs. However, after a period of time, advocates realized that the Rowley decision did not mean the erosion of rights earned for students with disabilities. The decision simply interpreted the intent of PL 94-142 and made the Individualized Educational Program (IEP) the key factor in determining an appropriate education (Turnbull, 1986).

Implications.   The implications of the Rowley case cannot be overemphasized. For the first time, the U.S. Supreme Court interpreted the intent of Congress as it related to how much schools are required to do to facilitate academic success of students with disabilities. The ruling ended the quest to maximize the educational opportunities for students with disabilities. At first glance this may seem to be a setback for students with disabilities. However, the court in fact said that students with disabilities should receive the same thing that nondisabled students receive from public schools; that is, a chance at a good, sound education. Put another way, because nondisabled students do not get "the very best," schools are not required to provide "the very best" to students with disabilities.

Defining Related Services

PL 94-142 resulted in schools providing a free appropriate education for students with disabilities, which includes both special education and related services. Related services have been defined as those services that are required to help a student benefit from special education. The extent of related services, however, was not specific in the law. It took a U.S. Supreme Court decision to help clarify the requirements for related services.

Irving Independent School District v. Tatro.   The second case dealing with PL 94-142 to reach the U.S. Supreme Court was *Irving Independent School District* v. *Tatro* (1984). In this case, the parents of Amber Tatro, a 3½-year-old child with spina bifida, filed suit requesting that the Irving Independent School District of Texas provide Clean Intermittent Catheterization (CIC). This procedure was necessary in order to prevent a chronic kidney infection. The CIC was needed every 3 to 4 hours and was considered a legitimate related service by the Tatro family (Vitello, 1986).

The school district refused to provide CIC based on the premise that the service was health related and that Amber Tatro was not intellectually impaired. The federal district court ruled in favor of the school district. However, the Fifth Circuit Court of Appeals reversed the decision, stating that the CIC was a supportive service that enabled Amber to access special education. On appeal, the Supreme Court upheld the right of Amber to receive CIC as a related service but reversed the appellate court's decision to award damages and attorney's fees (Vitello, 1986).

In its ruling, the U.S. Supreme Court (1) upheld the right of the courts to review the appropriateness of a child's IEP and (2) expanded the concept of related services. A key part of the ruling broadened "the related services construct to include not only services to enable a handicapped child to benefit from education but obtain access to beneficial educational services" (Vitello 1986, p. 355). This helped clarify one of the most nebulous issues of PL 94-142, accessibility to related services (Turnbull, 1993).

Implications.   The Tatro case, just like the Rowley case, finally gave school districts, state departments of education, and advocates for persons with disabilities some answers regarding the requirements of PL 94-142. In this case, the Court indicated that schools had to go a long way in providing whatever services might be necessary to enable a child to attend school and therefore benefit from special education. Although not rigidly defining the term *related services,* the ruling did suggest to schools that they should seek out every means available to facilitate a child's accessibility to school programs.

Educability

One other issue that was not clearly described in PL 94-142 was the school's limitations on responsibility for students too disabled to benefit from school programs. Or, were any students too disabled to benefit, under the requirements of the law?

Timothy W. v. Rochester School District. In May, 1989, the First Circuit Court of Appeals underlined its support for the zero reject principle. This principle generally accepts the notion that all children with disabilities can benefit from intervention programs. In the case of Timothy W., the Rochester School District determined that Timothy, a 13-year-old boy with profound mental retardation and other disabilities, was not capable of benefiting from an educational program and was therefore not educationally disabled. The state due process hearing officer ruled that Timothy was capable of benefiting from educational programming, and therefore ordered the school to provide a program. Upon appeal, the Federal District Court reversed the hearing officer's decision, stating that a determination should be made regarding the educability of children (*Victory for Timothy W.,* 1989).

The parents appealed this decision, and the appeals court reversed the district court's decision, stating that school districts could not exclude certain children on the basis of a determination of ineducability (*Victory for Timothy W.,* 1989). During the fall of 1989, the U.S. Supreme Court refused to hear the appeal from the First Circuit Court of Appeals, thus allowing the decision in Timothy W. to stand. This decision makes it very difficult for schools to avoid serving students with disabilities based on the severity of the disability (Turnbull, 1993).

Implications. The Timothy case basically means that schools are responsible for school-age children with disabilities, regardless of the severity of the disability. Although these students may not be able to benefit from traditional instructional programs, the courts are saying that they can benefit from some program made available through the schools. As a result, schools are attempting to provide some interventions even though the student may experience significant disabilities.

Liability Issues

How liable is a school for students with disabilities? Although the law is firm on the responsibility of the school to provide appropriate educational programs, does a child's disability eliminate certain responsibilities from the school?

Waechter v. School District No. 14-030 of Cassopolis, Michigan. In the Waechter case, the court ruled that a parent could receive damages from a school as a result of the death of their child with a disability. The particular case, filed in Michigan in 1991, focused on a student who died during a "gut run," a disciplinary action that several students were subjected to as a punishment for talking while standing in a line. The school and the student's teacher, who knew that the child was not supposed to exert himself physically, were held liable for the child's death. The student had been diagnosed as having a congenital heart defect that left him with symptoms of dizziness, fainting, chest pains, exhaustion, and rapid heart palpitations, as well as an orthopedic disability resulting from a short leg (Turnbull, 1993).

Implications. The Waechter case underlines the importance of taking into consideration all of the ramifications of a child's disability. Although laws and litigation have resulted in schools providing equal opportunities to students with disabilities, they do not remove the requirement that schools take special precautions with some students. Equal opportunity does not mean equal treatment or equal requirements. Schools must use common sense when applying discipline or certain standards to students with disabilities.

Emerging Issues

Although the landmark court cases that were discussed continue to have a major impact on special education and services to students with disabilities, there undoubtedly will be several legal issues over the next several years that will impact services. Some of these issues will include the following:

- *Inclusive education.* Issues related to inclusion include the role and responsibility of school personnel, due process procedures for students, grading requirements, homework requirements, and discipline. Many of these issues will be addressed in the courts.

- *Broadening definition of disabilities.* The Americans with Disabilities Act (ADA) and Section 504 of the Rehabilitation Act define disability much more broadly than IDEA. Students with AIDS, attention deficits, and behavior disorders may be considered as having disabilities by these legislative acts. Legal actions are very possible when determining which students are eligible for services.

- *Restructured education.* General education is currently undergoing major restructuring. The impact of this restructuring, which includes an emphasis on educational outcomes, will affect special education. Litigation could easily be a result of applying restructured ideas to special education.

- *Reduced funding.* Education and other governmental agencies are facing several years of reduced budgets. The impact of reduced funds on special programs will be significant and could result in significant levels of legal actions to guarantee continued levels of services.

- *Including students with severe disabilities.* Recent movements to include students with disabilities in regular education programs include students with severe disabilities. The result of placing students with severe problems in regular classrooms will likely include legal actions.

CHAPTER
EIGHT

PROGRAM
EVALUATION

School administrators spend a great deal of time absorbed in the process of evaluating educational programs (Dagley & Orso, 1991; Decker & Decker, 1992). Because most school reform efforts are lead by governors and state and federal legislators, evaluation has become a political issue, and thus, public attention has focused on the evaluation of programs. School administrators are responsible for all aspects of the educational program and, therefore, are required to ensure the appropriateness of special education programs through evaluation. In addition to other goals of program evaluation for the entire school program, administrators are required to assure that children with disabilities receive a free, appropriate public education, as mandated by PL 94-142 and the Individuals with Disabilities Education Act (IDEA) (Decker & Decker, 1992). Within this framework, principals must decide how to conduct evaluations (Glassman, 1986).

PROGRAM EVALUATION: PURPOSES AND PROCEDURES

Evaluation in education began as a process to determine the intellectual abilities of children or, more specifically, to determine how to separate, at an early age, the efficient learner from the poor learner. In the 1930s and 1940s, evaluation expanded to encompass the degree to which educational objectives had been met by the school program. In the late 1950s and 1960s, educational evaluation was again expanded to include the relationship between evaluation data and decision making, especially after passage of the Elementary and Secondary Education Act in 1965. By the 1970s, educational evaluation was expanded even more broadly. Glassman (1986) concluded that the focus of evaluation "was the measurement of individual differences in relation to the achievement of curricular objectives, and its function was to provide information to decision makers" (p. 11).

Today, the major concern at the national level, as noted in the deliberations of the National Governors Association, is to develop uniform educational goals and evaluation methods. Parents and the general public are demanding more school accountability and student achievement (Sapone & Sheeran, 1991). Program evaluation promises to be an even more important area for the administrator in the next few years as accountability and school reform agendas remain high on the national political agenda. With the movement to include more students with disabilities in regular education programs, program evaluation adds another significant component (Ysseldyke, Thurlow, & Bruininks, 1992).

Evaluation has become a major part of public education, requiring significant resources and the attention of school personnel (Audette & Algozzine, 1992). After relatively large amounts of federal funds became available to schools under a variety of programs, Congress demanded assurances that funds would be used efficiently and that programs they supported would have an impact on public schools (Borich & Nance, 1987). Today, even with significant reductions in the amounts and levels of federal funding, program evaluation activities are still important in the school reform effort. Indeed, educational evaluation is now considered the formal means of determining the quality of educational programs (Worthen & Sanders, 1987). When handled properly and at the appropriate level, program evaluation can result in numerous benefits for educational programs (Cummings, 1992).

Program evaluation in special education is intended to affirm the effectiveness of the school's special education program. In addition, there are also legal and legislative requirements for evaluating special education. With the passage of PL 94-142, there were specific program evaluation requirements. IDEA, the latest reauthorization of PL 94-142, requires that, in their annual program plans, states include "procedures for evaluating at least annually the effectiveness of programs in meeting the educational needs of children with disabilities, including evaluation of individualized education programs" (Sec. 121a. 146).

In addition, states must develop monitoring and evaluation procedures that include, at a minimum, (1) the collection of data and reports, (2) on-site visits, (3) audits of the use of federal monies, and (4) comparison of IEPs with actual programs (PL 94-142, Sec. 121a. 601).

In order to comply with federal evaluation requirements, states monitor local school districts at least once every three years to guarantee to the U.S. Department of Education that local schools are in compliance with IDEA. Although states vary in their evaluation processes, the majority of monitoring time is spent on the following activities (Field & Hill, 1988):

1. Reviewing student files to make sure that procedural guidelines are followed.
2. Making sure that time lines are met.
3. Ensuring that students meet eligibility requirements for the disabling conditions under which they are classified.
4. Ensuring that IEPs adequately document goals, objectives, the dates on which objectives were initiated and completed, the amount of time spent in the mainstream program, and parental knowledge of their rights. (p. 23)

Various states also require evaluation procedures of local education agencies. For example, Montana requires that (1) all schools be evaluated with both objective and subjective measures, (2) that the evaluation design measure the degree to which objectives have been accomplished, (3) that results are reported to facilitate decision making, and (4) that evaluation be ongoing and reports completed at least annually. The Tennessee State Plan for Part B of the Education of the Handicapped Act requires that local plans to provide special education services include a plan for evaluating services for children with disabilities. In North Carolina, the state education agency monitors local districts to determine compliance with state and federal regulations and requires local districts that have not been monitored in a year to complete a self-monitoring process and report the findings to them.

Evaluation has often been perceived merely as (1) a means of satisfying the requirements for receiving grants, (2) a method to provide accountability data to school boards (Callahan, Covert, Aylesworth, & Vanco, 1981), or (3) a means of meeting federal and state regulatory guidelines. However, there are other, more important, reasons for evaluation (Cummings, 1992). Without adequate evaluation, interested persons such as administrators, teachers, and parents are not able to determine if programs meet the needs of students (Cummings, 1992; Worthen & Sanders, 1987).

The continued use of self-contained classrooms, based on poorly designed research that was used to attest to their effectiveness, is a prime example of accepting a service delivery model as appropriate without valid information for making such a determination (Smith, Polloway, Patton, & Dowdy, in press; Smith, Finn, & Dowdy, 1993). In this case, evaluations that were conducted were often invalid due to flaws in the evaluation design. "Sampling was often inadequate, instrumentation was weak, and there was little knowledge of what actually transpired in the classroom" (Jones, Gottlieb, Guskin, & Yoshida, 1978, p. 589).

Evaluation is also necessary to determine:

- The quality of instructional environments (Ysseldyke & Christenson, 1987; Wang, 1987).
- The effectiveness of staff development (Orlich, 1989).
- The quality of special education programs (Borich & Nance, 1987).
- The appropriateness of supplemental materials in instructional programs (Miller & Sabatino, 1977).
- The effectiveness of interagency coordination efforts (Flynn & Harbin, 1987).
- The physical characteristics of special education rooms (D'Alonzo, D'Alonzo, & Mauser, 1979).
- The appropriateness of materials (Boland, 1976).
- The extent to which individual students are making progress toward goals and objectives (Schuncke, 1981).

When evaluation results show deficiencies in programs, steps can be taken to correct the problems and strengthen the program. Evaluation might also indicate that certain school personnel are not adequately carrying out their responsibilities. In these cases, administrators can intervene, provide personnel counseling and training, and conduct follow-up evaluations.

What Should Be Evaluated?

Because time and other resources in schools are limited, priorities for evaluation must be established. Schools must determine how much evaluation is enough (Cummings, 1992). Too often, schools focus merely on academic outcomes. In fact, focusing on outcomes has become the trend in evaluation (Ysseldyke, Thurlow, & Bruininks, 1992). Although the academic achievement of students should be a primary concern, evaluation must encompass more than student scores. Worthen and Sanders (1987) suggest the following areas as potential objects of formal evaluation:

- Student development and performance.
- Educator qualifications and performance.
- Curriculum design and processes.
- School organizational structure.

- Textbooks and other curriculum materials and products.
- Funded or unfunded projects.
- Any aspect of school operations (e.g., school transportation, food services, health services).
- School budgets, business, and finance.
- Facilities, media and libraries, equipment.
- Educational policies.
- School–community relations.
- Parent involvement in schools.
- School climate.
- Ideas, plans, and objectives. (p. 8)

School climate is an area that has not traditionally been considered important in evaluation but has become increasingly important in program evaluation as methods used in business have been introduced into education. The focus is clearly on the morale of teachers, staff, and students. This has often been used as an index of the effect of the administrative style and personality of the administration. Authoritarian or doctrinaire administrators in organizations tend to have less satisfied employees, higher absenteeism, and lower productivity. Conversely, more open environments have higher productivity and more cohesive staffs. However, climate is a subtle factor and there is no clear relationship between certain organizational variables and outcomes. Regardless, this is an increasingly important area of consideration as schools are moving more toward models of self-management or site-based management by teachers and parents. Although the assessment of climate variables can be time consuming, there are ways to quickly determine the school's climate, thus providing diagnostic data for organizational improvement (Fairman & Podemski, 1982).

A major problem in assessing school climate is in determining what the climate should include. Definitions focus on achievement, morale, and the interactions between them (Kelley, 1981). For example, Sagor (1981) described a high school in which overall achievement scores of the students were high, but some students were bored and others felt overworked. Applying Kelley's definition, it would appear that even though achievement was high, morale was low; and therefore there was room for improvement in the school's climate.

Administrative and support services in the school might also be evaluated. Often, administrators concern themselves with evaluating all aspects of the school except their own roles (St. John, 1991). Yet, if the administrative and support services provided to teachers and students are inadequate, the effect on the total school program can be devastating. Teachers who feel that the administration does not support them and students who feel that support services are inadequate may have difficulty achieving at their maximum levels.

An additional area of concern might be the relationship between the principal and special education administrators and personnel, especially in inclusion settings where traditional roles for special education personnel are altered to support regular class activities. Often, special education teachers are confused about who they are responsible to, the building principal or the special education supervisor. Although this may vary somewhat among districts, the building principal is generally considered in charge of all of the programs in his or her building (Decker & Decker, 1992). Accordingly, teachers in that building, whether they are special education teachers or regular education teachers, are responsible to the building principal.

As noted earlier, the major consideration in evaluating the special education program should be the effectiveness of the special education services offered by the school (Ysseldyke, Thurlow, & Bruininks, 1992). Prior to the current emphasis on educating children with disabilities in the least restrictive environment and the move toward inclusion, the majority of special education students were served in isolated, self-contained classrooms. However, as a result of studies that found that self-contained programs did not significantly benefit students in segregated settings, the resource room model became the primary setting for special education services (Smith et al., 1993; Smith et al., in press).

To evaluate the effectiveness of resource rooms, Jones et al. (1978) suggest that data be collected on (1) student achievement; (2) attitudes of administrators, teachers, and parents; (3) student adjustment; (4) student acceptance; (5) cost effectiveness; and (6) school attendance of students. Recently, more emphasis has been placed in evaluation on measuring student outcomes. Examples of outcomes that are included in the evaluation are (Ysseldyke, Thurlow, & Shriner, 1992):

- Graduation
- Reading achievement
- Math achievement
- Attendance
- Communication
- Status after high school
- Dropout rate
- Leadership
- Motivation
- Self-esteem
- Employment
- Independent living

Some states have moved to require schools to measure the effectiveness of programs using specific outcomes. Table 8-1 provides examples of the outcomes lists of various states.

The teacher–consultant model differs from the resource room model because it focuses on the skills of regular teachers rather than the remediation of students (Smith et al., 1993). This model more closely fits into the Regular Education Initiative and the inclusion concept, where most students with disabilities spend their entire days in regular classrooms. Evaluating the effectiveness of the teacher-consultant model will require a different approach from evaluating the quality of resource rooms. As schools move to include all students with disabilities in their regular education programs, specific areas for evaluation will continue to change (Smith et al., in press).

Table 8-1   Examples of Outcomes Lists

State	Outcomes
Connecticut	Participation, attendance, graduation rates, suspension Academic achievement in math, writing, and reading on Connecticut Mastery Test Attitudes and attributes: motivation, persistence, satisfaction Graduate follow-up
Florida	Mathematics Communication: reading, writing Functional literacy
Iowa	Background information High school program: course type, work experience, extracurricular activities Evaluation of school experience from student perspective Current lifestyle: marital status, living arrangements, leisure activities Post and current employment Contact with adult service providers
Nebraska	Employment history Independent living functioning Financial assistance Communication skills Earnings Job skills Social skills
New York	Attendance, promotion, graduation, and dropout rates Achievement on State and Regents exams District-level standards
New Hampshire	School-based measures of: absenteeism, suspension rates, dropout rates, graduation rates, school satisfaction
Oregon	Residential setting, independent living situation, recreational activities, absence of social maladjustment, social relationships, personal satisfaction, employment Program and Individualized Education Program (IEP) description Parent and teacher survey on student's satisfacton and quality

From "Expected Educational Outcomes for Students with Disabilities" by J. E. Ysseldyke, M. L. Thurlow, and R. H. Bruininks, 1992, *Remedial and Special Education, 13,* p. 24. Reprinted by permission.

Self-contained classrooms, resource rooms, and the consultant model are not the only areas in special education that should be evaluated. In fact, evaluation of special education programs should focus on programmatic aspects rather than on service delivery models. Other areas that should be evaluated include (Wiederholt, Hammill, & Brown, 1978):

- Physical environment
- Curriculum
- Time allocated for specific activities
- Factors that relate to the resource pupils
- Personnel involved in the resource effort
- Planning/monitoring process
- Reporting procedures
- Record keeping
- Materials used in the program
- Public relations activities (p. 87)

The implementation of full inclusion will have a significant impact on evaluation. One of the concerns of many advocates is that students with disabilities will some-how lose some of the advantages available in special programs. Evaluating student outcomes will become critical with this model if an accurate determination can be made about the quality of programs for this group of students.

Two specific programmatic areas that should be evaluated are the curricular approach used by special education teachers, especially with secondary students (Polloway, Patton, Epstein, & Smith, 1989), and the methodologies practiced by special education teachers. The curricular approach must be evaluated to determine the effectiveness of the school's academic program. And specific methodologies—such as study skills instruction, which has been gaining in use at the secondary level (Smith & Dowdy, 1989)—must be evaluated to ascertain their effectiveness.

Who Should Be Evaluated?

There are obviously many different groups and individuals who should be evaluated in attempts to determine the effectiveness of programs for students with disabilities, including students, teachers, administrators, and the community. When determining whom to evaluate, it may be necessary to make the determinations based on avail-ability of resources and the priorities set by statutory requirement.

Students.   Because the major objectives of special education programming are acade-mic achievement, behavioral modification, or a change in some other student variable, an obvious target of evaluation is the students, individually and collectively. And, as noted previously, with more emphasis being placed on specific outcomes, students are the predominant target for evaluating special education programs (Ysseldyke, Thurlow, & Bruininks, 1992). The IEP's short-range objectives and annual goals can provide much of the information needed to evaluate student progress in specific areas, provid-ing it is actually used in programming. Administrators may decide that the rate of achievement of annual goals by students is a good outcome measure of program effectiveness. Assessment of the degree to which a majority of students achieve annual goals can provide useful information about the IEP development process and its comprehensiveness (Schuncke, 1981). However, more frequent evaluation of student objectives has the advantage of (1) providing teachers with specific ongoing information related to the progress of students toward goals and objectives, (2) enabling teachers to modify individual programs, and (3) providing teachers with information indicating the student's readiness to progress toward the next objective in the sequence (Wehman & McLaughlin, 1981). Used in this manner—as a monitoring vehicle to gauge student progress—the evaluation process can be extremely effective.

Outcomes-oriented models are going to become more important in special education (Audette & Algozzine, 1992; Ysseldyke, Thurlow, & Bruininks, 1992; Ysseldyke, Thurlow, & Shriner, 1992). Thus administrators may need to devise different instruments and theories of assessment, rather than rely on norm-referenced tests. In moving to a more outcomes-oriented evaluation model, a first step is simply to identify the specific outcomes to be evaluated.

Teachers.   Although student evaluations provide information concerning program effectiveness, they may not reflect teacher effectiveness because students may achieve despite the actions of teachers. Because educating children with disabilities is currently a shared responsibility between special and regular educators, student achievement alone does not tell administrators which aspects of the program or which teaching personnel are most effective. To determine the overall effectiveness of programs and to identify areas where administrators can make improvements, the performance of teachers and other support personnel involved in special education programs must also be evaluated. Teachers, in effect, represent instructional treatments for students and therefore must be considered critical in the special education process (Popham, 1988). Their role in the attainment of educational outcomes cannot be overlooked.

Evaluation of teachers has become more and more popular with the accountability movement. As many schools are changing to team teaching, site-based management, reflective teaching, constructivist learning, and inclusive education, evaluation has become more complex. Problems have developed as a result of large-scale evaluations, including the enormous expense, a false sense of confidence on the part of policymakers, and too much time being spent by teachers preparing for the evaluation (Popham, 1988). For more than 40 years, educators have been trying to determine the criteria for teaching excellence (Smith & White, 1988). And although the effort has been increasing since the early 1980s, there is still a great deal of controversy concerning how best to evaluate instructional personnel (Buser & Pace, 1988).

Teachers often become defensive about the methods used in personnel evaluation systems. However, if the evaluation data are perceived as being used primarily to improve programs rather than to judge teachers, teachers will be more willing to participate actively in the evaluation efforts (McGreal, 1982). Therefore, it is important that administrators clarify the purpose of the evaluation.

There are numerous methods of evaluating teachers. Some of the most commonly used include (Popham, 1988):

- Administrative ratings
- Classroom observations
- Pupil test performance
- Student ratings
- Tests of teachers' competency/knowledge
- Professional portfolios
- Teacher appraisal interviews
- Teachers' self-evaluations
- Contract plans
- Teaching performance tests

There is no single, comprehensive evaluation method that always provides valid, reliable data. Wood (1992) suggests that administrators remain mindful that merely using paper/pencil checklists may result in their forgetting that they themselves are the primary instrument in evaluation. Administrators should utilize a combination of methods to get the overall estimate of performance (Buser & Pace, 1988). Teacher evaluation procedures are discussed in detail in chapter 9.

Administrators.   Many researchers have stressed the importance of administrators in special education programs, especially since the advent of the concept of "administrator as instructional leader" (Smith, Price, & Marsh, 1986; T. E. C. Smith, 1990; Johnson, 1989). In the administrative area, specific key individuals in the development and operation of special education programs should be targeted for evaluation. These include building principals, supervisors or directors of special education programs, and central office personnel.

St. John (1991) lists five reasons why administrative personnel should be included in the evaluation program. These include:

1. To improve overall job performance.
2. To determine how well annual goals are achieved.
3. To pinpoint specific performance strengths and weaknesses.
4. To identify specific professional development needs.
5. To increase understanding of the evaluation process. (p. 88)

Community.   More and more, the community is becoming a critical factor in the quality of public schools. Targets for evaluation in the community should include select community members such as parents and school board members. Support from these individuals is important in the successful operation of school programs. Without such support, financial resources, volunteers, and community services may not be available.

Particularly in the area of special education, community support is vital, because some special education programs are costly, require professional support from the community, or may be perceived as taking away resources from programs for students without disabilities. More and more special education programs are being implemented in community-based settings. As community-based instruction (CBI) becomes more widely adopted, evaluating the community becomes increasingly more important.

EVALUATION MODELS

This section describes several models that may be used in evaluating special education programs. However, additional information should be obtained before deciding upon a particular model. In some cases, further research on specific procedures may be needed to apply the model effectively.

Discrepancy Evaluation Model

The discrepancy evaluation model (DEM) is based on the premise that for any educational program, it is possible to identify performance descriptors for the program as it actually exists and also to articulate a standard of what the program should be. Any difference between program performance and the standard is termed a discrepancy. The discrepancy may be negative, when a performance does not achieve the standard, or positive, when the performance exceeds the standard (Yavorsky, n.d.). If the discrepancy is positive, actions may not need to be taken, because the program is outperforming expectations; if the discrepancy is negative, program alterations may be necessary.

There are five stages to the discrepancy evaluation model: (1) design, (2) installation, (3) process, (4) product, and (5) program comparison (Popham, 1988). Table 8-2 describes each of these stages.

The key process in using the discrepancy model is to determine whether or not there is a difference between the desired standard and the actual outcome. Yavorsky (n.d.) suggests that, in cases where the discrepancy is negative, it may be necessary to (1) reformulate an unrealistic standard, (2) exert greater supervision of the pro-

Table 8-2   Five Stages of the Discrepancy Evaluation Model (DEM)

Stage	Description
Design	Nature of the program is described, including (1) objectives of the program; (2) staff, students, and other resources needed to achieve objectives; and (3) instructional activities.
Installation	Comparison is made between what the program is and what it is supposed to be. Standard is compared to actuality to determine discrepancies.
Process	Determination is made regarding the achievement of enabling objectives. This is determined in light of any discrepancies detected.
Product	Focuses on whether or not the program has achieved its terminal objectives. Standards compared to postinstructional performance of students.
Program Comparison	Compares the cost-benefit of the program with other similar programs.

From *Educational Evaluation* (2nd ed.) by W. J. Popham, 1988, Englewood Cliffs, NJ: Prentice Hall.

gram, or (3) terminate the program. Determining which of these three actions to take will depend on the nature of the program being evaluated and on the type and importance of other variables impacting the program.

The DEM may be used to evaluate discrepancies in the following areas: (1) between program plans and actual operations, (2) between predicted and actual program outcomes, (3) between supposedly similar parts of a program, and (4) within the organization of the program.

Context, Input, Process, Product Evaluation Model

The context, input, process, product (CIPP) evaluation model examines the process of decision making. This model is an attempt by D. L. Stufflebeam to help administrators make good decisions based on a decision-oriented evaluation approach (Worthen & Sanders, 1987). It has been used frequently in educational settings (Brinckerhoff, Shaw, & McGuire, 1993). In the CIPP model, evaluation is defined as "the process of delineating, obtaining, and providing useful information for judging decision alternatives" (Stufflebeam et al., 1971). The CIPP model examines decision making from four different evaluation perspectives: (1) context evaluation, (2) input evaluation, (3) process evaluation, and (4) product evaluation (Stufflebeam & Webster, 1988).

Context Evaluation.   In context evaluation, fundamental evaluation data designed to facilitate decision making are collected. The evaluation determines the needs, problems, objectives, and opportunities of programs. These determinations are then used as the basis for the development of objectives to meet needs or deal with deficiencies (Stufflebeam & Webster, 1988). Context evaluation process requires (1) a description of the environment, (2) a determination of unmet needs and necessary resources, (3) an identification of deficiencies in meeting needs, and (4) a prediction of future deficiencies (Dressel, 1976).

Input Evaluation.   Input evaluation is used to make decisions concerning the use of available resources to achieve goals. Data that describes the strengths and weaknesses of the program and alternative strategies to achieve goals and objectives are collected (Orlich, 1989). This information is used to determine a plan that has the best chance for achieving the preferred product or program (Worthen & Sanders, 1987). The intent of input evaluation, therefore, is to determine available resources for programs and to make decisions concerning programs based on that information. Issues arising from input evaluation include the feasibility of meeting goals, the availability of resources to meet goals, the costs of needed resources, the advantages and disadvantages of alternative approaches, and the likely success of programs (Anderson, Ball, & Murphy, 1975).

Process Evaluation.   After the program has been implemented, process evaluation is used to provide ongoing monitoring of the program components (Stufflebeam & Webster, 1988; Orlich, 1989). Process evaluation has three major functions:

1. To enable those in charge of programs to detect problems in the program and to predict problems that are likely to occur.
2. To help in decision making during the course of the program.
3. To record information so that outcomes can be better interpreted.

Information collected during process evaluation is used to detect problems in procedures, determine the sources of problems, make program revisions, determine staff performance and use of resources, and project needed resources not previously identified (Dressel, 1976). In short, process evaluation permits program monitoring and implementation of changes without having to wait until the end product is evaluated.

Product Evaluation.   Product evaluation provides information concerning the attainment of original program goals and objectives. It is related to the final, overall decision-making process. This information can be used to determine whether the program should be continued in its current plan, modified, or terminated (Orlich, 1989). For example, product evaluation can assess the achievement of annual goals for a child with disabilities by the end of the school year while it assesses through regular monitoring the rate at which the child is moving toward those goals during the year.

Table 8-3 provides an example of applying the CIPP model to postsecondary programs for students with learning disabilities. Evaluating other programs for students with disabilities could generally follow this format.

Formative and Summative Evaluation

Formative evaluation is used to ensure that all project activities are running smoothly so that ultimately the goals of the program will be achieved (Orlich, 1989). It enables personnel to make interim decisions about a program, rather than waiting until the end of the project or activity (Decker & Decker, 1992). According to Hamm (1988), "formative evaluation provides continuous feedback to facilitate the improvement of a program during its development and implementation" (p. 405).

As an example, formative evaluation could be used to evaluate the curriculum for work-study students throughout the first year of a program. If the administrator does not want to wait an entire year before determining if the needs of the students are being met, formative evaluation can be used. At several times during the year, information such as test data from students, teachers, and objective sources is collected to determine if modifications in the curriculum are warranted. As the need for changes becomes apparent through the evaluation, the changes are implemented. Then, after a specified amount of time, those changes are again evaluated. Hopefully, the end product is a curriculum that meets the goals of the program and is appropriate for the students enrolled.

Sirotnik and Oakes (1981) suggest that a formative evaluation system be used for the entire school. In contrast to the "factory model" of evaluation where raw materials (uneducated children) exit periodically, the Sirotnik and Oakes system would

Table 8-3   Application of the CIPP Model to the Postsecondary LD Programs

	Purpose	Method
Context Evaluation	To determine whether the goals and objectives of the LD program are pertinent to the needs of students to be served as well as to the institution	Use of needs assessments, surveys, diagnostic data, institutional documents
Input Evaluation	To identify the services or approaches needed to assist students to meet program goals; to assess already existing campus resources (e.g., career counseling, mental health services, services for students with disabilities) to determine whether they can be adapted to assist students with learning disabilities	Review of the literature to determine effective interventions for students with learning disabilities; site visits to other institutions with exemplary LD programs; institutional "inventories" of other student services; consideration of staffing, space, and budgetary needs
Process Evaluation	To determine the extent to which LD program services are implemented, as well as the efficiency of service delivery; to gather data for use in modifying the program; to monitor student participation in LD services; to account for program expenditures (e.g., tutoring, equipment); to determine student satisfaction regarding LD services	Establishment of a systematic data-collection procedure and time line; identification of LD program staff roles and responsibilities for data collection; review of program records and documents (e.g., logs, contact hours); establishment of an advisory group including students, faculty, and appropriate administrative staff; conducting of interviews with and questionnaires for student consumers as well as campus personnel (e.g., faculty)
Product Evaluation	To determine the effects or outcomes of LD program services; to relate program outcomes to program objectives and procedures; to render judgments about program outcomes (both positive and negative) for the purpose of modifying the program to become more cost-effective and to better serve the needs of students with learning disabilities	Student pretest/posttest performance (e.g., self-efficacy surveys, *Learning and Study Strategies Inventory* [Weinstein, Palmer, & Schulte, 1987]); grade-point average data gathered over time; retention-graduation data; case studies of program participants; follow-up surveys of program graduates; experimental research designs including students with learning disabilities who received services and control groups (e.g., non-LD peers or documented students with learning disabilities who elected not to participate in LD services)

From *Promoting Postsecondary Education for Students with Learning Disabilities* (pp. 265–266) by L. C. Brinckerhoff, S. T. Shaw, and J. M. McGuire, 1993, Austin, TX: PRO-ED. Reprinted by permission.

assess not only the academic achievement of students but also such variables as teaching practices, school and classroom climates, staff working environments and morale, and parent and community attitudes. Thus, formative evaluation can be used both to assess a single program or curriculum and to evaluate entire school programs and processes.

Unlike formative evaluation, which provides ongoing monitoring of activities, summative evaluation examines the quality of a completed product or the effectiveness of a program after its implementation (Decker & Decker, 1992). When formative evaluation ends, summative evaluation begins. That is, after formative evaluation has facilitated the modification and improvement of programs, summative evaluation evaluates the effectiveness of the program and provides information to determine whether the program should be continued (Hamm, 1988). Although formative evaluation is used primarily by persons who administer ongoing operations of programs, summative evaluation is used by individuals who set policy, such as determining if a program should be continued or if the overall goals of a program are being met.

Another distinction between formative evaluation and summative evaluation is the relationship of the evaluator to the program. In formative evaluation the evaluator is a part of the program; in summative evaluation, the evaluator is independent of the program and its developers. This separation creates both the image and reality of objectivity.

Summative evaluation can be used to evaluate large programs, specific classroom programs, or even student performance. Teachers frequently use summative evaluation to assess student performance following a unit or course of instruction, thereby determining how well the objectives of the course have been achieved (Guyot, 1978).

Although frequently used in isolation, formative and summative evaluation can be used together to provide a very effective evaluation system. As noted by Dagley and Orso (1991), what is learned in formative evaluation and summative evaluation can be used together to form a stronger evaluation model, rather than only using one of the components.

Total Quality Management

During the past several years, the business community has been adopting a total quality management (TQM) system to evaluate and improve businesses. The principles of TQM can facilitate a movement toward more quality education. According to Blankstein (1993), the following 14 principles, developed by W. Edwards Deming, can easily be applied to educational settings:

1. Create constancy of purpose for improvement of product and service.
2. Adopt the new (Deming) philosophy.
3. Cease dependence on inspection to achieve quality. Build in quality in the first place.
4. End the practice of awarding business based on price alone.
5. Improve constantly and forever in every process.
6. Institute training on the job.
7. Adopt and institute leadership.

8. Drive out fear.

9. Break down barriers between staff areas.

10. Eliminate slogans, exhortations, and targets for the staff.

11. Eliminate numerical quotas for the staff and goals for management.

12. Remove barriers that rob people of pride of workmanship.

13. Institute a vigorous program of education and self-improvement for everyone.

14. Put everybody in the organization to work to accomplish the transformation. (p. 28)

Brandt (1993) also suggests that these 14 principles can easily be applied to education. For example, instituting training on the job could be related to revamping teacher education and staff development programs, and eliminating numerical quotas could be related to reducing the need to rely on standardized test scores for quality measures. However, when applying Deming's 14 principles, school personnel must take into consideration the unique ecology of each school setting (Hixson & Lovelace, 1993).

Bonstingl (1993) describes four "pillars" that must be present when adopting the TQM model to school settings. First, the school must focus on its suppliers and customers. Administrators, teachers, students, and parents must work together to identify quality and ways to achieve that quality. Second, everyone in the school must be dedicated to continuous improvement. This includes school personnel as well as students and parents. Third, schools must be considered as a system. Within the system, all parties must contribute to the overall goals related to quality. And fourth, the overall success of TQM rests with the top management of the school, that is, the superintendent and other school leaders.

TQM can be applied to school settings in numerous ways. Kaufman and Hirumi (1993) suggest the following 10 steps:

1. Be ready for a challenge.

2. Create and use a quality system that will collect performance data.

3. Define the ideal vision (results, not processes).

4. Determine gaps between current results and the vision.

5. Obtain agreement regarding how to come closer to achieving the vision, next year, in five years.

6. Identify results that would demonstrate achievement of the vision.

7. Define activities that would deliver such results.

8. Identify resources required to deliver such results.

9. Specify what each person in the system must do to facilitate the achievement of desired outcomes.

10. Continue to use a data-based quality system (p. 34).

School personnel need to be aware of some attitudinal barriers that might impede the implementation of the TQM concept in schools. These include defensiveness and a general attitude that programs used in the business world will not work in school settings. Table 8-4 briefly summarizes some of these attitudinal barriers.

Table 8-4   Attitudinal Barriers to Quality

The Word *Quality* Itself	Seen by many as a platitude, unobtainable, and overused by advertisers
The Corporate World as the Model	Skepticism about corporate example, rejection of customer orientation
Leadership	Low confidence in leader commitment, scant examples of quality-oriented leaders
Just Another Change	Regarded as another trend that will pass
One Year at a Time	Quality is a long-range commitment and schools plan on a year-by-year basis
I Know That Already	False perception that there is nothing new in a quality orientation
Students Don't Value School	If only the student worked harder, we wouldn't have to improve schools
It's Not My Fault	Changed social context of families presents insurmountable barriers to successful schools
A Question of Culture	Belief that quality management is only achievable in Japan's culture
Teacher as Self-Employed Entrepreneur	Teaching is an independent, isolated profession without the collaboration needed for a quality approach

From "Getting Started with TQM" by K. R. Freeston, 1992, *Educational Leadership, 50,* p. 13. Reprinted by permission.

TQM is not, in itself, the ultimate answer to program evaluation. It is, however, an attempt to adapt successful business practices to educational settings. Although it will likely be implemented in a variety of different ways, it should add significantly to the quest to improve the educational system for all children, including those in special education programs.

CONDUCTING EVALUATIONS

Before conducting special education evaluations, specific planning should be accomplished. Administrators must define the evaluation objections, select the evaluator, decide what information is necessary to complete the evaluation and how to collect it, analyze the information, and communicate the evaluation results. Haphazardly jumping into evaluation without ample preplanning is likely to result in inadequate or useless information, thus jeopardizing the entire evaluation process. Planning evaluations helps to prioritize evaluation areas, to allocate funding, and to clarify expectations of different groups (Stufflebeam & Webster, 1988). Table 8-5 describes a step-by-step method to plan for evaluations.

Table 8-5   Step-By-Step Method to Plan for Evaluations

Steps	Considerations
1. Consider the audience.	College administrators? Potential consumers (e.g., incoming freshmen, transfer students, nontraditional students)? Faculty? Program staff? Legislators? Research community? Governing boards?
2. Determine the purposes of the evaluation.	Justify program needs (e.g., staff, space equipment)? Monitor student achievement? Document compliance with Section 504? Monitor cost-effectiveness? Analyze use and effectiveness of program services? Assist in developing institutional policy (e.g., course-substitution policies)?
3. Focus the evaluation.	Context? Product? Input? Formative? Process? Summative?
4. Determine appropriate methods of evaluation.	Quantitative? Qualitative?
5. Collect and analyze data.	Time line established? Data collection instruments and procedures identified? Staff responsible for data collection identified? Data collection monitoring plan in place? Plan for organizing, coding, storing, and retrieving data? Data-analysis procedures identified?
6. Report and utilize data.	Format for reporting and communicating results (e.g., formal written reports, memos, presentations)? Plan in place for generating report? Follow-up activities planned?

From J. M. McGuire, 1992 [unpublished material], The University of Connecticut, A. J. Pappanikou Center on Special Education and Rehabilitation: A University Affiliated Program, Storrs. Reprinted by permission.

To assist local school districts in evaluating special education programs, many states have developed program evaluation and monitoring formats. These formats are frequently used by state education agency monitoring teams to determine local district compliance (Field & Hill, 1988). However, they may also be used by local district administrators for self-evaluation of special education programs.

The formats used by state education agencies to evaluate and monitor local special education programs are comprehensive, frequently including not only items related to the direct delivery of services but also items on such areas as budgets and personnel development. Thus, local districts may have to individualize their own program evaluation procedures.

The remainder of this chapter is intended to help general education and special education administrators develop program evaluation plans that are unique to the needs and objectives of their district. The tasks cited should be carried out in conjunction with the procedures required by the particular evaluation model selected by the administrator.

Planning for Evaluation

The first step in evaluation is to determine the purpose of the evaluation. Evaluations without purpose are time-consuming efforts that usually result in the collection of useless data and, ultimately, in invalid conclusions. The specific purposes of evaluation in education include the following:

- To determine the effectiveness of an educational program.
- To determine the effectiveness of a particular service delivery approach.
- To determine the extent to which particular curricular approaches are effective.
- To appraise teacher and support personnel.
- To appraise program materials.
- To determine compliance with state and federal requirements.
- To evaluate the comprehensiveness of a special education program.
- To compare the accomplishments of a program with projected objectives.

Defining Evaluation Objectives

After the purposes of the evaluation have been determined, specific evaluation objectives should be set. An objective might be, for example, to gather information concerning the special education resource room program in order to make a decision regarding the delivery model that best meets the needs of students with disabilities. Whatever the objectives, they should be clearly stated, measurable, and related to the purpose of the evaluation. There must be a direct relationship between the purpose of the program being evaluated and the evaluation objectives.

Selecting the Evaluator

The evaluation may require that individuals with certain specified relationships to the program be involved. For example, in formative evaluations, when the program is being refined, the evaluators should be people who are closely associated with it. This is in contrast to the role of evaluators in summative evaluation, where, as previously noted, the individuals selected should be external to the program being evaluated.

Frequently a team approach is better than an individual approach. An evaluation team consisting of both content area specialists and research/evaluation specialists can facilitate and improve the evaluation process (Callahan et al., 1981). Thus, for example, if a program for gifted and talented children were being evaluated, the evaluation team might consist of specialists in the area of gifted and talented education as well as specialists in evaluation.

In selecting members of the evaluation team, the potential for bias must be kept in mind. If their evaluation results are to be valid, the team members must be capable of reviewing the program objectively; biased evaluation results are useless. Moreover, program areas needing improvement might thereby be overlooked, creating the false impression that the program is adequate. In special education, in particular, objective evaluations are vital (especially in light of federal and state requirements that students with disabilities be afforded a free appropriate education and due process safeguards).

One member of the team should be designated as leader or coordinator. The specialty of the individual chosen—research/evaluation specialist or content-area specialist—must be determined in light of the particular local situation. Although not always the case, persons experienced in conducting evaluations are likely to perform better in such a leadership role and to better coordinate the team's evaluation efforts. Although budgetary constraints may restrict who can perform in the role as leader of the evaluation team, if possible, this individual should be a third party. If the team leader is not directly associated with the administration or the project being evaluated, the better the chances for a more diagnostic and accurate evaluation (Flynn & Harbin, 1987; Brinckerhoff et al., 1993).

Collecting Information

In the planning phase, a data collection plan should be developed. This plan should determine (1) the type of information to be collected, (2) how the information will be gathered, (3) the individuals responsible for the collection, and (4) timeliness for the collection.

Types of Information.   The type of information required for an evaluation will depend on the purposes of the evaluation. The information collected might include:

- Student achievement data from norm-referenced tests.
- Student achievement data from criterion-referenced tests.
- Program cost information.
- Statistical analyses.
- Interview data from program participants.
- Interview data from teaching and support personnel.
- Interview data from parents and other community members.
- Reports of student progress during the program.

- Observations of the program.
- Official reports from state or federal monitoring teams.

Once the type of information to be collected has been determined, the next step is to decide on appropriate methods for collecting each type of information. For example, if student achievement data are needed, it should be decided whether to use standardized tests, criterion-referenced tests, or teacher-made tests.

Methods.   The following methods may be used to collect the required data:

1. *Norm-referenced tests.* Most schools use standardized, norm-referenced tests to gather information concerning academic programs. The major advantage of norm-referenced over criterion-referenced and teacher-made tests is that school officials can compare the results in their district to the norm sample, which usually represents a national performance. If a major purpose of the evaluation is to determine how a program compares with national programs, norm-referenced testing can be a valuable source of data.

2. *Criterion-referenced tests.* Criterion-referenced tests determine the individual's skill in a particular area (Salvia & Ysseldyke, 1988). These tests do not compare students to a national norm group or other specific groups. They merely allow teachers to determine what skills a student has in a particular area, such as math or reading. In developing IEPs and evaluating individual progress toward educational goals, criterion-referenced tests are much more useful than norm-referenced instruments.

3. *Interviews.* Interviews are an efficient way of determining the perceptions that a person has about a situation or event, either current or historic. Though subjective, an interview schedule or protocol should be used. This is simply a questionnaire or question guide that provides continuity among the kinds of information collected from those interviewed.

4. *Attitude surveys.* Several types of attitude surveys are available for use in program evaluation. These include Likert scales, semantic-differential scales, and ranking statements. The particular format will depend on the type of information desired. Because their data are subjective, attitude surveys can uncover biases held by individuals and thus can yield helpful information (Smith, Price, & Marsh, 1986).

5. *Observations.* Observations may be one of two types: systematic or nonsystematic. Systematic observation is aimed at something specific, and nonsystematic observation is a more general review of a program or setting. Accordingly, observation methods range from very specific techniques, such as the use of systematic observation instruments, to sequential narratives of everything that occurs during the observation. In collecting information through observations, the ideal situation would be to have trained observers present for extended periods of time. Unfortunately, given limited resources, this is frequently not feasible. Alternatively, Wolf (1979) recommends that several observation periods of limited duration be used. For example, 40 15-minute observation periods could be used rather than 10 60-minute sessions. In this way, with each observation period, a fresh situation can be viewed.

Analyzing Information

After the evaluation data are collected, they must be analyzed and presented. Although this is a major activity, it frequently receives little attention. In reality, the importance of analysis is unsurpassed by any other element. If the data collected are not analyzed appropriately for easy interpretation, the entire evaluation effort could be meaningless (Worthen & Sanders, 1987).

In some evaluations, decisions are made solely on the basis of the descriptive information that has been collected. In other cases, however, extensive analysis must be made before decisions can be made. Often, such an analysis uses sophisticated statistical techniques, such as t-tests, analysis of variance, or regression procedures. Data are examined to determine if relationships among program variables are statistically significant. The type of analysis will depend on the particular set of data and the evaluation questions to be answered. In any event, in using statistical analysis, evaluators must remember that individual judgment is still a critical part of the process. Finally, even if high-powered statistical tests are used to determine such factors as relationships, treatment gain, and program effectiveness, individuals must still consider the results in relation to all other relevant variables before making evaluation decisions.

Communicating Evaluation Results

The final step in the evaluation of special education programs is to communicate the results. Unfortunately, evaluations frequently result in poorly written reports filled with jargon and meaningless statistics (Stufflebeam & Webster, 1988). Administrators must determine both the appropriate audience and the appropriate medium.

Appropriate Audience.   Knowing the audience can help evaluators write useful reports. In some cases, the agencies who pay for the evaluation have the opinion that they own the results and thus should have total decision-making authority in determining who receives the results. However, because schools are publicly supported institutions, they must disseminate the results of their evaluations broadly. Worthen and Sanders (1987) suggest that an audience analysis be conducted prior to writing and disseminating the report. Although the nature of the particular evaluation will in some ways dictate specific recipients, some of the individuals and groups who should be considered for the school evaluation reports are (1) students, both current and future, and their parents or guardians; (2) teaching personnel and ancillary staff; (3) the agencies who provided funding for the program; (4) administrators of similar educational programs; (5) community members, especially if the program has community interest; (6) members of the media; and (7) professionals concerned with the program content (Anderson et al., 1975).

Appropriate Medium.   After determining who will receive the results of the evaluation, the method to be used to transmit the results should be considered. Evaluation reports can be lengthy documents, detailing the entire program and evaluation process; or they can be brief and concise, focusing on the specific evaluation questions posed. Worthen and Sanders (1987) list the following types of evaluation reports:

- Written reports
- Photo essays
- Audiotape reports
- Slide-tape reports
- Film or videotape reports
- Multimedia presentations
- Dialogue/testimonies
- Hearings or mock trials
- Product displays
- Simulations
- Scenarios
- Portrayals
- Case studies
- Graphs and charts
- Test score summaries
- Questions/answers

Formal evaluation reports are generally of two types: interim or final. Interim reports are short summaries of activities during a particular time period. Their primary purpose is to keep individuals informed about the progress of the evaluation. Final reports are more extensive and include conclusions and recommendations. Final reports should include an overview of the program being evaluated, the evaluation methods used, and the outcome of the evaluation.

The exact format will vary with the nature of the evaluation and the particular desires of the administration and the evaluators. Reports should, however, be presented in such a manner that the content is easily understood by the audience receiving the information. This may require a slightly different report for each target group. For example, the report that goes to teachers might focus on aspects of the program related to instruction. Other groups, such as the media and parents, may require modified reports or special reporting methods. Administrators should also consider including brief summaries of evaluation data in local newspapers or school-based communication media. Regardless of the method used, all data collected during the evaluation should be accessible by groups or individuals who may wish to undertake additional analysis or replication, assuming that the data are not protected by requirements of confidentiality.

CHAPTER
NINE

PERSONNEL

Over the last decade, the emphasis of school reform has clearly been placed on enforcement measures for accountability while essentially ignoring the human factor. There has been only cursory mention of teachers in most of the "blue ribbon panels" or in most of the reform measures. However, as in other fields, management strategies have begun to focus on personnel as the most important element in improvement. And many grassroots trends in education have begun to focus on personnel as well. The global economy has forced all institutions to become more flexible, to rely more on workers, to develop adaptable forms of accountability, and to rely on team decisions.

It is difficult to believe that the problems of today's schools can be rectified with stricter standards, uniform procedures, or accountability measures, when the most important component is the interaction between teachers and students, as well as collaboration between teachers. The new culture, for both business and schools, is based on teamwork.

Over the last century, most curriculum development has been based on the needs of the bureaucracy, rather than on the needs of students or teachers. But new definitions of the curriculum are emerging, and these new definitions increasingly take into account the needs of teachers and other school personnel.

The curriculum is based on goals and objectives that address district, state, or national outcomes, but it permits teachers to use a variety of instructional approaches in meeting the diverse needs of a diverse student body. And this demands that school administrators carefully select personnel with diverse skills, rather than mere competence in one discipline or subject matter area.

A review of the various trends in school restructuring suggests common elements that relate to personnel (Reavis & Griffith, 1992), primarily site-based decision making in the areas of budget, staff development, curriculum and instruction, and personnel. Spence (1990) noted that "when placed in the same system, people, however different, tend to produce similar results" (p. 42). Levine (1992) has emphasized the importance of management focused on achievement of results rather than delivery of programs. Reavis and Griffith (1992) state that "decision-making authority is a key change in the restructured organization."

Of all the functions that the administrator must perform, the most important and time consuming is that involving personnel. And the demands of a new age, to garner more involvement of personnel in making decisions for the organization, increases the amount of time that administrators must spend dealing with personnel issues. Education is a labor-intensive industry that achieves its goals mainly through the efforts of people, rather than through capital investments or technology. In fact, 80 to 85% of the typical school district budget is devoted to personnel-related costs.

It is vital that administrators develop and maintain comprehensive personnel policies and procedures to ensure that the school district selects, develops, and maintains the most capable staff possible. There must be procedures to help administrators determine if staff members are performing adequately. Wise personnel policies can solve problems before they become serious and can help the administrator to develop the most important school resource—a good staff.

Although there was a general oversupply of teachers in most regular education teaching areas of the 1980s, a trend that continues into the 1990s, the overall teaching force is aging. It is anticipated that over one million teachers will retire by the end of the decade. It remains to be seen if there will be a large pool of candidates to replace these teachers. Depending upon certification requirements for special education, there may be a shortage of special education teachers, especially African-American teachers or teachers from minority ethnic backgrounds. Many states continue to issue emergency certificates to teachers of students with disabilities who do not have appropriate training. If the current trend toward inclusion and dual certification of classroom teachers continues, the classroom teacher may become the special education teacher as well. This possibility should heighten the concern of administrators about selecting new teachers. Administrators must establish sound personnel systems to help them in the identification, placement, development, and evaluation of all staff; but they must be particularly concerned about the abilities of classroom teachers to deal effectively with both the nondisabled students and the students with disabilities, who may likely be included in the same classrooms.

To carry out the intent of federal legislation, regular and special education teachers must understand each other's responsibilities and must work cooperatively. Indeed, the trends toward team teaching and site-based management may elevate this concern regardless of the nature of the curriculum or children involved. In the past, concern was about mainstreaming, but the new emphasis is likely to be on inclusion, which has implications for personnel selection, cooperative teaching, evaluation, and budgetary considerations. This requires the willingness of teachers to work together in meeting the needs of pupils as well as the needs of the school. Central to this relationship are the appropriate attitudes, knowledge, and skills that enable teachers to work together effectively. These factors should be clearly described in board mission statements and policy and should guide all aspects of the personnel function. It is particularly important that the district select and retain teachers who are willing and able to work with children with disabilities. Administrators must assist those teachers currently employed in developing the skills needed to work with children with disabilities. And efforts should be made to assure that new employees also have the prerequisite attitudes and skills.

For categorical programs, the special education administrator usually makes personnel decisions by using and adapting regular personnel procedures. Under policies of inclusion, routine personnel procedures may be used as well. In many districts a separate personnel division is administered by a personnel officer. In other districts, the personnel function is divided between central office and building-level administrators, with the superintendent assuming the major responsibility for overall monitoring. Regardless of the organizational structure, the special education administrator and the building principal should be actively involved in personnel decisions that relate to the delivery of services to children with disabilities.

The special education administrator should be consulted during the development and implementation of regular education personnel functions whenever those functions interact with the special education system. All of this will be determined by the extent of separation of special education services from the mainstream. A district bound by inclusion principles and/or certification will probably have a more integrated system or will probably move in that direction with the passage of time.

POSITION DESCRIPTIONS

Position descriptions communicate expectations for job performance, identify the supervisory and reporting system for each position, and serve as the fundamental criteria for activities in evaluation and staff development systems. Insofar as special education competencies are concerned, descriptions for all positions should be prepared by the special education administrator and the building principal, with staff assistance. Inclusion models of education will incorporate many special education requirements with the regular personnel system, and in such cases, teacher competencies related to the needs of children with disabilities should be included in position descriptions for the regular education teacher. This is important because studies of licensure requirements have indicated that most regular education teachers usually are required to have only a cursory exposure to the nature of disabilities and little knowledge of classroom accommodation strategies (Patton & Braithwaite, 1990; Reiff, Evans, & Cass, 1991). For categorical programs and for children not served in regular classrooms, a comprehensive position statement for each special education position must be developed.

Because of inclusion models, special education competencies should also be incorporated in position descriptions for all regular education administrators, especially building principals. The special education role of these administrators must be clearly stated in a position description and may include competencies related to federal and state laws and local district policy. The administrator must be able to ensure due process, interpret federal and state laws, use appropriate leadership styles consistent with board policies and/or site-based management expectations, resolve conflicts among program personnel, use evaluation data to make program revisions for exceptional learners, and determine staff functions and qualifications for educational programs for children with disabilities. Valesky and Hirth (1992) found that administrator licensure requirements in most states did not adequately address aspects of special education law, and hence, many potential candidates may not possess the requisite knowledge.

RECRUITMENT

The purpose of recruitment procedures is to ensure that the district, when filling vacancies, has an adequate number of candidates for a selection pool. The more qualified the candidates who apply, the greater the likelihood that a good selection will be made. Comprehensive recruitment policies and procedures are, therefore, very important for school districts that have difficulty attracting qualified personnel or that attempt to fill positions with a small selection pool of qualified candidates. Inadequate policies can lead to conflict, internal strife, and litigation. One aspect of policy is to clearly adhere to all laws and guidelines that affect hiring practices. Lunenburg and Ornstein (1991) identify several considerations including minorities, women, older workers, people with disabilities, veterans, and affirmative action programs. Laws pertaining to recruitment include:

• Equal Pay Act of 1963, which prohibits wage discrimination based on gender.

- Title VII of the Civil Rights Act of 1964, amended, prohibiting discrimination on the basis of race, color, religion, gender, or national origin.

- Age Discrimination in Employment Act of 1968, amended, which prohibits discrimination against persons forty and older.

- Occupation Safety and Health Act of 1970, requiring notification and procedures about safety and health hazards.

- Rehabilitation Act of 1973, requiring affirmative action in the employment and promotion of qualified persons with disabilities.

- Vietnam Era Veterans Readjustment Act of 1974, requiring affirmative action in the employment of Vietnam Era veterans with disabilities.

- Pregnancy Discrimination Act of 1978, which requires pregnant women and new postpartum mothers to be regarded as other employees in employment related activities.

Castetter (1981) identified five components of the recruitment process: (1) development of a policy, (2) specification of recruitment activities, (3) development of potential personnel sources, (4) coordination of the personnel search, and (5) evaluation of the entire process.

Recruitment Policy

Many districts do not develop a clear policy for recruitment; that is, a policy statement by the board of education regarding the attraction and selection of the types of professionals it intends to employ. Board policy provides direction to district administrators who seek and interview qualified candidates for potential employment. All recruitment policies should be written and disseminated among staff so that all are aware of the board's position.

It is also critical that the district consider its expectations for internal recruitment and for employing new individuals. It should seek to employ individuals who are capable of working both within its guidelines and with current staff. The board's recruitment policy must answer several questions:

- How widespread will recruitment be?
- To what extent will staff be involved in recruitment?
- What is the district's commitment to affirmative action?
- To what extent does the board want to encourage the selection and retraining of current personnel for new or vacant positions?
- What are the general levels of preparation and experience that the board expects of qualified applicants before consideration for a position?
- Which district employees are responsible for certain aspects of the recruitment process?
- What district resources will be allocated to the recruitment activities?

Castetter (1981) stressed the importance and acceptance of centralized recruitment and screening and decentralized selection as a procedure for permitting unit administrators to have a voice in the selection of personnel. With the spread of site-based management, many schools involve the teaching faculty more directly in selecting new personnel. District staff, including the special education administrator, bear the main burden in recruiting a wide, suitable pool of acceptable candidates for a position, but they must involve building administrators and staff in the final selection or rejection of candidates. Decentralized involvement is crucial because of the increasing need for personnel to be able to work together. Without site involvement, it is unlikely that a new employee or perhaps a promoted employee would fit into the work situation and be able to forge cooperative working relationships with teams of teachers.

Recruitment Activities

The general recruitment policy should serve as a guide for the development of position specifications for each vacancy as it occurs. This will give direction to the district when it advertises the vacancy and selects candidates for interviews. General position descriptions should serve as a beginning point for development of individual position specifications.

Care should be taken to involve district staff who will be working with a new employee. If there is a vacancy in special education, for example, the special education administrator might be the one to specify the competencies the candidate should possess. However, the building principal and the staff should also be involved and consulted for their views about the desirable characteristics of the employee, especially in inclusion settings. In filling regular education positions, the special education administrator and teachers have usually played a consultative role, but as the trend to inclusion gains momentum it seems likely that such distinctions will be less important.

Once position characteristics have been determined, it is necessary to determine other factors such as level of salary, fringe benefits, and teaching load. All of this information should be included in the vacancy announcement. The announcement should also include a general description of position benefits, application time lines, characteristics of the district and community, and a description of the type of information each candidate must submit. The submitted information may include, in addition to the completed application form, items such as a resume, letters of reference, a statement of the candidate's teaching philosophy, and a portfolio of previous work. At this point in the process, the district-level employee who is coordinating the application process must ensure that the following elements are in order: (1) appropriate application forms, (2) a system for processing applications and notifying individuals of their application status, (3) a time line for application procedures, (4) a procedure for screening applications and selection of finalists, and (5) a recruitment budget for advertising, travel, and other expenses.

Potential Personnel Sources

In selecting possible sources for recruitment, the administrator should not overlook the possibility of internal promotion or reassignment. In times of fiscal cutbacks, internal reassignment may be economical. Also, morale may be adversely affected if a highly qualified internal candidate is overlooked. It is possible that teachers in the district may be retrained, and student teachers who have been assigned to practice teach in the district may have already demonstrated competence and ability to collaborate. In cases of internal recruitment, the district has the advantage of previous knowledge of the capabilities of the candidate and the assurance that the candidate already knows district policies and procedures.

If external candidates are sought, the district should attempt to advertise the vacancy as widely as possible. External recruitment sources include college and university placement bureaus, public and private employment agencies and firms, professional associations, other school districts, professional meetings and conventions, professional journals, and direct solicitation of known candidates. The *New York Times* carries a Sunday supplement to advertise careers and is widely read throughout the country.

Personnel Search

In the personnel search, procedures are developed to process all application materials when they arrive, to notify applicants of their status, and to identify those applicants whose credentials match the position requirements. It is important that applications be processed as soon as they arrive and that applicants begin to assess the attractiveness of the district on the basis of these initial contacts; the administrator must, accordingly, seek to promote a positive district image.

As the applications arrive, each should be compared with the position description to determine the relative rank of the candidate. Some of the candidates will be considered in greater detail, and ultimately a certain number will be invited to visit the district for interviews. As appropriate, special and regular education administrators and other personnel should be actively involved in these activities.

Evaluation

In the final phase of the recruitment process, the administrator should seek to determine if the recruitment activities have been successful. Castetter (1981) suggested that certain questions be examined, such as:

- Have the costs incurred in the process been reasonable?
- Has a sufficient number of candidates applied?
- Has the quality of the applicants been adequate?
- Have personnel time and costs been reasonable?

Answers to these questions will also help the administrator determine what changes in the recruitment procedures, if any, should be made in subsequent recruitment efforts. If problems exist, certain steps can be developed to prevent them in the future.

SELECTION

Once the most qualified candidates have been identified, the next task is to select the candidate who best meets the position description. Though the information collected in the recruitment phase includes descriptions of the qualifications of each candidate, those descriptions are not sufficient to guide the selection of the individual who best meets the district's needs. To make this decision, additional information must be obtained through personal interviews and observations. This selection process consists of several possible stages: (1) establishment of a selection committee, (2) articulation of selection criteria, (3) review of application information, (4) selection of interview and observation questions, and (5) selection of the individual who meets the criteria (Castetter, 1981).

Selection Committee

Although the board of education alone has the authority to employ, most new employees are first screened and selected by a district committee, which then, through the office of the superintendent, recommends to the board that a certain individual be employed. This selection committee should consist of administrators, teachers, and other individuals who have knowledge and experience necessary to determine the degree to which the candidates meet the position requirements and fit into current district philosophy and operations. The district special education supervisor should assume primary responsibility for coordinating the work of the selection committee. The principal in whose building the vacancy exists should also be involved, because that individual will also have the supervisory responsibility for the new employee.

It is also advisable to involve representatives of the regular and special education faculties, when appropriate, because they will work closely with the new employee. However, the committee should consist of no more than five or six people so that it can be managed efficiently. When a regular education position is filled, it might be advisable to involve special education staff to ensure that the new regular education employee is knowledgeable about and sensitive to the needs of children with disabilities, especially in cases where inclusion models are used. The selection committee should be given release time to conduct its work and should be provided, by the district, with all the information necessary to make a wise decision.

Selection Criteria

To determine which candidate is the most appropriate, the selection committee must agree on the criteria by which the candidates will be assessed. In their discussion about criteria, the committee members will, in effect, translate general teacher characteristics into specific, district-related criteria and then determine ways to assess these characteristics during the interview. Every attempt should be made to select criteria that are specific to the individual vacancy.

Applicant Information

After the position criteria have been identified, the credentials of the applicants are reviewed and compared with the criteria. This may be done by the district's personnel director, the special education administrator, or by a member or members of the selection committee. The purpose of this review is to identify those few candidates whose credentials best meet the selection criteria and who will be invited for interviews.

Interview and Observation Questions

The interview is the most common technique for selecting an individual from a group of finalists. The format for the interview can be either formal or informal. In either case, it is important that the selection committee clearly specify in advance those procedures and expected outcomes of the interviews. All the interviews should follow the same format, so that the data will permit comparisons among the candidates.

The interview is very important, but it often has many flaws (Bolton, 1973; Drake, 1972; and Greene, 1971). Lunenburg and Ornstein (1991) recommend the use of a structured interview format, interviewer training, a written record of each interview, multiple interviewers, opportunity for the applicant to talk, and avoidance of the interview as the sole criterion for selection. They also note that interviewers are sometimes unfamiliar with the job, make premature decisions, emphasize negative information, interject personal biases that offend applicants, and make other errors.

The professional literature for years has abounded with suggestions for interview questions (Castetter, 1981; Diamond, 1974: Engel & Friedrichs, 1980; Koerner, 1969). But even the most structured interview can present incomplete or misleading information about a candidate. This is because interview data are verbally oriented and reflect only what the candidate says. But this may not necessarily correspond to how the candidate will actually behave after employment. If the applicant has a previous record, evaluations may be obtained from former employers, but this may be fraught with problems. Reliance on an unknown employer will not necessarily result in valid information, and sometimes employers will characterize their comments if they are trying to retain or release an employee. For new graduates, there is often little objective information available. One trend that may be helpful is the tendency to use portfolio assessment, whereby a candidate may provide videotapes of actual classroom performance. But for now it is necessary to rely on techniques that can elicit relatively accurate characterizations of the candidates' behavior, such as a comprehensive reaction to simulated activities described in a problem. Candidates may also be asked to write personal statements of their philosophy or attitudes toward some issue, such as regular and special education cooperation. These techniques can provide data about candidates' writing abilities and ability to think, as well as provide some insight into the candidates' teaching style.

Final Selection

After all candidates have been interviewed, the selection committee should review the data and offer the position to the individual who best meets the selection criteria. This is often a difficult decision because usually no one individual meets all of the criteria and because not all candidates are comparable in every respect. In addition, for a variety of reasons, the committee may be divided about the traits of various individuals. Committee members must keep their selection criteria firmly in mind in order to maintain maximum objectivity at this stage.

After a candidate has been identified as the most appropriate, the committee chairperson or other administrator designated to handle personnel matters should offer the individual the position and discuss the terms and conditions of employment, contingent upon board approval. The specific issues to be discussed should include working conditions, salary, specific assignments, the role of superiors, the length of the contract, the nature of provisional or tenure status, and other matters that are uniquely relevant to the local school. The agreement between the school and the candidate on these various points should be documented, as a basis for a contract to be recommended by the superintendent and approved by the board.

It is important that the terms of employment be clearly understood by the candidate prior to acceptance of the contract. Such understanding will foster the transition of the candidate into an integral role on the school staff, a candidate who is excited about the new challenges and opportunities of the position and who will concentrate on fulfilling the requirements of the position. It has long been known that employee satisfaction and productivity in the first year is greatly determined by the degree to which the employee's expectations match the organization's expectations (Kotter, 1973; Rubin, 1969; and Schein, 1962, 1970).

Personnel Shortages

Where personnel shortages exist, especially in rural areas or when certified racial or ethnic minority special education candidates are needed, the district may wish to encourage currently employed teachers to seek retraining. Partnerships between universities and local schools can often be targeted toward addressing specific personnel needs (King-Sears, Rosenberg, Ray, & Fagen, 1992). School districts may find that in the long run it is more economically feasible to provide release time, sabbaticals, or tuition reimbursement to retrain existing teachers, who will remain committed to the district, than risk hiring new staff or incurring recruitment expenses when the chance of finding a qualified candidate is low (McIntosh, 1986).

ORIENTATION

The orientation system serves several purposes. First, it provides an opportunity for the new employee to learn more about the culture of the school, the instructional and other resources of the district, the job expectations, and the procedures to follow in fulfilling expectations. More importantly, it helps the new employee become acquainted with his or her colleagues, thus facilitating the assimilation of the employee into ongoing working relationships within the organization. This human aspect of the orientation process is crucial, because the working relationships begun during this phase will carry over throughout the first year of the job and establish a foundation for the future.

District-Level Orientation

Most school districts have procedures for the general orientation of new faculty and staff. Often these procedures begin immediately after the new employee has signed the contract and may include such services as helping the new employee move to the district and find housing. In any event, some type of orientation is essential to inform the new employee about district procedures. The new employee should receive, for example, a district policy handbook, a teacher personnel handbook, and information about fringe benefits, as well as information about the community and community resources, personnel evaluation procedures, and instructional and other resources available in the district (including procedures for requesting and using such resources).

Building-Level Orientation

The orientation process should continue at the building level where the new employee is to be located. Information at this level needs to be much more specific and should be designed to help the new employee assume the job as soon as possible. It should include information on (1) building layout and facilities, (2) school schedules and routines, (3) the attendance system and other record keeping, (4) the building support staff and their functions, (5) procedures for ordering supplies and other materials, and (6) procedures for administrative supervision.

Some districts assign an experienced teacher to assist the new teacher, thus creating a collegial system upon which the new teacher can rely for ongoing information, personal support, and modeling. Such a system has merit because it frees the administrator from the need for constant supervision of new employees while it creates positive interpersonal relationships among fellow teachers. However, if such a system is employed, great care should be taken to ensure that the assigned teacher has positive work habits, displays appropriate attitudes toward students with disabilities, meets the highest standards of professionalism, and will work constructively with the new employee.

Special Orientation Problems

It is important, at the outset, that the district stress its expectation that the regular and special education staff will cooperate in all areas of curriculum and student activities. Newly hired regular education teachers should understand all aspects of the referral, placement, and evaluation procedures for children with disabilities; the nature of the special education services available and procedures for requesting services; and the nature of joint instructional planning between regular and special teachers. Some new teachers may express anxiety about dealing with children with disabilities and sharing instructional planning with other teachers. These anxieties should be dealt with as soon as possible. Individual counseling or other forms of instruction may be provided to help the teacher adopt the necessary positive attitudes and professional working relationships. Ideally, these factors would have been considered thoroughly before the contract was offered. In schools that use the inclusion model, regular classroom teachers will likely be required to have prior training and/or certification to meet the needs of students with disabilities in regular classrooms.

STAFF DEVELOPMENT

The orientation process serves as the initial staff development activity for new employees. Thereafter, the employee will continue to acquire new knowledge about current trends and procedures and to refine skills, knowledge, and attitudes. Continuing opportunities must be provided for the growth and development of the employee. This is a function of the staff development system.

Staff development is often required, either by the district or the state. As such, it may often include both informal training programs as well as college courses. A variety of options are available, however, ranging from teacher-directed staff development, as in the Dade County Public Schools of Florida, to training programs designed by local administrators to achieve certain goals of change. Herzberg (1987) refers to a system of motivation-hygiene theory that produces job enrichment rather than staff development. Herzberg maintains that it is important for the organization to motivate the employee to achieve outcomes that are both important to the employee and to the organization.

Regardless of the reasons, staff development can be perceived as an important activity for continuous staff improvement or as an imposition. Researchers present arguments both for and against staff development. For example, Lunenburg and Ornstein (1991) note that people learn best by doing, not by listening to speakers or attending workshops; that educators are highly trained and do not necessarily need more training; and that staff development is too expensive and time consuming. We believe, however, that despite the qualifications of employees when they enter a job, ultimately there will be changes that will require new training; teachers' knowledge can become outdated; and staff development can keep teachers current.

Bishop (1976) identified eight components of a staff development system that are still viable:

- Identification of needs and objectives.
- Determination of target groups.
- Determination of time, space, personnel, and material resources.
- Determination of program format.

- Specification of program responsibilities and logistics.
- Development of program content and materials.
- Implementation of the program.
- Evaluation.

Needs and Objectives

All staff development activities should be designed to achieve clearly articulated objectives. Without this focus, staff development activities will be poorly received and create apprehension regarding future staff development activities. Teachers themselves are an important source of needs data. Informal comments by teachers can be recorded, or more formal needs assessment questionnaires can be used. The survey need not be elaborate to be effective but should be constructed in such a way as to allow teachers to identify their perceived needs accurately and anonymously. In this connection, it should be noted that short-term workshops and training frequently leave teachers feeling uncertain about their abilities to deal effectively with a new concept or range of issues. The ability of teachers to acquire skills will take a sustained effort over a long period of time with adequate follow-up and follow through.

Because many teachers may not be aware of their own needs, multiple data sources should be used. Regular and special education administrators may identify training needs through supervision and evaluation of teachers; review of litigation, court rulings, and state and federal regulations; and examination of current research on teacher competencies. Needs data may identify staff development objectives in a variety of areas, including attitudes, curriculum, staff relationships, organizational procedures, staff knowledge and skills, use of resources and materials, and instructional operations and procedures.

Target Groups

To meet staff development objectives, the administrator must determine which individuals or groups should participate in staff development activities. Too often, administrators assume that all staff must participate. Although this may be an effective strategy for certain types of objectives, it should not become a routine procedure, because the needs of specific groups may differ. Also, large group activities do not meet individual needs or allow adequate individual participation and evaluation or effectiveness.

The administrator thus might choose to individualize staff development activities in terms of such special target groups as individual schools, staff subgroups, or individual staff members. Thus, individuals at a certain grade level, individuals with similar responsibilities or students, and staff specialists might be selected for special development activities. In some cases, participation of local community or business elements might be needed to accomplish certain instructional goals.

Relevant Resources

Most frequently, private or university consultants are hired to develop and organize training experiences. Such consultants have the advantage of being external to the politics of the local school. However, they should, of course, possess the expertise to provide training on a particular topic. If the cost of external consultants or their lack of relevant expertise makes the use of such personnel inappropriate, school administrators should consider the use of local teachers or other staff to provide training. Most schools have outstanding teachers who model exemplary teacher behavior. Such individuals feel honored when asked to train their peers. Also, they have the advantage of being familiar with the local situation, and their services will usually cost the district less than those of outside consultants. Other potential trainers include department of education officials, regional service center staff, and staff from neighboring districts.

The staff development training program should be conveniently located and have all the necessary facilities, such as audiovisual equipment and large and small group spaces, that are needed to accomplish the program's objectives. Comfort features, such as lighting, seating, and ventilation, should also be taken into account.

Probably the most difficult aspects of logistical planning are determining the amount of instructional time and selecting appropriate time periods. No time is convenient for everyone. Also, most teachers are hesitant to give up instructional time with children or to attend staff development after school without additional compensation. Often the amount of time that schools can devote to in-school staff development is restricted by teacher collective bargaining agreements. In any event, if at all possible, staff development should be conducted at times other than immediately after the instructional day. Also teachers should be paid for attending sessions that are not on school time. School district administrators should also consider the advantages of allowing staff development credit to count toward salary increments.

An important logistical issue concerns the nature and type of materials and equipment needed in the training. Items such as supplies and audiovisual equipment must be considered. The administrator will also need to determine whether existing training materials will be used or if new or revised materials need to be developed. The development of new materials will, of course, prolong the development lead time needed.

Program Format, Responsibilities, and Logistics

The development program format must match the objectives and needs of the participants; it should include active participation, self-directed learning, and demonstrations of classroom procedures with opportunities for practice. The administrator should consider the following alternative formats to improve the staff development experience or to achieve specific training objectives:

- A workshop or seminar, allowing for individual involvement.
- A task force, in which members actively explore a topic and make recommendations for changes in district procedures.

- A clinic, using hands-on experiences and demonstrations with children or other clients to demonstrate teaching or instructional techniques.
- Individual study, to help teachers develop new skills or improve existing capabilities.
- Teacher visitation, in which teachers receive release time to observe other teachers demonstrate a technique or skill.
- University courses, to the extent that they are designed to address specific staff development topics and are offered at times and in locations convenient for local school personnel.

The administrator should also consider cooperating with other schools and school districts to pool fiscal and personnel resources and thus lower the cost of staff development activities. Such interdistrict or regional programs are often stimulating and successful in that they allow teachers to share problems and solutions with colleagues from other districts.

Finally, someone must be given clear responsibility for coordinating the various activities of the development program. Each component must be monitored and coordinated with the other parts of the program. These components include:

1. Overall leadership and coordination.
2. Ongoing training.
3. Small group activity.
4. Preparation of materials.
5. Site and logistic arrangements.
6. Payment of bills and handling of expenses.
7. Program evaluation.
8. Mailing of agenda, invitations, and site directions.

Program Content and Materials

The content of staff development activity must be relevant to the specific objectives of the program. Too often, administrators try to modify previous training activities to meet program objectives for which they were not originally designed, and predictably, the results are deficient. Sound, instructional planning skills must be used to design the content of the staff development activities to match the objectives and meet the needs of the participants. Among these activities are (1) the planning and sequencing of events and (2) the development of the agenda, program materials, audiovisual materials, and evaluation forms.

Implementation

Most staff development activities will run smoothly if adequate planning procedures have been followed. However, the administrator should always anticipate the unexpected and use formative evaluation to monitor the ongoing progress of the training experiences and to adjust it as needed.

Evaluation

Using the evaluation procedures and forms that have been developed, the administrator should ensure that evaluation data are collected, analyzed, and shared with the participants. As usual, assessment may be used in the areas of attitudes, changed behavior, financial costs, and other traditional criteria for determining the effectiveness for the staff development efforts and assessing their implications for future programs.

PERSONNEL EVALUATION

Personnel evaluation in special education is important to ensure that district goals regarding instruction for students with disabilities are met. Without the evaluation of teachers and other support staff, one of the main variables in the accountability of the special education system would be missing. Data gathered through evaluation can be used to establish staff development objectives either for individual teachers or for groups. A systematic evaluation process also provides the documentation required to satisfy due process in the case of teacher dismissal. Personnel evaluation in special education, however, is problematic for several reasons:

1. Special education teachers may operate in a different instructional setting and often employ different instructional techniques than regular education teachers.
2. Lines of responsibility for evaluating special education personnel and the special education responsibilities of regular class teachers are often unclear between the special education administrator and regular education administrators, especially the building principal.
3. Responsibility for accomplishment of special education goals is shared jointly between regular education and special education teachers. In inclusion settings this shared responsibility, unless well clarified, is of particular concern.

Most school districts already have teacher evaluation systems in place. These are used primarily to evaluate regular class teachers as they deal with regular instruction in the regular class and the typical regular education student. Such systems consist of simple checklists, comprehensive performance appraisal models, or outcomes-based models. Regardless of the system used, it must be flexible enough to allow for meaningful evaluation of all aspects of the special education teacher. Many districts use the same evaluation criteria for regular education and special education teachers. This may be problematic, because the instructional setting for the regular teacher and the special educator may be very different. However, as more schools develop inclusion models, it may be that a more uniform system will emerge or that special evaluation procedures will be developed to account for the unique responsibilities of each. Or, new evaluation models may need to be developed to address cooperative teaching arrangements between regular and special education personnel who work together in the regular class.

Personnel Evaluation Models

All personnel evaluation systems are variations of one of three basic systems: (1) narrative, (2) checklist, and (3) performance objectives. Each of these systems has advantages and disadvantages that must be considered. To determine which system to use, the administrator should first ascertain its intended purpose; not all systems will accomplish all purposes equally well (nor would an administrator want to work with such a cumbersome system). Rather, the administrator should first determine exactly what the system should accomplish and then examine its procedure to see if, in fact, it is accomplishing these objectives. Following are specific alternative purposes for evaluation systems:

- Improve instruction.
- Provide information for staff development.
- Demonstrate accountability to the board or patrons.
- Facilitate retention, assignment, and nonrenewal decisions.
- Provide information on teacher salaries.
- Validate the selection process.
- Identify conditions that would increase teacher effectiveness.
- Improve teacher performance.
- Promote cooperative relationships between teachers and administrators.
- Ensure that district and building goals are met.
- Recommend probationary teachers for tenure or continuing contract status.
- Select teachers for supervisory or administrative positions.
- Provide information for reductions in force.

Narrative Model.   The narrative model is the simplest mode of evaluation. In this model, the evaluator observes the teacher and records a summary of the observation in narrative form. Some narrative forms contain headings to guide the observation on various aspects of teaching, such as instructional effectiveness, personal qualities, and professional characteristics.

The advantages of the narrative model are:

- It is simple to complete.
- It is adaptable to most situations.
- It has a flexible recording format.

The disadvantages are:

- It requires a great deal of skill to record observations accurately.
- It does not provide a uniform evaluation for all teachers.
- It makes it difficult to compare teacher ratings.
- It may or may not include suggestions for improvement.

Checklist Model.   With the checklist model, the evaluator observes and rates the teacher's behavior on a structured evaluation checklist. Each checklist format is unique to the local district, and it may included a Likert-type rating scale of 1 to 5 or use some other system of rating, such as "excellent, good, average, and poor." Most checklist formats have several broad categories to describe the total teacher-learning process, for example, instructional effectiveness, personal characteristics, professional qualities, and public relations skills. In each general category, lists of specific characteristics are used as the basis for the ratings.

The advantages of the model are:

- It provides a structured pattern for observation.
- It accommodates numerical ratings.
- It allows for comparisons of ratings.
- It is easy to complete in a short period of time.
- It communicates expected behaviors to teachers.

The disadvantages are:

- Categories do not deal with actual teacher effectiveness.
- Its profile ratings usually do not differentiate between the poor, good, and excellent teacher.
- It forces the evaluator to use a standard set of criteria, even though the class lessons and formats may vary widely.
- Its categories and items within categories vary in significance, and there is rarely an attempt to weigh their relative importance.
- Routine use of the checklist can encourage rash judgments and lack of reflection about observed behavior.
- It makes no suggestions for improvement.

Although the checklist model is by far the one most frequently used, the special and regular education administrator should understand that its frequent use is related more to historical precedent than to its advantages. In fact, the disadvantages of the checklist model are numerous.

Performance Objectives Model.   The performance objectives model is an attempt to structure the process of evaluation while individualizing the criteria used in the evaluation of teachers. The evaluator meets with each teacher to establish objectives for the performance of the teacher and the criteria and procedures to be used in assessment. The evaluator uses class observations and other means to monitor the success of the teacher in meeting performance objectives. The emphasis is on continuous instructional improvement and yearly reassessment of improvement goals.

The advantages of the performance objectives approach are:

- It encourages the evaluator and teacher to cooperate as a team.
- Its focus is on improvement of teacher behavior.
- The evaluator is viewed less as a threat.
- Its format is flexible and adaptable to most teaching situations.
- Its use of goals provides criteria for assessment progress.
- It documents procedures to enable the evaluator to help the teacher improve.
- It places primary responsibility for improvement on the teacher.

The disadvantages are:

- It is more time consuming than other methods.
- Teachers using it may have difficulty writing performance objectives.
- It may require training for the evaluator and the teacher.
- The evaluator may not have the interpersonal skills necessary to interact effectively with teachers.

Probably the most useful aspect of the performance objective model is that it gives the evaluator and the teacher complete flexibility in establishing the improvement objectives. Also, although these objectives usually deal with some area of instruction, they need not be confined to class behavior. However, the performance objectives approach requires a serious commitment of time and effort, because the evaluator and teacher must engage in face-to-face conferences, once to establish objectives and again to review progress in meeting the objectives. Yet this time investment can be quite productive, giving the evaluator greater insight into the instructional process and into the role of each teacher in the process. Further, the rapport developed through personal interaction with each teacher confirms the evaluator's willingness to cooperate with the teachers, to be concerned about their improvement, and to facilitate their career growth. Moreover, once established, that rapport will facilitate other areas of interaction between the evaluator-administrator and the teacher.

Outcomes Evaluation.   Various trends in school restructuring suggest such common elements as site-based decision making, a shift in instructional emphasis from pedagogical models to an emphasis on human cognition, and a shift from coverage of topics to a constructivist approach, helping students construct their own meaning (Reavis & Griffith, 1992). Such changes cause the system of evaluation of students and teachers to change, especially when teachers and groups of teachers have more authority in making their own decisions and the system is altered from evaluation of the teacher as a master of a body of knowledge. Alternative types of personnel evaluation systems will gain more popularity as the public becomes more concerned with educational results and disenchanted with the effectiveness of traditional evaluation systems to weed out poor teachers or to enrich marginal teachers.

One possibility is outcome assessment rather than process assessment of teachers. In other words, teachers should be viewed as more accountable to other teachers, to teams, and to their students. Darling-Hammond (1992) calls this "client-oriented accountability" because professional accountability is defined by client-oriented and knowledge-based decisions rather than definable moves and behaviors to be performed for an assessment audience. Rather than examining inquiry methods, time on task, eye contact during lecture, and other variables so popular in teacher assessment approaches (behaviors that may not exist with the same frequency if children are engaged in cooperative learning), assessment must reflect peer involvement.

If teachers are primarily employed to teach students rather than teach courses or content, an observation or rating by an administrator will not be adequate. As collaboration supersedes hierarchical structure in a modern organization, the focus will be more on the outcome (product, student) instead of the process. As education becomes more characterized by groups of teachers working collaboratively, by cooperative learning among pupils, and by the use of technology in teaching, new methods of evaluating pupils and teachers must emerge. Such an assessment system may require teachers to present portfolios with examples of their students' work or other student outcomes as evidence of accomplishing instructional goals. With an emphasis on human cognition rather than pedagogical models, evaluation must become less concerned with the teacher as skilled presenter and more concerned with teacher as collaborator, team player, and manager of classrooms and constructive learning. This will be especially true in inclusion settings in which teams of teachers work collaboratively with individual and groups of students.

Alternative Sources of Evaluation Data

The following methods can be incorporated in any of the evaluation systems mentioned as supplemental information sources about teaching effectiveness:

1. *Student ratings.* There are many forms available for use by students. These forms are used to record the students' perceptions of the effectiveness of the teacher and personal judgments about the teacher's relationship with the students. These data can help teachers develop insights into the effectiveness of their teaching style and class behavior. Some caution, however, should be exercised to ensure that the students are mature enough to make such judgments and that the format is geared to the age and grade level of the students.

2. *Self-ratings.* Many evaluation procedures require that the teacher complete some form of self-rating, based on the district's formal evaluation protocol. This self-assessment can be quite instructive, in that it forces the teacher to review and assess

personal performance and thus lays the groundwork for the evaluation conference between the teacher and the evaluator. However, evaluators should not force teachers to be overly critical of themselves or to misuse teachers' personal evaluation data. It requires a great deal of courage for individuals to be self-critical, and the evaluator should be sensitive to this fact.

3. *Peer ratings.* Peer ratings are an assessment of a teacher's performance by other teachers. This form of rating can be helpful to a teacher, especially if it is done by respected colleagues in a professional manner. However, many teachers resist evaluating other teachers because they believe that it is not their job; nor are they willing to be the subjects of such evaluation by other teachers, unless there is a team teaching arrangement where teachers are intimately aware of each other's performance. It is important that the teachers understand that the data collected in this manner will be confidential and used only to support the professional growth of the teachers.

4. *Parent or patron ratings.* Often an administrator receives unsolicited parent or patron evaluations of a teacher's performance. Such evaluative comments should be shared with the teacher in question, but they should be corroborated before they are taken into account. Still, similar comments about a teacher from several parents may indicate the existence of a problem or the existence of an outstanding teacher. However, most parent evaluation comments or ratings are used to judge the effectiveness of the entire instructional program rather than the performance of an individual.

SUPERVISION

Whereas personnel evaluation is designed to assure that teachers meet acceptable levels of performance, the purpose of supervision is to help teachers improve their teaching and identify goals for personal improvement. Sergiovanni (1991) indicates that administrative supervision of teachers is concerned with teachers' (1) knowledge about teaching, (2) ability to demonstrate this knowledge when observed, (3) ability to sustain competent teaching continuously, and (4) commitment to continuous professional growth. Supervision is also designed to ascertain the degree to which the school's curriculum is being implemented and instructional goals are being achieved.

In the area of special education, the supervision system is used to determine if the regular class teachers and the special education teachers are providing appropriate instruction for students with disabilities. Breton and Donaldson (1991) studied resource room teachers in Maine and found that the majority received minimal supervision, and many indicated that they never received any supervision at all. The building principal was reported as the primary supervisor in 39% of cases and the special education director in 53%. Professional supervision, when it occurred, was largely nondirective and unrelated to classroom duties, focusing more on nonteaching responsibilities such as due process procedures. These data indicate that professional supervision procedures are not being used to determine if special education teachers are meeting the needs of their pupils. And it is doubtful that regular class teachers receive supervisory help regarding accommodation strategies for the children with disabilities in their classes.

The fact that both the principal and the special education administrator may be involved in supervision can cause potential problems unless administrative responsibilities for each are clearly defined and both are trained in appropriate supervisory techniques. In the case of the regular class teacher, either administrator must be able to identify and recommend effective strategies for children with disabilities within the context of the regular curriculum and the culture of the regular class. In the case of the special education placement, either administrator must be able to identify appropriate special education techniques for different disabilities. Two widely used supervision systems are noteworthy: clinical supervision and contingency supervision.

Clinical Supervision

Clinical supervision consists of three major phases: (1) planning or preconference, (2) classroom observation, and (3) postconference. The unique aspects of clinical supervision are (1) that it focuses on the analysis of observable classroom behavior of individual teachers and (2) that it is related to performance improvement based on the teacher's own assessment of his or her behavior in conjunction with the assessment of the supervisor. The clinical process provides objective feedback about the instruction, focuses on solving instructional problems, helps to develop skills in self-diagnosis, and attempts to instill a positive attitude toward continuing professional improvement.

In the preconference, the supervisor encourages the teacher to identify concerns about the instructional process, to translate those concerns into observable behaviors, and then to identify a process for collecting information about those behaviors during the subsequent classroom visit. The preconference is important because it clarifies for the supervisor and the teacher the context in which the observation will take place and tailors the supervisory observation to the teacher's instructional goals for the lessons to be observed. Further, it serves to create rapport between the supervisor and the teacher. Acheson and Gall (1992) describe in detail a wide variety of observation techniques that can provide useful and complete information about the teacher's behavior. Included among these techniques are (1) selective verbatim, or the recording of key verbal interactions between the teacher and the students; (2) observational techniques that monitor teacher movement, teacher verbal behavior, or the degree to which students are exhibiting "at task" behaviors; (3) checklists or time-line codes to assess various aspects of teacher-student interactions; and (4) more comprehensive methods such as audio and video recording and anecdotal records.

During the observation phase the supervisor uses the data collection method, which was identified during the preconference to capture information about the behavior of both the teacher and the students. After the observation the supervisor leaves a copy of the observation data with the teacher, and the supervisor and teacher review and independently attempt to analyze the data prior to a postconference.

The postconference is designed for the teacher to share impressions and conclusions based on an analysis of the data collected during the observation. The supervisor attempts to validate the teacher's observations or help the teacher tease out more substantial issues from the data, if necessary. This analysis then is used to encourage the teacher to consider alternative methods or techniques to improve teaching in the immediate future. Improvement goals may be identified and means of assisting the teacher in achieving these goals may be specified, including staff development or observing other teachers, if necessary. The improvement goals then become the basis for initial discussion during the subsequent preconference as the clinical cycle begins again.

Clinical supervision is a successful supervisory technique because it is individualized and directly relates to actual teacher concerns. It is time consuming, however, and requires special training on the part of the supervisor and teacher. The benefits of this approach are worth the investment of time and training. This practice can be used to great advantage to help teachers focus on accommodation strategies for students with disabilities in the regular class or special class.

Contingency Supervision

Glickman (1985) believes that no one type of supervision strategy is appropriate for all teachers and that the type of strategy used should relate to the teacher's level of maturity, level of responsibility, and the type of concerns or problems that the teacher is having. He identifies three basic styles of supervision: nondirective, collaborative, and directive.

The nondirective approach is appropriate for the mature teacher who is willing and able to take responsibility for self-evaluation and improvement. The directive strategy is more useful for supervising the immature teacher who is unwilling or unable to identify significant instructional concerns or improvement strategies. In the collaborative approach, the supervisor and teacher work together so that the teacher will benefit from the resulting cooperative interaction.

Glickman believes that a variety of supervisory options, including informal methods, collegial interaction with other teachers and support staff, clinical supervision, and personal interventions, can be used depending on the situation and the ability of the teacher to accept personal responsibility for self-improvement. Glickman's supervision system is complex and requires that the supervisor be trained to understand how to analyze specific teacher circumstances and implement various supervisory methods. But this system holds promise because it recognizes each teacher as an individual, and teacher improvement must be individualized.

Peer coaching as described in the organizational arrangements chapter should be considered as an important strategy within a comprehensive supervision system. Peer coaching can exist between the consultant or itinerant special education teacher and the regular class teacher or even between pairs of regular class teachers. The research conducted on this technique indicates that teachers working together, even pairs of regular class teachers, can help each other identify successful instructional strategies to accommodate the learning needs of students with disabilities (Johnson & Pugach, 1991).

TEACHER DISMISSAL

The dismissal of a staff member is never easy because it has both organizational and personal implications. At the organizational level, the administrator must follow appropriate due process procedures required in termination, as well as deal with the organizational effects of losing a staff member. On a personal level, administrators are faced with the unpleasant task of telling teachers that they are not competent while trying to help them deal with the realities of the situation in a professional manner. But the staff dismissal process is made much easier if the administrator has an established, comprehensive personnel system, as described above. Such a system will help to ensure that competent staff are hired initially and that they are systemically evaluated and assisted in overcoming deficiencies in performance. In such a system, the need to dismiss staff is greatly reduced.

In any event, when a staff member is considered for termination, the administrator must be certain that proper dismissal procedures will be followed. The major issues involved in the termination process are tenure status and due process. Each state has specific laws governing the awarding of tenure and describing due process requirements.

Teacher Tenure

During the teacher's probationary period, administrators should provide careful supervision to determine how the teacher is performing. In the case of unsatisfactory performance, the administrator should make every attempt to help the teacher remedy the problem. Staff development procedures, discussed previously, can assist in such remediation. However, if remediation is not successful and the administrator concludes that the teacher does not show potential for acceptable performance, the contract should not be renewed.

If, however, after several years of successful performance in probationary status, the teacher is awarded tenure, the teacher can then be terminated only with just cause. Reasons for termination with cause include (1) incompetence, (2) immorality, (3) insubordination, (4) neglect of duty, (5) conviction of certain crimes, (6) physical or mental incompetence, and (7) elimination of the position.

Due Process

If the administrator determines that a tenured teacher should be terminated, due process must be followed. Due process procedures ensure that the contract rights of a teacher are not violated except with just cause. Two forms of due process must be followed: substantive and procedural. Substantive due process requires that the criteria used in evaluation are not arbitrary, but related to the person's job.

Procedural due process requires the administrator to follow process guidelines in notifying the teacher about the reasons for the intended termination and in assisting the teacher in remediation of relevant problems. Although state law may specify different due process procedures for probationary and tenured staff, general due process guidelines should be specified in board policy and followed.

COLLECTIVE BARGAINING

Special education issues may be introduced at the bargaining table, especially when new philosophies of accommodation, such as inclusion, are introduced. New procedures require new behaviors, and change is always threatening to some. With respect to the potential impact of collective bargaining, both the regular and special education administrator should:

- Be involved in the formation of the board's bargaining issues, particularly those concerned with the organization of special education services.
- Be appointed as members of a negotiations advisory committee to help the board review the implications of issues being discussed in the negotiation process.
- Be allowed to review all items as they near final agreement and to discuss with the board negotiations team the implications of such items for achieving the district's special education goals.

FISCAL POLICY

* This chapter was written by Dr. James Hale,
Professor of Educational Administration,
University of North Florida.

Public financing of programs for students with disabilities is inextricably bound to the financing of all elementary and secondary education programs. Such has not always been true. The concept of equal educational opportunity has long existed among basic American values of liberty and equality, but children with disabilities were often excluded from public schools. Rooted in the founding fathers' expressions of need for universal free public education, each state adopted constitutional or statutory provisions for teaching children to read and write. A typical expression of law would call for a system of free education for children of school age who could benefit. And by definition, children with disabilities could not benefit because there was no program of instruction to meet their needs. That exclusion posited responsibility for educating children with disabilities with the parents of those children. In some instances of severe malady, the state or charitable organizations offered residential custodial care.

Recognition of the economic contributions made by education to individuals and to society at large has changed our view of expenditures for public education. Where social expenditures for education were once seen as consumption, they are now viewed by most economists as attractive capital investments (Becker, 1975; Benson, 1978; Benson & O'Halloran, 1987; Cohn, 1979; Psacharopoulos, 1973; Psacharopoulos & Woodall, 1985). Investments in education have been evaluated traditionally with regard to their private rate of return. Findings that public investments in educational programs have competitive rates of return to society are increasingly evident from research (Benson, 1988). Investments in educational programs for children with disabilities would seem to show similar results, given the logic and processes of human-capital formation and rate-of-return analysis. Yet, the struggle for support of public elementary and secondary education is unrelenting. There are a number of merit goods, such as health, transportation, safety, and recreation, that compete for limited resources.

The financing and budgeting of public education programs are like mileposts on a journey. The data offer reference points in the search for equity, adequacy, and excellence in the provision of education programs for all children. The public demand for new vistas rise and fall as the collective perceptions of educational needs gain or lose prominence on the public agenda. Historical linkages between public values of educational equity and efficiency and the practices of schooling remain loosely coupled. Perhaps that is because the historical road map of state support for elementary and secondary education in the United States shows long periods of fiscal neglect.

Similarly, the organized study of education finance is only a relatively recent phenomenon. Cubberley's (1906) seminal cartography of public elementary and secondary school fiscal policy has probably been read more often in the past 20 years than it was the first 50 years following its publication. With a few notable exceptions, the early neglect by scholars was perhaps due to the collective perception that education was a private investment. Also, the minor roles of states in the support of elementary and secondary education prior to the end of World War II established the locus of fiscal control with local school districts. The latter were largely uninterested in studies of funding equity.

Table 10-1 notes trends in the percentages of contributions to school district revenues for all instructional programs made by federal, state, and local governments

Table 10-1 Trends in Percentages of Elementary and Secondary School Revenues by Governmental Source

Year	Federal (%)	State (%)	Local/Intermediate (%)
1930	0.4	17.0	82.6
1940	1.8	30.3	67.2
1950	2.9	39.8	57.3
1960	4.4	39.1	56.5
1970	7.0	38.4	54.6
1976	7.8	44.0	48.2
1980	9.2	49.1	41.7
1981	9.0	49.7	41.4
1983	7.0	48.1	44.8
1985	6.2	49.0	44.8
1987	6.2	50.0	43.8
1989	6.4	48.8	44.5
1990	6.4	48.7	44.9
1991	6.2	49.3	44.5

From *Digest of Educational Statistics,* 1930 through 1979, by W. Grant and C. Lind, 1979, Washington, D.C: U.S. Government Printing Office; *Estimates of School Statistics,* 1980, 1981, 1983, 1985, 1987, 1989, 1991, National Education Association.

for selected years. *Local/intermediate* refers to the local school district contribution plus any intermediate education unit contribution. The latter include instructional programs supported and operated by units of government such as county cooperatives in California and Boards of Cooperative Educational Services (BOCES) in New York State. The intermediate units often offer programs for children with disabilities, among others. The increasing federal participation in supporting school district programs is noted for the 50 years between 1930 and 1980. Since 1980, however, the percentage of federal contributions to school district budgets has declined by one-third. The proportion of school district program budgets assumed by state governments almost tripled between 1930 and 1987, and the proportion contributed by local/intermediate governments declined by almost one-half.

The path to equity in state assumption of responsibility for the financing of programs for children with disabilities was more recently established, and it is paved with a plethora of personal sacrifices and frustrations of advocates. Yet, they persisted and they prevailed in advancing alternative views of public education; vistas that included students with disabilities in regular attendance in day-school programs and more recently in classrooms with nondisabled children and inclusion in other special programs such as Chapter One and Vocational Education. Widespread barriers to access were successfully removed through the courts (e.g., *Mills* v. *Board of Education of the District of Columbia,* 1972; *PARC* v. *Pennsylvania,* 1972), and increased fiscal support was achieved through successful lobbying of individual state legislatures and the federal government (PL 94-142). And the states, although seemingly at times to be fiscal laggards, have in the past 20 years reformed their education policies to include support for children with disabilities beyond the traditional state residential schools.

Attainment of the goal of providing educational programs of excellence begins with offering equality of educational opportunity for all children. Whether schools succeed or fail in their dual missions of daily establishing equity and recreating excellence depends largely on community support. Although support of schools may take on many forms, each may be characterized as child advocacy expressed through varied forums. Many of those important community support issues are reviewed in other chapters. Here we have delimited the discussion to fiscal issues, such as the funding of equal educational opportunity in schools.

The chapter begins by looking briefly at the role played by the federal government in financing programs for children with disabilities. The second section reviews and evaluates approaches taken by states to support school district efforts to provide special programs for children with disabilities. Critiques are made of each measure of need used by states and of the taxpayer and child equity issues associated with each funding model. Fiscal data and their implications regarding the regular education initiatives (mainstreaming) are discussed. A concern is expressed regarding the need for participation of children with disabilities in the school reform movement. Fiscal issues related to inclusion are addressed. The chapter closes with a brief discussion of budgeting programs for children with disabilities.

FEDERAL SUPPORT

Debate on the proper federal role in education matters is not new. Perhaps what has changed in the last 30 years is that the question of *ought* is asked rarely. Only questions of amounts and for what priority purposes federal aid should be appropriated are discussed in current literature. In a decade of public "finger pointing" of responsibility for declining national achievement scores, increasing dropout rates, declining parental involvement in their children's education, and increasing teen pregnancies and drug abuse, it is also noted that the federal government has abrogated leadership in both policy research and program support. That conclusion is supported by data presented in Table 10-1 and by the Verstegen (1987) and Verstegen and Clark (1988) analyses.

The powers of the federal government are delegated and enumerated and are not inherent powers. The Tenth Amendment reserves to the states powers not delegated to the federal government by the U.S. Constitution. Therefore, provision for public education, not being an enumerated power, is the responsibility of the states. This conclusion and the finding that education is not a right guaranteed by the U.S. Constitution were articulated clearly by the U.S. Supreme Court in *San Antonio* v. *Rodriguez* (1973). Yet, the federal government has a long history of involvement in education.

Although that general history of federal participation and influence in the formation of education policy is important to our discussion here, space does not permit a thorough review. There are a number of references that may be secured to review the development and the provisions of federal aid to education (e.g., Allen, 1950; Guthrie, Garms, & Pierce, 1988; Johns, Morphet, & Alexander, 1983; Monk, 1990; Odden & Picus, 1992; Tiedt, 1966; Verstegen, 1987). This chapter, however, presents selected fiscal data and discusses briefly the federal role in financing elementary and secondary education generally and programs for children with disabilities specifically.

It is clear from Table 10-1 that there was growth in federal support of elementary and secondary education each decade between 1930 and 1980. The federal percent of public elementary and secondary education budgets more than quadrupled in the 1930s (depression years) but less than doubled in the 1940s (most of that growth was after World War II). Although vocational education has a long history of federal support, large amounts of federal funding for targeted instructional programs began with the passage of the Elementary and Secondary Education Act (PL 89-10). The growth in federal participation during the 1960s was largely during the second half of the decade. Similarly, the 1976 data highlights the first year of federal support for PL 94-142, and it is important to note that substantive increases were made during the second half of that decade. The decline in federal participation between 1980 and 1985 negated 20 years of prior commitment and leadership, and the decline continued through 1991.

Federal Assistance for the Education of Students with Disabilities

Two federal initiatives directly support instructional programs for students with disabilities. The fundamental difference between them is the state-determined location of managerial and operational responsibilities of programs for target populations. Are the programs operated by the state or are the programs operated by local education agencies?

Local Managed and Operated Programs.   The much heralded Public Law 94-142, the Education for All Handicapped Children Act (1975), first established roots as Title VI in the 1966 amendments (PL 89-750) to the equally heralded 1965 compensatory education program, the Elementary and Secondary Education Act (PL 89-10). Title VI authorized grants for states to initiate, expand, and improve educational programs for children with disabilities, and the amendments created the Bureau of Education for the Handicapped in the U.S. Office of Education (now the Department of Education). Increased federal fiscal support and leadership exercised by the new bureau stimulated state and school district expansion of educational offerings for children with disabilities. Title VI was replaced with the Education of the Handicapped Act (PL 91-230, 1970). Part B of the latter became law in 1971 and reinforced the federal commitment to individuals with disabilities. The 1974 amendments (PL 93-380) set forth six prerequisites to receiving federal funds under Part B. Each state was required (1) to establish a goal of providing full educational opportunities for all children with disabilities, (2) to establish a timetable for accomplishing the full educational opportunity goal, (3) to establish nondiscriminatory testing procedures, (4) to establish policies and procedures to protect the confidentiality of information about individuals with disabilities, and (5) to establish procedures that ensure due process to children with disabilities and their parents. Each of these provisions has associated costs to the states and school districts, if they accept funding under the Act.

As a result of these programs, the comprehensive Education for All Handicapped Children Act (1975) blossomed. Of particular interest here is the promised federal largess to states and school districts for support of programs for children with disabilities. It was anticipated that the federal government would support 40% of the excess cost of providing programs for children with disabilities by the early 1980s. That goal has not been met. Approximately $25 billion was budgeted for programs for students with disabilities during the 1989-90 school year, but less than 10% of that amount is provided by PL 94-142.

Table 10-2 presents comparisons of trends in federal support for three selected instructional programs: (1) *compensatory,* which refers to the total compensatory education for the disadvantaged, including grants to states for individuals with disabilities (under Chapter 1 ESEA); (2) *special education,* which refers to the total education for individuals with disabilities grants; and (3) *vocational/adult,* which refers to the total vocational and adult education appropriations.

The data show that support for special education programs has been the most favored among the three areas, followed by vocational and adult education, and then by compensatory education. The total increase between the 1981 appropriations and the 1989 requests was about 113% for special education, 42% for vocational and adult education, and 29% for compensatory education. Averaging the percentages of change would seem to indicate sustained federal commitment (although relatively small in two cases). However, since 1980, there has been a sharp reduction in federal participation.

Verstegen and Clark (1988) have offered an incisive analysis of the diminution in federal expenditures for education in the 1980s. Their data demonstrate there was disinvestment in elementary and secondary programs for the years 1981–88 when adjusted for inflation. They reported that, when adjusted for inflation, education for individuals with disabilities decreased 6%, and rehabilitative services and support for individuals with disabilities (not included in Table 10-2) decreased 5%. Also, when adjusted for inflation, compensatory education support from the federal government decreased 25%, and vocational and adult programs experienced a 41% decrease. Although the Verstegen and Clark reasons for concern about federal disinvestment

Table 10-2   Trends in Federal Support of Selected Priority Instructional Programs for Selected Years

Year	Compensatory Amount*	% change	Special Education Amount*	% change	Vocational/Adult Amount*	% change
1981	3,670	—	947	—	781	—
1983	3,200	(12.8)	1,199	26.6	824	5.5
1985	3,696	15.5	1,321	10.2	838	1.7
1987	3,952	6.9	1,742	31.9	995	18.7
1989	4,570	15.6	1,961	12.6	1,054	5.9
1991	6,215	36.0	2,467	26.0	1,246	18.0
1993	6,699	8.0	2,966	20.0	1,475	18.0

* In millions of dollars.

From February, 1984, *Education, USA*. The other selected data were taken from *Education, USA*, Data Banks, for various years.

are arguable, their citation of research findings that the public prefers increases in federal spending on education over other federal outlays is not.

Fiduciary responsibilities accrue to states that accept funds under the provisions of PL 94-142. Only New Mexico rejected funds initially on the basis that compliance would disrupt its comprehensive plan for statewide program development. At this writing, all states receive federal aid under PL 94-142. In order to receive aid, states must demonstrate that 80% of the funds flowed through to local educational agencies, that the funds were spent in accord with the general provisions of Chapter I (Title I of PL 89-10), and that funds were spent on programs and services contained in the state education plan for students with disabilities. Important to this discussion is the Chapter I provision that funds must supplement and not supplant expenditure entitlement accruing to children with disabilities as though they were not placed in a special educational program. A state may claim the federal revenues as state support and be free of the Chapter I nonsupplanting provision if the state can show it is full-service. However, the requirements for demonstrating full-service are onerous, and that may be the reason why no state has been able to petition successfully to do so (one child not served appropriately may be grounds for noncompliance).

State Managed and Operated Programs.   Enacted in 1965 as an amendment to Title I of the Elementary and Secondary Education Act (PL 89-10), the Federal Assistance to State Operated and Supported Schools for the Handicapped Act (PL 89-313) provided funds to state agencies to supplement the education of children with disabilities and youth in state operated schools. The 1974 amendments (PL 93-380) required that all children in participating agencies be provided an education commensurate with their special needs and that funds appropriated under the aegis of PL 89-313 follow deinstitutionalized children into schools in their own communities. States may withhold 20% of PL 94-142 allocations for state managed programs, cooperative programs between school districts, and special initiatives that benefit targeted populations of children with disabilities. All safeguards and general reporting requirements of Chapter I encumber programs supported under this Act.

In 1981 the federal government provided approximately $146.5 million for state agency programs for individuals with disabilities under Chapter I, Grants for the Disadvantaged. That amount increased to approximately $151.3 million in 1989. The General Accounting Office has recommended that this program, which serves approximately 259,000 children with disabilities in schools and state-operated institutions, be merged with other special education efforts (Viadero, 1989). Federal support for Rehabilitation Services and Handicapped Research was in excess of $1.6 billion in 1989. Those amounts are not included in the above analyses.

STATE SUPPORT

States provided approximately $354 million for elementary and secondary schools in 1930. Those appropriations grew to almost 100 times that amount in 1978 at $35 billion. State appropriations more than doubled again by 1987 when states provided $80.4 billion (Webb, McCarthy, & Thomas, 1988). Total spending for elementary and secondary schools is expected to increase through 1993 but at a much slower rate than recorded for the 1980s. It has been noted that spending rose by 23% between 1982 and 1987 but will increase by only 13% by 1993. That increase will be only 9% when adjusted for projected inflation (Staff, *Education Week,* April 26, 1989, p.3). Over one half of the projected modest increases will come from state governments.

Cost Finding

The U.S. Department of Education, Office of Special Education (1985) reported that costs of programs for individuals with disabilities are usually higher in small school districts than in large districts. Similarly, costs are known to be higher in rural areas and for programs having a low incidence of enrollment. The reason for these higher costs is primarily due to a diseconomy of scale in each instance cited. The report also cited training centers as the most expensive method of providing services and the itinerant teacher as the least expensive delivery system. Studies by Clemmons (1974) in Minnesota, J. O. Garcia (1976), J. P. Garcia (1976), and Hale (1976) in New Mexico, Cambron (1976) and Hale (1979) in Florida, and Hartman and Mitchell (1987) in Oregon support the delivery system findings. The conclusion that cost finding should focus on cost variances among program delivery methods and factors that affect economies of scale is supported by the seminal national cost study by Rossmiller, Hale, and Frohreich (1970); the Sorensen (1973) study in Illinois; the Marriner (1977) study in New York; the Alexander and Hale studies in West Virginia (1977), Arkansas (1978), Louisiana (1978), and North Carolina (1978); the Hale and Cambron (1978, 1979) studies in Tennessee; and the Geske and Johnston (1985) study in Illinois.

Slobojan (1987) reviewed a number of the earlier special education cost studies and reported extensively on the application of a cost-finding model that he used in a Maryland school district. Like the studies he reviewed, he too found that the data bases available in the school districts' accounting systems rarely support the data demands of the cost model selected. It has also been our experience, since the seminal study done for the National Education Finance Project (Rossmiller et al., 1970), that the various studies are simply not comparable because they use different definitions and assumptions about (1) special program populations, (2) special program expenditures, (3) regular program populations, and (4) regular program expenditures. Yet, the inability to compare studies does not negate their use for contextual interpretations. Further, they consistently support the proposition that programs for children with disabilities are more expensive than programs for the nondisabled.

The Search for Equity

There are two fundamental equity goals that need to be appraised in each state's school finance policies. There is child equity and there is taxpayer equity. A simple view of child equity requires that in providing equal educational opportunities, equals be treated equally and that nonequals be treated unequally in meeting educational needs. It is the determination of educational needs that creates legitimate differences among children as being equals or nonequals for purposes of meeting the goal of equal educational opportunity. A similarly simplistic view of taxpayer equity requires that equal revenue be available for equal tax effort (see Berne & Stiefel, 1984). The unit of government best positioned to ensure equal revenue for equal tax effort among school districts is the state.

The basic unit of state support of programs for children with disabilities is, more often than not, the same unit of support used by the state to fund other elementary and secondary instructional programs. There are three basic measures of educational need used by states to fund education programs: (1) pupil unit, (2) teacher unit, and (3) budget guarantee. The general provisions of each funding measure will be reviewed and their application to and impact on funding programs for children with disabilities will be appraised.

The Pupil Unit

The pupil-unit measure of educational need is used to provide a revenue grant or guarantee to school districts based on pupil measures. The latter are reported as numbers of students enrolled in average daily attendance, in average daily membership, or in full-time-equivalency (FTE) by program. These measures of resource-need are modified in a number of states to reflect differences in program support, commonly termed *weighted-pupils*. The methods of pupil accounting vary among the states but are mostly either average-daily-membership (ADM) or average-daily-attendance (ADA), the latter being the more popular. The FTE measure has been selected by some states that use the weighted-pupil approach to funding and by several other states in combination with ADA or ADM to fund part-time kindergarten programs.

ADA is determined by summing the number of days attendance during the school term and dividing by the total number of days in the school term. For example, if a student is absent for any reason during 5 of the 180 days he or she is in membership during the school term, then 175/180 equals 0.972 ADA for funding purposes. Further, if the state guarantee for each student in ADA is $1,000, then the district would have available $972.

The ADM method accounts for each student during the time of school membership for the term regardless of one being present each day. In the preceding example, the school district would not be penalized for the student's absence if funding were based on ADM. However, if a student enrolled after the term started or withdrew from school before the last day of the term, then the district would be funded for the fraction of the student's school-term membership only.

The FTE approach accounts for fractions of time that a student spends in an instructional program during the school week and assigns a portion of the week to each instructional program in which the student participates. For example, if a school week is defined as 25 hours of instruction and a student attends regular classes for 23 hours and attends speech therapy for 2 hours, then the student is accounted in the regular program at 0.92 FTE (23/25) and in the speech therapy program at 0.08 FTE (2/25). Using this method, kindergarten children enrolled in half-day programs would each be counted as 0.5 for funding purposes. The determination of the number of

FTE students to be funded in each program is made by taking a census two or more times during the school term of each child's program participation.

Infrequent enrollment surveys may not position this pupil accounting measure to stimulate school attendance as would ADA, nor would it capture late arrivals to programs and early departures from programs. Use of a combination FTE with ADA or ADM would overcome the deficiency of infrequent surveys but would increase the onerous task of FTE accounting of pupils by programs on a daily basis. No states are known to do the latter for all programs, but electronic data processing could readily facilitate such a policy.

Weighted-pupil measures of educational need are becoming increasingly popular state education fiscal policy provisions. Paul Mort (1924) found in his early research that the average elementary school classroom accommodated more students than did the average secondary school classroom. He advocated that the state provide additional support for high schools to compensate for the diseconomy of scale. (A modern twist on that policy is the state of Florida's provision for funding grades K through 3 at higher levels for pedagogical reasons.) Mort's early research was the forerunner of modern weighted-pupil funding.

The weighted-pupil measure is a combination of a selected pupil-unit measure and a program cost factor. For example, a weight of 2.0 would indicate that for funding purposes a particular program would generate twice as much guaranteed revenue per pupil-unit than a program assigned a weight of 1.0, the assumption being that to obtain child equity (equivalent educational services), one program requires twice the amount of resources, measured in dollars. Once the program weights are determined, they are applied to the pupil measure (ADA, ADM, or FTE) to create (1) weighted-average-daily-attendance (WADA), (2) weighted-average-daily-membership (WADM), or (3) weighted-full-time-equivalency (WFTE).

Finally, the weighted measure may be applied either by add-on or by integrated indexing. The add-on weight would provide (for each child enrolled in a particular program) a specific funding weight to be added to the child's basic program weight. For example, if a fourth grader has a basic funding weight of 1.0 ADM and she receives three hours of physical therapy each week, and the physical therapy service weight is 0.5 ADM, then this child's funding unit would be 1.5 ADM (basic plus special weights). Note that the 0.5 weight is determined to generate resources necessary to provide the special services. Pupil accounting rules must be established to support the part-time enrollment.

The use of indexing does not require special accounting rules associated with WADA or WADM because each special program is indexed to a basic program, and FTE pupil accounting is used. Part-time special program participation weights must be established on a resource cost basis to accommodate the higher cost of services and the variable length of participation by each student. For example, the fourth grader cited previously would be funded for $22/25 \times 1.00$ for regular program participation and $3/25 \times 6.00$ for special program participation, assuming a weight of 6.0 per FTE for the physical therapy program ($22/25 \times 1.0 + 3/25 \times 6.0 = 1.5$ WFTE). However, the end result of both add-on and indexing must be such that they arrive at an adequate resource support level; and they will if they are cost-based and, as in this case, the add-on approach becomes, conceptually, a special form of indexing.

Application of Pupil-Unit Measures to Students with Disabilities.   Use of an unweighted-pupil measure to fund programs for children with disabilities would deny the reality that programs for students with disabilities require greater resources than programs for nondisabled children. Although most states at one time or other in their histories funded school districts on a pupil-unit basis without regard to special needs, such is not the case today. All states provide for students with disabilities differentially in some manner.

The choice of pupil-unit funding measure (ADA or ADM) is largely based on two values. Those who favor ADA argue that it will help enforce the state's compulsory attendance law. Those who favor ADM argue that program costs are not reduced when children must remain home during times of illness. This issue may be exacerbated in programs for students with disabilities. That is, if it can be shown that students with disabilities are absent more often than students without disabilities due to reasons such as malady related visits to physicians, then use of ADA as the funding unit would impact more harshly on programs for students with disabilities than would the ADM measure.

Further, use of either ADA or ADM assumes that uniform funding will provide for all educational needs, an assumption that is contrary to research findings and one that violates the child-equity principle. In *Serrano v. Priest* (1971), the court articulated the equity principle, which requires programs with unequal expenditures for children with disabilities to provide service parity with nondisabled children. However, if program weights are associated with ADA or ADM, the equity principle is not violated. In this instance, however, accounting for part-time enrollments becomes a major problem. If students with disabilities are enrolled in full-time, self-contained classrooms, the WADA or WADM measures may be assumed to address the cost experience. A state policy could establish a rule that funding would be based on the program in which most of the student's time was spent (South Carolina did this at one time). But that would cause programs such as speech therapy and physical therapy to be underfunded (because less than 50% of a student's school week is spent in such programs) and perhaps some other special programs to be overfunded. The latter problem demonstrates the need for other pupil-accounting rules to preserve child equity. Any attempt to account for part-time participation in programs ultimately leads to establishing measures of FTE. At last count, 19 states used some form of weighted-pupil measure to fund programs for children with disabilities.

The state of Florida has been a leader among states using integrated indexing of pupil weights by program. The 1973 reform initiative had 22 distinct programs indexed to a basic program. That year the basic program was defined as Grades 4 through 9 and was weighted as 1.00. In 1992 the number of weighted programs had grown to 54 indexed to a basic program defined as Grades 4 through 8. Of these programs, 15 were programs for students with disabilities based largely on maladies, 8 requiring full-time and 7 offering part-time participation. There were also three categories of grade levels indexed to the basic program and entitled mainstream (inclusion). The program weights associated with physical and mental characteristics of students ranged in value from 14.506 for students enrolled in part-time programs for individuals with visual impairment to 1.918 for students enrolled in programs for the gifted. Florida guaranteed $2,423.65 per unweighted FTE that year, which means that

1.0 FTE for the part-time program for individuals with visual impairment generated $35,157. Although this may seem to be a large amount of money for 1.0 FTE, one must keep in mind that it may take a caseload of a dozen or more students with visual impairment receiving part-time services to equal a 1.0 FTE. The 1991–92 Florida Educational Finance Program Calculation (Florida Department of Education, 1992) reported 133,643 total exceptional education unweighted-full-time-equivalent (UFTE) students in special programs and 3,021 UFTE students in mainstream programs K–12. The report further showed 378,189 WFTE students in special programs for students with disabilities and 6,043 WFTE students with disabilities in mainstream basic K–12 programs. Combining the WFTE in special programs and the WFTE in mainstream programs produces 384,232 WFTE funded that year. Given the base student allocation support level of about $2,432 per UFTE, the state guaranteed a total of over $931 million for instruction and support services of students with disabilities.

It may be shown, using any state's data, that mainstream programs are less expensive than are part-time or self-contained programs (Cambron, 1976; Clemmons, 1974). However, the educational efficacy of placing students with, for example, emotional disturbance or profound disability in mainstream or part-time programs remains a fundamental pedagogical issue before it becomes a fiscal issue.

New Mexico indexed two programs for children with disabilities (moderate and severe) to a basic program defined as Grades 4 through 6. They used ADM as the pupil accounting measure and weighted the special programs as 1.90 and 3.50, respectively. Students were enrolled full-time in these programs, and the program weights emphasized severity of malady rather than separate impairments. They also provided for speech therapy and resource rooms as funded delivery systems and weighted them at 20.0 for funding purposes. This rather unique approach of identifying resource needs was established in the 1974 school finance reform (Hale, 1976). The logic that increased severity of disability requires additional resources is supported by research, in New Mexico (Garcia, J. O., 1976; Garcia, J. P., 1976) and elsewhere. Funding a resource room at 20.0 could ensure adequate revenue to fund pupil services even when faced with small enrollments in the program (diseconomy of scale) if state policy so provided. More often than not, however, a typical state policy will allow for the funding of a fraction of the resource room based on a standard caseload. Although a full-funding method could become very expensive if not closely controlled, its use in predominately rural areas would seem appropriate. States could also use PL 94-142 revenue to offset a diseconomy of scale. In New Mexico, caseloads of 45 students with speech impairments and 18 students with learning disabilities are required in order to receive full funding for a resource room.

Utah was another early adopter of the program indexing approach to measuring educational needs. In 1977, Utah indexed 12 programs for students with disabilities measured by ADM to a basic program defined as the average of ADA and ADM in Grades 1 through 12. The designated program weights ranged from 0.5 for speech impairment to 3.09 for emotional disturbance. Further, the weights were add-on values, that is, in addition to the basic program funding. New Jersey also uses the add-on approach.

The preceding three examples illustrate several important policy differences used by states to apply the weighted-pupil indexing approach to funding educational programs. These differences further support the caveat, noted earlier, that one may not compare program weights used by states. First, note that each state uses a different definition for a basic program. New Mexico's Grades 4 through 6 would tend to capture the lowest cost among instructional programs because they suffer least from diseconomy of scale. Florida's Grades 4 through 9 designation of a basic program would similarly benefit from economy of scale but would average expenditures for more grades to arrive at the basic program cost. The Utah approach would average costs for 12 grades, which, given the higher expenditure for high school programs, would increase the basic program cost compared to the other two states. Second, they each use different pupil accounting measures; thus they cannot be compared. And third, they define their special programs differently.

Mainstreaming and part-time programs would seem to provide the least restrictive placement alternative, although not, perhaps, always the most educationally appropriate. Operationally, mainstreaming and self-contained classrooms offer the lowest cost placements, and part-time and homebound programs are the highest cost delivery approaches (Cambron, 1976; Clemmons, 1974; Slobojan, 1987). The reason for those differences is mostly diseconomy of scale due to low incidence and hence small enrollments or small enrollments established for pedagogical purposes. Wood, Sheehan, and Adams (1985) reviewed opinions of a number of fiscal policy analysts and exceptional student program specialists and concluded that more weight of authority favors the weighted-pupil approach to funding.

The Teacher Unit

The teacher-unit measure of educational need has two dimensions that are not differentiated clearly in school finance literature: the simple teacher unit and the instructional unit. The simple teacher unit may be characterized as a state salary schedule used to classify each teacher in a school district according to training and experience and to provide salary support to the district based on some predetermined amount for each cell in the matrix. This does not mean that the district could hire the teacher for that amount; the state grant must be supplemented with amounts generated from local revenue sources. Delimitations are placed on the minimum pupil-teacher ratio that the state will support to prohibit unwarranted raids on the state treasury. North Carolina, West Virginia, and other states have used this approach, although they each apply the concept differently.

The second teacher-unit funding approach, sometimes referred to as an instructional unit, expands the notion of teacher-salary support to include support for supplies, some equipment, and purchased services such as heat, light, water, and other current expense. States such as Louisiana and Texas have used this funding approach. The appropriation may also include amounts to support supervision. Typically, there is only one amount used to support the instructional unit, but the instructional unit may differentiate among instructional levels or programs regarding the number of students (ADA or ADM) necessary to receive the amount authorized. The latter approach creates a category of support that could be termed weighted-instructional-unit.

Application of Teacher-Unit Measures to Students with Disabilities.   The Texas approach to teacher-unit funding, prior to the mid-1980s reform that shifted state funding policy to weighted pupil-unit funding, was typical among states using weighted instructional units to define school district resource needs. An instructional unit required 20 students in ADA for Grades 7 through 9 and 18.5 students for Grades 1 through 3. They had nine categories of programs (based on maladies) for students with disabilities. Each category had an enrollment range requirement for funding. For example, the instructional unit for students with educable mental retardation required 8 to 11 students in ADA as did programs for students with trainable mental retardation, visual and hearing impairment, and orthopedic disability. Other programs required either more or less students for funding purposes.

Louisiana used an approach similar to Texas except that Louisiana funded 11 categories of programs for children with disabilities, used ADM as their pupil measure, and used wider instructional unit ranges. For example, the Louisiana funding ranges were 8 to 19 for the program for students with educable mental retardation, 4 to 9 for the program for students with trainable mental retardation, and 6 to 17 for the program for students with hearing impairment. The different choices of pupil measures account for some of the qualifying range differences but not the major parts. On a statewide average basis for all states, ADA would be approximately 90% of average-daily-membership. The unit measures between Texas and Louisiana vary more than that amount. Therefore, one may assume that the differences were for planned-program reasons.

Delaware used ADM to determine instructional units for 14 categories of programs. Eight of the programs were for children with disabilities, and they required six students each for full funding for a program for students with trainable mental retardation and for a program for students with hearing impairments. Fifteen students in ADM were required for full funding for a program for students with educable mental retardation. The single measure, unlike the enrollment range, does not address the economy of scale experienced by most school districts. Typically, if a district has a fraction of a teacher unit earned, it will be proportionally funded for that fraction. The school district has the burden of raising sufficient additional resources to provide appropriate services.

The Budget Guarantee

The third general approach used by states to fund educational programs is the budget guarantee. In this method the state chooses a base year and then supports incremental increases in the budgets of school districts. The growth rates may be applied differentially as a function of other measures (usually district revenue capacity). Colorado used this approach for a number of years, and California used it the year following the widely reported Proposition 13, which cut local revenues substantially and shifted more school revenue burden to the state. The funding unit guarantee is noted as an approved budget amount per pupil (ADA or ADM) that is within the delimited growth increment, usually expressed as a percentage. The budget guarantee method is not a popular approach to funding educational programs in general but is used often by states to fund categorical (specific purpose) programs.

State assumption of all or part of an approved district budget for programs for students with disabilities has a long history in Wisconsin, and it is used by several other states. A more popular policy is one that funds a portion of the excess pupil cost. There is little conceptual difference in the latter approach and the approved budget approach. It is largely a matter of dividing by the number of pupils served in the latter policy. For example, the district determines a program budget and expresses it on the basis of per pupil unit served. The state subtracts the amount of pupil-unit support for nondisabled students (because that amount has already been funded under the general funding policy) and then funds all or part of the excess cost. More states use this funding approach for programs for students with disabilities rather than for programs for nondisabled students. At last count, 19 states used either the budgeted pupil excess cost or the total approved budget approach. It can be argued that the weighted pupil and the weighted instructional units are also excess cost funding measures. That is why it is important to emphasize the concept of budget guarantee for this approach; it seems to avoid unnecessary debate over fidelity of categories.

Which measure of educational need best meets the child-equity principle? Several could be both adequate and equitable. Equity requires that needs of students in any program be met proportional to needs of students in other programs, based on discriminating measures of educational need required to provide equality of educational opportunity. Adequacy answers the question of whether sufficient resources were available to meet all needs. It may be argued that some states spread educational poverty equitably due to inadequacy of funding. We are not willing to use space here to argue an operational definition of adequacy; we simply say, like Wise (1968), that we know when it is not present.

However, Judge Corns did define adequacy in a Kentucky case (see *Rose* v. *Council for Better Education,* 790 S.W. 2nd 212), which, like Serrano (1971), required differential funding based on children's educational needs. We believe that it has been shown in the preceding text that the weighted pupil approach, whether per pupil unit or per teacher unit, meets the child-equity criterion and that the budget guarantee of excess cost may establish the same funding relationship among programs for students with disabilities. The critical issue is whether the final funding relationships are cost-based with regard to resource needs of special programs. We have noted however, in our work with legislative committees in over a dozen state school finance reform studies, that legislators would prefer to talk about increased appropriations to meet children's educational needs rather than to focus increased appropriations on teacher salary increases.

Categorical Funding

The use of categorical funding in state educational policy means special purpose funding. The qualitative policy characteristic of categorical funding is that an audit trail is established to ensure that appropriated revenues are expended for the specified purpose(s). States use this funding approach for a large number of support programs (e.g., textbooks, transportation, construction, and food service) and for a smaller number of instructional programs (e.g., writing skills improvement and special reading services). It may be argued successfully that excess cost funding for students with disabilities or others, whether weighted-pupil, weighted instructional unit, or budget guarantee, is categorical funding because it is special purpose and more often than not has expenditure limitations.

For example, Florida requires that 80% of the funds generated by a program must be spent in that program at the school level. For this purpose all funding to a school district for students with disabilities is viewed as funding for one program. This designation allows local program managers to shift funds among programs for children with disabilities and to meet the 80% school-level criterion on a districtwide basis as opposed to a school-by-school basis, as other programs are required to do. Clearly, expenditure requirements associated with programs for children with disabilities meet the definition requirement of categorical programs. Such designations do not change the critique given each funding measure above but do influence the accountability of local program managers.

Taxpayer Equity

Taxpayer equity is included in the state elementary and secondary education policy to the extent that taxpayers in school districts of the state carry equal burden for support of the state's education programs. Where a school district does not have sufficient taxing capacity to fund the state requirements, the state must provide sufficient resources such that the equal treatment of equals and the unequal treatment of nonequals criterion is met. How a state meets the equity criterion is not a debated issue, only a matter of preference. The fact that a state does or does not meet the equity criterion is measurable (Berne, 1988; Berne & Stiefel, 1979, 1984) and justiciable, that is, subject to litigation (see Alexander, 1981; Wise, 1968; and cases such as *Robinson* v. *Cahill,* 1973, in New Jersey; *San Antonio* v. *Rodriguez,* 1973, in Texas; and *Serrano* v. *Priest,* 1971, in California). For a review of state preferences in funding models such as district power equalizing, flat grant, guaranteed yield, foundation program, and percentage equalization, the reader is referred to school finance texts such as those cited elsewhere in this chapter.

The Pursuit of Fiscal Equity

The federal court ruled in *McInnis* v. *Shapiro* (1968) that its competence did not extend to developing a school finance program for Illinois that would treat all children equitably. That problem, the court said, belonged to the people of Illinois. Wise (1968) stated that future litigation seeking distribution equity of state resources should follow the successful pattern established by civil rights plaintiffs. That is, do not ask the court to define equalization or equity, but ask the court to declare that it does not exist based on evidence submitted and to maintain jurisdiction until such a plan is presented to the court that meets its approval. The litigants in *Serrano* v. *Priest* (1971) did that in California state court, and that case became a model for school finance litigation in other states and for *San Antonio* v. *Rodriguez* (1973) in federal court.

The purpose of these initiatives was to gain revision of state distributions of resources to school districts. Given that education is a state function, plaintiffs sought relief in state courts after the U.S. Supreme Court ruled in *Rodriguez* that there was no federal issue in the equity question presented. The Court reasoned that rich people live in poor school districts and poor people live in rich school districts, and therefore wealth was not a suspect classification (like race, sex, and age). The *Serrano* Court articulated an axiom that school finance specialists call the principle of fiscal neutrality when it said that a child's education should not be a function of the wealth of his or her parents and neighbors but the wealth of the state as a whole.

At about the same time as the tide of taxpayer equity reform was rising, the National Education Finance Project reports were being released and disseminated widely. Among those reports were descriptions of cost-finding activities that clearly demonstrated that costs of instructional programs for students with disabilities were substantially higher than programs for nondisabled children. The *Serrano* Court was clear also in recognizing program cost differences when it said that equity did not mean expenditure of equal amounts of dollars per pupil and that program parity may demand higher expenditures for some children.

Ward (1988) notes that 19 states had major school finance reforms in the five-year period following *Serrano*. A review of those state reforms shows major changes in the funding of programs for students with disabilities, both in method and in amount and by inclusion of previously excluded children, the latter perhaps prompted by the *Mills* (1972) and *PARC* (1972) litigations.

Some have suggested that the success of a number of early state reform efforts have been marginal with regard to equitable distributions of per pupil revenues (Carroll, 1982). However, what was missed in those conclusions was that two of the states, Florida and New Mexico, had redefined child equity by creating a system of indexing program weights. Distribution of resources on the basis of program weights will discriminate among school districts, as it is intended to do, with regard to program needs and not with regard to other pupil measures. Research has demonstrated that there is an unequal distribution of children with disabilities among school districts, and therefore some districts have higher program cost burdens than others (see Slobojan, 1987).

The constellation of diverse litigation, one group seeking taxpayer equity and another seeking child equity, and fiscal policy research, demonstrating clearly unmet educational needs, prompted all state legislatures to review their school finance policies. An important outcome of the school finance reforms of the early 1970s was that states included in their revised fiscal policies provisions for educating children with disabilities in the school districts where they lived.

Equity and the School Reform Movement

The search for equity during the school finance reform movement of the early 1970s focused on expenditure differences resulting from revenue disparities among school districts. Faced with a tidal wave of court decisions that swept aside a number of existing state-aid formulas, state legislatures tried to support their school finance policies with new reallocation formulae and increased state revenue. It was soon clear that costs were rising while school enrollments were falling. National college placement test scores and local reading-ability scores were not improving–they were in fact declining. The increased political activism of governors and key legislators within states during the school finance reform movement, coupled with increased state assumption of education expenditures, provided the means for launching a new education reform movement in the late 1970s and early 1980s to improve quality.

A review of the literature reveals that few researchers have attempted to determine the costs of nationwide reform proposals. Those who have are forced to make a number of arguable post hoc assumptions that do not reflect individual state funding capacity or needs. For example, cost estimates assume that implementation of initiatives is across all districts and is thorough and timely and that resources are distributed equitably (Wagner, 1984). Actually, implementation is likely to be fragmented and incremental. Some reform items will be judged as too expensive and will be rejected by legislatures and local school boards. Jordan and McKeown (1984) suggest that cost estimates based on incremental projections would be the most accurate; that projections based on stable state-local interactions would be somewhat less accurate; and that projections based on innovative projects and in need of new sources of funding would be the least accurate.

Many educators are not comfortable when discussing costs because the linkages between costs and instructional outcomes have not been clearly determined. School finance specialists have not contributed substantially to the development of a new linkage terminology because their foci have been on questions of inter-district equity (Odden, 1984). The aggregate data used in school finance models are not tied to student or teacher performance or to classroom data on student characteristics and instructional methods (Kirst, 1983). The growing literature on school reform has identified variables that are the most powerful determinants of student achievement. Among the variables that do not appear to directly affect performance are the level of spending per pupil, the quality of the physical plant and facilities, the school or class size, and the organizational structure (Rossmiller, 1983). It is precisely these variables, however, that have captured the attention of school finance reformers.

Although Odden (1986) suggested that the quality improvement initiatives had not impacted gains made during the equity movement, Levin (1975) and others disagree. Levin focuses concern on lack of participation in the school improvement reforms by students who are disadvantaged. Our concerns echo that major omission and note that there are changes in measures of overall equity. For the most part, new state revenue for quality improvement bypassed the state's school finance formula in favor of categorical aid appropriations that are tracked to specific programs. In doing so, the appropriations are not subject to the equalization model established to create fiscal equity for taxpayers and program equity for children.

Use of categorical appropriations to bypass the equalization model is not new. Those who have measured changes in school fiscal policies have also observed erosion in equity provisions through growth in categorical program appropriations. Any school reform, whether fiscal policy or improvement of practices, (1) affects taxpayer equity if it circumvents the equalization provisions of state policies and (2) affects child equity provisions if all students are not recipients of reform benefits in proportion to their educational needs.

The national reform reports reflect a policymaking bias and an implementation model characteristic of their corporate sector authors. The reports assume a rational, hierarchical, industrial model, wherein policy made at the top management level is implemented at the lower managerial and technical levels. As for the reforms themselves, they call for more of what schools are already doing: more classes, more time, more money. Concomitant with more of the same are demands for improvement: better teaching, better curriculum, and better school management.

School improvement research, however, focuses on school-site variables that significantly affect student performance. Local community values are taken into consideration giving administrators, teachers, and parents important roles in the implementation of effective school reforms. Although the organizational structure is more complex in comparison to the industrial model, effective school research has been able to link specific instructional and climatic variables to higher student achievement (Brandt, 1987; Joyce, Hersh, & McKibbin, 1983).

Governors and state legislators rarely differentiate between educational reform proposals that originate from national reform reports and school improvement research. State officials often share values and organizational perspectives reflected in national movements such as Education 2000. It is incumbent upon educators to clearly link selected school reforms to better schooling. If educators do not relate reforms to measures of education excellence, the program costs will become the primary basis of policy choices.

For over 20 years, school finance reformers have been communicating with state officials on ways to equalize educational opportunities for all students regardless of whether they live in property-rich or property-poor districts. Although it is difficult to compare state efforts and to generalize, there are some common characteristics relevant to this discussion. First, school finance reform has its roots in educational equity concerns. Despite differences in approaches, the aim of finance reform across the states has been to establish increased levels of pupil funding along with child equity and taxpayer equity. Second, the unit of analysis has always been the school district. And third, there is also a concern for quality, but its measure has been fugitive.

Contrary to these efforts, differences in quality among schools exist. Kirst (1983) states that "the blame falls not on finance reform or on finance research but on changing fiscal conditions, politics, and instructional policies." A state's fiscal condition and its politics are inseparable. Reforms are expensive, and most school districts cannot meet the increased revenue demands. The willingness of state residents to pay those added costs is influenced by a number of political factors: the election of a proactive governor (McLaughlin, 1983); a key legislator (Wirt & Kirst, 1982); and perhaps most importantly, the state's political culture, which is manifest by the historical relationship between state and local governments. The political culture is reflected in the state's proportion of the average school district's educational budget (see Table 10-1).

Educators can play a significant role in the politics of education by responsibly addressing the costs needed for school reform. There is a pervasive American willingness to spend more on education (note the success of the Clinton campaign in articulating the education issue), but the current reform era can fail to achieve its educational goals if the public is faced with big-ticket items posited in the same reform package as those items linked by research to improve schools. What is needed are school finance models that incorporate instructional variables identified in school improvement research, because money that reaches student learning variables will have a greater effect on schools than money spent elsewhere. Sherman (1985) called for a concentration of resources in areas that related directly to educational quality. The tools exist to concentrate resources on student instruction; it is a matter of school finance specialists addressing such problems (Kirst, 1983; Rossmiller, 1983).

INCLUSION: FISCAL IMPLICATIONS

Both Clemmons (1974) and Cambron (1976) reported research that evaluated delivery system costs of special services to children with disabilities. For example, Clemmons audited existing instructional programs and determined program costs for (1) regular classroom with special consultant, (2) regular classroom with itinerant special teacher, (3) regular classroom with resource room, (4) part-time special education classroom, and (5) self-contained special education classroom. Cambron addressed similar categories of delivery but established a cost-model for each rather than auditing existing instructional programs. Obviously, each followed the alternative program identifications articulated by Reynolds (1962), Deno (1970), Bruininks and Rynders (1971), Dunn (1973), and Chaffin (1974). However, both Clemmons and Cambron found few practices in their Minnesota and Florida samples that differed from full-time or part-time instructional settings. The dates of the preceding citations testify to the fact that the technology for cost-finding delivery models among programs for children with disabilities has been demonstrated for over 20 years.

It is unclear at this time what the fiscal implications of the inclusion movement might be at either the state or the local level. Finance formulae must be altered to reflect a changing reality if children with special needs are served within the regular classroom and support services are targeted to the child in regular classes, not to pull-out and special programs. Florida has done so in its state policy.

The National Association of State Boards of Education in a report advocating inclusion (NASBE, 1992) argues that current finance systems for special education:

- Reinforce the dual system of special/regular education and create barriers to inclusion.

- Tie funding to student labels rather than learning outcomes and the appropriateness of the instructional environment for the student with disabilities.

- Create an incentive to overidentify students with disabilities and encourage districts to place students in more highly restrictive placements than necessary so as to receive the maximum amount of funding.

- Provide more funding for special and residential placements and provide less funding for similar services for students in their home districts.

- Forward-funds schools for expensive, restrictive out-of-state placements and reimburse districts at the end of the academic year for expenses accrued in district-based programs.

In order to support an inclusion philosophy, the NASBE recommends: "State boards, with state departments of education, should sever the link between funding, placement and handicapping label. Funding requirements should not drive programming and placement decisions for students" (p. 30). The report, in describing recent funding changes in Oregon and Pennsylvania, appears to advocate a flat funding approach based on averages.

We agree in some respects with the NASBE Study Group's advocacy for inclusion of students with disabilities in regular classrooms. We also find fault with some current state funding practices. We must, however, take exception to their recommendation to sever links between funding, placement, and person to be served. Those of us who have studied instructional practices and funding of special education programs know that:

- Misplacement of students in programs for the purpose of increasing funding is both incompetent and illegal behavior. To say it does not happen is to be naive. To say the practice is widespread would seem to be insulting to the profession and contrary to years of substantive audit reports.
- Current weighted-pupil funding used by states developed from exemplary practice. If exemplary practice changes, we have the cost accounting technology to identify other configured costs of services.
- An audit trail must be made between allocation purpose and expenditure or the purpose will become subordinate in practice.
- State funding of instructional programs should be based on costs.
- Flat grant funding based on averages negates (1) that children with disabilities are not uniformly distributed among school districts and (2) that it will overfund some districts and underfund others. Such approaches have long been held to be neither equitable nor efficient.

We agree with the report that school districts should explore how additional funding sources such as migrant education, Chapter 1, Chapter 2, Medicaid, and vocational supplements can be combined to support more comprehensive and inclusive special education programs. The success of the inclusion movement will clearly depend upon the willingness of local school boards, educators, and citizens to integrate rather than segregate children with disabilities. As inclusion continues, new funding models will also be required.

SCHOOL DISTRICT BUDGETING

The school district budget functions to translate proposed educational programs and services into a financial plan that, when adopted, expresses community commitment to the schools. It further identifies the goals and priorities established by the school board to fulfill its mandate to administer the state plan for public education in the community (Johns et al., 1983). The budgetary processes include management functions of planning, coordinating, interpreting, presenting, approving, administering, and appraising (Roe, 1961) the fiscal activities of the school district on a year-round calendar (also see Jordan, McKeown, Salmon, & Webb, 1985).

The budgetary processes ultimately are cast into a budget document that is characterized by accounting language (Tidwell, 1985), program language (Hartley, 1968), or planning language (Hentschke, 1986). That is, budgets are said to be line-item, program, or zero-based. The most comprehensive modern statement that demonstrates the myriad of issues that school leaders must address in the budgeting processes is provided by Hartman (1988). The school business management texts cited in this chapter offer detail about a number of budget items, but the finance texts cited offer only brief reviews. Our purposes delimit this offering to less than any of the preceding. We merely want to point the reader to substantive literature on this topic.

Budgeting standards are prescribed by the state but are often supplemented by school districts to increase the amount of information provided to the community. The school district budget has two basic schedules (revenue and expenditure) and four or more parts (operations, capital outlay, debt service, and special revenue, the latter being for categorical programs and services). The operations portion of the budget expresses planned revenue and expenditures necessary to accommodate what is sometimes called current expense. The revenues would include federal, if general, noncategorical, such as Area Impacted Aid (PL 81-874); state noncategorical, such as the equalization aid; and local noncategorical, such as tax revenue for operations. The expenditure accounts of the operations portion of the budget would provide for expenses such as salaries, benefits, purchased services, and supplies and materials. The operations budget will often provide for capital outlay purchases delimited to equipment replacement.

The capital outlay budget part is intended to define the fiscal plan for purchases of land, buildings, and equipment. It offers a revenue statement that identifies sources by governmental levels. For example, this budget may include dedication of federal revenues transferred from another budget part for purchases of new equipment to be used in programs for children with disabilities; state revenue dedicated to the purchase of land, buildings, and equipment; and local revenue and nonrevenue (sale of property and the sale of bonds) dedicated for capital improvements.

The debt service part of the budget is intended to describe the fiscal plan for paying principal and interest due during the budget year that resulted from past year(s) borrowing, including bonds. It consists of a revenue schedule identifying sources, state and local, and an expenditure schedule identifying purposes.

The special revenue part of the budget provides for the receiving and disbursing of specific obligations. Federal revenue distributed by states as a school district's entitlement under PL 94-142 creates a special obligation for the district to expend those receipts according to the state approved district plan. Similarly, if the local Lions Club, for example, offered to pay for the purchase of vision screening equipment, the receipt of the revenues and the disbursement for the purchase would be accommodated through this budget part. An audit trail is established for each revenue receipt and for each purchase.

A number of other budget parts may be established by school districts to accommodate fiscal control. For example, an enterprise budget may be established to control revenue receipts and expenditures for school food services or a separate capital outlay budget may be created to control replacement of equipment, including textbooks. Tidwell (1985) offers suggestions of appropriate budget parts and identifies acceptable standard accounting practices used with each.

The expenditure dimension of the school district budget is translated into individual cost center budgets (schools and support units) to facilitate the school board's plans. Thus the three basic dimensions of program budgeting and accounting are: (1) accounting (salaries, benefits, etc.), (2) program (basic K-3, special learning disabilities, etc.), and (3) location (specific elementary school). Electronic data processing allows for tracking of expenditures to programs and establishes state audit trails. The latter may facilitate state monitoring of policies, such as one that requires a certain percentage of the funds generated by a particular program to be spent for services in that program at the school level.

Finally, cost accounting by program establishes the statewide data base for appraising the efficiency of program cost indices. When combined with program efficacy reviews, program cost factors may be adjusted to reflect current expenditure experiences of school districts. These practices, program budgeting and accounting by school site and program adequacy reviews, combine to offer data for the periodic evaluation of the weighted-pupil funding indices.

We have now come full circle in this discussion. We have identified the roles of the federal, state, and local governments in the support of elementary and secondary education and programs for students with disabilities particularly. Our emphasis has been on state fiscal policy because education is a state responsibility. We have identified strengths and weaknesses of various state policies used to fund programs for children with disabilities. Our affinity for policy structures that index funding by programs, on either pupil basis or on teacher basis, places us among a large number of fiscal policy specialists and special educators, because structure must lead to funding parity to meet child-equity criteria. We have no definition of funding adequacy; we only recognize its presence or absence.

Schenkat (1988) wrote about the promise of restructuring for special education. Although most of the issues of that paper are covered in other chapters of this text, we offer here a brief word about the fiscal impact of restructuring. Restructuring, as used in the corporate sense and as used by Schenkat, assumes divestiture of some assets to liquidate selected liabilities. We are not convinced that either the language or the policy implications are applicable to schooling and the financing of schools. We have no evidence that the $25 billion or more being spent on programs for children with disabilities in the United States during 1990 was in need of redistribution. Neither do we find that amount adequate to meet the needs of students with disabilities. We have already discussed the fiscal issues of placement and reiterate here that funding strategies must follow pedagogical purposes.

FACILITIES AND TRANSPORTATION

FACILITIES

School administrators not only have to be involved with the programmatic aspects of the special education program but also with support activities such as transportation and facilities. This responsibility starts with the district superintendent and is delegated to building principals or to central office personnel with expertise in transportation and facilities. In some districts, supervisors of the special education program have partial responsibility for services in these two areas and must coordinate their efforts with other administrators who have the overall responsibility.

Although many administrators may not view their roles as including facilities and transportation, the simple fact is that a free appropriate public education is impossible without adequate attention to these two areas. Students with disabilities must get to school safely, and the facilities must be accessible and conducive to learning. For example, space that is well organized "cuts down on time loss by children and staff and reduces confusion and discipline problems" (Decker & Decker, 1992, p. 158).

Legal Requirements

Four federal legislative acts that affect facilities are PL 94-142, PL 99-457, PL 101-336, and Section 504 of the Rehabilitation Act of 1973 (PL 93-112). Although PL 94-142 does not specifically mention or deal with facilities, its basic intent is to ensure that every child with a disability is afforded a free and appropriate education in the least restrictive setting, which inherently requires accessibility to programs.

Section 504 is explicit, stating:

> No otherwise qualified handicapped individual in the United States, as defined in Section 7 (6), shall, solely by reason of his handicap, be excluded from the participation in, be denied the benefits of, or be subjected to discrimination under any program or activity receiving Federal financial assistance. (PL 93-112, 1973)

Because schools receive substantial federal financial assistance, they fall under the purview of this section. The regulations implementing Section 504 are also explicit in their relationship to facilities. A major subsection of the regulations focuses on program accessibility:

> No qualified handicapped person shall, because a recipient's facilities are inaccessible to or unusable by handicapped persons, be denied the benefits, be excluded from participation in, or otherwise be subjected to discrimination under any program or activity to which this part applies (Federal Register, 1977, Sec. 504, Sec. C, 84.21).

This means that school buildings must be accessible to children with disabilities to such an extent that the required programs are accessible.

Section 504 regulations require that programs, not buildings and classrooms, be accessible to children with disabilities. The specific methods used by schools to ensure program accessibility will vary from one school to another. Some of the methods that schools can use include assigning aides, redesigning equipment, making home visits, and reassigning classes or other services to an accessible building. Structural changes are not required in existing facilities if other methods are effective. The key is to use methods that provide program opportunities in as integrated a setting as possible (Sec. C, 84.22). In other words, districts would be on shaky ground if they made one building accessible for children with disabilities and required all children with disabilities in the district to attend that one school. This, in effect, would lead to the segregation of children with disabilities, which is unacceptable (Nondiscrimination Provisions, 1977).

For construction started after the implementation date of Section 504 (June 3, 1977), regulations require that buildings be designed to make all or part of the facility accessible to students with disabilities. In designing new construction, recipients are required to comply with the accessibility standards of the American National Standards Institute (Sec. C, 84.23).

The Americans with Disabilities Act (ADA) is similar in its physical accessibility requirements to Section 504. The ADA, basically a civil rights law for persons with disabilities, requires that schools make their programs accessible to students with disabilities (Hecker, 1991). As with Section 504, this means that the programs must be accessible, not the buildings or classrooms. Also, similar to Section 504, the accessibility of programs should occur in as integrated an environment as possible, not in a separate building that just happens to be accessible (Americans with Disabilities Handbook, 1992).

The ADA requires schools to address facility accessibility in three areas: (1) new construction requirements, (2) renovations, and (3) program accessibility. Program accessibility is the key requirement of the ADA for public schools (Hecker, 1991). When it is not feasible to physically alter buildings, schools are required to implement other means to make programs accessible to all students with disabilities.

Close examination of the regulations of Section 504 and the ADA indicate that barrier-free schools means more than simply placing a ramp for wheelchair access into a building. It also includes:

> Access to grounds and buildings through curb cuts, entrance ramps, 32-inch door openings; access to primary building facilities such as classrooms, the library, the gymnasium; access to convenience and support facilities such as bathrooms, the cafeteria, lockers. (*Quick! Tell Me How To Buy*, 1978, p. 10)

The task required of schools, therefore, is very complex and requires a great deal of thought and planning.

PL 99-457, passed in 1986, was an amendment to PL 94-142. This law lowers the age of mandatory services for children with disabilities to 3 years, a mandate extended with passage of the Individuals with Disabilities Education Act (IDEA) Amendment of 1991, or PL 102-119. The legislation also provides financial incentives for schools that provide services to children from 0 to 2 years of age (Smith et al., 1993; T. E. C. Smith, 1990). As a result of programs for young children and because of the differences between and needs of very young children and infants, there are implications for classroom space and design (Decker & Decker, 1992).

Role of Administrators

The basic function of administration in education is to facilitate teaching and the education of children. In special education, this includes the education of children with disabilities. Indeed, the principal is expected to take major responsibility in direct service to pupils and in all supervisory and evaluation aspects of personnel administration. All that takes place within the building is generally conceded to be the major responsibility of the principal (Smith et al., 1993).

The school building and grounds must facilitate the educational program in the school. For example, if the education program is self-contained, the self-contained classroom must be large enough to permit a variety of activities; if daily living skills are taught in the program, such facilities as a kitchen, laundry, bathroom, and sewing equipment must be available; and if the program takes place in a resource room, there must be space for equipment and room for centers so that several children in the room at the same time can work independently on a variety of activities (Westling & Koorland, 1988). The extent to which children with disabilities are placed in regular classrooms under the mainstreaming concept or the newer inclusion model will dictate alterations to existing classrooms that previously were used for nondisabled students.

Facility Planning

School administrators must plan effectively to avoid unnecessary pitfalls (Skaller, 1992). To plan adequately for appropriate facilities, four kinds of information are necessary: (1) a conceptualization of the type and philosophy of program that will be provided, (2) a projection of the school population that would utilize the facilities, (3) a plan for using existing facilities, and (4) an estimate of the availability of funds.

In any facility planning effort, the district must ensure that the plan developed is based on the school district's philosophy of special education services (Johns & Ryden, 1989). For example, if the district has a philosophy that all students with disabilities be integrated into regular programs for the majority of the school day, the facilities plan will be different than if the philosophy were based on self-contained services.

Although it seems that an inclusion philosophy would have limited impact on facilities, the exact opposite could occur. A philosophy that emphasizes inclusion may have even more dramatic implications. Full inclusion of students with disabilities might result in all regular classrooms being made accessible. It could also mean that room for aides and ancillary equipment be set aside in each classroom space. Therefore, a full inclusion model could impact an entire facility, as opposed to lesser inclusion models where only some of the facilities might be affected. Table 11-1 describes the implications of a full inclusion service model on facilities.

There are two types of facility planning for new or renovated facilities: (1) long-range planning and (2) short-range planning. Both types of facility planning are important for schools. If schools do one and not the other, they may not be prepared to meet the needs of all students.

In the long-range planning process, the following must be considered (Abend, Bednar, Froehlinger, & Stenzler, 1979):

- Projected populations and student enrollments
- Organizational patterns
- Evaluation of existing facilities
- Health, building, and fire code requirements
- Legislation and regulations related to the education of children with disabilities
- Class size
- Staffing patterns
- Site criteria
- Transportation alternatives
- Population to be served
- Financial requirements
- Program accessibility
- Student placement practices
- Specific services required

Information from these areas is critical in developing a long-range plan for school facilities. School personnel must know the projected population figures for their district, as well as information from all of the other areas.

Planning new or renovated facilities requires more immediate tasks. First, any new or renovated facility should meet the needs determined by the long-range planning process. Districts should not consider facilities for immediate use without first examining the overall long-term needs of the district. In matching immediate needs to the long-term plan, the most important components are "the education programs and services required for disabled students to be served" (Abend et al., 1979). In this way, potential pitfalls can be avoided, and the end result will be a well-conceived and well-developed plan.

An important part of the planning process for new or renovated facilities is the utilization of individuals from various representations. Whether the resulting group is called the facility planning committee, the building committee, the special educa-

Table 11-1   Implications of Full Inclusion on Facilities

- All programs must be accessible for students with all types of disabilities.
- School grounds must be accessible for students with all types of disabilities.
- Focus on different types of disabilities, including visual and hearing impairments, cognitive impairments, mental/emotional problems, and mobility impairments.
- Ensure accessible restroom facilities in sufficient numbers in all parts of the school.
- Consider accessibility for parents and family members who may have disabilities.
- Provide staff development for all school personnel, including ancillary professional staff, lunchroom workers, bus drivers, teachers' aides, etc.
- Ensure accessibility of extracurricular activities to students with all types of disabilities.

---

tion facility committee, or something else is unimportant. The important thing is that it has representation from as broad a background as possible. Groups of individuals that should be represented on the planning committee should include (1) the central school administration, (2) the board of education, (3) the local building administration, (4) teachers and other instructional personnel, (5) support personnel, (6) parents, and (7) students (Brockett, 1993). Table 11-2 describes the unique information brought to the planning process by these different groups.

Regardless of committee membership, the superintendent of the local district is responsible for the entire planning process. However, tasks can be delegated to other individuals, such as the educational facility planner, the building principal, or a consultant. In some cases, the director or supervisor of special education might be the appropriate person to coordinate the planning activities. In particular, (1) local school administrators are needed to provide input concerning their schools' programs; (2) administrative personnel in special education should be available to contribute information concerning the special education program needs; (3) school finance specialists should provide financial projections; and (4) parents should be given an opportunity to provide input into the special education program from the ground up.

Table 11-2   Unique Information for Planning Purposes

Source	Information
Board of Education	Board of education has ultimate responsibility, therefore members should be involved. Board members will have information regarding the district's long-range plans and fiscal capacity.
Superintendent	The superintendent is the board's primary instrument to implement board policy. The superintendent will have information regarding the district's instructional and fiscal capacity.
Teachers	Teachers will have to implement appropriate instruction for students with disabilities. They can provide information about specific instructional requirements.
Parents	Laws currently require that parents of students with disabilities be involved in their children's education. Parents have unique information about the instructional and support needs of their children.
Students with Disabilities	Students with disabilities are the ultimate consumer of services. Through their own experiences, they have unique knowledge concerning their needs as they relate to facilities.
Architects	Architects who design facilities have expertise concerning building capabilities.
State Consultants	State department of education consultants have knowledge concerning how other districts have made services available to students with disabilities through facilities. Their experience can prevent districts from making the same mistakes other districts have already made.

Also, depending on the nature of the program to be housed, various specialists might be needed in the planning process. For example, if the facility is to provide educational services for children with emotional problems, a specialist in the education of such children will be needed to provide information concerning their special physical needs, such as time-out rooms. When designing facilities for children with physical disabilities, a specialist in this area could provide very relevant information regarding design needs.

Although the planning group may thus become rather large, it is better to include all relevant persons, rather than leave some out to minimize the size. In fact, smaller subgroups will do most of the work; thus, the large size of the total group should not be a major barrier in achieving the goals of the planning process.

In any planning process, certain pitfalls should be expected and methods to alleviate them should be preplanned (Skaller, 1992). However, even with the best planning, some potential problems will not be identified. Therefore, procedures should be established for dealing with problems as they arise. These may include establishing a core committee to take up any problems in the process, convening the entire committee periodically to review subgroup activities and provide input regarding problem areas, or having the superintendent and/or the board make decisions on problem areas. Regardless of the method used, districts should be able to anticipate problems during the process and have methods available to deal with them.

The planning process requires (1) preliminary budget development, (2) educational specifications, (3) schematics, (4) design development and construction documentation, (5) furniture and equipment, (6) orientation and in-service programs, and (7) evaluation. Some of these will be dealt with simultaneously; others will be handled in sequence.

Proper facilities planning is a time-consuming process (Brockett, 1993). However, without such planning, the end result could be disastrous. For example, a lack of input from certain groups might lead to problems when the facility is completed; improper budget planning could mean an end of funds before the project is completed; and the exclusion of certain specialists in planning could result in a facility that does not adequately meet the needs of the particular group of children with disabilities to be served or that does not meet minimum state and federal requirements. The key to any facilities project is planning (Skaller, 1992); though the program may be delayed a short time, the end result is likely to be more successful if the proper planning or preplanning is accomplished.

General Design of Facilities

The information presented throughout this section focuses on the unique facilities required for offering the full range of instructional and related services to students with disabilities. For most schools this will require a blend of adaptations to the regular class and specialized facilities for the students with disabilities. The design of specialized facilities will depend on the unique needs associated with each disability. As inclusion models are more widely implemented, it is evident that accommodations will need to be made to the regular class as appropriate to help meet the needs of students with disabilities. However, the full extent of these accommodations to the regular class is currently unclear as full-inclusion models are still in the beginning stages. Nonetheless, facility design characteristics that were formerly used for special classes may be adapted for the regular class.

Parking Areas.   Many persons with disabilities drive their own vehicles. This must be considered in planning programs, especially for secondary pupils with disabilities. At the elementary level, although the students will not be driving themselves, parking facilities must be made available for their parents or others who deliver the students. Special parking areas should be established conveniently in parking lots. The Americans with Disabilities Act Accessibility Guidelines (ADAAG) indicate that the accessible parking spaces must be a minimum of eight feet wide and should be located on the shortest possible route from the parking area to an accessible entrance. The number of accessible parking spaces required will depend on the overall size of the parking lot. Table 11-3 provides the minimum number of spaces required based on the size of the lot (ADAAG Guidelines, 1990).

Table 11-3   Number of Accessible Parking Spaces Required

Total Parking in Lot	Required Minimum Number of Accessible Spaces
1 to 25	1
26 to 50	2
51 to 75	3
76 to 100	4
101 to 150	5
151 to 200	6
201 to 300	7
301 to 400	8
401 to 500	9
501 to 1000	2 percent of total
1001 and over	20 plus 1 for each 100 over 1000

Except as provided in (b), access aisles adjacent to accessible spaces shall be 60 in (1525 mm) wide minimum.

(b) One in every eight accessible spaces, but not less than one, shall be served by an access aisle 96 in (2440 mm) wide minimum and shall be designated "van accessible" as required by 4.6.4. The vertical clearance at such spaces shall comply with 4.6.5. All such spaces may be grouped on one level of a parking structure.

From Federal Register, Vol. 56, No. 144, July 26, 1991, Rules and Regulations, p. 35612.

Walks and Ramps.   Walks and ramps are generally necessary for movement from the parking area to the building. They should be a minimum 3 feet wide, with walks having a slope of no greater than 1 inch in 20 inches and ramps having a slope of no greater than 1 inch in 12 inches. Handrails are required on both sides if the ramp has a slope of greater than 6 inches (ADAAG, 1990). Handrails allow individuals in wheelchairs to pull themselves up and provide a stabilizer for individuals on crutches or for individuals with balance problems. Handrails should be easy to grasp. The top of the handrails should be between 34 and 38 inches. The surfaces of walks and ramps should be smooth, firm, and slip resistant (ADAAG, 1990). Figure 11.1 depicts standards for ramps.

Doors and Doorways.   After individuals with disabilities have traveled from the parking area to the door, further accommodations must be available. Doorways must be a minimum 32 inches wide to allow the passage of wheelchairs. Doors must be easily opened so that persons in wheelchairs, on crutches, or with limited strength can operate them, especially fire doors, which shall have the minimum opening force allowable by the school administration (ADAAG, 1990).

Lighting.   Many of the learning activities in a school are visual in nature. Thus, the lighting is an important aspect of the instructional environment (Clark & Herbert, 1991). If possible, a variety of lights should be used, such as drop lights, desk lights, and undershelf lighting, and should be set at various heights. Such lighting helps establish the mood of the room and enables children to exercise some control over their immediate space (Birch & Johnstone, 1975). Also, if a separate reading area or work area is set up, "care must be taken not to shut off a light source, although subdued lighting may be suitable for a 'quiet' area" (Westling & Koorland, 1988, p. 16).

Figure 11.1   Standard for Ramps

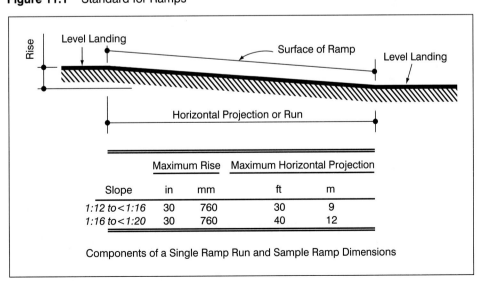

Slope	Maximum Rise		Maximum Horizontal Projection	
	in	mm	ft	m
1:12 to <1:16	30	760	30	9
1:16 to <1:20	30	760	40	12

Components of a Single Ramp Run and Sample Ramp Dimensions

From Federal Register, Vol. 56, No. 144, July 26, 1991, Rules and Regulations, p. 35635.

Acoustics   Just as lighting is an important aspect of the learning environment, factors that affect hearing should also be considered (Clark & Herbert, 1991). Acoustics concerns the way sound is absorbed, reflected, and distributed, as well as the sources and transmission of sounds (Abend et al., 1979). The importance of acoustics with regard to particular types of children with disabilities cannot be overlooked. For example, children with visual impairments rely on their auditory channel for most of their learning; children with hearing losses must make the most of their residual hearing skills; children with auditory perceptual problems require acoustic controls; children with speech difficulties rely on their own articulation to monitor their speech efforts; and children with behavior disorders are frequently triggered into atypical behavior by unusual sounds (Birch & Johnstone, 1975). The special needs of children with disabilities may require the soundproofing of walls and the use of carpet and other floorings and acoustical ceiling tiles to reduce outside noises that might prove distracting (Westling & Koorland, 1988).

Some materials are better for soundproofing than others. The following provides characteristics of various materials (Clark & Herbert, 1991, p. 48):

Material	Characteristics
Damage resistant ceiling boards	Good
Better quality mineral boards	Better
Cement/wood board with various backings	Good-to-Best
Perforated metal acoustical roof deck	Better-to-Best
Acoustical structural glazed tile	Good
Slotted concrete block with various filers	Good-to-Better

Climate.   Variables that affect climate include the amount and type of activity in the room, solar heat gain and loss, the physiological characteristics of individual students, and the capacity of equipment to maintain an even temperature. To maintain quality of air and a range of acceptable temperature, the following should be considered (Abend et al., 1979):

1. The climate of each area should be related to the type and level of room activity required by each special population.
2. Teachers must be able to rely on climate control or have access to the controls for specified areas.
3. Fresh air must be provided by the ventilation system in the appropriate quantity and quality.
4. Heating and cooling systems must be able to maintain temperatures in the desired range.
5. Temperatures must be stable.
6. Pollutants must be eliminated by the ventilation system.

In all situations, proper ventilation must be maintained. Good ventilation is not only good for health but also improves the learning environment. Make sure vents are open and working at all times (Westling & Koorland, 1988).

Bathrooms.   Many children with disabilities are capable of using regular bathroom facilities. However, for some children with physical impairments and some children with other disabilities, regular bathroom facilities create difficulties and thus represent major barriers. Problems include a lack of space for wheelchair maneuvering and toilet stalls that are not large enough for wheelchairs and wheelchair transfers. Three types of facilities are needed in barrier-free bathrooms: (1) regular facilities for those who require no modifications, (2) facilities designed for wheelchair use, and (3) large-area facilities for cleaning up children who have occasional accidents or who do not have urinary and bowel control (Birch & Johnstone, 1975).

Bathrooms designed for wheelchair access should adhere to the standards shown in Figure 11.2. Mirrors and other accessory items should be no higher than 40 inches (ADAAG, 1990).

Figure 11.2   Standards for Bathrooms

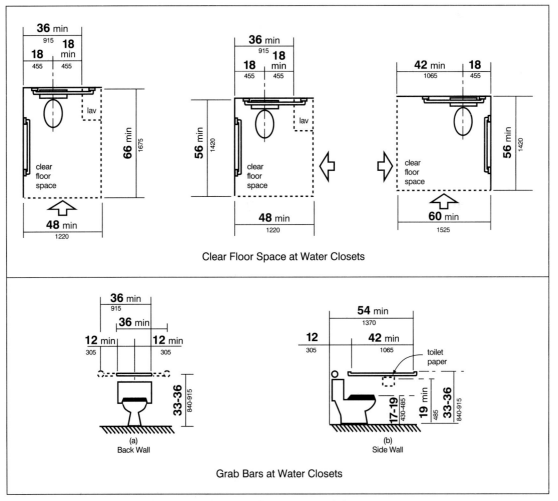

From Federal Register, Vol. 56, No. 144, July 26, 1991, Rules and Regulations, p. 35635.

Water Fountains.   To make water fountains accessible to students in wheelchairs, the height of the spout shall be no higher than 36 inches from the floor and should be mounted at the front of the unit. A flow of water at least 4 inches high must be possible. If higher fountains are used, a cup dispenser must be provided (ADAAG, 1990).

Furniture and Equipment.   Stationary furniture and equipment, such as blackboards, should be located in positions that are easily accessible to children with disabilities. To accommodate their use, chalkboards and tack boards should be floor-to-ceiling in rooms where children are in wheelchairs. Otherwise, blackboards should be hung on walls with the distance from the floor dependent on the types of disabilities and the ages of the children who need to use them (D'Alonzo, D'Alonzo, & Mauser, 1979). Other furniture and equipment should be designed to allow wheelchair accessibility. Movable partitions should be present to allow for space changes dictated by different programs and services (Johns & Ryden, 1989).

The design criteria for furniture is similar to that for persons without disabilities. The major difference is that children without disabilities can usually adapt to modifications in furniture design, and children with disabilities cannot. As a result, strict adherence to basic designs should be followed. As a general rule, furniture used in a classroom with students with disabilities should (1) be age-appropriate, (2) should be available for all students with specific needs, (3) should be in good usable condition, and (4) should be the appropriate size (Westling & Koorland, 1988).

Lunch Room.   Physical modifications for lunch rooms should be minimal. Examples of possible modifications would include lowering the height of benches, tables, and tray lines, and modifying entrances to include ramps and doorways wide enough for wheelchair access (ADAAG, 1990; "Food Services for the handicapped," 1979).

Fire Safety.   Because of fire and building codes, adequate provisions must be made for speedy evacuation of children from schools. Unfortunately, that may not be enough to ensure the safe evacuation of children with disabilities. Although most buildings are accessible, at least to some degree to students with disabilities, some attention must be devoted to getting students out of the building in the event of a fire or other emergency. As a result, egress for students with disabilities is beginning to receive a great deal of attention by facilities planners and administrators (Agron, 1989).

Because most students with disabilities are integrated part of the day with nondisabled students, it might appear to make sense to assign nondisabled students the responsibility of getting students with disabilities out of the building in emergency situations. This may, however, be unfair to the nondisabled students and not a very reliable method of ensuring the evacuation of students with disabilities (Agron, 1989). It also provides the basis for litigation. All attempts should be made to ensure safe evacuation for children with disabilities, on their own, when at all possible.

Special provisions may be required (1) for children who are immobile and not able to move quickly or easily, (2) for children who are hearing impaired who may not be able to hear an audible fire alarm, (3) for children with limited intellectual capacities who may not respond well in atypical situations, and (4) for children who may be restricted in standing tables or braced to furniture or other equipment. In these cases, obvious modifications must be made to guarantee adequate fire safety.

A well-developed plan for evacuating students with disabilities must be in place and understood by all students and staff. This plan should be explained to students and rehearsed to ensure its potential for success (Agron, 1989). Also, any new plan should be an elaboration or modification of the existing plan. Examples of possible modifications include fire alarms that have a visual signal, additional exits to the exterior of the building, exits located close to the special education room, and escape routes outside the building that are accessible by wheelchair and by other children with disabilities. In addition, fire drills should be held on a regular basis, and teachers should be instructed in procedures for evacuating the special needs student. Students must know proper procedures during a fire drill, teachers should know the location of fire extinguishers, and substitute teachers must be apprised of fire exit plans (Birch & Johnstone, 1975).

Outdoor Play Areas.   Play frequently provides children with their first learning experiences; when used properly, it can facilitate the development of visual motor skills, spatial relationships, social relationships, and physical development (Birch & Johnstone, 1975). Abend et al. (1979) suggest that, for children with disabilities:

1. Play areas be removed from hazardous areas, such as roads, service drives, and extreme slopes.
2. Walkways be provided to a large part of the school's exterior to facilitate movement of students with impaired mobility.
3. Elevated areas be accessible by wheelchairs and children on crutches in activities that involve sand, water, and plants.
4. Play areas provide a continuum of possibilities for segregated play, as well as activities that integrate children with disabilities and nondisabled children.
5. Overhead shading be provided as necessary for some children.
6. Bathrooms be in close proximity to play areas.
7. Handrails be installed as necessary for some play activities.
8. Modified equipment be made available if required for some activities.
9. Spacing between various types of play equipment be modified as necessary to accommodate wheelchairs.

Specific Design Criteria

In addition to general building design criteria, service providers for children with disabilities must consider design criteria for a broad range of specific special education and related services. These range from instructional services in self-contained classrooms, resource rooms, and regular classrooms to a wide variety of related services provided in special settings, such as physical therapy rooms. In determining the design criteria for this broad range of services, certain factors must be considered.

Nature of the Educational Program.   The most important design criteria is the nature of the instructional program and the district's philosophy of special education. As districts implement inclusion models, the traditional uses of resource and self-contained classrooms will change as will, of course, the design and use of regular classrooms. When planning and renovating facilities, special and regular education administrators must be sure that all other facility design elements are subordinated to the intent of the district's instructional philosophy and the manner in which it is to be implemented through the instructional program.

Age of Students.   Different age levels of students may dictate different designs of physical space (Decker & Decker, 1992). For example, secondary students generally are provided services using a three-curriculum model: vocational, general, and college preparatory (Polloway, Patton, Epstein, & Smith, 1989); these different curricular tracks may require different physical arrangements. And students at the elementary level may require smaller, more compact classrooms (Decker & Decker, 1992). However, classrooms for young children often have several different specialty areas. Safford (1978), for example, suggests that classrooms for young children with disabilities have socio-drama play areas, sand and water tables, group listening centers, carpentry areas, block areas, fine motor areas, and reading corners. In addition, the room should be large enough for motor activities.

Activities.   Another important factor in determining specific design criteria is the nature of the activities to be carried out in the room. For example, one popular intervention strategy is teaching study skills to students at the secondary level (Smith & Dowdy, 1989). If this were the nature of the activities in the resource room, limited space would be required. Tutoring is another instructional approach frequently used (Polloway et al., 1989) that will require minimal physical space as well. Whereas, if motor activities are commonplace, large areas are necessary.

Space Requirements.   The amount of space required will vary with the type of program. The exact amount of space will depend, therefore, on several factors, including the type of children served, the type of service delivery system being used, the age of the children, and the nature of the activities. Support service areas, such as physical therapy rooms, will also vary in space requirements.

Resource Rooms.   Resource rooms are special education classrooms where students attend only parts of each day. They receive the majority of their instruction in regular classrooms and attend the resource room only for special interventions (Smith, Price, & Marsh, 1986). The resource room is currently the most popular special education classroom model in public education (Smith, 1990). Resource rooms should be as similar to regular classrooms as possible in appearance and location. Because one of the goals of integrating students with disabilities is to reduce stigma, calling attention to the resource room defeats the purpose of the resource-room approach.

Self-Contained Classrooms.   Self-contained special education classrooms, one of the predominant models used to serve students with disabilities, are now the second most popular type of arrangement. Students receiving special education services in self-contained classrooms remain in the classroom with the same teacher for most of the instructional day (Smith, 1990). Attempts should be made to reduce the stigma associated with self-contained rooms by designing them as similar to regular classrooms as possible while still taking into consideration the needs of the students.

Because they serve students on a full-time basis, self-contained classes require space and room arrangements to facilitate the instructional program. In addition to academic facilities, self-contained rooms may require equipment and space for training in self-help and prevocational, vocational, and home-living skills.

Regardless of the population served in self-contained classrooms, provisions must be made for toilet use and toilet training for some age and functional levels. Self-contained classrooms may also need space for physical and occupational therapy, for grooming skills training, and for motor training. Attempts to locate a self-contained special education room in a classroom that is smaller than a regular classroom will create problems in the facilitation of the instructional program. In order to accommodate all of the activities that may occur in a self-contained classroom, various partitions may be used to divide the space into specialty areas (Westling & Koorland, 1988).

Specific Subject Areas.   Design criteria for specific subject areas must be considered to accommodate the needs of students with disabilities. Table 11-4 describes subject area design criteria.

Related Services.   Federal legislation requires that schools provide related services necessary to help children with disabilities benefit from special education. Although not all related services require special criteria in building design, some require specialized space. For example, school administrators must take into consideration the need for space and special equipment for providing physical therapy, speech therapy, occupational therapy, and counseling. When designating space for these activities, professionals who provide services should be consulted to determine specific needs.

Facilities Evaluation

To determine if current facilities for special education programs are appropriate, an evaluation of the facilities should be conducted on a regular basis. Evaluation of facilities cannot be accomplished effectively without also evaluating other aspects of programs, including the curriculum, personnel, support services, and student progress. Educational evaluation is a complex process that involves many different aspects (Hamm, 1989). Evaluating the physical facilities is only one part of an overall, comprehensive evaluation model that schools should use.

Table 11-4   Design Criteria for Subject Areas

Area	Space Requirements	Furniture/Equipment
Art	Too little space inhibits use of some equipment, and too much space makes it difficult for proper teacher supervision. Recommendation: 55 sq ft per pupil up to 20 students; Not less than 800 sq ft for elementary and 1,000 for secondary.	Furniture has to be related to the specific needs of the children with disabilities. For example, disruptive children should be seated with distance between them and other students. Cut-out and stand-up tables might be required for some children with physical disabilities.
Home-living skills	Space required will depend on the type of activities. For example, if cooking classes are conducted, ample room for appliances and clean-up is required. Sewing requires space for machines and maneuverability.	Equipment depends on the activities taught. They might include washers and dryers, beds, kitchen utensils, and appliances.
Industrial arts	There is no need for space modifications to accommodate students with disabilities. General space requirements include 150 sq ft for storage, 50 sq ft for observation, 300 sq ft for lecture, plus required space for various industrial arts activities.	Specific equipment will depend on the types of programs offered. Safety requirements should be a major consideration. Handrails or handgrips may be necessary, as well as custom-made coats or aprons for protection for some students with physical disabilities.
Physical education	Recommended space requirements are a range of 700 sq ft to 3,000 sq ft for elementary students and 800 sq ft to 1600 sq ft for secondary students. This space is in addition to regular P.E. space, with the exact needs determined by the number and type of students served and type of equipment used.	Typical equipment may be modified or specialized equipment acquired for children with disabilities.
Elementary music	There is no need for modifications to regular music space requirements: 60 sq ft per person for 10 to 12 students, with an additional 25 sq ft for up to 20 and an additional 15 sq ft for up to 30.	No major modifications needed, with the possible exception of seating with special chairs or standing tables.
Science	Counters, tables, and equipment must be made accessible by students. No major modifications in space needed except to ensure adequate room for mobility.	Needed equipment might include a mirror above the demonstration table, handrails or grips, and custom-made lab coats for students with physical disabilities.

Adapted from *Facilities for Special Education Services: A Guide for Planning New and Renovated Schools* (pp. 61–88) by A. C. Abend, M. J. Bednar, V. J. Froehlinger, and Y. Stenzler, 1979, Reston, Va.: Council for Exceptional Children. Copyright 1979 by the Council for Exceptional Children. Adapted by permission.

The following aspects of the physical environment should be evaluated: (1) general accessibility of the building, (2) location of the special education program, and (3) the physical characteristics of the special education classroom.

General Accessibility of the Building.   Some public schools have developed checklists to determine the general accessibility of buildings and building components. Although these checklists vary, they generally include the following areas:

1. Parking lots
2. Walks
3. Ramps
4. Entrances/exits
5. Doors and doorways
6. Stairs and steps
7. Floors
8. Rest rooms
9. Water fountains
10. Public telephones
11. Elevators
12. Controls for light, heat, ventilation, etc.
13. Signage
14. Warning signals
15. Hazards
16. Special rooms

With the passage of the Americans with Disabilities Act in 1990 has come a new set of guidelines that must be adhered to by public facilities. School personnel should obtain checklists that are developed based on this legislation to ensure that their school buildings and programs are accessible. A short checklist that addresses ADA guidelines is included in Figure 11.3.

Location of the Program.   Location is an important consideration in maximally integrating children with disabilities into the regular activities of the school. It is particularly pertinent in providing easy access to entrances and exits, bathroom facilities, lunchroom facilities, and ancillary services. Relevant questions that could be asked to determine the appropriateness of the location of these rooms and other aspects of the special education program include the following:

1. Does the location facilitate scheduled participation in regular classes and transfer to and from regular classes and provide maximum opportunities for children with disabilities to test reality?
2. Does the location provide flexibility in the use of the school facilities?

Figure 11.3   A "Quick Look" Checklist for Accessibility.

ITEM TO BE PERFORMED	YES	NO
Building Access		
1. Are 96" wide parking spaces designated with a 60" access aisle?	_____	_____
2. Are parking spaces near main building entrance?	_____	_____
3. Is there a "drop off" zone at building entrance?	_____	_____
4. Is the gradient from parking to building entrance 1:12 or less?	_____	_____
5. Is the entrance doorway at least 32 inches?	_____	_____
6. Is door handle easy to grasp?	_____	_____
7. Is door easy to open (less than 8 lbs. pressure)?	_____	_____
8. Are other than revolving doors available?	_____	_____
Building Corridors		
1. Is path of travel free of obstruction and wide enough for a wheelchair?	_____	_____
2. Is floor surface hard and not slippery?	_____	_____
3. Do obstacles (phones, fountains) protrude no more than four inches?	_____	_____
4. Are elevator controls low enough (54") to be reached from a wheelchair?	_____	_____
5. Are elevator markings in Braille for the blind?	_____	_____
6. Does elevator provide audible signals for the blind?	_____	_____
7. Does elevator interior provide a turning area of 51" for wheelchairs?	_____	_____
Restrooms		
1. Are restrooms near building entrance/personnel office?	_____	_____
2. Do doors have lever handles?	_____	_____
3. Are doors at least 32" wide?	_____	_____
4. Is restroom large enough for wheelchair turnaround (60" minimum)?	_____	_____
5. Are stall doors at least 32" wide?	_____	_____
6. Are grab bars provided in toilet stalls?	_____	_____
7. Are sinks at least 30" high with room for a wheelchair to roll under?	_____	_____
8. Are sink handles easily reached and used?	_____	_____
9. Are soap dispensers, towels, no more than 48" from floor?	_____	_____
Personnel Office		
1. Are doors at least 32" wide?	_____	_____
2. Is the door easy to open?	_____	_____
3. Is the threshold no more than ½" high?	_____	_____
4. Is the path of travel between desks, tables wide enough for wheelchairs?	_____	_____

From *ADA Self-Evaluation Guide for Public Entities* (p. 25), Washington, DC: U.S. Government Printing Office.

3. Are there enough pupils to provide suitable groupings by age, ability, and achievement?

4. Is participation with nondisabled children in activities such as sports, physical education, music, plays, school activities, and social events facilitated by the location?

5. Is maximum use made of the school library, cafeteria, auditorium, shops, home economics suite, health services suite, gym, swimming pool, and outdoor recreation areas?

6. Is the necessary specialized equipment available?

7. Does the location facilitate transportation?

8. Are audiovisual aids, maps, globes, labs, computers, and other equipment available to the location?

9. Does the location facilitate the most efficient use of school and ancillary personnel, maximize the use of supervisors, foster relationships among special education and other school personnel, facilitate teamwork among special education personnel and between regular and special educators, and increase the likelihood that family members will attend school with their children with disabilities?

10. Will the location enhance participation by parents of children with disabilities in school activities and increase the opportunities for all children to take advantage of academic and social enrichment activities?

11. Does the location assist in keeping building costs down and in developing positive community relations?

Physical Arrangement of the Classrooms.   Although a school may have accessible rooms, furniture, equipment, and materials, the arrangement of individual classrooms often presents a dilemma for teachers. Should desks be arranged in, for example, straight rows, circles, or small clusters? The importance of the physical arrangement of furniture and materials in a classroom is obvious. The best of lesson plans will be ineffective if students cannot access materials, and behavior problems may develop or be exacerbated if freedom of movement is inhibited by classroom arrangement (Guernsey, 1989).

One suggestion for arrangement is to have three different kinds of spaces. One area should be for group activities, one for individual work, and one for free-time activities (Minner & Prater, 1989). If the size of the classroom does not allow such flexibility, movable partitions might be useful. Ensuring that every student has work space is important. With resource rooms and students coming and going, many special education teachers do not realize the importance of "ownership" in a work environment.

Another consideration concerns the reduction of extraneous stimuli. For many years, special education professionals have been aware of the highly distractible nature of some students. Therefore, arrangement of the physical environment to reduce unwanted visual and auditory distractions and interruptions is important. Because outside windows and doorways are key areas for distraction, teachers should arrange their space to avoid students facing or being too near these two primary sources of distraction (Minner & Prater, 1989).

Some special education teachers prefer to organize their classrooms to emphasize the differences between their rooms and regular rooms where students often experience failure. Special education teachers want students to feel accepted and to have a comfortable working environment. Unfortunately, this may convey expectations to students that are inaccurate. If students perceive the special education room to be significantly different from the regular classrooms, they may attach a lesser importance to the setting, with lowered academic expectations. Therefore, teachers should not make their rooms that much different from regular classrooms. Teachers can convey warmth and acceptance in other ways.

Organizational Sources of Assistance

In planning new facilities or remodeling existing ones, several sources of information and assistance are available:

- The President's Committee on Employment of the Handicapped, Washington, D.C. 20210
- The National Center for a Barrier-Free Environment, Seventh and Florida, N.E., Washington, D.C. 20020
- The National Easter Seal Society for Crippled Children and Adults, 2023 W. Ogden Avenue, Chicago, Illinois 60612
- Mainstream, Inc., 1200 15th Street, N.W., Washington, D.C. 20005
- Arts, Box 2040, Grand Central Station, New York, New York 10017
- Architectural and Transportation Barriers Compliance Board, Washington, D.C. 20201

TRANSPORTATION

Transportation is equally important to facility accessibility for pupils with disabilities. Without adequate transportation, the mandate of a least restrictive environment may be unrealizable. Developing appropriate transportation for students with disabilities provides many challenges for school administrators (O'Donnell, 1992). Because difficulties in arranging transportation for a child are not justifiable reasons for denying an appropriate educational program, schools must consider transportation needs and arrange for suitable and safe transportation.

A primary consideration when developing accessible transportation for students with disabilities is safety (Stroup, Stout, Atkinson, Doll, & Russell, 1991). When considering safety issues, school personnel should:

1. Discuss transportation needs in advance.
2. Take into consideration personal characteristics of individual children.
3. Ensure that restraint systems used are functional.

4. Ensure that parents, transportation personnel, and students understand the equipment instructions.

5. Ensure that drivers are familiar with the transportation system being used (Stroup et al., 1991).

Public school transportation is a major enterprise in our country. Each day approximately 350,000 school buses travel 18 million miles and transport 22 million students (Making school transportation safe, 1989). This translates into more than 4 billion miles annually. Providing transportation for students without disabilities is commonplace. Providing appropriate transportation for students with various disabilities can present several difficulties. Administrators may find that they are most vulnerable to litigation in matters of transportation, and they should take steps to decrease liability, contain costs, and provide policy and procedures related to transportation (Linder, 1991). Table 11-5 summarizes general safety rules for parents, professionals, and children.

Legal Requirements

Public Law 94-142, the Americans with Disabilities Act, and Section 504 of the Rehabilitation Act of 1973 require that schools determine the nature of appropriate trans-

Table 11-5   Bus Safety Rules for Parents, Professionals, and Children

- Always cross in front of the bus in full sight of the driver.
- Wait for the bus on the curb, not in the street.
- Remain seated quietly during the entire bus ride.
- If safety belts are available, be sure to use them throughout the ride; only release them when the bus comes to a complete stop.
- Sit up straight on the bus seat or in the proper safety seat with hips up against the back of the bus seat or car safety seat.
- A safety belt should be secured and snugly tightened low on the hips. (A safety belt placed across the abdomen could result in internal injury in the event of an accident.)
- A safety belt should lie flat across a child's hips; it should not be twisted.
- A child who uses a wheelchair should transfer to the bus bench seat where a safety belt, car safety seat or other restraint system can be used.
- All child safety seats require a seat belt for securement.
- When a child cannot be transferred to the bus bench seat, the wheelchair should be secured in a **forward-facing** position. Dynamically tested, four-point tie-down systems are the most reliable means of securing a wheelchair.
- The child and the wheelchair should be secured independent from one another.

From "School Bus Safety" by K. B. Stroup, J. Stout, B. L. Atkinson, J. P. Doll, and R. Russell, 1991, *Exceptional Parent, 21,* p. 82. Reprinted by permission.

portation services for children with disabilities. Section 504 requires that transportation be provided as a nonacademic service: "A recipient shall provide non-academic and extracurricular services and activities in such a manner as necessary to afford students with disabilities an opportunity for participation in such services and activities" (Federal Register, 1977, Sec. 504,37).

Public Law 94-142 includes transportation as a related service. As defined in the Final Regulations of PL 94-142, services include "transportation and such developmental, corrective, and other supportive services as are required to assist a handicapped child to benefit from special education" (Federal Register, 1977, 121a. 13). Transportation is defined to include (1) travel to and from school and between schools, (2) travel in and around school buildings, and (3) specialized equipment (such as specially adapted buses, lifts, and ramps), if necessary to provide special transportation for a child with disabilities.

The right to receive transportation services has been upheld in hearings for several degrees and types of disabilities. In a state education agency decision in Massachusetts, a hearing officer ruled that the school was responsible for the transportation of a child with learning disabilities to and from a private school (*Robin G.* v. *Acushnet Public Schools,* 1980). In a New York case, the state education agency ruled that an emotionally disruptive child was still eligible for transportation even though the student had been unruly on the bus (In the Matter of Application of a Handicapped Child, 1980, 502:214). Another state case resulted in a decision that a child with a hearing impairment was eligible for transportation to and from daily therapy (Los Angeles United School District, 1981).

Responsibility for the transportation of children with disabilities, therefore, belongs to the schools if the IEP specifies that transportation is an appropriate related service or if the child lives in an attendance zone in which transportation to school is provided to all children. The person responsible for arranging the required transportation services is the principal. In some districts, this responsibility is delegated to the special education supervisor.

Schools may use a variety of means to meet the transportation requirements. These include (1) owning the vehicles, (2) contracting for transportation, (3) renting the vehicles, (4) sharing ownership of the vehicles with area schools, and (5) reimbursing individuals who provide transportation. If parents provide transportation, schools should reimburse them at an appropriate mileage rate. In some instances, where the school district serves only a few students who require specialized transportation, this may be the best solution if parents are willing.

Transportation Plan

To ensure the adequate transportation of children with disabilities in a district, school administrators should develop a plan (Stroup et al., 1991). This written document should state the policy of the district in providing transportation, including the various means that might be required for different children. The individuals who should provide input for the plan include the administrators, the special education supervisor, the special education teacher, a district transportation specialist, and the parents of the children who require transportation. The plan should be sufficiently flexible to accommodate children with varying degrees and types of disabilities and provide guidance to personnel in meeting the needs.

Some students with disabilities may live nearby and be able to walk. Providing some extra accommodations for these students to facilitate walking might be all the school needs to do to meet the obligation. Schools need to take into consideration the needs of all students, including those with disabilities, in developing transportation plans (Ponessa, 1988).

Children with disabilities, who require transportation as a related service, should have specific transportation procedures written into their IEPs. Whenever appropriate, these procedures should (1) ensure all reasonable transportation that the child requires in order to participate fully in all parts of the program and (2) take into account all conditions that must be met in order to safely transport the child (Higgins, 1977).

Vehicle Accessibility and Special Equipment

Without ramps and lifts, vehicle accessibility depends on the availability of individuals to physically lift students into the vehicle. However this alternative may be unsafe, may not meet the needs of most students, or may be stigmatizing for the students who are lifted on and off buses on a regular basis. Lifts and ramps offer two alternatives to make the boarding or off-loading of students easy and safe.

Manual ramps are the cheapest modification for vehicles. Their advantages, in addition to cost, are that they are virtually maintenance-free and can be made to fit most vehicles without major alterations. Electric/hydraulic lifts, although easier to use, require a more substantial financial outlay initially as well as in routine maintenance. Fully automatic lifts cost about 40% less but provide equal accessibility with a minimum of activity from operators (Lifts and Ramps, 1982).

In the bus, appropriate estimates might include carry straps, restraining wheelchairs, or individual seat belts. For extremely small children, car seats may be required. Regardless of the type of restraint selected, the safety of the child must be a major consideration in providing transportation services.

Transportation Personnel

Transportation personnel, including bus drivers and transportation aides, are vital to the appropriate and safe transportation of students (O'Donnell, 1992). Higgins (1977) suggests that bus drivers be required (1) to receive training to become familiar with the special needs of children with disabilities, (2) to report any unruly rider to the principal, (3) to attempt disciplinary measures only in an extreme case when the safety of the group is at stake, and (4) to evict riders from the vehicle only after following proper procedural due process to guarantee the rights of the child.

In-service training for bus drivers is essential. The training may be conducted by special education teachers, special education administrators, or other school personnel and should cover the policy areas mentioned earlier. Transportation personnel must recognize that they are acting as official district personnel and must follow established procedures in dealing with the unique needs of children with disabilities. Without prior training, bus drivers may not react well to the behavior problems or safety needs associated with some children with disabilities.

Transportation aides may be required for some students, to ensure their safety and well-being. In particular, aides are required for children who need special attention or who could distract bus drivers. Transportation aides should be school employees, not simply volunteers over whom the school has no control (Higgins, 1977).

Transportation Evaluation

Districts should regularly evaluate the transportation services available for students with disabilities. The evaluation, though ongoing, should be formalized at least twice during the school year. The following questions should be asked in the evaluation:

- Does the district provide transportation at no cost to students with disabilities?
- Are appropriate lifts and ramps available on buses to provide manual lifting?
- Are adequate restraint systems in place in buses to ensure the safety of students with disabilities?
- Do the IEPs for individual students contain transportation provisions?
- Have bus drivers been trained concerning the needs of riders with disabilities?
- Are aides present on routes where riders with disabilities require assistance and monitoring?
- Is door-to-door transportation being provided to students with disabilities who require such service?
- Is the riding time for students with disabilities in line with that of students without disabilities?

Although these questions are not exhaustive, they should provide distinct evaluation data needed to evaluate transportation services for children with disabilities.

CHAPTER
TWELVE

SCHOOL AND
COMMUNITY
RELATIONS

A strong school-community relations program is essential for an effective special education program. There are many different definitions of the scope of a school community relations program. For some, this concept simply means the school will keep the community informed of school activities. However, given the criticism of schools over the last decade and the requirements of special education laws, administrators will seek to involve parents and patrons more fully in school programming and, thus, will need to employ a comprehensive philosophy of school community relations. Clearly, any relations between school and community must rest on the active involvement of citizens and staff in the educational decision-making process through the use of two-way communications. Although such involvement may be problematic for the regular and special education administrator, we believe that it will ultimately result in a more effective special education program.

IDEA specifically addressed the rights of parents in the education of their children regarding:

- Written consent before an initial evaluation.
- Written consent before placement in special education.
- Independent evaluation.
- Evaluation at public expense.
- Participation on the committee that determines evaluation, placement, and programming.
- Inspection and review of records and ability to challenge information.
- A copy of the information in the child's educational record.

In addition to respecting and guaranteeing these rights, the school can actively pursue a proactive plan to prevent problems and conflicts with parents and patrons in the community.

COMMUNICATING WITH THE EXTERNAL COMMUNITY

Both special and regular education administrators frequently deal with community organizations and representatives and, therefore, must be able to use effective communication and interpersonal skills and special community relations techniques. In these endeavors, the administrator should work as much as possible through the district's regular school-community relations vehicles. Many districts employ a director of communications or a publications specialist who can assist in developing general communication strategies or specific communication methods.

General Communication Strategies

A major aim of a school-community relations strategy is to share information about the special education program with all district patrons. Members of the community should be aware of the available special education services and should know how to request them. To keep the community informed, the special and regular education administrator should employ a combination of communication strategies. The specific media used will depend on the nature of the community, the message that is being communicated, the availability of resources, and past success with specific techniques (Lunenburg & Ornstein, 1991). Following is a list of methods for communicating with the external public:

- A brochure that describes the special education program in general, including the district's philosophy of services to individuals with disabilities.
- Specialized brochures, each describing a specific aspect of the program.
- A parent handbook that describes the IEP process, forms, and the role of the parent.
- Articles in the district newspaper, school building paper, or local newspaper.
- A special newsletter that focuses on special education news.
- A regular newspaper column written by the special education administrator.
- Speeches to community groups or civic clubs.
- Telephone contacts with individual parents, civic leaders, or other citizens.
- Annual reports.
- Displays at locations such as schools, civic meeting places, and shopping malls.
- Speeches at gatherings of local neighborhood groups.
- Special education open houses.
- Public service announcements on radio and television describing some aspect of the special education service, for example, child find.
- Letters to individuals and groups.
- Videotapes.

The administrator should take great care in preparing the information to be communicated through these media, because "how it is said may be as important as what is said." The following are some general guidelines:

1. Have a particular audience in mind.
2. Tailor the message to the audience.
3. Be concise and to the point.
4. Avoid jargon and explain unfamiliar terms.
5. Use pictures, graphics, or audiovisual media.
6. Pretest materials with a small, representative group or focus group and revise as necessary.

Citizen Advisory Committees

Establishing a citizen advisory committee is a method of involving the community formally in the decision-making process. Citizens can contribute their expertise and energy to help the school explore alternatives, implement new programs, and evaluate various aspects of the school. The administrator may also wish to foster citizen involvement to deal with potentially difficult or controversial decisions, thereby minimizing future criticism by citizens. The advisory committee provides an additional means of dealing with the demands of various advocacy groups for individuals with disabilities and developing positive working relationships with these groups.

However, the administrator should be aware of some disadvantages and potential pitfalls associated with use of a citizen advisory committee:

1. Advisory committees can consume a great deal of the administrator's time.
2. Committee members often lack perspective and background information about educational issues.
3. Special interests of individual committee members can dominate.
4. Committee members may not be aware of past school practices or how the school operates.
5. Committee members may not understand group dynamics or group decision-making procedures.
6. Final recommendations can exceed the committee's original charge or overstep its authority.
7. The committee may search for problems or issues to justify its existence (Podemski & Steele, 1981).

To overcome these potential pitfalls, the administrator may employ the following techniques (Gorton, 1983; Podemski & Steele, 1981):

1. Set up ad hoc committees to deal with specific issues. Permanent committees soon outgrow their original purpose and then look for other issues to justify their existence. Committee size should be between 5 and 10 members; groups of this size facilitate group interaction, yet are large enough to provide for adequate representation of relevant perspectives.
2. Select committee members with care, and be sure that each member has time to contribute to the committee and is willing to work with other committee members to achieve a consensus.
3. Provide the committee with a comprehensive written charge, describing all constraints that the committee must keep in mind, the dates reports are due, and the formats in which the reports are due and should be presented.
4. Provide the members of the group with the information they need to accomplish their task. Be available to speak with the group or even participate in its deliberations as needed. Some groups may even need training in group decision-making processes.
5. Show sincere appreciation for the work of committee members and the committee as a whole. The participants give a great deal of their time and energy to the committee's work and should receive official and personal acknowledgement.

6. Attempt to implement as much of the committee's recommendations as possible. If the administrator has done a good job of defining the task and monitoring the committee's activity, most of the recommendations should be realistic and implementable. Failure to act on the recommendations will damage the administrator's credibility and make it less likely that the members will serve on future committees.

Volunteers and Paraprofessionals

Many volunteers serve in schools and are increasingly used in inclusion settings. Volunteers and paraprofessionals can be a valuable asset to the school; such service can provide members of the community opportunities to contribute their talents and learn more about the school. Almost anyone is a potential volunteer, for example, working and nonworking parents, business persons, college and high school students, members of civic organizations, and senior citizens. The motives that prompt individuals to volunteer are as varied as the individuals themselves, for example, the desire to help others, the desire to get out of the house, lack of anything to do, wanting to help bring about change, wanting to feel needed and appreciated, or "repaying" the school. In any case, because of their considerable potential to support and improve the delivery of special education services, the administrator should actively seek the services of volunteers to help complement and maximize the work of special education professionals.

Volunteers can be used in a variety of ways in the special education program:

1. Support tasks
   - Driver
   - Receptionist
   - Clerk
   - Library aide
   - General housekeeping
   - General office tasks

2. Client-based tasks
   - Assisting teacher to individualize instruction
   - Grading papers
   - Tutoring
   - Home visitor
   - Mobility assistance
   - Record keeping
   - Monitoring
   - Health screening

3. Creative tasks
   - Art work
   - Craft instruction

- Musical entertainment
- Organizing sports activities
- Assisting in producing plays

4. Administrative tasks

- Fund raising
- Grant writing
- Recruiting other volunteers
- Conducting surveys
- Assisting in school census

Administrators should deal with volunteers in much the same way as they deal with the professional staff, imparting to the volunteer the need for loyalty, dependability, and quality effort. Special problems arise when parents of children with disabilities work in the same classrooms with their children. Particularly influential parents, those with informal power because of relationships to others in the community or in the school, may also be potentially troublesome. In such cases, the administrator should seek involvement and guidance of other administrators and superiors in the district.

Administrators should develop systematic plans for using volunteers and monitoring their work; without such supervision and guidance, volunteers can interfere with the normal operations of the school and thus negate their potential usefulness. The plan should encompass recruitment, selection, orientation, evaluation, and means of appreciation. In such a plan the special education administrator might wish to implement the following activities:

1. Recruitment

- Coordinate activities with ongoing district volunteer programs, such as the Volunteers in Public Schools (VIPS).
- Advertise the need for volunteers through public service announcements on radio and television, in newspapers, and by word of mouth. Target retirement communities, nursing homes, and senior citizen programs.
- Develop volunteer application forms to request applicant identification information, past work experience, services the volunteer would like to perform, times available, and reasons for wanting to volunteer.
- Develop a job description for volunteer activities that describe specific duties, unique requirements, the environment in which the duties are performed, times when the volunteer services are needed, and financial considerations and benefits, if any.

2. Selection

- Question applicants about their reasons for wanting to volunteer, their work experience, hobbies, skills, and previous experiences in working with children.
- Explain general volunteer duties and responsibilities. Stress the importance of commitment and dedication.
- Give applicants an opportunity to ask questions and provide them with honest answers.

- Attempt to assign volunteers to jobs that match their abilities, personalities, and interests.

3. Orientation
   - Provide training about the needs and behavior of children with disabilities.
   - Involve the teachers with whom the volunteers will work.
   - Prepare a volunteer handbook that describes general school procedures and schedules, emergency procedures, the school layout, procedures for evaluating volunteers, dress codes, and procedures for notifying the school when unable to meet scheduled appointments.
   - Make sure the volunteers know the limits of their authority, to whom they report, and the exact nature of their responsibilities.
   - Provide a tour of the building and introduce the volunteers to other staff.
   - Allow time for questions and answer honestly.
   - Make all orientation sessions short, interesting, and to the point.

4. Evaluation
   - Develop a written evaluation form that is tied to the job description for the position.
   - Instruct teachers about the role you wish them to play in the evaluation of volunteers.
   - Supervise the volunteers regularly.
   - Review evaluations with the volunteers regularly and, if necessary, suggest improvements. If volunteers are not performing satisfactorily, determine if they should be assigned other types of duties or suggest that volunteering may not be the most appropriate means for them to be of service.

5. Showing appreciation
   - Encourage professional staff members to show their appreciation.
   - Provide volunteers with parking spaces; meals; reimbursement for expenses; uniforms, arm bands, or badges; and a lounge area.
   - Use formal methods to show appreciation, such as certificates and awards, appreciation banquets or ceremonies, recognition at faculty meetings, announcements in district newspapers or newsletters, and personal letters of appreciation.

As with all other aspects of the special education program, the administrator should periodically evaluate the procedures used in the volunteer program and determine if changes are needed. Careful attention to the success of a volunteer and paraprofessional program will pay great dividends in the quality of services to children with disabilities.

COMMUNICATING WITH PARENTS

Generally, federal legislation stipulates that school organizational procedures be designed in such a way as to give parents every opportunity to participate in the decisions that affect the educational programs for their children, from which a policy of parental involvement has grown over the years. The trend toward site-based management also incorporates the intention to broaden the authority of teachers and parents, students, and others in the community (David, 1989). In the area of special education, the administrator must make sure that all parental communications are conducted in a professional manner so as to fulfill not only the letter but also the spirit of parental involvement, as mandated in federal law; but this may be a minimum requirement.

Understanding Parents

Lareau (1989) has provided a unique view of the relationship of school personnel to parents, finding differences associated with the social class of the parents. Most importantly, Lareau reports that most schools seem to want one-way communication—for parents to receive instructions from school personnel but not to accept direction from parents (teachers and administrators being in the role of expert). Although teachers report that they want more parent involvement and ask for it, especially in the early years of schooling, they do not want a partnership, which implies a relationship between equals. Lareau reports that a more accurate description is a professional-client relationship, wherein teachers want to control the amount of interconnectedness between home and school. Many administrators may take the same view, perhaps even more so.

Also, there is an association between the social class of parents and their involvement in schooling. Parents of a lower social class tend to be less involved in schooling and to ask fewer questions or not seek assistance. The higher the educational level and/or social status of parents, the greater the potential for conflict if parents are dissatisfied or ask questions of school practices. Thus, working-class parents are more likely to defer to the professional role of teachers, and parents of the professional class are more likely to question the authority of teachers and schools.

According to Lareau (1989), in a working-class community, there is a separation between home and school, education being compartmentalized as something that occurs in a different place under the supervision of teachers. In upper-middle-class communities, there is an interconnectedness of family life and educational institutions. Parents who are dissatisfied with a school may employ consultants and tutors and challenge the school. Teachers in such schools are often displeased with parental involvement because upper-middle-class parents may view teachers as servile, thus disrupting the professional-client relationship. Accordingly, the special education administrator may have very different sets of problems and opportunities in different kinds of schools and communities.

Though parents of a child with disabilities obviously want the school to provide the most appropriate education for their child, they often are not knowledgeable about proper procedures to follow, or they may have been mistreated by school employees and thus become frustrated and angry. This hostility can be misinterpreted by school personnel and lead to antagonistic and nonproductive parent-school relationships. An understanding of the parent's point of view can help administrators deal more effectively with all types of parent behavior and create organizational procedures to make the parents feel more trusting in their interactions with the school.

An examination of the parent-professional relationship from the perspective of parents indicates many reasons why parents may feel uncomfortable in dealing with educational personnel about instructional programming for their child with disabilities. The following descriptions of parental feelings and attitudes may help school personnel to overcome problems stemming from negative feelings and attitudes by parents:

- The IEP process places parents in the position of asking the school to provide help for their child. As a result, depending upon the parents involved, some parents may feel inferior to school professionals and vulnerable, and others may feel superior.

- School personnel who maintain a formal, detached, professional manner, communicate a lack of empathy, understanding, or caring.

- School personnel who do not have children with disabilities of their own may not understand the difficulty that parents often have in raising such a child. A child with disabilities may compound the difficulties normally faced in bringing up children, resulting in parental feelings of distress, anxiety, and even exhaustion. School personnel should not misinterpret these parental behaviors but should be supportive and understanding.

- The parents may feel responsible for their child's disability. Parents frequently search for the cause behind their child's disability, often blaming themselves, especially in such cases as autism, emotional disturbance, and schizophrenia. School personnel often reinforce these guilt feelings through their actions and thus create additional barriers to effective communication with parents.

- The parents may feel that school personnel discount their observations and opinions. Parents may be offended by school officials who believe that their "professional" opinion is more valid.

- The parents may perceive that school officials view them as adversaries. Even though the parents are trying to do what they think is best for the child, school personnel often view such advocacy as unreasonable or extreme. This posture makes many parents more adamant in their demands and serves to widen the gulf between the parents and the school.

- The parents may feel that the school labels them, based upon their behavior. School personnel may misinterpret the concern of parents for their child and thus label parents as uncooperative, angry, demanding, and so on. However, parents usually try to communicate their real concerns for their child. The educational professional should listen carefully and attempt to understand their motivations.

As administrative and teaching staff learn to empathize with the feelings and motivations of parents of children with disabilities, they will be in a better position to deal effectively with parental anxiety and concern for the child's educational welfare. The special education administrator should offer staff development training and other opportunities for the staff to develop this sensitivity to the parental perspective. This will be most important in inclusion settings where regular teachers will increasingly work with children with disabilities and their parents.

Lunenburg and Ornstein (1991) have identified four barriers to effective communication. One is an inappropriate "frame of reference" where messages are ineffective because of unintentional distortions of the message between people. Another barrier, filtering, involves the change and alteration of information that is "filtered" from one level to another, as in the case where administrators and subordinates have differing perceptions of statements. In communicating with parents, it is possible to filter information again, unless primary documents are used. The structure of communication or the climate in which communication takes place can also have adverse effects on the success of communication. Thus, the more people are directly involved in face-to-face meetings, the more accurate will be the information presented. And semantics, or different meanings for the same words, can also present a barrier, particularly if educational jargon is used. For example, one parent was concerned that his child would be harmed if given a "battery" of tests, apparently understanding battery to be similar to electric shock treatment.

Improving Parent-Teacher Conferences

Most educators have not had formal training in dealing with parents. Consequently, conferences are often poorly planned and conducted, resulting more often in one-way communication from the school official to the parent, rather than a mutual exchange or information-sharing. Walton (1989) makes it clear that two-way communication is the most satisfactory method in all important encounters. Care must be taken to assure that parents can understand written materials that will be provided, because much written material that is disseminated is beyond the reading level and comprehension of many adults (Egos, 1990).

There are strategies available to enable administrators and teachers to improve the participation of parents in the IEP and other educational planning conferences. These strategies require preplanning by the special education administrator, close management of the conference itself, postconference follow-up, and the training of educational staff in techniques for communicating with parents.

Conference Preplanning.   A district usually has an established IEP conference format. Such a format is helpful in that school staff thereby know what to expect in the conference and hence can better plan for it. However, the administrator should guard against the conference format becoming so routine that conference participants forget the unique needs of a particular child or that for many parents such conferences are new and potential anxiety-producing experiences.

Planning for the IEP conference will increase the likelihood that the conference will run smoothly and be productive. The following are some conference preplanning suggestions (Marsh & Price, 1980; Price & Marsh, 1985; Swick, Flake-Hobson, & Raymond, 1980):

- Select a site that is comfortable, private, well lighted and well ventilated, and close to district records and materials. Arrange the site with adequate, yet informal, seating.
- Establish a conference date and time that is convenient for the parents. An evening conference may have to be considered.
- Send advance written notices about the conference to all participants, including the time, location, date, purpose, and estimated length.
- Determine the objectives of the conference by reviewing the student's file and all teacher comments, test data, and other available information. Identify the information that will be used in the conference and make sure it is readily accessible.

Conference Management.   The use of sound conference management procedures will help put the parents at ease and facilitate positive conference outcomes. While conducting the conference, it is important to remember the needs of the parents and to attempt to deal with their anxieties caused by their unfamiliarity with the conference structure or with group decision-making practices. The following procedures should be considered (Price & Marsh, 1985; Kroth, 1978):

- Develop a written conference agenda, give it to the parents at the beginning of the conference, and stick to it.
- Listen to what the parents have to say and take note of important data they mention.
- Always begin and end the conference on a positive note. Informal conversation might help get the conference off to a pleasant start.
- Refer to the parents and the child by name.
- Explain unfamiliar terms and do not use jargon.
- Share test data and ask the parents to present their own observations and information.
- Consider whether taking notes during the conference will make the parents uncomfortable. If notes are taken, explain their purpose to the parents and verify their content with the parents before the conference is completed.
- Help the parents develop ways they can work with the child at home.

In implementing these procedures, the administrator or other conference coordinator should monitor the progress of the meeting and the behavior of the parents. Meetings will take less time if the administrator keeps the focus of the conference on the agenda, does not allow unnecessary discussion, and summarizes progress regularly. Goldstein and Turnbull (1982) described increases in parent participation during the conference when school counselors attended the IEP conference in the role of parent advocates.

Postconference Follow-up.   In addition to normal postconference instructional and placement follow-up activities, the administrator should initiate special activities to help the parents maintain their positive attitude toward the school. Chapman and Heward (1982) describe the use of recorded telephone messages to help improve teacher-parent information-sharing about the instructional activities. They suggest this medium might also be used for two-way communication between the parents and the school.

The administrator might also consider sending the following items to the parents as part of normal conference follow-up:

1. A copy of the IEP.

2. A note expressing appreciation for the parents' time and participation and offering additional assistance whenever they need it.

3. Materials that may help the parents implement at-home instructional activities related to IEP goals.

Staff Training.   In all parent-teacher conference activities, staff should be trained to deal with parents in a professional and constructive manner. As noted earlier, the parents may feel hesitant or at a disadvantage when dealing with the educational system. Also, because parents will react differently, depending on the situation, staff members must be prepared to work with various parental ages, backgrounds, behaviors, attitudes, and interpersonal skills. Sawyer and Sawyer (1981) have described a training approach to help teachers improve their ability to communicate and work with parents of children with disabilities. The training session covers many of the topics discussed in this section and also makes use of videotaped instruction followed by discussion and role-playing. The goal of such training is to help teachers model relevant behaviors, rather than merely describe them.

Dealing with Advocacy Groups

Often the special education administrator must deal with the parents of children with disabilities, not as individuals but as members of advocacy groups. Advocacy groups are of three general types (Mayer, 1982):

- *National associations for individuals with disabilities* (such as the Council for Exceptional Children, the National Association for Retarded Citizens, the Association for Children with Learning Disabilities, the National Center for Law and the Handicapped, and the American Epileptic Society). Many of these associations have state and local chapters.

- *Local groups of parents of the disabled.* These are groups of parents in the same geographic area who have common needs for information and support.

- *Private parent/child advocacy agencies.* These nonprofit agencies have their own lawyers, testing specialists, and counselors and provide independent tests and other support services for parents. They also assist parents in their due process activities with local schools.

These groups seek to advocate the rights of individuals with disabilities, provide information for their members and others, serve as support groups for parents who are experiencing difficulty, lobby legislatures and local school boards through political action networks, and participate in community awareness activities. Frequently they advocate parent/child rights in disputes with local school districts. Such advocacy might concern the program for a particular child; it might involve a class action suit concerning the rights of many children with the same or similar condition; or it might focus directly on changes needed in the general operating procedures of a school district.

The administrator's relationship with advocacy groups can be problematic. On the one hand, such groups can assist the school in parent education and parent support and can exert influence on the local board of education to support the needs of individuals with disabilities. On the other hand, the administrator and the advocacy group can become adversaries when they do not agree on the nature of services being offered for a child or by the school generally, especially if such disagreements end in litigation.

We believe that administrators should seek to develop positive working relationships with advocacy groups for individuals with disabilities. Further we would encourage administrators (1) to provide opportunities for their staff to address the potential for an advocacy dilemma (i.e., when an educator's desire to advocate the rights of a child conflicts with the school's stated or implied directives or procedures) and (2) to develop procedures to ensure that their staff advocate the needs of children in a professional manner.

Dealing with Angry Parents

Administrators regularly encounter parents who disagree with the school regarding the instructional placement or the nature of services provided their child. The entire IEP process is designed to allow parents the opportunity to participate fully and rationally in planning their child's education and, if they desire, to challenge school decisions through a due process hearing. Parental disagreements may be directed at the administrator personally or at other members of the staffing team, including teachers. However, on occasion, they may erupt in confrontation, hostility, and displays of anger.

Dealing with anger is never pleasant; however, the administrator must anticipate the potential for parents to become angry and be prepared to deal with both the anger and its potential effects. An inability to do so could have profound negative effects on all those present during the confrontation, on the future effectiveness of the administrator, and on the relationship between the parents and the school.

Parents who conclude that the school has not or will not provide the special placement they believe their child needs, feel protective and defensive about their child. They may experience frustration because they believe that they have tried everything, to no avail. Or they may feel self-righteous because they believe that their position is the right one and the one supported by PL 94-142 and IDEA. All of these feelings may have been building for some time and are then released unpredictably in the form of anger.

Thus, anger may actually be a sign of frustration, a call for someone to understand and help. The administrator should monitor parents for relevant verbal or physical cues, such as a tightening of the hands or facial muscles or changes in breathing that indicate the possibility of anger, and should deal with such manifestations before they erupt in angry behavior. Specifically, in the event of displays of anger, the administrator should (Podemski & Childers, 1986):

- Stay calm. Do not reciprocate with anger, thereby losing personal control of the situation. Anger by the administrator will reinforce the parent's behavior and cause the situation to get out of hand. Be as gentle and honest as possible. The administrator must maintain self-control, thus helping the parent regain personal control and self-respect.

- As long as there is no potential for violence, allow the parent to release the pent-up emotion. This catharsis is often all that the parent needs to bring the anger under control.

- Do not take the anger personally. Remember that anger is a display of the parent's frustration and a plea for understanding and help.

- Attend to and visually focus on the parent. Nonattentive behavior, such as looking away or trying to look busy, will only incite the parent's anger further.

- After the parent has calmed down, acknowledge the anger using carefully selected words that accurately describe the intensity of the anger. Do not over-dramatize the situation by indicating that the display of anger was worse than it actually was.

- Work with the parent to identify the cause of the anger, and deal with the cause rather than the angry behavior itself. This can be done by asking the parent to specify the facts of the situation as the parent sees it, identifying a problem on the basis of the facts and exploring alternative solutions to the problem.

- After the incident is over, follow up on the discussion, maintaining contact with the parent while attempting to solve the problem.

Administrators may also wish to involve their teachers in role-playing situations dealing with parental anger so that they will also know how to anticipate such behavior and deal effectively with it.

COMMUNICATING THROUGH THE MEDIA

Television, radio, and newspapers are powerful forces in today's society. These media can be either allies of the special education administrator or constant sources of frustration. The posture adopted by the administrator toward the media will largely determine how the relationships develop.

Positive ties with the media are essential, because the administrator will want to use these vehicles to disseminate information about the school and its activities. For example, in child-find procedures, radio, television, and newspapers should be used to publicize the fact that the school is interested in identifying all children who are suspected of having a disability. Generally, the special education administrator wants the community to be aware of the success of the school program and seeks the help of the media in publicizing that success. In order to make wise use of the media, the administrator must first understand what is "news" and foster a working relationship with reporters.

Defining the News

Both the print (newspapers) and broadcast (television and radio) media view their mission as making the news available to the public. However, the definition of the news is often different for the various media sources and, more importantly, may be at odds with what educators believe should be reported. Kindred, Bagin, and Gallagher (1984) state:

> One of the most common errors made by educators is to assume that something is newsworthy just because it is of interest to them. The editor has a different yardstick: How many readers will the item interest? Answering this one question will encourage many stories to be written and will cause others to be rejected. (p. 212)

Further, each editor's definition of the news is affected by the news medium for which the editor works, the amount of news available at any given time, and the degree to which the editor believes the public is interested in an item. Thus, the administrator should talk with local news editors and determine what they believe is newsworthy and the type of stories about which they would like to be informed.

Newspapers. Newspapers can provide thorough, comprehensive coverage of a wide range of events, from new school programs or activities to board meetings; advisory committee meetings; special school events; or outstanding accomplishments by students, staff, or volunteers. Newspapers are also willing to run advance announcements of meetings and deadlines for obtaining school services. Coverage of an item will depend on whether the paper is a local, township, city, or regional paper and on the frequency with which it is published. Many districts have a regular education column that can be used to carry special education news.

Newspapers differentiate between hard news, which is the reporting of facts, and events and feature stories, which deal with interesting activities or people. Newspaper editors often call schools to inquire about possible topics for feature articles. Once written, feature articles will not necessarily appear in print immediately but will be kept on file until space permits. Hard news must appear immediately after the event or it loses its newsworthiness. Newspapers also offer opportunities for letters to the editor, guest editorials, and brief news fillers.

Television. For a special education item to be newsworthy to the television editor, it must have some visual potential. In any event, because television stations potentially cover a broader geographic area than do local newspapers, the television editor is unlikely to cover local education news unless the story is dramatic or the issue has general appeal. Television editors normally do not run routine announcements or reports during a hard-news period, but they may offer the school the opportunity to air such items as public service announcements at other times throughout the day.

Radio.   In contrast with television, radio has a limited usefulness as a news medium. Few radio stations cover hard news regularly; most offer only headline coverage. However, radio is ideal as a medium for emergency messages because its signal covers a wide area and its programming can be changed quickly. Most radio station managers will gladly run school announcements as long as the proper notification procedures are followed, and they will immediately broadcast emergency information after verifying the identity of the school official.

Working with Reporters

Unless the specific education administrator develops an ongoing relationship with local reporters, it is possible that the first encounter with the press will take place during some school controversy, thus placing the administrator at a disadvantage. A good working relationship with reporters will increase the likelihood that school news will be regularly reported and, during times of controversy, that the issues will be dealt with fairly and honestly. To develop such a relationship, the following steps are suggested (Armistead, 1981; Henry, 1979; Kindred et al., 1984; Orsini, 1979):

- Get to know the reporters who cover education news on a first-name basis. Develop at least one contact with each news outlet. Remember that reporters also are concerned about their credibility and their ability to do a competent job.

- Send news releases frequently but do not be discouraged when everything you send is not used. Find out what time lines, formats, or other logistics you need to take into account in sending information.

- Call reporters regularly and let them know what is happening. Suggest possible stories or follow-up of previous stories.

- Always be honest and accurate. If you do not know something, say so and get the appropriate information as soon as possible. Do not mislead or distort the facts. A good reporter will get the information anyway and will only be "burned" once.

- Never say, "No comment." It sounds defensive and intimates that you have something to hide. If you are unable to comment, explain the reason, such as board policy or the nature of the issue. "No comment" invites reporters to search deeper for the "real" story.

- Remember that all school reports, surveys, and data are public documents. Share them as requested and be willing to provide adequate explanations of their content.

- Know that off-the-record comments must be agreed to in advance by both you and the reporter and still do not guarantee that you will not be quoted.

- Talk with reporters when there is a crisis or in the event of negative news. Be honest. If a critical event is about to happen, consider calling the reporters in advance and sharing all relevant information. They will most likely find out anyway and will appreciate the tip.

- Compliment the reporters when they have done a good job. Also be careful about criticizing them if the news is not completely accurate. Much of what gets printed or shown on television is determined by the news editor and can be changed by the copy editor, headline editor, or others without the reporter's knowledge. Do not complain unless the facts are completely wrong and the school's image has been damaged. Then note the misinformation and ask for a retraction.

COMMUNICATING WITH THE INTERNAL COMMUNITY

Although positive communication between the school and the external public is important, the special education administrator spends more time communicating with staff members and others within the school. Communication with these internal publics provides the vehicle by which the administrator sets expectations for staff performance, develops interpersonal relationships with staff, and describes procedures that the organization will follow in delivering special education services.

To develop an efficient internal communications network, the administrator must involve all personnel in the school who in any way contribute to the special education program. The administrator should be careful not to leave out seemingly unimportant groups, because effective goal accomplishment requires that all groups and individuals have the opportunity to exchange ideas and develop strong working relationships. Also, internal groups communicate constantly with members of the community; hence, when provided with adequate, factual information about the school, they can become a powerful resource in the district's overall school-community relations program.

At a minimum, the following internal publics should be included in the special education administrator's communication network: (1) special education teachers; (2) regular education teachers; (3) principals; (4) other administrators; (5) professional specialists, such as guidance personnel, health and social workers, educational examiners, psychologists, nurses, librarians, and instructional coordinators; (6) uncertified personnel, such as secretaries, aides, and clerks; (7) service personnel, such as food service workers, maintenance personnel, bus drivers, and mechanics; and (8) students. Because members of these groups play a vital role in the total special education program, the administrator should attempt to understand each group's perspective and get to know the group members as individuals. The resulting two-way communication then becomes the basis for establishing positive, trusting working relationships. As principals increasingly deal with special education students in inclusion settings, they will also have to define their communication network.

Written Communications

Much of the administrator's time is spent in attempting to develop meaningful, clear, written descriptions of the various aspects of the special education program. The administrator also relies on written forms of communication to keep in touch with individual staff members or staff groups.

Written communications have certain advantages over other communication forms. In the form of official directives, documents, or, comments, they may be kept and filed for future reference and can serve as a reminder that certain tasks must be completed or that specific feedback is expected. The ability to write well and clearly is obviously a valuable administrative skill.

In selecting the appropriate written communication medium, the administrator must give careful attention to the characteristics of the receiver, the message, and the medium and attempt to blend all three into an effective communication process. First, the administrator should tailor the message and the medium to the receiver. Some media are more effective with individuals than with groups. The specific characteristics of the individual or group receiver will also affect the selection of the medium. Second, the characteristics of the message—such as importance, length, complexity, formality, urgency, and need for confidentiality—should be taken into consideration. Third, the administrator should determine the necessity for feedback and then select a medium that will increase the likelihood that such feedback will ensue.

The administrator has a wide variety of written communication vehicles from which to choose (Lunenburg & Ornstein, 1991). Following are some written communication formats frequently used in schools:

- *Policy and personnel handbooks.* The administrator should be sure that these formal documents are carefully written and always up to date. Staff should receive updates regularly, and the administrator should frequently review with the staff the use of these documents in describing and directing their efforts.

- *Memoranda.* These are probably the most frequently used but least effective means of internal communication. Although memoranda are quick and convenient, they are impersonal and do not promote feedback. When staff are deluged with memoranda, they tend to develop a disdain for this type of communication and may disregard future memoranda. Thus, this medium is most effective in communicating relatively unimportant information or when used in combination with other media. The administrator should not use memoranda as a convenient substitute for interpersonal communication.

- *Letters.* Letters are most frequently used to communicate with members of the external public, but they can also be used effectively to convey official notices or personal messages of appreciation to members of the staff. Form letters should be discouraged, because they are typically poorly reproduced. However, schools increasingly have access to word processing systems that can be used to "personalize" form-letter types of communication.

- *Staff newsletters.* This is a useful vehicle for sharing general information with the staff. Announcements of meetings, in-service activities, staff accomplishments, sharing of teaching techniques, and new equipment purchases can be conveyed in staff newsletters. They can also be used to help the staff develop a comprehensive view of the special education program and the contributions of the internal staff.

- *Flyers or bulletins.* These are easier to produce than formal newsletters. They should be used on a weekly basis to keep the staff informed of current events and activities, calendar updates, schedule changes, and meeting places. Copies may be distributed to all staff and posted in prominent places.

- *Information forms.* Special information-collection and documentation forms, such as the IEP, should be designed with care, because these forms serve as the basis of communication among staff about student needs and the ability of the special education program in meeting those needs. The forms should help staff document the information they need in a manner that is convenient and useful.

- *Special publications.* Special publications might be used to describe new policy or to suggest procedures to implement policy. Examples are publications on referral procedures, the conduct of parent-teacher conferences, discipline practices and techniques, and guides for homework.

- *Bulletin board posters.* Although these are more frequently used by teachers in the classroom, they can also be used to remind staff of certain events or to display the creative efforts of students.

- *Communications with external publics.* The administrator should make sure that the staff receive copies of newsletters, newspapers, and other general communications sent to parents or other citizens. In this way, staff members can keep abreast of current information relating to the district.

Internal Advisory Committees

Internal advisory committees give staff the opportunity to express their concerns, impact new policy, and help change elements of the system that are not working well. Personal staff communications with the special education administrator are often infrequent and do not carry the weight of formal advisory committee meetings. In addition, such meetings provide an opportunity for staff to share information, thus creating horizontal communication patterns that can promote staff cooperation.

The success of an advisory committee will depend on the administrator's willingness to share information and decision-making authority with staff representatives and ability to structure and organize the workings of the committee. The caveats associated with citizen advisory committees, discussed earlier, are also relevant to internal advisory groups. Nonetheless, internal groups can be productive and can help the administrator improve the effectiveness of the special education program.

Procedures For Conducting Meetings

Administrators normally spend a great deal of time preparing for, conducting, summarizing, and evaluating meetings. However, without such opportunities for individual and small group contact, administrators would be out of touch with the staff and unable to provide effective leadership. Further, meetings provide the staff with opportunities to express and satisfy their emotional and psychological needs by directing their creative talents and energies toward improving their work. Thus, poorly conducted meetings can hinder staff morale, contribute to ineffective organizational behavior, and result in poor goal accomplishment. As in other aspects of administration, planning and preparation for the meeting should be based on goals; an agenda; coordination among all parties; keeping records of what happens; and conduct of the meeting, evaluation, and follow-up.

Although all group members should share in these leadership tasks, the administrator frequently assumes the major responsibility. Thus, the administrator should:

- Prepare and disseminate an agenda in advance of the meeting.
- Set a time limit for the meeting.
- Make certain that all necessary documents and other resources will be available.
- Select a comfortable meeting site and carefully arrange seating. Creature comforts are important. Make sure that there are desks or tables to write on and that all individuals can see each other.
- Start the meeting on time.
- Review the agenda, making sure that everyone understands it. Revise it, if necessary, before moving to the first item of business. Discuss the ground rules for achieving group decisions, such as the use of motions, parliamentary procedure, and procedures for being recognized to speak. Set time limits for the discussion of each agenda item and stick to those limits.
- If the meeting is not progressing well, stop and analyze the causes. Notice the roles the members are playing and deal with behaviors that are nonproductive. Try different techniques, such as brainstorming or the nominal group approach, to help minimize the undue influence of individuals. If the task is too complicated to be dealt with in a large group, try breaking it into subtasks or divide the group into smaller groups, each dealing with a subtask and then reporting back to the larger group.
- Try to develop consensus. Consensus does not require voting or majority rule. It simply means that sufficient members of the group understand the alternative being discussed, believe it to be reasonable, and are willing to give it a try, even though they may not personally think it is the best idea. Consensus is easier to reach than total agreement and may be all that is necessary to get the group moving in a positive direction.
- Monitor group participation. Draw out silent members and help to put the dissenting comments in perspective. Group decision making is more effective if all group members participate. Restrict the discussion to agenda items.
- Conclude the meeting on time.
- Prepare and disseminate the written minutes of the meeting. Identify those who have responsibilities for implementing the outcomes and time lines and the items that need to be addressed at the next meeting.

REFERENCES

Abend, A. C., Bednar, M. J., Froehlinger, V. M., & Stenzler, Y. (1979). *Facilities for special education services: A guide for planning new and renovated schools.* Reston, VA: Council for Exceptional Children.

Acheson, K. A., & Gall, M. D. (1992). *Techniques in the clinical supervision of teachers* (3rd ed.). New York: Longman.

Adelman, H. (1970). An interactive view of causality. *Academic Therapy, 6,* 43–52.

Agron, J. (1989). Balancing the scales of handicapped egress. *American School and University, 61,* 74–75.

Alexander, K. (1981). The potential of due process for school finance litigation. *Journal of Education Finance, 6*(4), 456–470.

Alexander, K., & Hale, J. (1978). *Educational equity: Improving school finance in Arkansas.* Little Rock, AR: Advisory Committee of the Special School Formula Project.

Alexander, K., & Hale, J. (1977). *Our children's educational needs: Reforming school finance in West Virginia.* Gainsville, FL: Education Finance and Research Institute.

Alexander, K., & Hale, J. (1978). *Equitable school finance in North Carolina.* Raleigh, NC: Governor's Council on Public School Finance.

Algozzine, B., Christenson, S., & Ysseldyke, J. (1982). Probabilities associated with the referral to placement process. *Teacher Education and Special Education, 5*(3), 19–23.

Allen, H. (1950). *The federal government in education.* New York: McGraw-Hill.

Allen, J. P., & Turner, E. (1990, August). Diversity regions. *American Demographics,* 34-39.

Alper, S., Parker, K., Schloss, P., & Wisniewski, L. (1993). Extended school year programs: A community-driven curriculum model. *Mental Retardation, 31,* 163–170.

Ambert, A., & Dew, N. (1982). *Special education for exceptional bilingual students: A handbook for educators.* Milwaukee Midwest National Origin Desegregation Assistance Center.

Americans with disabilities act accessibility guidelines. (1990). Washington, DC: U.S. Government Printing Office.

Americans with Disabilities Act handbook. (1992). Washington, DC: U.S. Government Printing Office.

Anderson, S. B., Ball, S., & Murphy, R. T. (1975). *Encyclopedia of educational evaluation.* San Francisco: Jossey-Bass.

Archer, R. (1987, June 14). Black conservatives want to silence pied-piper. *Arizona Republic.*

Armistead, L. (1981, February). Working with the media develops good news. *NASSP Newsletter,* 5–6.

Armstrong v. Klein, 513 F. Supp. 425, 629 F.2d 269 (3d Cir. 1980).

Association for Persons with Severe Handicaps (1992, July). CEC slips back; ASCD steps forward. *TASH Newsletter,* 18, 1.

Audette, B., & Algozzine. B. (1992). Free and appropriate education for all students: Total quality and the transformation of American public education. *Remedial and Special Education, 13,* 8–18.

Axelrod, S., & Bailey, S. L. (1979). Drug treatment for hyperactivity: Controversies, alternatives, and guidelines. *Exceptional Children, 45,* 544–550.

Ayers, G. (1994). Statistical profile of special education in the United States, 1994. Supplement to *Teaching Exceptional Children, 26*(3), 1–4.

Ayres, B., & Meyer, L. H. (1992, February). Helping teachers manage the inclusive classroom: Staff development and teaming star among management strategies. *The School Administrator,* 30–31, 33–37.

Bartlett, L. (1989). Disciplining handicapped students: Legal issues in light of *Honig v. Doe. Exceptional Children, 55*(4), 357–366.

Baumeister, M., & Morris, R. K. (1992, Summer). Rural delivery model for vocational education. *Teaching Exceptional Children, 24*(4), 40–43.

Becker, G. (1975). *Human capital* (2nd ed.). New York: National Bureau of Economic Research.

Bennett, R. E., & Ragosta, M. (1984). *A research context for studying admissions tests and handicapped populations.* Princeton, NJ: Educational Testing Service.

Benson, C. (1978). *The economics of public education* (3rd ed.). Boston, MA: Houghton-Mifflin.

Benson, C. (1988). Economics of education: The U.S. experience. In N. Boyan (Ed.), *Handbook of research on educational administration* (pp. 355–372). White Plains, NY: Longman.

Benson, C., & O'Halloran, K. (1987). The economic history of school finance in the United States. *Journal of Education Finance, 12*(4), 495–515.

Berne, R. (1988). Equity issues in school finance. *Journal of Education Finance, 14*(2), 159–180.

Berne, R., & Stiefel, L. (1979). Concepts of equity and their relationship to state school finance plans. *Journal of Education Finance, 5*(2), 109–132.

Berne, R., & Stiefel, L. (1984). *The measurement of equity in school finance.* Baltimore, MD: The Johns Hopkins University Press.

Birch, J. W. (1974). *Mainstreaming.* Minneapolis: University of Minnesota, Leadership Training Institute/Special Education.

Birch, J. W., & Johnstone, B. K. (1975). *Designing schools and schooling for the handicapped.* Springfield, IL: Charles C. Thomas.

Bishop, L. (1976). *Staff development and instructional improvement: Plans and procedures.* Boston: Allyn and Bacon.

Blankstein, A. M. (1993). Applying the Deming corporate philosophy to restructuring. *The Education Digest, 58,* 28–32.

Board of Education, Hendrick Hudson School District v. Rowley, 458 U.S. 176 (1982).

Boland, S. K. (1976). Instructional materialism—Or how to select the things you need. *Teaching Exceptional Children, 8,* 156–158.

Bolton, D. L. (1973). *Selection and evaluation of teachers.* Berkeley, CA: McCutchan.

Bonstingl, J. J. (1993). The quality revolution in education. *Educational Leadership, 50,* 4–9.

Borich, G. D., & Nance, D. D. (1987). Evaluating special education programs: Shifting the professional mandate from process to outcome. *Remedial and Special Education, 8*(3), 7–16.

Boscardin, M. L. (1987). Local-level special education due process hearings: Cost issues surrounding individual student differences. *Journal of Educational Finance, 12,* 391–402.

Brady, M., McDougall, D., & Dennis, H. F. (1989). The schools, the courts, and the integration of students with severe handicaps. *The Journal of Special Education, 23*(1), 43–55.

Brandt, R. (1987). On leadership and student achievement: A conversation with Richard Andrews. *Educational Leadership, 45*(1), 9–16.

Brandt, R. (1993). On Deming and school quality: A conversation with Enid Brown. *Educational Leadership, 50,* 28–31.

Breton, W. A., & Donaldson, G. A., & Gordon, A., Jr. (1991). Too little, too late? The supervision of Maine resource room teachers. *Journal of Special Education, 25*(1), 114–125.

Brinckerhoff, L. C., Shaw, S. F., & McGuire, J. M. (1993). *Promoting postsecondary education for students with learning disabilities.* Austin, TX: Pro-Ed.

Brockett, D. (1993). *Designing schools and schooling for the handicapped.* Springfield, IL: Charles C. Thomas.

Brooks-Gunn, J., & McCarton, C. (1991). *Effects of drugs in-utero on infant development.* Washington, DC: National Institute of Child Health and Human Development, Report to Congress.

Brophy, J., & Good, T. (1974). *Teacher-student relationships: Causes and consequences.* New York: Holt, Rinehart, and Winston.

Brown v. Board of Education of Topeka, 1954, 347 U.S. 483, 74 S.Ct. 686.

Bruininks, R., & Rynders, J. (1971). Alternatives to special classes for educational mentally retarded. *Focus on Exceptional Children, 3,* 8.

Burrello, L. C., & Sage, D. D. (1979). *Leadership and change in special education.* Englewood Cliffs, NJ: Prentice-Hall.

Buser, R. L., & Pace, V. D. (1988). Personnel evaluation: Premises, realities, and constraints. *NASSP Bulletin, 72*(512), 84–87.

Callahan, C. M., Covert, R., Aylesworth, M. S., & Vanco, P. (1981). Evaluating a local gifted program: A cooperative effort. *Exceptional Children, 48*(2), 157–163.

Cambron, N. (1976). *A model for the cost analysis of alternative delivery systems for exceptional child education programs.* Unpublished doctoral dissertation, University of Florida, Gainesville.

Campbell, R. F., Cunningham, L. L., Nystrand, R. O., & Usdan, M. D. (1985). *The organization and control of American schools* (5th ed.). Columbus, OH: Merrill.

Cannon, G. (1992). Educating students with mild handicaps in general classrooms: Essential teaching practices for general and special educators. *Journal of Learning disabilities, 25*(5), 300–317.

Carmichael, D. J., Dyer, J. A., & Blakely, C. H. (1992). Potential impacts of site-based management on special student populations: The pursuit of equity. *Texas Researcher,* Winter (3), 39–56.

Carpenter, L. (1983). *Communication problems of children from non-English homes.* Paper presented at the BUENO Center First Annual Symposium on Evaluation and Interdisciplinary Research in Bilingual Education, Vail, CO.

Carroll, S. J. (1982). The search for equity in school finance. In W. McMahon & T. Geske (Eds.), *Financing education: Overcoming inefficiency and inequity.* Urbana, IL: University of Illinois Press.

Carter, T. P., & Segura, R. D. (1979). *Mexican Americans in school: A decade of change.* New York: College Entrance Examination Board.

Cartwright, G. P., Cartwright, C. A., & Ward, M. E. (1989). *Educating special learners.* Belmont, CA: Wadsworth.

CASE. (1993). Case position paper on delivery of services to students with disabilities. *CASE Newsletter, 34*(5), 2–3.

Castetter, W. B. (1981). *The personnel function in educational administration* (3rd ed.). New York: MacMillan.

CEC. (1993). *Council for exceptional children (CEC) policy on inclusive schools and community settings.* Reston, VA: Council for Exceptional Children.

Chaffin, J. (1974). Will the real mainstreaming program please stand up! (or . . . Should Dunn have done it?). *Focus on Exceptional Children, 6,* 13.

Chalfant, J. C., & Pysh, M. V. D. (1981, November). Teacher Assistance Teams—A Model for within-building problem solving. *Counterpoint,* 16-21.

Chalfant, J. C., & Pysh, M. V. D. (1989). Teacher Assistance Teams: Five descriptive studies on 96 teams. *Remedial and Special Education, 10*(6), 49–58.

Chalfant, J. C., Pysh, M. V. D., & Moultrie, R. (1979). Teacher assistance teams: A model for within-building problem solving. *Learning Disability Quarterly, 2*(3), 85-96.

Chapman, J. E., & Heward, W. L. (1982). Improving parent-teacher communication through recorded telephone messages. *Exceptional Children, 49*(1), 79–82.

Children's Defense Fund. (1975). *School suspensions: Are they helping children?* Cambridge, MA: Author.

Clark, E. M., & Herbert, R. K. (1991). Optimizing the hearing/learning environment. *American School and University, 64,* 46–49.

Clemmons, A. (1974). *An assessment of variations in special education program costs in six selected Minnesota school districts.* Unpublished doctoral dissertation, University of New Mexico, Albuquerque.

Cohn, E. (1979). *The economics of education.* Cambridge, MA: Ballinger.

Cubberley, E. (1906). *School funds and their apportionment.* New York: Teachers College, Columbia University.

Cummings, O. W. (1992). Evaluation: How much is enough? *Measurement and Evaluation in Counseling and Development, 24,* 150–154.

Cummins, J. (1984). *Bilingualism and special education: Issues in assessment and pedagogy.* Clevedon, Avon, England: Multilingual Matters Ltd.

Dagley, D. L., & Orso, J. K. (1991). Integrating summative, formative modes of evaluation. *NASSP Bulletin, 75,* 72–82.

D'Alonzo, B. J., D'Alonzo, R. L., & Mauser, A. J. (1979). Developing resource rooms for the handicapped. *Teaching Exceptional Children, 11*(3), 174–178.

Darling-Hammond, L. (1992). Accountability for professional practice. In M. Levine (Ed.), *Professional practice schools* (pp. 81–104). New York: Teachers College Press.

David, J. L. (1989). Synthesis of research on school-based management. *Educational Leadership, 46,* 45–53.

Davis, W. E. (1989, February). The regular education initiative: Its promises and problems. *Exceptional Children, 55*(5), 440–447.

Decker, C. A., & Decker, J. R. (1992). *Planning and administering early childhood programs.* New York: Merrill/Macmillan.

De Leon, J., & Gonzales, E. (1991). An examination of bilingual special education and related training. *Teacher Education and Special Education, 14,* 5–10.

Deno, E. (1970). Special education as developmental capital. *Exceptional Children, 37*(3), 229–237.

Diamond, S. (1974). The group interview. *National Association of Secondary School Principals Bulletin, 58*(386), 56–60.

Diana v. California State Board of Education, No. C-70 37 RFP (District Court of Northern California, February, 1970).

Division for Learning Disabilities. (1993). *Inclusion: What does it mean for students with learning disabilities?* Reston, VA: Council for Exceptional Children.

Dobbs, R. F., Primm, E. B., & Primm, B. (1991). Mediation: A common sense approach for resolving conflicts in education. *Focus on Exceptional Children, 24,* 1–12.

Doe v. Koger, 480 F. Supp. 225 (1979).

Doe v. Maher, 795 F.2d 787 (9th Cir. 1986).

Drake, J. D. (1972). *Interviewing for managers.* New York: American Management Association.

Dressel, P. L. (1976). *Handbook of academic evaluation.* San Francisco: Jossey-Bass.

Dulay, H., Burt, M., & Krashen, S. (1982). *Language two.* New York: Oxford University Press.

Dunn, L. (1973). *Exceptional children.* New York: Holt, Rinehart, and Winston.

Edmister, P., & Ekstrand, R.E. (1987). Lessening the trauma of due process. *Teaching Exceptional Children, 19*(3), 6–10.

Egos, R. L. (1990). *Oral and written communications.* Newbury Park, CA: Sage Publications.

Ekstrand, R. E., & Edmister, P. (1984). Mediation: A process that works. *Exceptional Children, 51*(2), 163–167.

Engel, R. A., & Friedrichs, D. (1980). The interview can be a reliable process. *National Association of Secondary School Principals Bulletin, 64*(432), 85–91.

Erickson, M. T. (1978). *Child psychopathology: Assessment, etiology, and treatment.* Englewood Cliffs, NJ: Prentice-Hall.

Evans, L. D. (1992). Severe does not always imply significant: Bias of a regression discrepancy model. *Journal of Special Education, 26*(1), 57–67.

Fairman, M., & Podemski, R. S. (1982). Pinpoint your school's strengths and weaknesses. *Executive Educator, 4*(6), 19–20, 36.

Fairweather, J. S. (1989). Transition and other services for handicapped students in local education agencies. *Exceptional Children, 55*(4), 315–320.

Federal Register. (1977, August 23). Washington, DC: U.S. Government Printing Office.

Field, S. L., & D. S. Hill. (1988). Contextual appraisal: A framework for meaningful evaluation of special education programs. *Remedial and Special Education, 9*(4), 22–30.

Florian, L. D., & West, J. (1989). Congress affirms the rights of children with handicaps. *Teaching Exceptional Children, 21*(4), 4–7.

Florida Department of Education (1992). *Division of public schools 1991–92 Florida education finance program fourth calculation.* Tallahassee, FL: The Department of Education.

Flynn, C. C., & Harbin, G. L. (1987). Evaluating interagency coordination efforts using a multidimensional, interactional, developmental paradigm. *Remedial and Special Education, 8*(3), 35–44.

Food services for the handicapped. (1979). *American School Board Journal, 166*(5), 14.

Frymier, J., & Gansnedner, B. (1989). The Phi Delta Kappan study of students at risk. *Phi Delta Kappan, 71*(2), 142-146.

Fuchs, D., Fuchs, L. S., Bahr, M. W., Fernstrom, P., & Stecker, P. M. (1990). Prereferral intervention: A prescriptive approach. *Exceptional Children, 56*(6), 493-513.

Fuchs, D., Fuchs, L. S., & Fernstrom, P. (1993). A conservative approach to Special Education reform: Mainstreaming through transenvironmental programming and curriculum based measurement. *American Educational Research Journal, 30*(1), 149–177.

Fuchs, L. S. (1992). Classwide decision making with computerized curriculum-based measurement. *Preventing School Failure, 36*(2), 30–33.

Garcia v. Miera, 17 F. 2d 650 (10th Cir. 1987).

Garcia, J. O. (1976). *Cost analysis of bilingual, special, and vocational public school programs in New Mexico.* Unpublished doctoral dissertation, University of New Mexico, Albuquerque.

Garcia, J. P. (1976). *Cost analysis of bilingual, special, and vocational public school programs in New Mexico.* Unpublished doctoral dissertation, University of New Mexico, Albuquerque.

Garcia, S., & Ortiz, A. (1988). *Preventing inappropriate referrals of language minority students to special education. New Focus,* No. 5. Wheaton, MD: Maryland National Clearinghouse for Bilingual Education.

Garcia, S. B. (1984). *Effects of student characteristics, school programs and organization on decision-making for the placement of Hispanic students in classes for the learning disabled.* Unpublished doctoral dissertation, The University of Texas at Austin.

Gartner, A. (1986). Disabling help: Special education at the crossroads. *Exceptional Children, 53*(1), 72-76.

Gearheart, B. R. (1980a). *Learning disabilities: Educational strategies.* St. Louis: Mosby.

Gearheart, B. R. (1980b). *Special education for the 80s.* St. Louis: Mosby.

Geiger, G., & Lettvin, J. Y. (1987). Peripheral vision in persons with dyslexia. *The New England Journal of Medicine, 316*(20), 1238–1243.

Geske, T., & Johnston, M. (1985). A new approach to special education finance: The resource cost model. *Planning and Changing, 16*(2), 105–117.

Gickling, E. E., & Thompson, V. P. (1985). A personal view of curriculum-based assessment. *Exceptional Children, 52,* 205-218.

Glassman, N. S. (1986). *Evaluation-based leadership: School administration in contemporary perspective.* New York: State University of New York Press.

Glickman, C. D. (1985). *Supervision of instruction: A development approach.* Boston: Allyn & Bacon.

Goldberg, S. S., & Kuriloff, P. J. (1991). Evaluating the fairness of special education hearings. *Exceptional Children, 57,* 546–552.

Goldstein, S., & Turnbull, A. P. (1982). Strategies to increase parent participation in IEP conferences. *Exceptional Children, 48*(4), 360–361.

Goodman, G., & Poillion, M. J. (1992). ADD: Acronym for any dysfunction or difficulty. *Journal of Special Education, 26*(1), 37–56.

Gorton, R. A. (1983). *School leadership and administration.* Dubuque, IA: William C. Brown.

Greene, J. E. (1971) *School personnel administration.* Philadelphia: Chilton.

Guernsey, M. A. (1989). Classroom organization: A key to successful management. *Academic Therapy, 25,* 55–58.

Guthrie, J., Garms, W., & Pierce, L. (1988). *School finance and education policy: Enhancing educational efficiency, equality, and choice* (2nd ed.). Englewood Cliffs, NJ: Prentice-Hall.

Guyot, W. M. (1978). Summative and formative evaluation. *Journal of Business Education, 54*(3), 127–129.

Haberman, M. (1991). The pedagogy of poverty versus good teaching. *Phi Delta Kappan, 73,* 290–294.

Haddock, P. (1991). High technology employment: Another view. *Monthly Labor Review, 11,* 26–30.

Hale, J. (1976). School finance in New Mexico, evolution and revolution. In E. Tron (Ed.), *Selected papers in school finance, 1976.* Washington, DC: United States Office of Education.

Hale, J. (1979). A case study in Florida of federal and state programs for children with special, bilingual, or compensatory education needs. In E. O. Tron (Ed.), *Selected papers in school finance 1979.* Washington, DC: U.S. Office of Education.

Hale, J., & Cambron, N. (1978). *Cost analysis of educational programs in Tennessee.* Nashville, TN: Tennessee School Finance Equity Study.

Hale, J., & Cambron, N. (1979). *Reexamination of education costs in Tennessee, 1979–80.* Nashville, TN: Tennessee School Finance Equity Study.

Hamm, R. W. (1988). Educational evaluation: Theory and a working model. *Education, 108*(3), 404–408.

Hampton, D. R., Summer, C. E., & Webber, R. A. (1982). *Organizational behavior and the practice of management* (4th ed.). Glenview, IL: Scott, Foresman, & Company.

Harper, J. R. (1979, Spring). Perceptual and perceptual-motor tests. *Learning Disability Quarterly, 2*(2), 70–75.

Harris, K. C. (1991). An expanded view on consultation competencies for educators serving culturally and linguistically diverse exceptional students. *Teacher Education and Special Education, 14*(1), 25–29.

Hart, S. (1992). Differentiation-way forward or retreat? *British Journal of Special Education, 19*(1), 10–12.

Hart, S. N. (1987). Psychological maltreatment in the schools. *School Psychology Review, 16,* 169–178.

Hartley, H. (1968). *Educational planning-programming-budgeting: A systems approach.* Englewood Cliffs, NJ: Prentice-Hall.

Hartman, W. (1988). *School district budgeting.* Englewood Cliffs, NJ: Prentice-Hall.

Hartman, W., & Mitchell, B. (1987). Creation of a funding formula: Regional programs for severely handicapped in Oregon. *Journal of Education Finance, 12*(3), 331–350.

Hecker, B. (1991). How will the Americans with disabilities act affect you? *American School and University, 64,* 59–61.

Helge, D. I. (1981). Problems in implementing comprehensive special education programming in rural areas. *Exceptional Children, 47*(7), 514–520.

Henry, W. E. (1979). Working with the media. *National Association of Secondary School Principals Bulletin, 63*(423), 10–16.

Hentschke, G. (1986). *School business administration: A comparative perspective.* Berkeley, CA: McCutchan.

Herzberg, F. (1987). One more time: How do you motivate employees. *Harvard Business Review, 65,* 109–112.

Higgins, S. T. (1977). *Special education administrative policies manual.* Reston, Va: Council for Exceptional Children.

Hirth, M. A., & Valesky, T. C. (1990). Principals' knowledge of special education law. *National Forum of Educational Administration and Supervision Journal, 6*(3), 131–141.

Hixson, J., & Lovelace, K. (1993). Total quality management's challenge to urban schools. *Educational Leadership, 50,* 24–27.

Hobson v. Hansen, 369 F. Supp. 401, 514 (D.D.C., 1967).

Hodgkinson, H. (1988). The right schools for the right kids. *Educational Leadership, 45*(5), 10-14.

Hollis, J., & Gallegos, E. (1993). Inclusion: What is the extent of a school district's duty to accommodate students with disabilities in the regular classroom? *Texas School Administrators' Legal Digest, 9*(9), 4–7.

Honig v. Doe, 484 U.S. 108 S.Ct. 592, 98 L.Ed. 2d 686 (1988).

Hoover, J. J., & Collier, C. (1991). Meeting the needs of culturally and linguistically diverse exceptional learners: Prereferral to mainstreaming. *Teacher Education and Special Education, 14*(1), 30–34.

Ingraham v. Wright, 430 U.S. 651 (1977).

In the matter of application of a handicapped child. (December 8, 1980). *Education for the handicapped law report,* 502:214.

Irving Independent School District v. Tatro, 104 S. Ct. 3371 (U.S. Sup. Ct. 1984).

James, K. F. (1963). *Corporal punishment in the schools* (Education Monograph No. 18). Los Angeles: University of Southern California.

Johns, A., & Ryden, J. E. (1989). Designing for independence. *American School and University, 61,* 27–28.

Johns, R., Morphet, E., & Alexander, K. (1983). *The economics and financing of education* (4th. ed.). Englewood Cliffs, NJ: Prentice-Hall.

Johnson, L. J., & Pugach, M. C. (1991). Peer Collaboration: Accommodating students with mild learning and behavior problems. *Exceptional Children, 57*(5), 454–461.

Johnson, N. A. (1989). Criteria for assessing the effectiveness of schools and principals. *Education Canada, 29*(2), 14–19.

Jones, R. L., Gottleib, J., Guskin, S., & Yoshida, R. K. (1978). Evaluating mainstreaming programs: Models, caveats, considerations, and guidelines. *Exceptional Children, 44*(8), 588–601.

Jordan, F., & McKeown, M. (1984). *Fiscal policy implications of the educational reform reports.* Paper presented at the annual meeting of the American Educational Research Association. (ERIC Document Reproduction Service No. 245 326)

Jordan, F., McKeown, M., Salmon, R., & Webb, D. (1985). *School business administration.* Beverly Hills, CA: Sage.

Joyce, B., Hersh, R., & McKibbin, M. (1983). *The structure of school improvement.* New York: Longman.

Joyce, B. R., & Weil, M. (1986). *Models of teaching.* Englewood, Cliffs, NJ: Prentice-Hall.

Kagan, S. (1989). Early care and education: Beyond the schoolhouse doors. *Phi Delta Kappan, 7*(2), 107-112.

Kaskowitz, D. H. (1977). *Validation of state counts of handicapped children. Volume II—Estimation of the number of handicapped children in each state.* Prepared for DHEW, Bureau of Education for the Handicapped (Contract No. 300-76-60513); Menlo Park, CA: Stanford Research Institute.

Kaufman, R., & Hirumi, A. (1993). Ten steps to "TQM plus." *Educational Leadership, 50,* 33–34.

Kavale, K. A., & Forness, S.R. (1987). Substance over style: Assessing the efficacy of modality testing and teaching. *Exceptional Children, 54*(3), 228–239.

Kelley, E. A. (1981). Auditing school climate. *Educational Leadership, 39,* 180–183.

Kindred, L. W., Bagin, D., & Gallagher, D. R. (1984). *The school and community relations* (3rd ed.). Englewood Cliffs, NJ: Prentice-Hall, Inc.

King-Sears, M. E., Rosenberg, M. S., Ray, R. M., & Fagen, S. A. (1992). A partnership to alleviate special education teacher shortages: University and public school collaboration. *Teacher Education and Special Education, 15*(1), 9–17.

Kirmer, K., Lockwood, L., Mickler, W., & Sweeney, P. (1984). Regional rural special education programs. *Exceptional Children, 50,* 306–311.

Kirst, M. (1983). A new school finance for a new era of fiscal constraint. In A. Odden & L. Webb (Eds.), *School finance and school improvement linkages for the 1980s.* Cambridge, MA: Ballinger.

Koerner, T. F. (1969). Interviewing: Asking the right questions. *Clearing House, 44,* 102–104.

Koontz, H., O'Donnell, C., & Weihrich, H. (1986). *Essentials of Management.* New York: McGraw-Hill.

Kotter, J. (1973). The psychological contract: Managing the joining up process. *California Management Review, 15,* 91–99.

Krashen, S. (1982). *Principles and practice in second language acquisition.* New York: Pergammon Press.

Krauss, M. W. (1990). New precedent in family policy: Individualized family service plan. *Exceptional Children, 56*(5), 388–395.

Kronstadt, D. (1991). Complex developmental issues of prenatal drug exposure. *The Future of Children, 1*(1), 36-49.

Kroth, R. (1978). Parents—powerful and necessary allies. *Teaching Exceptional Children, 10*(3), 88–90.

Kumar, D. D. (1991). Curriculum concerns of science-technology-society education in the United States of America. *Science, Technology & Society,* (82), 7–14.

Lareau, A. (1989). *Home advantage: Social class and parental intervention in elementary education.* London: Falmer Press.

Larry P. v. Riles, No. C-71-2270-RFP (N.D. Cal., October 16, 1979).

Larsen, L., & Hammill, D. D. (1975). Relationships of selected visual perceptual abilities to school learning. *Journal of Special Education, 9,* 281–291.

Larue, A. (1989). *Home advantage: Social class and parental intervention in elementary education.* New York: Falmer Press.

Laski, F. (1974). Civil rights victories for the handicapped. *Record, 1,* 15–20.

Lau v. Nichols, 414 U.S. 563; 39. L. Ed 2d 1, 94 S. Ct. 787 (1974).

Lawrence, P. R., & Lorsch, J. W. (1967). *Organization and environment.* Boston: Harvard University, Graduate School of Business Administration, Division of Research.

Learning Disabilities Association of America (1993). Position paper on full inclusion of all students with learning disabilities in the regular education classroom. *Texas Key LDAT,* No. 1013, 15.

Lehr, D., & Haubrich, P. (1986). Legal precedents for students with severe handicaps. *Exceptional Children, 52*(4), 358–365.

Lemley. C. R. (1982). Disciplining the handicapped student. *Catalyst for Change, 11,* 13–15.

Levin, H. (1975). *The limits of educational reform.* New York: D. McKay Co.

Levine, M. (Ed.). (1992). *Professional practice schools.* New York: Teachers College Press.

Lewis, A. C. (1991). Churning up the waters in special education. *Phi Delta Kappan, 73*(2), 100–101.

Lifts and ramps for buses. (1982). *American School Board Journal, 169*(1), 6.

Linder, D. (1991). Special education transportation: An eight-point tune-up. *School Business Affairs, 57*(7), p.26–28.

Los Angeles United School District. (1981). Due process hearing resulting in transportation services. Case No. 81-87.

Ludlow, B. L., & Lombardi, T. P. (1992). Special education in the year 2000: Current trends and future developments. *Education and Treatment of Children, 15*(2), 147–162.

Lunenburg, F. C., & Ornstein, A. C. (1991). *Educational administration.* Belmont, CA: Wadsworth.

MacMillan, D. L., Hendrick, I. G., & Watkins, A. V. (1988). Impact of *Diana, Larry P.,* and P.L. 94-142 on minority students. *Exceptional Children, 54,* 426–432.

MacMillan, D. L., Keogh, B., & Jones, R. (1986). Special educational research on mildly handicapped learners. In M. C. Wittrock (Ed.), *Handbook of research on teaching* (3rd ed.). New York: Macmillan.

Maheady, L., & Algozzine, B. (1991). The regular education initiative—Can we proceed in an orderly and scientific manner? *Teacher Education and Special Education, 14*(1), 66–73.

Making school transportation safe. (1989). *American School and University, 61,* 54–55.

Mallory, B. L., & Kerns, G. M. (1988). Consequences of categorical labeling of preschool children. *Topics in Early Childhood Special Education, 8*(3), 39–50.

Marriner, L. (1977). The cost of educating handicapped pupils in New York City. *Journal of Education Finance, 3*(1), 82–97.

Marsh, G. E., II, & Podemski, R. S. (1982). Special education assessment: Problems and procedures for the school principal. *NASSP Bulletin, 66*(453), 88–99.

Marsh, G. E., II, & Price, B. J. (1980). *Methods for teaching the mildly handicapped adolescent.* St. Louis: Mosby.

Marsh, G. E., II, Price, B. J., & Smith, T. E. C. (1983). *Teaching mildly handicapped children: Methods and materials.* St. Louis: Mosby.

Martin, G., & Pear, J. (1978). *Behavior modification.* Englewood Cliffs, NJ: Prentice-Hall.

Mayer, C. L. (1982). *Educational administration and special education: A handbook for school administrators.* Boston: Allyn & Bacon.

Mayson v. Teague, 749 F.2d 652 (11th Cir. 1984).

McAfee, J. K. (1987). Emerging issues in special education tort liability. *Teacher Education and Special Education, 10*(2), 47–57.

McCarthy, M. M., & Cambron-McCabe, N. H. (1987). *Public school law: Teachers' and students' rights* (2nd ed.). Boston: Allyn & Bacon.

McFadden, A. C., Marsh, G. E., II, Price, B. J., & Hwang, Y. (1992). An examination of race and gender bias in the punishment of handicapped children. *The Journal of Behavior and Treatment of Children, 15*(2), 140–146.

McGreal, T. L. (1982). Effective teacher evaluation systems. *Educational Leadership, 39,* 303–305.

McInnis v. Shapiro, 293 F. Supp. 327 (1968).

McIntosh, D. K. (1986). Problems and solutions in delivery of special education services in rural areas. *The Rural Educator, 8*(1), 12–15.

McLaughlin, M. (1983). State involvement in local educational quality. In A. Odden & L. Webb (Eds.), *School finance and school improvement linkages for the 1980s.* Cambridge, MA: Ballinger.

Meers, G. (1992). Getting ready for the next century: Vocational preparation of students with disabilities. *Teaching Exceptional Children, 24*(4), 44–48.

Miller, S. R., & Sabatino, D. A. (1977). Evaluating the instructional effectiveness of supplemental special education materials. *Exceptional Children, 43*(7), 457–461.

Mills v. Board of Education of the District of Columbia, 348 F. Supp. 886 (D.D.C. 1972).

Minner, S., & Prater, G. (1989). Arranging the physical environment of special education classrooms. *Academic Therapy, 25,* 91–96.

Mohavongsanen v. Hall, 529 R. 2d 488 (5th Cir.), 1976.

Monk, D. (1990). *Educational finance: An economic approach.* New York: McGraw-Hill.

Mort, P. (1924). *The measurement of education need.* New York: Teachers College, Columbia University.

NASBE. (1992, October). *Winners all: A call for inclusive schools.* Alexandria, VA: National Association of State Boards of Education.

National Assessment of Educational Progress. (1985). *The reading report card.* Princeton, NJ: Educational Testing Service.

National Education Goals Panel (1992). *World class standards for American education.* Washington, DC: U.S. Department of Education.

Neill, D. M., & Medina, N. J. (1989). Standardized testing: Harmful to educational health. *Phi Delta Kappan, 70*(9), 688–697.

Nevin, A. (1979). Special education administration competencies required of the general education administrator. *Exceptional Children, 45*(5), 363–365.

Nondiscrimination provisions of the HEW section 504 regulations. (1977). *Amicus, 2,* 23–32.

Odden, A. (1984). Financing educational excellence. *Phi Delta Kappan, 65*(5), 311-318.

Odden, A. (1986). A school finance research agenda for an era of education reform. *Journal of Education Finance, 12*(1), 49–70.

Odden, A., & Picus, L. (1992). *School finance: A policy perspective.* New York: McGraw-Hill.

Odom, S. L., Yoder, P., & Hill, G. (1988). Developmental intervention for infants with handicaps: Purposes and program. *The Journal of Special Education, 22*(11), 11–24.

O'Donnell, E. (1992). Special needs for special programs. *American School and University, 64,* 57–60.

Ohanian, S. (1990). P.L. 94-142: Mainstream or quicksand? *Phi Delta Kappan, 72,* 217–222.

Okolo, C. M., & Sitlington, P. (1988). The role of special education in LD adolescents transition from school to work. *Learning Disabilities Quarterly, 11*(3), 292–306.

Orlich, D. C. (1989). Evaluating staff development. *The Clearing House, 62,* 370–374.

Orsini, B. (1979, February). Press coverage can be positive. *National Association of Secondary School Principals Newsletter,* p. 8.

Ortiz, A. A. (1984). Choosing the language of instruction for exceptional bilingual children. *Teaching Exceptional Children, 16,* 208-212.

Ortiz, A. A. (1990, Fall). Using school-based problem-solving teams for prereferral intervention. *Bilingual Special Education Newsletter, 10*(1), 3-5.

Ortiz, A. A., Garcia, S. B., Holtzman, W. H., Jr., Polyzoi, E., Snell, W. E., Jr., Wilkinson, C. Y., & Willig, A. C. (1985). *Characteristics of limited English proficient Hispanic students in programs for the learning disabled: Implications for policy, practice, and research.* Austin, TX: The University of Texas, Handicapped Minority Research Institute on Language Proficiency.

Ortiz, A. A., Garcia, S. B., Wheeler, D., & Maldonado-Colon, E. (1986). *Characteristics of limited English proficient students served in programs for the speech and language handicapped: Implications for policy, practice, and research.* Austin, TX: The University of Texas, Handicapped Minority Research Institute on Language Proficiency.

Ortiz, A. A., & Maldonado-Colon, E. (1986). Recognizing learning disabilities in bilingual children: How to lessen inappropriate referrals of language minority students to special education. *Journal of Reading, Writing, and Learning Disabilities International, 1*(1), 47-56.

Ortiz, A. A., & Wilkinson, C. Y. (1991). Assessment and intervention model for the bilingual exceptional student (AIM for the BEST). *Teacher Education and Special Education, 14*(1), 35–42.

Ortiz, A. A., & Yates, J. R. (1981). *Exceptional Hispanics: Implications for special education services and manpower planning.* Austin, TX: Council for Personnel Preparation for the Handicapped, Texas Education Agency.

Ortiz, A. A., & Yates, J. R. (1982). Teacher training associated with serving exceptional bilingual students. *Teacher Education and Special Education, 5*(3), 61-68.

Ortiz, A. A., & Yates, J. R. (1983). Incidence of exceptionality among Hispanics: Implications for manpower planning. *Journal of the National Association for Bilingual Education, 7*(3), 41-53.

Ortiz, A. A., & Yates, J. R. (1988). Characteristics of learning disabled, mentally retarded, and speech-language handicapped hispanic students at initial evaluation and reevaluation. In A. A. Ortiz & B. A. Ramirez (Eds.), *Schools and the culturally diverse exceptional student: Promising practices and future directions* (pp. 51–62). Reston, VA: The Council for Exceptional Children.

Patton, J. M., & Braithwaite, R. (1990). Special education certification/recertification for regular educators. *The Journal of Special Education, 24*(1), 117–124.

Pearman, E. L. (1992). Educating all students in school: Attitudes and beliefs about inclusion. *Education and Training in Mental Retardation, 27*(2), 76–82.

Pennsylvania Association for Retarded Children (PARC) v. Commonwealth of Pennsylvania, 343 F. Supp. 279 (E.D. Pa. 1972).

Peters, T., & Austin, N. (1985). *A passion for excellence.* New York: Random House.

Pino, E. C. (1988, December). Tools of the trade for more effective instructional leadership. *NASSP Bulletin, 72*(512), 60–63.

PL 81-874. Impact Aid Act of 1950, 20 U.S.C.A. §236 *et seq.* (1951).

PL 89-10. Elementary and Secondary Education Act of 1965, 20 U.S.C.A. §236 *et seq.* (1985).

PL 89-313. School Districts—Federal Aid of 1965, 20 U.S.C. §238, 241, 635, 646, 647 *et seq.* (1989).

PL 89-750. Elementary and Secondary Amendments of 1966, 20 U.S.C.A. §238, 240 *et seq.* (1989).

PL 90-247. Bilingual Education Act of 1968, 81 Stat. 783 816.

PL 91-230. Education of the Handicapped Act of 1970, 20 U.S.C. 2701, 84 Stat. 121 (1970).

PL 93-112. Rehabilitation Act of 1973, 504, 29 U.S.C.A. §794 (1992).

PL 93-380. Education Amendments of 1974, 20 U.S.C.A. §237 *et seq.* (1979).

PL 94-142. Education for All Handicapped Children Act of 1975, 20 U.S.C. 1400, 89 Stat. 793.

PL 101-336. Americans with Disabilities Act of 1990, 42 U.S.C.A. §12101 *et seq.* (1992).

PL 101-476. Education of the Handicapped Act, Amendments of 1990, 20 U.S.C. §1400 *et seq.* (1992).

PL 102-119. Individuals with Disabilities Education Act, Amendments of 1991, 20 U.S.C. §1400 *et seq.* (1992).

Podemski, R. S. (1981). School district policy and Public Law 94-142. *Education Unlimited, 3*(2), 28–30.

Podemski, R. S., & Childers, J. H. (1986). How to deal with angry people: Human relation strategies that work. *Principal, 66*(1), 55–58.

Podemski, R. S., & Steele, R. (1981). Avoid the pitfalls of citizen committees. *American School Board Journal, 168*(4), 40, 42.

Policy Analysis for California Education (PACE). (1989). *Conditions of children in California.* Berkeley: University of California School of Education.

Polloway, E. A., Patton, J. R., Epstein, M. H., & Smith, T. E. C. (1989). Comprehensive curriculum for students with mild handicaps. *Focus on Exceptional Children, 21,* 1–12.

Ponessa, J. M. (1988). Students must be considered in planning. *American School and University, 61,* 30–31.

Popham, W. J. (1988). *Educational evaluation* (2nd ed.). Englewood Cliffs, NJ: Prentice-Hall.

Prasse, D. P. (1986). Litigation and special education: An introduction. *Exceptional Children, 52,* 311–312.

Prasse, D. P. (1988). Legal influence and educational policy in special education. *Exceptional Children, 54,* 302–308.

Prasse, D. P., & Reschly, D. J. (1986). Larry P.: A case of segregation, testing, or program efficacy? *Exceptional Children, 52,* 333–346.

Price, B. J., & Marsh, G.E., II. (1985). Practical suggestions for planning and conducting parent conferences. *Teaching Exceptional Children,* Summer, 274–278.

Psacharopoulos, G. (1973). *Returns to education.* San Francisco, CA: Jossey-Bass.

Psacharopoulos, G., & Woodall, M. (1985). *Education for development: Analysis of investment choices.* New York: Oxford University Press.

Pugach, M. C., & Johnson, L. J. (1989). The challenge of implementing collaboration between general and special education. *Exceptional Children, 56*(3), 232–235.

Putnam, M. L. (1992). Characteristics of questions on tests administered by mainstream secondary classroom teachers. *Learning Disabilities Research and Practice, 7*(3), 29–36.

Quick! Tell me how to buy . . . Renovation for handicapped students. (1978). *American School Board Journal, 165*(7), 10.

Rabe, B. G., & Peterson, P. E. (1988). The evolution of a new cooperative federalism. In N. J. Boyan (Ed.), *Handbook of research on educational administration* (pp. 476–486). New York: Longman.

Ramirez, M., III, & Casteneda, A. (1974). *Cultural democracy, bicognitive development and education.* New York: Academic Press.

Reavis, C., & Griffith, H. (1992). *Restructuring Schools: Theory and Practice.* Lancaster, PA: Techonomics.

Reiff, H. B., Evans, E. D., & Cass, M. (1991, September/October). Special education requirements for general education certification: A national survey of current practices. *Remedial and Special Education, 12*(5), 56–60.

Reiher, T. C. (1992). Identified deficits and their congruence to the IEP for behaviorally disordered students. *Behavioral Disorders, 17*(3), 167–77.

Reynolds, M. (1962). A framework for considering some issues in special education. *Exceptional Children, 28,* 367–370.

Reynolds, M. C. (Ed.). (1975). *Special education and school decentralization.* Minneapolis: University of Minnesota, Leadership Training Institute/Special Education.

Reynolds, M. C., & Birch, J. W. (1977). *Teaching exceptional children in all America's schools.* Reston, VA: Council for Exceptional children.

Reynolds, M. C., Wang, M. C., & Walberg, H. J. (1987). The necessary restructuring of special and regular education. *Exceptional Children, 53*(5), 391–398.

Riley, R. (1993, Fall). A conversation with the U.S. Secretary of Education. *National Forum, 73*(4), 5–7.

Robin G. v. Acushnet Public Schools. Massachusetts Case No. 80-238. 6 EHLR 1003.

Robinson v. Cahill, 62 N.J. 473 (1973).

Roe, W. (1961). *School business management.* New York: McGraw-Hill.

Rose v. Council for Better Education, 790 S.W. 2nd 186, 212 (KY 1989).

Rossmiller, R. (1983). Resource allocation and achievement: A classroom analysis. In A. Odden & L. Webb (Eds.), *School finance and school improvement linkages for the 1980s.* Cambridge, MA: Ballinger.

Rossmiller, R., Hale, J., & Frohreich, L. (1970). *Educational programs for exceptional children: Resource configurations and costs.* Madison, WI: University of Wisconsin.

Rubin, I. (1969). The process of joining up: Individuals and organizations. *Education Opportunity Forum, 1,* 35–38.

Ryckman, D. B. (1981). Searching for a WISC-R profile for learning disabled children: An inappropriate task? *Journal of Learning Disabilities, 14*(9), 508–514.

S-1 v. Turlington, 635 F.2d 342, 5th Cir. (1981).

Safford, P. L. (1978). *Teaching young children with special needs.* St. Louis, MO: Mosby.

Sage, D. D., & Burrello, L. C. (1986). *Policy and management in special education.* Englewood Cliffs, NJ: Prentice-Hall.

Sagor, R. (1981). A day in the life—technique for assessing school climate and effectiveness. *Educational Leadership, 39,* 190–193.

St. John, W. D. (1991). Comprehensive performance valuation includes evaluation of administrative team. *NASSP Bulletin, 75,* 88–95.

Salvia, J., & Ysseldyke, J. E. (1978). *Assessment in special and remedial education.* Boston: Houghton-Mifflin.

Salvia, J., & Ysseldyke, J. E. (1988). *Assessment in special and remedial education* (4th ed.). Boston: Houghton-Mifflin.

San Antonio Independent School District v. Rodriguez, 411 U.S. 1 (1973).

Sapone, C. V., & Sheeran, T. J. (1991). A fourth wave model for supervision and evaluation. *NASSP Bulletin, 75,* 66–70.

Sawyer, H. W., & Sawyer, S.H. (1981). A teacher-parent communication training approach. *Exceptional Children, 47*(4), 305–306.

Schein, E. H. (1962). *Problems of the first year at work.* Monterey, CA: Office of Naval Research.

Schein, E. H. (1970). *Organizational psychology.* Englewood Cliffs, NJ: Prentice-Hall.

Schenkat, R. (1988, November 16). The promise for restructuring for special education. *Education Week, 11,* 36.

Schmidt, T., & Stipe, M. (1991). A clouded map for itinerant teachers: More questions than answers. *Perspectives in Education and Deafness, 9*(4), 6–7.

Schuncke, G. M. (1981). The uses and misuses of evaluation. *Clearing House, 54,* 219–222.

Schwarz, S. L., & Taymans, J. M. (1991). Urban vocational/technical program completers with learning disabilities: A follow-up study. *Journal for Vocational Special Needs Education, 13*(3), 15–20.

Selby, D., & Murphy, S. (1992). Graded or degraded: Perceptions of letter-grading for mainstreamed learning-disabled students. *B.C. Journal of Special Education, 16*(1), 92–104.

Sergiovanni, T. (1991). *The principalship: A reflective practice perspective* (2nd ed.). Boston: Allyn & Bacon.

Serrano v. Priest, 487 P 2d 1241 (1971).

Shaw, S. T., & Braden, J. P. (1990). Race and gender bias in the administration of corporal punishment. *School Psychology Review, 19,* 378–383.

Shepard, L. A. (1987). The new push for excellence: Widening the schism between regular and special education. *Exceptional Children, 53*(4), 327–329.

Shepard, L. A., & Smith, M. L. (1983). An evaluation of the identification of learning disabled students in Colorado. *Learning Disability Quarterly, 6*(2), 115-127.

Shepard, L. A., & Smith, M. L., with Davis, A., Glass, G. V., Riley, A., & Vojir, C. (1981). *Evaluation of the identification of perceptual-communicative disorders in Colorado.* Boulder: University of Colorado, Laboratory of Educational Research.

Sherman, J. (1985). *Resource allocation and staffing patterns in public schools.* Paper presented at the annual meeting of the American Educational Research Association. (ERIC Document Reproduction Service No. 263 687)

Shinn, M. R., & Habedank, L. (1992). Curriculum-based measurement in special education problem identification and certification decisions. *Preventing School Failure, 36*(2), 11–15.

Simpson, R. L., & Myles, B. S., (1990). The general education collaboration model: A model for successful mainstreaming. *Focus on Exceptional Children, 23*(4), 1–10.

Sirotnik, K. A., & Oakes, J. (1981). A contextual appraisal system for schools: Medicine or madness? *Educational Leadership, 39,* 164–173.

Skaller, L. D. (1992). Planning against pitfalls. *American School and University, 64,* 64–70.

Slobojan, A. (1987). Descriptive cost analysis of special education. *Journal of Education Finance, 13*(1).

Smith, J. D., Polloway, E. A., & West, G. K. (1979). Corporal punishment and its implications for exceptional children. *Exceptional Children, 45,* 264–268.

Smith, N., & White, W. F. (1988). The criterion and measurement problem in teaching. *Education, 108* (3), 385–392.

Smith, S. W. (1990). Individualized education programs (IEPs) in special education: From intent to acquiescence. *Exceptional Children, 57*(1), 6–14.

Smith, T. E. C. (1981). Statutes of due process hearings. *Exceptional Children, 48,* 232–236.

Smith, T. E. C. (1990). *Introduction to education* (2nd ed.). St. Paul: West.

Smith, T. E. C., & Dowdy, C. A. (1989). The role of study skills in the secondary curriculum. *Academic Therapy, 24,* 479–490.

Smith, T. E. C., Finn, D. M., & Dowdy, C. A. (1993). *Teaching students with mild disabilities.* Ft. Worth, TX: Harcourt, Brace, & Jovanovich.

Smith, T. E. C., & Podemski, R. S. (1981). Special education hearings: How to do them correctly. *Executive Educator, 3,* 22–24.

Smith T. E. C., Polloway, E. A., Patton, J. R., & Dowdy, C. A. (in press). *Teaching students with special needs in inclusive setting.* Boston: Allyn & Bacon.

Smith, T. E. C., Price, B. J., & Marsh, G. E., II. (1986). *Mildly handicapped children and adults.* Boston: West.

Sorensen, F. (1973). *A cost analysis of selected public school special education systems in Illinois.* Springfield, IL: Office of the Superintendent.

Special education, the attorney fees provision of Public Law 99-372. (1989). Washington, DC: U.S. General Accounting Office.

Spence, P. M. (1990). *The fifth discipline: The art and practice of the learning organization.* New York: Doubleday.

Staff. (1989, April 26). Spending slowdown ahead? *Education Week, 3.*

Staff. (1991a, August 9). New faces at school: How changing demographics are reshaping American education. *Education Daily* Special Supplement, 1-6.

Staff. (1991b, March 22). New faces at school: How changing demographics are reshaping American education. *Education Daily,* 5-8.

Stenner, J., Horabin, I., Smith, D. R., & Smith, M. (1988). Most comprehension tests do measure reading comprehension: A response to McLean and Goldstein. *Phi Delta Kappan, 69*(10), 765–767.

Stotland, J. F., & Mancuso, E. (1981). U.S. court of appeals decision regarding *Armstrong v. Kline:* The 180 day rule. *Exceptional Children, 47,* 266–270.

Stroup, K. B., Stout, J., Atkinson, B. L., Doll, J. P., & Russell, R. (1991). School bus safety. *Exceptional Parent, 21*(6), 80–82.

Stuart v. Nappi, 443 F. Supp. 1235 (D. Conn. 1978).

Stufflebeam, D. L., Foley, W. J., Gephart, W. J., Guba, E. C., Hammond, R. L., Merriman, H. O., & Provus, M. (1971). *Educational evaluation and decision making.* Itasca, IL: Peacock.

Stufflebeam, D. L., & Webster, W. J. (1988). Evaluation as an administrative function. In N. J. Boyan (Ed.). *Handbook of research on educational administration.* New York: Longman.

Swick, K. J., Flake-Hobson, C., & Raymond, G. (1980). The first step—Establishing parent-teacher communication in the IEP conference. *Teaching Exceptional Children, 12*(4), 144–145.

Theobald, N. D. (1991). A persistent challenge: Staffing special education programs in rural schools. *Journal of Research in Rural Education, 7*(3), 39–50.

Thurlow, M. L., O'Sullivan, P. J., & Ysseldyke, J. E. (1986). Early screening for especial education: How accurate? *Education Leadership, 44*(3), 93–95.

Tidwell, S. (1985). *Financial and managerial accounting for elementary and secondary school systems* (3rd ed.). Reston, VA: Association of School Business Officials.

Tiedt, S. (1966). *The role of the federal government in education.* New York: Oxford University Press.

Tikunoff, W. J. (1985). *Applying significant bilingual instructional features in the classroom.* Rosslyn, VA: National Clearinghouse for Bilingual Education.

Timothy W. v. Rochester School District, EHLR 559:480 (D.N.H. 1988).

Torres, S. (Ed.). (1977). *A primer on individualized education programs for handicapped children.* Reston, VA: Foundation for Exceptional Children.

Tsang, M. C., & Levin, H. R. (1983). The impacts of intergovernmental grants on educational spending. *Review of Educational Research, 53,* 329–367.

Tucker, J. (1981). *Sequential stages of the appraisal process: A training manual.* Minneapolis, MN:

National School Psychology Inservice Training Network.

Turnbull, A. P., & Schulz, J. B. (1979). *Mainstreaming handicapped students: A guide for the classroom teacher.* Boston: Allyn & Bacon.

Turnbull, A. P., Strickland, B., & Turnbull, H. R. (1981). Due process hearing officers: Characteristics, needs, and appointment criteria. *Exceptional Children, 48,* 48–54.

Turnbull, A. P., Strickland, B. B., & Brantley, J. C. (1982). *Developing and implementing individualized education programs.* Columbus, OH: Merrill.

Turnbull, H. R. (1986). Appropriate education and Rowley. *Exceptional Children, 52*(4), 347–352.

Turnbull, H. R. (1993). *Free appropriate public education* (4th ed.). Denver: Love.

U.S. Department of Education. (1985). *Seventh annual report to Congress on the implementation of Public Law 94-142: The Education for All Handicapped Children Act.* Washington, DC: U.S. Government Printing Office.

U.S. Department of Education. (1988). *Tenth annual report to Congress on the implementation of the Education of the Handicapped Act.* Washington, DC: Author.

USA Today. (1991a). USA snapshots. Monday, November 11, 1A.

Valesky, T. C., & Hirth, M. A. (1992). Survey of the states: Special education knowledge requirements for school administrators. *Exceptional Children, 58*(5), 399–406.

Verstegen, D. (1987). Two hundred years of federalism: A perspective on national fiscal policy in education. *Journal of Education Finance, 12*(4).

Verstegen, D., & Clark, D. (1988). The diminution in federal expenditures for education during the Reagan administration. *Phi Delta Kappan, 70*(2).

Viadero, D. (1989, June 7). All handicapped must be served, court concludes. *Education Week, 8*(37), 1.

Victory for Timothy W. (1989). The Association for the Severely Handicapped (TASH). *Newsletter, 15*(8), 1.

Vincent, L., Salisbury, C., Strain, P., McCormick, C., & Tessier, A. (1990). A behavioral-ecological approach to early intervention: Focus on cultural diversity. In S. Meisels & J. Shonkoff (Eds.), *Handbook of early intervention* (pp. 173–195). Cambridge: Cambridge University Press.

Vitello, S. J. (1986). The Tatro case: Who gets what and why. *Exceptional Children, 52*(4), 353–356.

Waechter v. School District No. 14-030, 773 F.Supp. 1005 (W.D. Mich. 1991).

Wagner, A. (1984). The national reports: Financing improvements in educational quality. In F. Demmer, W. Vogt, & A. Wagner (Eds.), *Challenges from without: Analyses of the recommendations advanced by five national education task forces and their policy implications for pre-college and higher education.* The Rockefeller Institute Special Report Series, No. 4. (ERIC Document Reproduction Service No. 259 064)

Wagstaff, L., & Reyes, P. (1993). *Report on school site-based management.* Austin, TX: College of Education, The University of Texas at Austin.

Walton, D. (1989). *Are you communicating? You can't manage without it.* New York: McGraw-Hill.

Wang, M. C. (1987). Toward achieving educational excellence for all students: Program design and student outcomes. *Remedial and Special Education, 8*(3), 25–34.

Wang, M. C., Reynolds, M. C., & Walberg, H. J. (1986). Rethinking special education. *Educational Leadership, 44*(1) 26–31.

Ward, J. G. (1988). The political ecology of reform: American public school finance in the 1970s and 1980s. *Journal of Education Finance, 14*(2).

Wayson, W. W. (1985). The politics of violence in schools: Doublespeak and disruptions in public confidence. *Phi Delta Kappan,* October, 127-132.

Weatherman, R. F., & Hollingsworth, S. A. (Eds.). (1974). *Administration of special education for rural and sparsely populated areas.* Minneapolis: University of Minnesota.

Webb, L., McCarthy, M., & Thomas, S. (1988). *Financing elementary and secondary education.* Columbus, OH: Merrill.

Wehman, P. (1992). Transition for young people with disabilities: Challenges for the 1990's. *Education and Training in Mental Retardation, 27*(2), 12–18.

Wehman, P., & McLaughlin, P. J. (1981). *Program development in special education.* New York: McGraw-Hill.

Wehman, P., Wood, W., Everson, J. M., Goodwyn, R., & Conley, S. (1988). *Vocational education for multihandicapped youth with cerebral palsy.* Baltimore, MD: Brookes.

Weick, K. E. (1976). Educational organizations as loosely coupled systems. *Administrative Science Quarterly, 21,* 1-19.

Weick, K. E. (1982). Administering education in loosely coupled schools. *Phi Delta Kappan, 63*(10), 673–676.

Weinstein, C. E., Palmer, D. R., & Schulte, A. C. (1987). *Learning and study strategies inventory.* Clearwater, FL: H & H Publishing.

Weintraub, F. J. (1977). Understanding the individualized educaional program. *Amicus, 2*(3), 26–31.

Westling, D. L., & Koorland, M. A. (1988). *The special educator's handbook.* Boston: Allyn & Bacon.

White, E. (1981, February). P.L. 94-142's toughest topics: Health care, discipline, summer school. *American School Board Journal, 168,* 19–23.

White, S., & Bond, M. R. (1992) Transition services in large school districts. *Teaching Exceptional Children, 24*(4), 44–47.

Wiederholt, J. L., Hammill, D. D., & Brown, V. (1978). *The resource teacher: A guide to effective practices.* Boston: Allyn & Bacon.

Wilkinson, C., & Ortiz, A. (1986). *Characteristics of limited English proficient and English proficient learning disabled Hispanic students at initial assessment and reevaluation.* Austin, TX: The University of Texas, Department of Special Education, Handicapped Minority Research Institute on Language Proficiency.

Will, M. (1986). *Educating students with learning problems—A shared responsibility.* Washington, DC: U.S. Department of Education, Office of Special Education and Rehabilitation Services.

Wirt, F., & Kirst, M. (1982). *The political web of American schools.* Boston, MA: Little, Brown, and Co.

Wise, A. (1968). *Rich schools poor schools.* Chicago, IL: University of Chicago Press.

Wolf, R. M. (1979). *Evaluation in education: Foundations of competency assessment and program review.* New York: Praeger.

Wood, C., Sheehan, R., & Adams, J. (1985). State special education funding formulas: Their relationship to regular education placement. *Planning and Changing, 15*(3), 131–143.

Wood, C. J. (1992). Toward more effective teacher evaluation: Lessons from naturalistic inquiry. *NASSP Bulletin, 76,* 52–59.

Wood, R. C., & Carros, D. (1988). Special education hearings in Indiana: An analysis of fiscal issues. *Planning and Changing, 19*(3), 150–156.

Worthen, B. R., & J. R. Sanders. (1987). *Education evaluation.* New York: Longman.

Yates, J. R. (1981). *Matrix organizational structure and its effects upon education organizations.* Paper presented at the meeting of the Council for Exceptional Children, New York. (ERIC Document Reproduction Service No. ED 208 475)

Yates, J. R. (1987, May). Current and emerging forces impacting special education (Part I). *Counterpoint, 7*(4), 4-6.

Yates, J. R. (1988). Demography as it affects special education. In A. Ortiz & B. Ramirez (Eds.), *Schools and the culturally diverse exceptional student: Promising practices and future directions* (pp. 1–5). Reston, VA: The Council for Exceptional Children.

Yates, J. R., & Ortiz, A. A. (1991). Professional development needs of teachers who serve exceptional language minorities in today's schools. *Teacher Education and Special Education, 14*(1), 11-17.

Yavorsky, D. K. (n.d.). *Discrepancy evaluation: A practitioner's guide.* Charlottesville, VA: University of Virginia Evaluation Research Center.

Young, M. W. (1993, Fall). Countdown: The Goals 2000 Educate America Act. *National Forum, 73*(4), 3–4.

Ysseldyke, J. E. (1991). *Public school choice: What about students with disabilities?* (Report No. 2). *Enrollment options for students with disabilities.* The University of Minnesota. (ERIC Document Reproduction Service No. ED343362)

Ysseldyke, J. E., Algozzine, B., Richey, L., & Graden, J. (1982). Declaring students eligible for LD services: Why bother with the data? *Journal of Learning Disabilities, 5,* Winter, 37–44.

Ysseldyke, J. E., & Christenson, S. L. (1987). Evaluating students' instructional environments. *Remedial and Special Education, 8*(3), 17–24.

Ysseldyke, J. E., Thurlow, M. L., & Bruininks, R. H. (1992). Expected educational outcomes for students with disabilities. *Remedial and Special Education, 13,* 19–30.

Ysseldyke, J. E., Thurlow, M. L., & Shriner, J. G. (1992). Outcomes are for special educators too. *Teaching Exceptional Children,* Fall, 36–49.

Zuckerman, D. (1991). Drug-exposed infants: Understanding the medical risks. *The Future of Children, 1*(1), 26-35.

SUBJECT INDEX

NAME INDEX